I0048371

HUMAN RIGHTS AND HOUSING ESTATES REGENERATION

By Shemi Esquire

Exclusively for JEB

This text analyses human rights under ECHR/ HRA 1998 in relation to Housing Estate regeneration enforced by CPOs. Although there are similarities with other UK devolved areas like Scotland, the acts here largely refer to England and wales.

Thanks to all those who made comments on the draft thesis chapter.[1]

---

[1] S Keenan -supervisor

Table of contents

Introduction

The aim of this text is to assess whether human rights law is an effective mechanism to challenge the harm caused by housing estate regeneration effected by the use of compulsory purchase orders in the United Kingdom.

The focus of this text relates to the actions of local authorities or public bodies that attract the jurisdiction of the ECHR and the applicable international human rights law.[2]

The book analyses any potential or existing human rights breaches associated with estate regeneration under the ECHR regime and briefly discusses the relevant international human rights law. International human rights law although discussed briefly below requires a separate chapter in terms of assessing how international human rights law safeguards against violations associated with CPO enforced estate regeneration. The ECHR rights examined here which are associated with the use of CPOs in housing estate demolition, include the right to a peaceful and quiet enjoyment of one's home, *respect for the home (Art 8), fairness, transparency and the expeditious nature of the whole process (Art 6), equality of treatment (Art 14), freedom of association, expression (Art 9 and 10), Art 13 dealing with Just compensation or the appropriate legal remedies, Art 2(right to life), Equal treatment, impact on children and applicable international law as indicated in detail below.*

The ECHR rights above are juxtaposed with the underlying practical policies, practices, decisions and impact on individuals or the wider community. Commencing with the initial decisions, consultation process, internal processes, viability reports, environmental issues, equality matters, planning permission and the eventual adverse impact on residents in the respective communities. The impact on communities is assessed by examining fundamental life indicators like employment, finances, culture, health, the disproportionate impact on racial minorities[3] and whether the statutory compensation is fair or equitable.[4]

By simple definition, compulsory purchase orders [5](CPOs) are a legal mechanism deployed by acquiring authorities to acquire land[6] which may be occupied or encumbered with competing property or legal interests through compulsion.[7]

---

[2] https://www.un.org/en/universal-declaration-human-rights

[3] 'It's not for us': Regeneration, the 2012 Olympics and the gentrification of East London, City, 2013

[4] Alice Belotti, Estate Regeneration and Community Impacts https://www.unicef.org/child-rights-conventionChallenges and lessons for social landlords, developers and local councils,2016

[5] Compulsory purchase orders , https://www.legislation.gov.uk/ukpga/1981/67/section/1

[6] /Knock It Down Or Do It Up pdf, https://www.london.gov.uk

[7] https://www.legislation.gov.uk/ukpga/1981/67/section/1

CPOs *'require approval of a confirming minister under the Acquisition of Land Act 198'.*[8] There are various enabling powers available and the determination to authorise will partly depend on the specific powers used. Such public bodies with statutory powers include 'local authorities, national parks, some executive agencies, the Homes and Communities Agency, health service bodies and government ministers. This is discussed in greater detail in other chapters.

There is a detailed process of CPO processes and various statutory requirements, discussed in other chapters. The focus of this book is not to discuss the detailed statutory CPO process but rather a detailed analysis of the detrimental impact on parties with interest in the land and whether such detrimental effects are compatible with human rights law.

Chapter 1

Overview of aspects of human rights law related to estate regeneration through the use of CPOs

Human rights[9] should be fundamental consideration in the authorisation process of compulsory purchase orders although this is not always the case in practice as discussed in greater detail below. Adherence to human rights law during the CPO process is emphasised in the government guidance, which states that *'the purposes for which the compulsory purchase order is made',* should *'justify interfering with the human rights of those with an interest in the land affected.*[10] But the guidance also refers to a public sector duty requirement[11] which by interpretation indicates that a failure to 'have proper regard to the public sector equality duty', related to affordable

[8] f-guidance-on-compulsory-purchase-and-the-crichel-down-rules-for-the-disposal-of-surplus-land-.

[9] See "Tesco Stores Limited v Secretary of State for the Environment and Others (Full Report)". *Journal of planning and environment law* (0307-4870), p. 581.

[10] Guidance-on-compulsory-purchase-and-the-crichel-down-rules-for-the-disposal-of-surplus-land-pdf

[11] In R (on the application of Reading BC v SoS DCL

housing, social infrastructure contributions and a vacancy credit policy[12] could be found to be unlawful.

The Government guidance further states that *'all public sector acquiring authorities are bound by the Public Sector Equality Duty as set out in section 149 of the Equality Act 2010. In exercising their compulsory purchase and related powers (e.g. powers of entry), these acquiring authorities must have regard to the effect of any differential impacts on groups with protected characteristics. For example, an important use of compulsory purchase powers is to help regenerate run down areas. Although low income is not a protected characteristic, it is not uncommon for people from ethnic minorities, the elderly or people with a disability to be overrepresented in low-income groups. As part of the Public Sector Equality Duty, acquiring authorities must have due regard to the need to promote equality of opportunity between persons who share a relevant protected characteristic and persons who do not share it.*

This might mean that the acquiring authority devises a process which promotes equality of opportunity by addressing particular problems that people with certain protected characteristics might have (e.g. making sure that documents are accessible for people with sight problems or learning difficulties and that people have access to advocates or advice.[13]

Despite the clear government, guidance above it appears that adherence to such guidance is often inadequate or arguably non-existent. To the extent that even a council lawyer expressed doubt or surprise, as to how the PSED[14] would apply to racial minorities.[15]

---

[12] Saira Kabir Sheikh QC, JPL, 2015

[13] CPO guidance, https://assets.publishing.service.gov.uk

[14] Nlp_ex_33b_appendix_2_legal_note.pdf , https://www.london.gov.uk/sites/default/files/

[15] Lambeth council lawyer, apart from disability, his client did not understand how THI applied to racial minorities; https://twitter.com/saveWestburySW8; https://www.facebook.com/Savewestburysw8-804075296314550/; Human Rights today blog

The CPO process in many respects is deemed to be unfair because the acquiring body or authority is also the main driver of the process as[16] documented by various reports highlighted above in detail, by entities like independent observers,[17] the Runnymede trust,[18] academics[19] among others.

In summary, the effects on residents include displacement,[20] financial disenfranchisement, dispossession,[21] environmental hazards,[22] disproportionate effect on racial minorities,[23] adverse health impact on residents, especially children, elderly and vulnerable adults. This is worsened by the unfair process, imbalance of resources and lack of adequate or meaningful access to an independent decision maker during the process, [24]which makes recourse to courts a complicated, cumbersome and expensive affair. From such observations, it would appear that there is at the very least prima facie evidence of possible incompatibility with human rights law, which is discussed in more detail below. The various aspects of the relevant human rights law are discussed below starting with ECHR which incorporates HRA 98.

---

[16]DCLG Guidance-on-compulsory-purchase-and-the-crichel-down-rules-for-the-disposal-of-surplus-land

[17] Anna Minton, GROUND CONTROL, Fear and Happiness in the Twenty-First Century City, by Anna Minton, Published by Penguin Books, paperback original, 26th June 2012; Anne Rendell (2017) 'Arry's Bar: condensing and displacing on the Aylesbury Estate, The Journal of Architecture, 22:3, 532-554, DOI: 10.1080/13602365.2017.1310125;

[18] UK NGOs' Alternative Report Submission to the UN Committee on the Elimination of Racial Discrimination with regard to the UK Government's 21st to 23rd Periodic Reports June 2016 Drafted by THE RUNNYMEDE TRUST

[19] Hubbard P and Lees L, "The Right to Community?" (2018) 22 City 8

Social exclusion, Paul Watt (2013) 'It's not for us', City; Paul Watt, Housing Stock Transfers, Regeneration and State-Led Gentrification in London Article in Urban Policy and Research.

Social exclusion, Paul Watt (2013) 'It's not for us', City; Paul Watt, Housing Stock Transfers, Regeneration and State-Led Gentrification in London Article in Urban Policy and Research.

[20] Alice Belotti, Challenges and lessons for social landlords, developers and local councils, 2016

[21] Demolition-watch-submission,http://www.demolitionwatchlondon.com, 14-march-2017,

[22] https://www.theguardian.com/environment/2019/may/04/brownfield-site-new-homes-building-wrecking-health-southall

[23] Jessica Perera, The-London-clearances-race-housing-and-policing, http://www.irr.org.uk

[24]Alice Belotti, Challenges and lessons for social landlords, developers and local councils, 2016;

Dispossession, The great social housing swindle, https://www.dispossessionfilm.com,

Chapter 2

ECHR Jurisdiction

The UK is a signatory to the ECHR,[25] which incorporated the Human Rights Act 1998 fundamental freedoms into UK domestic law. This therefore implies that the HRA 98 Act has to be read and given effect in compatibility with convention rights by public authorities, in terms of their processes, decisions, effect or impact thereof which by virtue of s3 of the HRA 1998.[26] Section 4 of the HRA 1998[27] refers to declaration of compatibility of local legislation with the HRA 98 while Section 6 of HRA 98 makes it unlawful for a public authority to act in a manner that is incompatible with convention rights and may apply to organisations which perform public functions.[28]

Furthermore, although UK courts do not have a requirement to make identical decisions to the ECHR, they have to take into account ECHR decisions.[29] Any person affected can bring a legal complaint but victims need to have standing under the CPO and the court can look at substance rather than form. A pressure group can be a victim if it shows that it is affected but it is for public authorities to show compatibility with ECHR rights. There is however a possibility of the complaint being rejected if it is raised too late.[30]

---

[25] The Law of compulsory purchase, third edition, Guy Roots et al

[26] http://www.legislation.gov.uk/ukpga/1998/42/section/3; Also See *nutshells, Human rights ;(state year?) See also HA1985-s7-*

Compulsory purchase/Human rights act guide to practitioners-Christopher Baker.

[27] http://www.legislation.gov.uk/ukpga/1998/42/section/4

[28] http://www.legislation.gov.uk/ukpga/1998/42/section/6

[29] https://www.legislation.gov.uk/ukpga/1998/42/section/4

[30] https://www.legislation.gov.uk/ukpga/1998/42/contents

In dealing with the implementation of the ECHR incorporated rights or decisions, states possess a margin of appreciation in areas such as housing. It is argued that this is due to housing being part of the social economic policy of a state and this could require unique solutions unless there is a manifest unreasonable foundation.[31]

However, that assertion could be interpreted differently from the perspective of the international convention rights as highlighted by the UN Rapporteur on human rights.[32] The alternative argument would be that since housing is a basic human need, nothing warrants derogation from protection of that basic human need (shelter) especially in economies that have extensive resources such as the UK.[33]

Specific ECHR rights and relation to Estate regeneration

The rights protected by the ECHR are sixteen in total. These are categorised as absolute, limited or qualified as indicated by Andrew Drzemczewski.[34] From a strictly legal perspective, property rights fall in the qualified category but are human rights that are no lesser than any other human rights As already highlighted above, the most applicable human rights articles associated with CPOs include, *Art 2, Art 8, A1P1, Art 6, ART 14, Art 3, 10, 11, 13, 41 of the ECHR* incorporating the HRA 1998 and international convention on human rights.

 As a summary and as indicated above, Art 3[35] relates to inhuman and degrading treatment, Art 6 protects the right for a fair, expeditious and impartial process[36], Art 8 protects respect for a home and home environment,[37] while Article 1 of the first

---

[31] ECHR; https://www.echr.coe.int/Convention_ENG.pdf

[32] Special Rapporteur on extreme poverty and human rights; https://www.ohchr.orgExtremePoverty

[33] https://data.oecd.org/united-kingdom.htm

[34] https://scholarlycommons.law.wlu.edu/cgi/

[35] ECHR, https://www.echr.coe.int

[36] ECHR, https://www.echr.coe.int

[37] ECHR, https://www.echr.coe.int/Convention_ENG.pdf

protocol,[38] safeguards against unjustifiable, disproportionate interference in the peaceful and quite enjoyment of one's home and possessions[39].

Art 2 protects the right to life and by default health. In estate regeneration, the argument advanced here is that projects which threaten public health or public safety may trigger proceedings under article 2. ART 10 protects freedom of expression, Art 11 protects freedoms of association, ART13 deals with compensation and Art 41 specifies remedies. Article one of the first Protocol refers to principles of law and international law underlining the payment of compensation in as far as money can be compensation.[40] A1P1[41] refers to principles of international law by payment of compensation in as far as money can compensate the affected persons.

However, when considering compensation per se, under the official CPO guidance cited above, a distinction is made between a CPO where land is taken and where land is not taken. This is because a CPO could proceed through imposition of restrictions, which amount to a taking or interference with the use or enjoyment, or ownership of the land but no actual physical land is taken. Therefore, it is arguable that to maintain fairness, in terms of compensation, there is a need for balancing that distinction with the public interest, as highlighted by both statute[42] and human rights law.[43]

Other jurisdictions related to estate regeneration and human rights law

International law [44]

[38] Referred to as A1P1 for brevity

[39] ECHR, https://www.echr.coe.int/Convention_ENG.pdf

[40] ECHR, https://www.echr.coe.int/Convention_ENG.pdf

[41] ECHR, https://www.echr.coe.int/Documents/Guide_Art_1_Protocol_1_ENG.pdf

[42]ECHR, https://www.legislation.gov.uk/ukpga/1973/26/section/1

[43] ECHR, https://www.echr.coe.int/Documents/Guide_Art_1_Protocol_1_ENG.pdf

As mentioned above, among the key protections for those affected by estate regeneration mandated by CPOs, is A1P1, which makes an explicit reference to principles of international law.[45] A1P1 states that, …'*every natural person or legal person is entitled to the peaceful enjoyment of his possessions and no one shall be deprived of his possessions except in the public interest and subject to the conditions provided for by law and by the general principles of international law*'.[46]

Such reference to international law therefore necessitates an examination of the wider international human rights law applicable to estate regeneration using CPOs. It is also important to point out that the UK is party to the Universal Declaration of Human rights[47]and other related conventions such as[48]the United Nations convention on economic, social and cultural rights which invoke 'the right of everyone to an adequate standard of living for himself and his family, including adequate housing.[49]

However, in notable cases[50] reference to principles[51] of international law, [52]was stated to be limited to persons who are not nationals. This restriction to non-nationals reflected in these cases requires further exploration. It would appear or it is possible part of the reasoning is that the architects of ECHR intended to allow non-nationals to secure their convention rights directly without the inbuilt disadvantages they would

---

[44] OHCHR, https://www.ohchr.org

[45] Egon Scweb, The Protection of the Right of Property of Nationals under the First Protocol to the European Convention on Human Rights, *The American Journal of Comparative Law*

Vol. 13, No. 4 (Autumn, 1964), pp. 518-541

[46] Guide on Article 1 of Protocol No. 1 to the European Convention on Human Rights Protection of property Updated on 31 August 2019, https://www.echr.coe.int/Documents/Guide_Art_1_Protocol_1_ENG.pdf
[47] http://www.un.org/en/universal-declaration-human-rights/

[48] incidentally I write this in the UN HW library in Geneva-7th1019

[49] OCHCHR, https://www.ohchr.org/Documents/ProfessionalInterest/ccpr.pdf

[50] in Lithgow v UK and James v UK

[51] Deborah Rook, Property Law and Human rights, 2001

[52] https://www.ohchr.org/en/professionalinterest/pages/internationallaw.aspx

face in the national legal system. Such disadvantages could include discrimination on the grounds of nationality, race or other grounds generally associated with being a non-national of a specific country, which would not necessarily apply to nationals. It could also be argued that nationals could be arguably protected by their local jurisdiction but this remains a very unclear rationale which needs further scrutiny.

Apart from the direct provisions of international law, there is also international scrutiny and domestic pressure to comply with international law[53] as evidenced by a report from the UNRA rapporteur on human rights, about issues that are arguably inextricably[54]linked to housing, socio-economic policies and therefore the wider issue of social housing. This has a direct policy link with large-scale CPO estate demolition,[55] which contributes to fuelling the housing problems in the UK[56]. It should not be read in isolation but in synthesis with the recognition of detrimental effects like dispossession, displacement and disenfranchisement that come with loss of a home, a sense of agency and support networks,[57]which is directly similar to the effects of CPO associated regeneration.[58]Therefore, any international scrutiny consistent with international law or public policy is a potential positive step in dealing with the detrimental social and economic impact that CPO affected residents face.

In his report, Professor Philip Alston observes that a wealthy country with the fifth largest economy in the world should not be 'patently unjust and contrary to British values that so many people are living in poverty'.[59] He quotes the Institute for Fiscal Studies which foresees, 'a 7% rise in child poverty between 2015 and 2022, and various sources predict child poverty rates of as high as 40%'. Professor Alston's

---

[53] UK NGOs' Alternative Report Submission to the UN Committee on the Elimination of Racial Discrimination with regard to the UK Government's 21st to 23rd Periodic Reports June 2016 Drafted by THE RUNNYMEDE TRUST

[54]Statement on visit to the United Kingdom, by Professor Philip Alston, United Nations Special Rapporteur on extreme poverty and human rights, https://www.ohchr.org/Documents/Issues/Poverty/EOM_GB_16Nov2018.pdf

[55] Anna Minton, Ground Control: Fear and Happiness in the Twenty-First-Century City; His-estates-10-year-wait-for-regeneration, https://www.insidehousing.co.uk

[56] Anna Minton, big capital who is London for

[57] Anna Minton, Ground control, fear and happiness in the 21st century

[58] https://haringeydefendcouncilhousingblog.wordpress.com/

[59] Professor Philip Alston, United Nations Special Rapporteur on extreme poverty and human rights

report further notes that 'almost one in every two children to be poor in twenty-first century Britain is not just a disgrace, but a social calamity and an economic disaster, all rolled into one'. He emphasises that, 'many of the recent changes to social support in the UK have a disparate impact on children'. Citing evidence from the Equality and Human Rights Commission which predicts that 'another 1.5 million more children will fall into poverty between 2010 and 2021/22 as a result of the changes to benefits and taxes, a 10% increase from 31% to 41%.' The report points to the legal aid cuts, 'in England and Wales since 2012 which overwhelmingly affected the poor and people with disabilities, many of whom cannot otherwise afford to challenge benefit denials or reductions and are thus effectively deprived of their human right to a remedy'. The report highlights ' the LASPO Act (Legal Aid, Sentencing and Punishment of Offenders Act) gutted the scope of cases that are handled, ratcheted up the level of means-tested eligibility criteria, and substituted telephonic for many previously face-to-face advice services'. According to Professor Philip Alston, the Social Metrics Commission, states that 'almost a third of children in the UK live in poverty. After years of progress, child poverty is rising again, and expected to continue increasing sharply in the coming years.'

As described above, this report has a direct policy link with large-scale CPO estate demolition,[60] which contributes to fuelling the housing problems in the UK.[61]

Prof. Alston concludes that 'It was a British philosopher, Thomas Hobbes, who memorably claimed that without a social contract; life outside society would be "solitary, poor, nasty, brutish, and short....many of the public places and institutions that previously brought communities together, such as libraries, community and recreation centres and public parks, have been steadily dismantled or undermined'.[62]

Arguably, Professor Philip Alston's report is acutely relevant to CPO affected residents in various respects. Such as the legal aid cuts in England and Wales since 2012, which overwhelmingly affected the poor or people with disabilities. A theme that is consistent with CPO affected residents who face a lack of access to legal aid

---

[60] Anna Minton, Ground Control: Fear and Happiness in the Twenty-First-Century City; His-estates-10-year-wait-for-regeneration, https://www.insidehousing.co.uk

[61] Anna Minton, big capital who is London for

[62] Report from UNRA rapporteur on human rights, by Professor Philip Alston, United Nations Special Rapporteur on extreme poverty and human rights https://www.ohchr.org/Documents/Issues/Poverty/EOM_GB_16Nov2018.pdf

which has a disproportionate impact on children, racial minorities, the disabled, elderly and historically disadvantaged communities. An issue that is highlighted by both the Institute on Racial relation[63] among others and would appear to be inconsistent with international conventions and international law. Such as the Universal Declaration of Human Rights[64], ICCPR (referred to1st generation rights)[65], ICESCR (referred to as second generation rights,)[66]CERD,ICE (in relation to racial discrimination)[67] and CROC (convention on the right of children 1989.[68]

These conventions aim to protect economic, social, political rights of individuals or groups, such a rights relating to protection for the home, family, health, racial minorities, access to justice and due process. The Universal Declaration on Human rights, specifically refers to a common understanding of a set of values applicable to the treatment of individual human beings, irrespective of their race, religion, gender or other protected characteristics. Furthermore, the European Social charter, protects health, family, property and against discrimination, among other rights.[69] Although enforceability and applicability and legal jurisdiction over member states remains a potent legal hurdle.[70]

Firstly, because such relief would require measures to be implemented by the faulting nation states through protracted legal and political mechanisms. Secondly, there is difficulty in terms of pursuing the international human rights law route due to the complexity of the law, lack of resources and technical support to those affected. Even at a national level, it remains a cumbersome, long and expensive process to pursue legal action against the acquiring authorities who often have access to extensive legal and financial resources. In comparison, residents or communities

[63]Jessica Perera, THE LONDON CLEARANCES A BACKGROUND PAPER ON RACE, HOUSING AND POLICING 2019, Institute of Race Relations

[64] Universal Declaration of Human rights, http://www.un.org/en/universal-declaration-human-rights/

[65]International convention on civil and political rights, https://www.ohchr.org/EN/ProfessionalInterest/Pages/CCPR.aspx

[66] International convention on social and economic rights,https://www.ohchr.org/en/professionalinterest/pages/cescr.aspx

[67] Committee on elimination of racial discrimination, https://www.ohchr.org/en/hrbodies/cerd

[68] Convention on the right of a Child, https://www.ohchr.org

[69] https://www.coe.int/european-social-charter

[70] https://www.un.org/en/universal-declaration-human-rights/

affected in some cases are litigants in person who use pro bono assistance, which therefore limits the degree of assistance available or other sources of funding just to initiate legal action. In addition to the many other day-to-day practical problems, they face due to compulsory acquisition of their homes.[71] Nevertheless, it is critical that there is a transnational approach and potential avenue for redress given that CPOs, eminent domains, forceful land acquisition or land grabbing in general, have wider long-lasting detrimental effects on particular communities and demographics, which are historically disadvantaged, marginalised, disenfranchised and oppressed. Therefore warranting an international redress mechanism and a degree of international legal intervention.[72]

Chapter 3

Individual ECHR Articles related to estate regeneration through the use of CPOs

As briefly discussed above, among the applicable articles of the ECHR, that are arguably directly triggered by CPOs, are Articles 8, A1P1 Art 6, Art 14, 2 and 3 and their relevance as a mechanism to challenge estate regeneration activities under human rights law. These will be discussed in the order highlighted above.

The subsequent chapters shall examine the statutory compensation regime, the adequacy of the current legal remedies to provide a more rounded understanding of the issue, suggested proposals for reform and a determination as to whether human rights law indeed is an effective mechanism for challenging CPOs.

Article 8 ECHR and estate regeneration through the use of CPOs

---

[71] Alice Belloti, Estate community regeneration and community impact, Case report 99, http://sticerd.lse.ac.uk/dps/case/cr/casereport99.pdf

[72] UK NGOs' Alternative Report Submission to the UN Committee on the Elimination of Racial Discrimination with regard to the UK Government's 21st to 23rd Periodic Reports June 2016 Drafted by THE RUNNYMEDE TRUST

Article 8 of ECHR,[73] states that:

1. 'Everyone has the right to respect for his private and family life, his home and his correspondence.

2. There shall be no interference by a public authority with the exercise of this right except such as is in accordance with the law and is necessary in a democratic society in the interests of national security, public safety or the economic well-being of the country, for the prevention of disorder or crime, for the protection of health or morals, or for the protection of the rights and freedoms of others'.

Before examining in depth the legal details or Art 8, it needs to be emphasised that just like other ECHR articles, there is a multitude of various areas of day-to-day life that could fall under the protections of Art 8. The focus here is on the relevant provisions that could be applicable to CPOs under estate regeneration.

Jurisdiction

Art 8 protects the respect for private and family life including one's home or correspondence[74] and could also be invoked in conjunction with A1P1. Observers, [75] point to a minute difference between these two articles in terms of the level of protection provided which may turn on particular facts of a specific applicant.

Scope of Art 8

---

[73] https://www.echr.coe.int/Documents/Guide_Art_8_ENG.pdf

[74] Aida Grigic, Zvonimir Mataga, Matija Longar and Ana Vilfan, The right to property under the ECHR, A guide to implementation of the ECHR, Human rights Hand Book no 10, https://rm.coe.int/168007ff55

[75] Aida Grigic, Zvonimir Mataga, Matija Longar and Ana Vilfan, The right to property under the ECHR, A guide to implementation of the ECHR, Human rights Hand Book no 10, https://rm.coe.int/168007ff55

Art 8[76] safeguards respect for a home and against deprivation of a home by way of access or occupation. It safeguards the right to live without interference and intrusion in one's family or private life and correspondence. Art 8 also refers to personal information being kept private or confidential and requires a positive step from a public authority.

Definition of a home

In brief and in this specific context of art 8, is a settled place where one lives, including a home one has the intention to move to,[77] described as an autonomous concept not based on domestic law categorisations.[78] In *Gillow V UK,* the court held that even though the applicants had not occupied the house for nineteen years[79] it was still their home. The applicants had not established domicile anywhere else and intended to live in the house.

To engage Art 8 protection, there has to be a determination on facts relating to continuous links and rights which cannot be interfered with, unless there is a reasonable justification.[80] Art 8 does not provide a general right to housing under HRA 98 or ECHR[81], except protection for respect for a home or unjustifiable interference of the peaceful and quiet enjoyment of one's home or possessions, under Art 8 and A1P1 respectively.

 Instead, Art 8 emphasises the need for the state to have a positive obligation to be proactive in regulating non-state interference and to provide remedies against

[76] ECHR

[77] Gillow v UK91986) ECHR 14

Donoghue V Poplar Housing association(2001)EWACA Civ 595

[78] https://www.echr.coe.int/Documents/Guide_Art_8_ENG.pdf

[79] CASE OF GILLOW v. THE UNITED KINGDOM (Application no. 9063/80)

[80] https://www.echr.coe.int/Documents/Guide_Art_8_ENG.pdf

[81] https://www.echr.coe.int/Documents/Guide_Art_8_ENG.pdf

harassment of individuals in and around their home as discussed in detail other chapters.[82]

The ECHR[83] further classifies a home as one that merits protection under the respect for a home legal principle. Which extends to property where the complainant is not an owner, a tenant, in long-term occupancy as well as a relative's house or a 'care' facility.[84] However, this may not apply to a home that one intends to build.[85]

Art 8[86] also appears to put emphasis on a home as being non-transient or exceedingly short term, like a hotel room. Although in *Buckley v UK,* [87]*which involved the retrospective denial of planning permission,* the notion of a home was not restricted to being lawfully established. Therefore, the designation or interpretation of what a home is or is not appears subjective.

In the context of a compulsory acquisition of social housing homes, such subjective academic notions of what is or is not a home per se, appears irrelevant for most residents due to the fact that they are actual physical owners and occupants of specific their homes either as secure tenants, leaseholders or freeholders. However, even for those that may not fall in those categories, there appears to be sufficient standing under Art 8 for them to assert their rights. Given that, they are non-transient accommodation or hotel rooms. Many live in these properties as their main homes with their families hence engaging Art 8. In terms of wider estate regeneration, conducted through the powers of CPOs, public authorities,[88] as social housing providers attract the jurisdiction of HRA 1998 and Art 8 of ECHR.[89] Mainly because

---

[82] Marckx x Belgium(1979)ECHR 2

[83] https://www.echr.coe.int/Documents/Convention_ENG.pdf

[84] https://www.echr.coe.int/Documents/Guide_Art_8_ENG.pdf

[85] Louizdou V Turkey(1996)ECHR 70

[86] https://www.echr.coe.int/Documents/Convention_ENG.pdf

[87] https://minelres.lv/coe/court/Buckley.htm

[88] Connors V UK(2005) 40 EHRR 9 'gypsies' removal from a locality was violation of art8

[89] R (weaver v London & Quadrant Housing Trust(2009) EWCA Civ 587

the issue here involves home and family life which must be only interfered with in 'accordance with the law'.[90]

Therefore, residents affected by CPOs, could rely on Art 8(1) in asserting their human rights if the public authorities do so in contravention of the law as held in the case of Malone, where it was affirmed that the 'exercise of powers must be in accordance with the law'.[91] The issue in *Malone* involved determination of infringement of rights by surveillance and the court held that although this was consistent with domestic law, discretionary use or application by officers was arbitrary. Therefore being incompatible with Art 8 of ECHR, although in this case the issue involved a tangential issue of surveillance not necessarily confiscation of a home.

Nevertheless, it falls within the remit of Art 8 and it also highlights the principle of a requirement of public authorities acting in accordance with the law, which is applicable to CPO affected parties. The wider point that must be further emphasised here is that planning and public authorities possess opaque, extensive discretionary powers[92], which are susceptible to arbitrary use.[93] Such abuse could be detrimental to individuals affected by decisions arising from CPOs, such as the demolition of housing estate homes, inadequate compensation, environmental hazards, displacement, dislocation, low or disputed valuations and the need for rehousing. Hence, raising potential incompatibility with Art 8, if CPOs are applied unlawfully or where there are illegitimate aims and disproportionate actions.[94] Furthermore, there are implied positive obligations where environmental factors directly and seriously affect private and family life. For example in estate regenerated areas like Southall, Westbury in Lambeth and other areas like Hackney there are increased complaints of environmental pollution especially in areas where the developers are building on contaminated land such as in Southall and the Westbury estate in Lambeth, South

---

[90] https://swarb.co.uk/malone-v-the-united-kingdom-echr-2-aug-1984/

[91] Malone v UK (1984) ECHR 10

[92] Greg Brown & Sean Yeong Wei Chin (2013) Assessing the Effectiveness of Public Participation in Neighbourhood Planning, Planning Practice & Research, 28:5, 563-588, DOI: 10.1080/02697459.2013.820037

[93] Too-poor-to-play-children-in-social-housing-blocked-from-communal-playground, https://www.theguardian.com/cities/2019/mar/25/

[94] Lustig-Prean and Beckett v UK(1999)ECHR 71 relating to UK military ban on LBGT due to 'operational' issues

London[95]. Although there is protection against interference within Art 8 in tandem A1P1, such a provision does not guarantee peaceful enjoyment of property.

The rationale under A1P1, which appears to offer qualified guarantees, appears both outdated and puzzling. Given that environmental or construction hazards associated with CPOs, pose serious and sometimes an existential threat to the health of residents or those exposed to such exposure. Such construction hazards include asbestos, lead, co2, benzene, industrial noise, dust, and fumes among other toxins. So the question has to be asked if those hazards exist how can it be that those affected are not guaranteed a peaceful and quiet enjoyment of their homes or home environment?

Is it possible to completely separate the two aspects of environmental protections with the interference in the peaceful and quite enjoyment of one's life? It is possible that given the current ubiquitous and front stage environmental campaigns, the facts and impact on those affected by estate regeneration construction or demolition could have potential challenges that could force a revisit of the courts approach or conclusions on environmental protection under Art8 and A1P1. It therefore appears that under the current ECHR Art 8 regime, save in exceptionally serious cases, environmental protections for CPO construction affected parties remains uncertain under Art 8 and A1P1 OF ECHR.

Chapter 4

Other Associated rights under Art 8 during CPOs in Estate regeneration

Among other potential safeguards provided under Art 8, discussed in detail below, are associated with issues such as succession, contracts of parties and the protection of a positive duty for the integration of children since family law matters relate to a family home.[96] This protection under Art 8 extends to state benefits or

---

[95] https://www.theguardian.com/environment/2019/may/04/brownfield-site-new-homes-building-wrecking-health-southall

allowances emphasising respect for family life[97]but is not applicable to fiancées. This is critically relevant to residents facing CPOs, which could determine re-housing, compensation or succession rights, not just for individuals, but for those they share their homes with or their relatives.

Tenancies and Art 8 in CPOS

Among other issues, the impact on the various types of tenancies is one of the areas that may engage protection under Art 8 including CPO affected estate regeneration residents or affected parties. There may be preconditions imposed on residents under CPO schemes, [98]whose occupation rights had ceased or those who are short-term occupants after displacing secure tenants[99]during the so-called callously named decanting process.[100]

The relevance here is that due to welfare cuts, high rents, low pay and job insecurity, short or informal arrangements such as sub renting or sharing homes is the most affordable way to live[101] or work in some cities[102]. It is arguable that such homes need a level of protection beyond the narrow confines of statutory or contractual arrangements.[103] This was highlighted in *Chapman V UK,[104] where* the concept of a home was expanded to cabins, bungalows stationed on land irrespective of the lawfulness under national law as well as second homes.[105] A principle that could be

---

[96] https://www.echr.coe.int/Documents/Convention_ENG.pdf

[97] https://www.echr.coe.int/Documents/Guide_Art_8_ENG.pdf

[98] http://estateregeneration.lambeth.gov.uk/key_guarantees#homeowners

[99] Part IV of HA 1985, amended by HA1988 and HA 96.

[100] Alice Belotti LSE Housing & Communities, Estate Regeneration and Community Impacts Challenges and lessons for social landlords, developers and local councils, Case report 99, March 2016

[101] Fenton, Alex. "Housing benefit reform and the spatial segregation of low-income households in London." (2011).

[102] Hamnett, Chris. "Moving the poor out of central London? The implications of the coalition government 2010 cuts to Housing Benefits." *Environment and Planning A* 42.12 (2010): 2809-2819.

[103] Michael Edwards (2016) The housing crisis and London, City, 20:2, 222-237, DOI: 10.1080/13604813.2016.1145947

[104] Chapman-v-united-kingdom-application-no-2723895

asserted by CPO affected residents who may not be long-term occupants or have formal tenancies.

There may however be limitations where there has been minimal occupation or weak links to the property to the extent that they are expunged. Therefore, sufficient nexus or occupation is necessary for recognition of a right to a home. Hence a mere possibility of inheritance may not give rise to a connection to a home under Art 8[106]al though altering the terms of tenancy[107] was found to be an interference with Art 8.[108]

It is nevertheless, evident that on the face of it, CPO processes, interfere with the respect for a home. Despite the fact, that such interference can be qualified under A1P1[109] to allow a member state some latitude in implementation, [110]if certain criteria are attached to the measures.[111] However, if the right in point is critical to the individual's enjoyment of personal intimate rights, the courts minimise the margin of appreciation.[112] Such as where there is demolition of homes[113] leading to[114] compulsion to move and hence a clear interference in the respect to a home under Art 8.[115] This rationale was unambiguously emphasised in Connors v. UK[116] where the court held *inter alia*, 'that the loss of one's home is a most extreme form of interference with the right to respect for the home'. In addition, since there was no justification for such interference, such as what the court referred to as a *pressing*

[105] https://www.echr.coe.int/Guide_Art_8_ENG.pdf

[106] https://www.echr.coe.int/Guide_Art_8_ENG.pdf

[107] Loretta Lees,The Urban Injustices of New Labour's "New Urban Renewal": The Case of the Aylesbury Estate in London, 2013

[108] (*Berger-Krall and Others v. Slovenia*, § 264);

[109] (*Howard v. the United Kingdom*,

[110] Alec Samuels, The planning process and judicial control: the case for better judicial involvement and control,J.P.L 1570

[111] *Noack and Others v. Germany*

[112] (*Connors v. the United Kingdom*, § 82).

[113] (*Aboufadda v. France* (Dec.));

[114] *Selçuk and Asker v. Turkey*, § 86; *Akdivar and Others v. Turkey* [GC], § 88; *Menteş and Others v. Turkey*, § 73).

[115] *Noack and Others v. Germany* (Dec.));

[116] Application no. 66746/01

social need or a legitimate aim, the court concluded that there was a violation of Art 8 pf ECHR[117]. This judgement accurately reflects the predicament of CPO affected residents by housing estates regeneration and could potentially provide an avenue to challenge such interference.

Estate regeneration disrepair or blight and Art 8 associated with CPOs

Another issue to consider is that in areas where CPO processes are enacted or merely announced, disrepair or neglect is a common feature.[118] Observers believe this appears to be managed decline to hasten what is termed as the decanting process.[119] A term that reflects the inhumanity and sanitisation of the arguably inhumane process of home expropriation[120]. The use of language and other phrases like brownfield sites or opportunity area drain or minimise any human association or presence in the areas or homes being expropriated. Coupled with the disrepair, blight and the consequential anti-social behaviour, the communities become ripe for targeted added claims by the acquiring authorities of an urgent need for regeneration,[121] which then softens the CPO approval process.

Disrepair has been found to be an infringement of Art 8 even[122]after examining the existence of procedural guarantees to determine the margin of appreciation. Disrepair, neglect and blight are also associated with *nuisance in the legal context under the pollution act 1972 or a public nuisance which falls under criminal law. This*

[117] CASE OF CONNORS v. THE UNITED KINGDOM (Application no. 66746/01) JUDGMENT STRASBOURG, 27 May 2004,https://www.refworld.org/cases,ECHR

[118] Estate Regeneration and Community Impacts Challenges and lessons for social landlords, developers and local councils, Case report 99,Alice Belotti LSE Housing & Communities March 2016;

See also Save Cressingham gardens; Save Central Hill: @savewetburysw8

[119] (*Khamidov v. Russia*,

[120] States and real estate private equity firms questioned for compliance with human rights, https://www.ohchr.org

[121] Estate Regeneration and Community Impacts Challenges and lessons for social landlords, developers and local councils, Case report 99,Alice Belotti LSE Housing & Communities March 2016;

[122] *Novoseletskiy v. Ukraine*, §§ 84-88).

is therefore another aspect that could come under the remit of Art 8 where parties who may not possess direct proprietary interest may seek to pursue their property rights from that perspective under Art 8. This is especially during construction related to CPO enforced estate regeneration. Such as in a case where a tree was felled into a neighbour's garden.[123] This is applicable to parties affected by CPO construction nuisances, asbestos or other contaminants as sighted in the Westbury and Southall cases[124] above. As mentioned such a nuisance could attract criminal sanctions under the codes such as the Asbestos Code 2012[125], as well as arising to the standard that breaches the respect for a home or home environment, hence being in contravention of Art 8 of ECHR.

Although Art 8 does not offer an inherent protection of a clean environment per se, planning decisions interfere with people's home and family lives, therefore triggering Art 8 and A1P1.[126] Moreover, since the convention is considered a living instrument, [127] it should be interpreted to fit present day conditions[128]to balance the rights of residents affected with a CPO due to public authorities' actions, which fall under the purview of art 8.[129]

It is arguably due to such hazardous intrusion or exposure that heightens the sense of dangerous impact on communities[130], which compels them to move away from their locality, family and their support networks.[131] There by essentially destroying the '*essential ingredient of a family ... the right to live together, enjoy each other's*

---

[123] *Lane V The Royal Borough of Kensington and Chelsea London Borough Council(2013)EWHC 1320(QB)*

[124] https://www.theguardian.com/environment/2019/may/04/brownfield-site-new-homes-building-wrecking-health-southall

[125] http://www.hse.gov.uk/asbestos/regulations.htm
[126] *J.P.L 2010,3 298-309*

[127] *Tyrer V UK*

[128] *J.P.L 2010, 3 298-309*

[129] https://www.echr.coe.int/Documents/Guide_Art_8_ENG.pdf

[130] Paul Watt (2013) 'It's not for us', City, 17:1, 99-118, DOI: 10.1080/13604813.2012.754190

[131] Tom Slater (2009) Missing Marcuse: On gentrification and displacement, City, 13:2-3, 292-311, DOI: 10.1080/13604810902982250

company[132] and relationship development'[133] consistent with the 'notion of family life being an autonomous concept'.[134]

Private life and Art 8 in CPOs

Under ECHR, private life is interpreted widely to include 'personal and physical integrity'.[135] The relevancy to CPOs is the excessive unjustifiable intrusion into people's lives culminating to eventual displacement[136]instigated and characterised by collection of personal data,[137] especially in circumstances where many residents could be vulnerable[138]with no access to independent advice or support. Furthermore, such intrusion and demand for disclosure requires justification to avoid contravention of Art 8[139] especially where the acquiring authority is the intruding party, which arguably gains competitive negotiating, commercial and legal advantage.

It appears that even providing information for census purposes may be an interference of rights under Art 8, including surveys, under the realm of Art 8 jurisdiction.[140]Furthermore, intrusion in private life also includes the loss of support networks in the locality, which disrupts employment and professional associations[141]

---

[132] Olson v Sweden

[133] Marckx v Belgium

[134] Marckx v Belgium; https://www.echr.coe.int /Guide_Art_8_ENG.pdf

[135] X and Y v the Netherlands(1985) ECHR 4

[136] Jane Rendell (2017) 'Arry's Bar: condensing and displacing on the Aylesbury Estate, The Journal of Architecture, 22:3, 532-554, DOI: 10.1080/13602365.2017.1310125

[137] *http://newmanfrancis.org/projects/westbury-lambeth/*

[138] https://www.ucl.ac.uk/engineering-exchange/sites/engineering-exchange/files/fact-sheet-health-and-wellbeing-social-housing.pdf

[139] As held in, Hilton V UK Application no,12015/86

[140] Z v Finland(1997) 25 EHHR 371

which appears to be an example where there seems to be a convergence of Art 8 with A1P1 where interference in one is private, personal, or family life could lead to a legitimate challenge under both Articles. As held, In *Niemietz v Germany[142]*, where the applicant's complaints of entry and seizure of the documents in the lawyer's office was found to be disproportionate and inconsistent with the expectation of confidentiality *'inherent in the lawyer's profession'[143]*, although in Niemietz, the court *did not find any 'separate issue under A1P1.'[144]*

Moreover, as indicated above, circumstances that could potentially lead to breach of Art 8 are more extensive than just physical possessions per se since art 8 protects attributes that are consistent with the preservation of family life and associated human dignity. Consequently, the court has also found[145]the loss of employment for a *breach of oath* to trigger Art 8, due to the impact it has on *relationships, material well-being, fami*ly and reputation. This is applicable to CPO affected parties, in the sense that compulsion to move from one's home has spiral effects on access to employment, education, support networks, well-being, family life and consequently one's human dignity and reputation as mentioned in the reports above. The other consideration for potential breach of art 8 is the fairness of the associated process which is discussed in detail below under art 6 but briefly in the paragraphs below under art 8.

Fair process and Art 8 during CPOs in Estate regeneration

Public authorities often use bureaucratic and inscrutable language or opaque processes. CPO decisions and processes may not be understood or formalised during a disruptive protracted process for residents. Valuations, advance payment

---

[141] Volkov Ukraine(21722/11) 2013 IRLR 480(ECtHR),

[142] 13710/88, [1992] 16 EHRR 97, [1992] ECHR 80

[143] Guidance Note 10, The right to property under ECHR

[144] Guidance No 10, The Right to property under the ECHR, pg 21

[145] Practical Law UK practice Note 8 835 5732

and negotiations for compensation or rehousing require specialist technical advice or access to financial resources.[146] Specifically, valuations are determined largely by the acquiring authority with limited independent oversight and imposition of pre-conditions in case of a valuation dispute.[147]This is worsened by the seeming lack of clear reasoning or timely information provided to residents, especially those that face measures that lead to eviction, which attracts protection under Art 8.[148]

The process is characterised by a lack of transparency, imbalance of resources, state self-interests or conflicts of interest due to decision makers being the acquiring party.[149] Planning decisions leading to CPOs [150] are sometimes authorised by the same acquiring party, which would appear to be a manifest conflict of interest with devastating detrimental impact in some cases.[151] An issue highlighted by Anna Minton, in her report 'Scaring the living daylight', [152]a situation which is acutely relevant to victims of estate regeneration enforced through CPOs.[153] In a nutshell, CPO affected residents who are in effect removed and therefore evicted from their homes and community[154] are subjected to obscure, broad, arbitrary and vague language without access to independent legal advice.[155]

[146] Stuart Hodkinson, Chris Essen, (2015) "Grounding accumulation by dispossession in everyday life: The unjust geographies of urban regeneration under the Private Finance Initiative", International Journal of Law in the Built Environment, Vol. 7 Issue: 1, pp.72-91, https://doi.org/10.1108/IJLBE-01-2014-0007

[147] Estate Regeneration and Community Impacts Challenges and lessons for social landlords, developers and local councils, Case report 99,Alice Belotti LSE Housing & Communities March 2016; See also Save Cressingham gardens;

See inter alia Hackworth & Smith, 2001; Glynn, 2008; Lees et al., 2008; Shaw, 2008, argue that Stock transfer in London can be understood through the lens of state-led 'third-wave gentrification', a widespread phenomenon across British, North American and Australian cities.

[148] Donoghue, above

[149]See inter alia Hackworth & Smith, 2001; Glynn, 2008; Lees et al., 2008; Shaw, 2008, argue that Stock transfer in London can be understood through the lens of state-led 'third-wave gentrification', a widespread phenomenon across British, North American and Australian cities.

[150] Buckley v. the United Kingdom, § 60);

[151]Siobhan O'Sullivan, et al. "Hearing the Voices of Children and Youth in Housing Estate Regeneration." Children, Youth and Environments, vol. 27, no. 3, 2017, pp. 1–15. JSTOR, www.jstor.org/27.3.0001.

[152] http://spinwatch.org/images/Reports/Scaring_the_living_daylight_final_27_March_13.pdf

[153] Estate Regeneration and Community Impacts Challenges and lessons for social landlords, developers and local councils, Case report 99,Alice Belotti LSE Housing & Communities March 2016; See also Save Cressingham gardens;

[154] Jane Rendell (2017) 'Arry's Bar: condensing and displacing on the Aylesbury Estate, The Journal of Architecture, 22:3, 532-554, DOI: 10.1080/13602365.2017.1310125

The Kate Barker Report, regarding the use of land for planning[156] further highlights the problems associated with the procedural unfairness in the planning process. It refers to 'planning decisions as policy decisions or expediency decisions, conducted in an anomalous manner'. An observation or description that would be consistent with the view that CPOs are imbalanced, favour acquiring parties, lack transparency and there is no real independent scrutiny, as highlighted in the various reports above.

Although, there is a possibility of judicial review it characteristically, largely focuses on procedural flaws, requires extensive resources and is characterised with structural impediments, which are looked at in more detail, under Art 6 below. As an example of such impediments, challenging such arbitrary decisions through judicial review would require a duty to give reasons by a public authority, documentation of the facts and any associated detrimental impact. However, requested information is not always provided, often delayed, deducted when provided, vague or broad even when conducted through freedom of information requests under the FOI Act.[157] Specifically, in areas like Southwark[158], Lambeth[159] and others, [160] residents' demand for due process remains a distant or box ticking exercise.

Therefore, the importance for a public authority to provide reasons for its actions or decisions cannot be understated. Such importance, to give reasons, in matters such as CPOs is captured in the law gazette article, in dramatic language. The article

[155] Duty to give reasons, :https://www.lawgazette.co.uk/legal-updates/local-government-duty-to-give-reasons

[156] J.P.L 1570

[157] https://www.whatdotheyknow.com/request/quantity_of_freedom_of_informati#incoming-1055418; https://www.whatdotheyknow.com/request/information_related_to_the_impac#outgoing-950497; http://www.brixtonbuzz.com/2017/12/lambeth-council-refuses-to-admit-how-many-empty-homes-are-on-cressingham-gardens-estate/

[158] http://35percent.org/heygate-regeneration-faq/ https://www.theguardian.com/cities/2018/sep/12/london-council-aylesbury-estate-development-southwark-financial-risk

[159] https://www.socialhousingsoundarchive.com/westbury-estate, https://savewestburysw8.wordpress.com/2015/04/14/the-westbury-residents-main-concerns/

[160] https://haringeydefendcouncilhousingblog.wordpress.com/

points to *'Shakespeare's decadent, drunken and corpulently challenged knight, Falstaff, when pressed to give reasons to verify an obvious lie, robustly declined. He declared that if '… reasons were as plentiful as blackberries, I would give no man a reason upon compulsion. But although Falstaff as a private individual was presumably within his rights to deny reasons, public authorities cannot be so cavalier.*[161] Despite the Shakespearean dramatization, there is a very serious point about accountability, transparency, protection against abuse of office or at worst impunity especially where 'the decision-maker is disagreeing with a considered and reasoned recommendation', as Lewison LJ, observed in the Court of Appeal'.[162]

Such intrusive and detrimental actions necessitate a need for the estate regeneration process to be conducted in a manner that respects the human dignity of affected persons and gives respect to their home,[163] giving appropriate weight to individual circumstances.[164] A point that was highlighted in *Connors V UK*[165] where it was held that the so called *gypsies* removal from a locality was in violation of Art 8, since the authority in question, appeared to evade statutory issues by making the applicant's wife sign a notice to quit without due regard to respect for his home. These actions effectively evaded any proper, fair or adequate due process. The emphasis on proper due process appears to be also reflected in *McCann*, where it was reiterated that 'any person at risk of an interference of this magnitude should in principle be able to have the proportionality of the measure determined by an independent tribunal in the light of the relevant principles under Article 8.*[166]

Therefore, for many CPO affected parties facing loss of their homes and the spiral detrimental effects that follow such potential displacement or dispossession, [167]the need for a fair and expeditious due process is an issue that cannot be minimised as indicated above.[168] It is however important to point out that despite the inherent

---

[161] Local government, duty to give reasons, *https://www.lawgazette.co.uk*
[162] Local government, duty to give reasons, *https://www.lawgazette.co.uk*

[163] (*Rousk v. Sweden*, §§ 137-142).

[164] (*Gillow v. the United Kingdom*, §§ 56-58).

[165] (2005) 40 EHRR9

[166] *McCann v. the United Kingdom, § 50*

[167] Such as loss of employment, extraction from school, effect on wellbeing, financial hardship or disruption

unfairness of the process and decisions, in some cases, such as Horada,[169] the initial decisions were overruled. In *Horada,* the court stopped the plans to demolish shepherds bush market, which would displace and dispossess thousands of local small businesses. It is however noticeable that these were businesses as opposed to homes and it's not clear whether that contributed to the reasoning in the final decision, an issue that needs further scrutiny which will be discussed in further detail in the later chapters detailing CPOs on a case by case basis.

In nutshell, as discussed above, Art 8, both substantively and procedurally appears to at least in law, provide a potential mechanism for challenging housing estate expropriation by public authorities. But such further relief under Art 8 appears inextricably linked with other rights under Art 6 and A1P1, such as the guarantee of the peaceful enjoyment of possessions, safeguard for ownership and other property rights under A1P1, as long as certain criteria are met. However, it is important to emphasise that while these protections appear intersectional with procedural rights under art 6 or protections under A1P1, there appears to be no unfettered protection given the various qualifications or limitations.

Art 6

Art 6 (1) of the ECHR states that," In the determination of his civil rights and obligations or of any criminal charge against him, everyone is entitled to a fair and public hearing within a reasonable time by an independent and impartial tribunal established by law'.

Art 6(1) is applicable to property rights, privacy matters, internal hearings or processes in terms of procedural fairness, access to an independent tribunal or equality of arms. Although Art 6 is not absolute,[170] it refers to some procedural limits

[168] Dispossession, the great housing swindle, https://www.dispossessionfilm.com/

[169] [2016] WLR(D) 148, [2016] PTSR 1271, [2016] EWCA Civ 169

[170] Ashingdale v UK(1985) 7 EHRR 528

as acceptable without procedural guarantees at every stage and stresses access to a court with full jurisdiction.[171]

As mentioned above, the focus here is about the relevant provisions of art 6 and others that could be applicable to estate regeneration through the use of CPOs. In analysing such relevance, a key issue therefore is a determination as to whether a civil right in Art 6 is 'a private right as opposed to a public right'.[172] In the context of estate regeneration, which is a housing matter, there is no ambiguity that this is consistent with a civil right in the context of ECHR and international conventions.[173] It is therefore the civil arm of Art 6 that is applicable to estate regenerations which therefore requires an identifiable issue over rights that have jurisdiction in domestic law[174]and consideration of the application of those rights.[175] In estate regeneration, there is an array of issues that require an expeditious, fair and independent determination as under art 6 stipulations. Such issues include the various competing interests between CPO affected parties, a need for examination of the consultation process,[176] a fundamental need for fair hearings as well as expeditious just compensation and adequate rehousing.[177]

The civil arm of Art 6 provides procedural guarantees in resolving disputes concerning property and ensures access to a court as well as a fair independent tribunal to safeguard the rights of those affected, although it covers permissible

[171] Golder V UK (1975) EHRR 524

[172] Alec Samuels, The planning process and judicial control: the case for better judicial involvement and control,J.P.L 1570

[173] Kenna, P. (2008). Housing rights: positive duties and enforceable rights at the European Court of Human Rights. European Human Rights Law Review, 13(2), 193-208

[174] H V Belgium(1987) 8 EHH 123 and GEorgiadis V Greece

[175] Bentehm V Netherlands(1985 8 EHRR

[176] Bokrosova v LLB http://www.bailii.org/ew/cases/EWHC/Admin/2015/3386.html

[177] Begum v London Borough of Tower Hamlets(2003) UKHL 5

[178] Handbook n0 10, Property rights under ECHR

[179] CASE OF DRAON v. FRANCE, (Application no. 1513/03), https://hudoc.echr.coe.int

interferences. To be admissible under Art 6 any potential applicant needs to have an existing interest or legitimate expectation in terms of possession or property rights under A1P1. However, where the eventual outcome is final after determination, it appears that no such prior requirement is mandated under Art 6[178]. It would also appear that emphasis will be placed on A1P1 if there is an issue that calls for the finality or decisiveness of the domestic legal actions but will be placed on Art 6 If the issue is about process. For instance, In *Draon v France,*[179] the court found a breach of the applicant's right to property due to a law limiting compensation associated with disability prior to the conclusion of the proceedings. Similarly, in the case of *Canea Catholic Church v Greece,* the court found that denying the applicant's legal personality was in breach of Art 6 after refusing to entertain the church's contention that such a rejection would deprive the church of the possibility of taking part in legal proceedings.

A question that arises is whether this is a clear signal that the court will take a pragmatic view rather than a uniform approach, as to what strand of specific issues are entertained and how to channel such issues when considering property rights under its jurisdiction. Whatever the answer to this question is , a potential lesson for CPO estate regeneration potential applicants, in terms of strategic and timely positioning of any potential legal actions under Art 8, A1P1 and Art 6, is that applicants should be cognizant of the fact that although there might be a prima facie case of breach ECHR rights, a strategic positioning of specific issues to determine a specific legal principle would appear to have a chance of success than a wider claim of breach of property rights.

The difficulty for almost all potential CPO estate regeneration affected applicants is that their main and prime goal is to preserve their property, homes and associated rights or livelihoods. As opposed to setting legal principles under the ECHR, which is a costly, protracted and academic process.

Access and delays

As discussed above, briefly, the other aspect that estate regeneration CPO affected parties face during housing estate expropriation is a lack of access to an expeditious fair process and independent tribunal. This is made worse by high costs, extensive

time constraints and lack of parity between the competing parties. Furthermore, residents are faced with the prospect of proceedings such as valuation disputes not being determined by an independent tribunal.[180] A situation which is consistent with *Ali V UK*,[181] where it was held that an applicant should have been afforded access to a fair hearing before an independent and impartial tribunal.

Similarly, resolutions should be consistent with the individual circumstances of those concerned which is consistent with HRA/ECHR art 6 which a fair process part of which would require an expeditious process or remedies such as just compensation or suitable adequate rehousing. Otherwise CPO affected potential applicants could be successful in alleging a breach of art 6 rights due to a delayed process or decision such as in *Robins v UK, where* there was a breach of Art 6[182] due to an unreasonable delay. CPO processes characteristically take years to conclude, [183]with detrimental effect on residents on various areas of their lives. Yet acquiring authorities have extensive resources unlike individuals who are compelled to accept offers such as lower valuations that would otherwise be unacceptable.[184] The decision making process is characteristically structurally advantageously skewed in favour of or conducted by acquiring authorities' to secure their legal, financial and political interests.[185]

Even when those affected pursue successful legal action related to unfair procedural issues, the acquiring authorities could circumnavigate the ruling by essentially starting the process again. For example Lambeth council was held to have failed to follow lawful process in reaching its decisions. A decision that residents affected thought would cause the council to abandon the entire scheme. However, the council did not abandon the scheme although residents have since applied for the right to

[180] See DCLG guidance; https://www.gov.uk/government/publications/compulsory-purchase-process-and-the-crichel-down-rules-guidance

[181] Ali V UK(2016) 63 HRR 20,

[182] https://www.echr.coe.int/documents/guide_art_6_eng.pdf file:///T:/002-7866.pdf

[183] Dispossession the great social housing swindle : https://www.dispossessionfilm.com

[184] Stuart Hodkinson, Chris Essen, (2015) "Grounding accumulation by dispossession in everyday life: The unjust geographies of urban regeneration under the Private Finance Initiative", International Journal of Law in the Built Environment, Vol. 7 Issue: 1, pp.72-91, https://doi.org/10.1108/IJLBE-01-2014-0007

[185] Alice Belotti, Estate regeneration and community impact, http://sticerd.lse.ac.uk/dps/case/cr/casereport99.pdf

manage successfully[186]. Whether this will force the council to abandon the demolition f cressingham gardens[187] remains to be seen.

This was in the case of *Bokrosova V Lambeth,*[188] where it was held that Lambeth acted unlawfully due to a failure to observe procedural issues in reaching its decisions. The court stated that the process of consultation, '*must include sufficient reasons for the proposals to enable consultees to consider them, and respond to them intelligently; enough time must be given for that; and the consultation responses must be taken conscientiously into account when the decision is taken…. ensure public participation in the local authority's decision making process and … in order for consultation to achieve that objective, it must fulfil basic minimum requirements'.*[189]

However, despite the ruling, that essentially quashed their decisions, the council still pursued the regeneration by restarting the process.[190] The council's ability to do this raises questions about the effectiveness of judicial review as a mechanism to challenge CPOs. Since then the residents of Cressingham gardens have secured the right to manage as mentioned above[191] and it is interesting to see how Lambeth council will respond or how that affects the overall housing estate demolition programme[192] under Lambeth council.

As already highlighted above, part of a fair process requires access to an independent and impartial tribunal. Although pursuing legal action could theoretically attempt to meet the requirement of access to a fair and impartial hearing or tribunal, it is a costly and long process for CPO affected residents. Prohibitive costs bar aggrieved residents from instigating legal action especially in the case of leaseholders who risk cost orders,[193] even if they satisfy the impeding requirements

---

[186] Right-to-transfer-determination-cressingham-gardens-estate, https://www.gov.uk

[187] http://cressinghampeoplesplan.org.uk/

[188] (2015)EWHC 3386(ADMIN)

[189] Citing *'one aspect of the Coughlan test'*

[190] https://savecressingham.wordpress.com/2016/12/21/residents-vow-to-fight-on-after-high-court-decision/

[191] right-to-transfer-determination-cressingham-gardens-estate

[192] https://savecressingham.wordpress.com/

such as seeking leave to commence legal proceedings.[194] Parties with deep pockets such as public bodies or property developers may unreasonably delay or deny their rights without the opportunity for the full circumstances ought to be fairly, diligently and impartially   determined to prevent abuse of process or punitive penalties.[195] Such tactics are often deployed by the acquiring authorities in concert with developers or interested parties.[196] Therefore, CPO affected residents could have Art 6 engaged if they were subjected to processes that amount to barring them from bringing civil actions against the acquiring authority as was the case in *Z and others V UK,* [197]where the court clarified that, *'the inability of applicants to sue the local authority flowed from the principles governing the substantive right of action in negligence`* and art 6 was therefore engaged. In other words rejecting the argument was being advanced to prevent the applicants from suing the authorities.

However, even when there is an avenue of access to an independent, fair and impartial process, there are other criteria necessary that CPO affected parties would have to satisfy due to the fact engagement of Art 6 requires a disputable implementation of national law in a specific matter.[198]

An issue that was considered in *Lithgow,* where the nationalisation of property, under a local Act,[199] was found to engage Art 6 after the applicants alleged a lack of statutory compensation.[200] In this case, there was an undisputable right of a property owners' claim to statutory compensation, legislated for under the s39 of the Land Compensation Act 1973,[201] which in this particular case appears not to have been

---

[193] part-44-general-rules-about-costs,www.justice.gov.uk/courts/procedure-rules/c

[194] H V UK, Application no 11559/85

[195] Osman V UK(2000) 29 EHRR 245 (1998) ECHR 101 (1999) 1 LGRT 431

[196] Anna Minton, Scaring the living day light of people, https://www.annaminton.com/single-post/2016/03/21/Scaring-The-Living-Daylights-Out-Of-People

[197] Z and others V UK(2001) ECHRR 333, (2002) 34 EHRR 9

[198] Lithgow v UK

[199] Aircraft and Shipbuilding industries ACT 1977

[200] Practical Law Practice note 835 5732

satisfactorily implemented by the state. Therefore, where the local authorities do not apply the relevant ECHR rights, such as art 6, it is plausible that there is a real possibility of a justiciable issue by the affected parties.

That could be in instances where there are unreasonable or disproportionate barriers to a person's rights, derived from state actions, or an issue of a decisive nature in relation to the rights of an affected party,[202] such as a home or business affected by a CPO, that could lead to life changing intergenerational detriments. As was the case in *Koning V Germany*[203], where a civil right, under ECHR, was considered to be of substantive character and defined autonomously irrespective of the characterisation under national law.[204] Similarly, in *Brugger V Austria*, it was held that the complainant was entitled to an oral hearing especially that judicial review was not available as remedy in the local jurisdiction. Therefore, it would appear that once there is a clear determination of a right at peril under Art 6, the courts are prepared to provide latitude or opportunity for such determination, which is a potential positive trend for CPO, affected parties due to estate regeneration, which ofcourse have direct effect on the UK as a signatory to the ECHR but also via the HRA 98 which incorporates the ECHR rights.

However, as indicated above, the recent curtailment of legal aid is an inherent disadvantage, which makes it almost impossible for disenfranchised residents to challenge detrimental decisions associated with CPO decisions. Particularly leaseholders who may have the value of their homes taken into account as capital and therefore could fall outside the threshold for legal aid eligibility hence risk substantial cost orders that would be attached to their homes. Despite the fact fundamental rights associated with home expropriation, are at issue here which make legal aid arguably necessary in such civil proceedings.[205]This also raises a legitimate question as to whether there is overall property ownership in light of state dispossession through the use of the law. This is a wider question that will be covered in detail in the chapters below.

---

[201] http://www.legislation.gov.uk/1973

[202] Practical Law Practice note 835 5732

[203] Koning V Germany(1978) 2 EHRR 170

[204] Practical law practice note,J.P.L, 2010,3, 298-309

[205] Stars and Chambers v Procurator-where appointment of a temporary sheriff was held to be incompatible with Art 6. One local authority proposed to appoint its own mechanisms of final arbitration

However, the central theme appears to be the manifest imbalance of power and appearance of conflicts of interest in planning processes characterised by a lack of fairness or equality of arms, procedural fairness or propriety or access to an independent adjudication.[206] An inherent imbalance which is arguably worsened, where local authorities' planning or cabinet decisions appear to favour the interests of the acquiring party which are usually the same Local Authority, in the case of estate demolitions, such as in Lambeth[207], Southwark[208] and Haringey[209] among others. For example, in documented cases, during the CPO related proceedings, residents are accorded less time to argue their case or rebuttal of disputable facts and refused access to information[210]. This seems to be inherently incompatible with Art 6, as was the case in *Borgers v Belgium*[211], where a defendant who could not hear or make responses to official arguments was said to have had his art 6 rights breached.[212] Even where it would be assumed that the process was fair, planning conditions are reportedly changed, breached after the process[213] or at least not implemented as issued.[214] A practice that raises pertinent questions about the integrity of the whole process and whose interests are being served.[215]

Lack of access to information by residents

---

[206] R v (Wright v SOS for health and another(2009) UKHL 3

[207] https://www.opendemocracy.net/en/shine-a-light/residents-challenge-lambeth-plans-to-demolish-homes/

[208] https://www.newstatesman.com/politics/2013/11/look-heygate-estate-whats-wrong-londons-housing

[209] https://www.theguardian.com/commentisfree/2017/jul/03/britain-power-contempt-grenfell-labour-haringey-social-housing

[210] https://newsfromcrystalpalace.wordpress.com/tag/campaign-for-freedom-of-information/

[211] Borgers v Belgium(1993) 15 EHRR 92

[212] Practical law practice note public sector.

[213] Council tenants win 'segregated' garden rule fight, https://www.bbc.com/news/uk-england-london-

[214] https://www.theguardian.com/cities/2019/mar/25/ too-poor-to-play-children-in-social-housing-blocked-from-communal-playground

[215] Anna Minton, Big Capital, who is London For

Another common complaint by CPO affected residents is the lack of access[216] to material information and the need to be heard which is critical to the equality of arms.[217] In any process of challenging or asserting one's rights from public authorities or such entities, information from such public authorities is critical. However, freedom of information requests are protracted affairs and substantial information is either not timely provided[218] denied, [219]deducted or is in vague broad language whilst access to hearings in public is not always guaranteed.[220]

Lack of independent review

Another common feature is the fact that the unfairness of the process is heightened by the fact that there appears to be no genuinely independent review mechanisms, save for the court system whose encumbrances, such as cost or complexity have been documented above. This is not assisted by the increasing perception that planning functions and permission granting processes conducted by local authorities [221] appear to be more political, are not always based on statutory grounds[222] and objections do not lead to a hearing per se as part of due process.[223] This makes the need for a fair balance between the rights of the community or potential applicants to be presided over by an independent and impartial decision maker, from the beginning more urgent than ever. Especially when faced with the most intrusive action of all the loss or demolition of one's home.

The imbalance and the lack of impartiality is highlighted in *Tsfayo v UK (2007) ECHR 656*, where the issue involved an applicants' renewal for housing and council tax, which was rejected by the review board. The ECHR found that the board was not an

[216] https://newsfromcrystalpalace.wordpress.com/2018/11/26/lambeth-council-refuse-to-answer-foi-questions-made-by-news-from-crystal-palace/

[217] Feldbrugge V Netherlands(1986) 8 EHRR 425, see practice note above

[218]https://www.whatdotheyknow.com/request/asbestos_enquiry#incoming-1327131

[219]https://www.whatdotheyknow.com/request/somerleyton_road_steering_group_2321`11

[220] https://www.dailymail.co.uk/news/article-4656656/Kensington-councillor-DEFENDS-decision-meet-secret.html

[221] Bryan V UK(1995) 21 EHRR 342

[222] DCLG guidance

[223] R (Adlard V SOS for environment(2002) EWCA

independent tribunal and the possibility of judicial review was not a reprieve from the lack of independence and included councillors. Since public authorities review, their decisions by committees often staffed by councillors, such as in the CPO process, the lack of a fair and impartial consideration would appear to engage Art 6 given that the imminent loss of a home, such as that associated with a CPO, *ought to be a serious consideration.*[224] There should be procedural measures and safeguards to protect parties' convention rights,[225] with scrutiny placed on the protection of the residents' legitimate interests.[226] The court appeared to agree with the view that the vesting of land subject to a CPO *'cannot comply with Art.6 of the Convention, unless the courts have a jurisdiction to examine that decision on broad public law grounds'.*[227] Therefore, a similar decision by a public body, associated with a CPO could be *'unlawful if it were made for a purpose not recognised in the compulsory purchase order*[228] *or unconnected with the reason for the grant of those powers.'*[229]

Furthermore, where environmental or nuisance complaints are raised, during demolition or construction, some local authorities with confidential s106 agreements explained above, as agreements which essentially enable a scheme that would not be approved to proceed[230] or other agreements with developers[231] may have their impartiality or practical ability to enforce any planning regulations compromised. Therefore, potentially leading to planning conditions being ignored or breached[232] during and after grant of planning permission.[233] For example, on the Westbury Estate,[234] residents' repeated formal and informal requests or demands to have the HSE investigate the safety measures in place to protect residents from exposure to

---

[224] (*Ivanova and Cherkezov v. Bulgaria*)

[225] (*Irina Smirnova v. Ukraine*, § 94).

[226] (*Orlić v. Croatia*, § 64; *Gladysheva v. Russia*, §§ 94-95; *Kryvitska and Kryvitskyy v. Ukraine*, § 50; *Andrey Medvedev v. Russia*, § 55)

[227] Jonathan Ferris, 2010, Journal of Planning & Environment Law Compulsory purchase: is there a general right to judicial review to challenge the decision to vest land the subject of a confirmed compulsory purchase order?

[228] (*Grice v Dudley*8; *Capital Investments Ltd v Wednesfield Urban DC*9).

[229] *Congreve v Home Office*11; and *R. v Birmingham Licensing Committee Ex p. Kennedy*12).

[230] See www.Lambeth.gov.uk Westbury estate

[231] Council tenants win 'segregated' garden rule fight,https://www.london.gov.uk/sites/default/files/berkley_group.pdf

[232] https://www.bbc.com/news/uk-england-london-

[233] https://www.theguardian.com/cities/2019/mar/25/too-poor-to-play-children-in-social-housing-blocked-from-communal-playground

[234] Westbury-a-year-after-Grenfell, http://housingactivists.co.uk/grenfell

asbestos were reportedly routinely ignored[235] and were often referred to the developers themselves namely the Berkeley group.[236] Residents' concerns[237] appear to be supported by the findings of the HSE report[238]after concerted pressure from the local M[239]P and other parties. The HSE report found that procedures like using water suppression, covering dust, storage of asbestos[240] were not satisfactory or acceptable despite the initial claims by Lambeth Council.

Overall, the inherent impediments associated with instigating legal challenges to the planning process or decisions made by the local authorities. This adds to the manifest imbalance and inherent unfairness experienced by CPO affected parties. Planning policies, such as a CPO process infringe the rights of enjoyment of one's home and property . CPO processes under estate regeneration may further reduce market value because arguably buyers would avoid buying CPO affected properties and worse the planning process is regarded as favourable to developers intent on maximising profits by raising the prices of the new properties while minimising the values of the existing properties owned by residents.[241] The process is characterised with disputed valuation processes[242] without fair appeal processes, which prejudice residents' rights without the proportionality of the measures in question being determined by an independent tribunal. Cumulatively, this creates a hindrance for CPO challengers[243]and objectors from having a fair crack of the whip through a transparent, independent process as well as timely access to any requested related material.[244] Therefore creating a prejudicial effect to the probative value of such material at a later stage in the process, [245]which could be a potential breach of Art 6

[235] Families hit out at London gasworks redevelopment, Brownfield-site-new-homes-building-wrecking-health-southall, https://www.theguardian.com/environment/2019/may/04/

[236] The Lambeth and London 'estate clearances: PRESENCE of still uncovered believed to be hazardous construction soil , https://humanlawyerist.blogspot.com/2019/04/the-lambeth-and-london-estate;

[237] Homes for Lambeth Review, https://moderngov.lambeth.gov.uk

[238] Agenda and draft minutes, Cabinet Monday 4 March 2019 5.00 , https://moderngov.lambeth.gov.uk

[239] Kate Hoey(MP) for Vauxhall
[240] https://humanlawyerist.blogspot.com/2019/04/the-lambeth-and-london-estate.html

[241] https://www.theguardian.com/cities/2015/jun/25/london-developers-viability-planning-affordable-social-housing-regeneration-oliver-wainwright

[242] Westbury-a-year-after-Grenfell, http://housingactivists.co.uk/grenfell

[243] Peter Harrison Qc, Glimpsed views of the legal land scape,

[244] R (on the application of Vieira) v Camden LBC

and an infringement of Article 8.[246] Hence providing a potential avenue for estate regeneration affected residents to assert their human rights once they overcome the hurdles associates with instigating legal action.

Chapter 7

Article 1 of the first protocol of the ECHR[247] and CPOs

Overview

A1P1 states that, *'every natural person or legal person is entitled to the peaceful enjoyment of his possessions and no one shall be deprived of his possessions except in the public interest and subject to the conditions provided for by law and by the general principles of international law. The preceding provisions shall not, however, in any way, impair the right of a state to enforce such laws, as it deems necessary to control the use of property in accordance with the general interest or to secure the payment of taxes or other contributions or penalties'.*

The three main rules which describe the degree of interference[248] under A1P1 include *non-interference with possession, no deprivation of property except in the public interest and that state control may only be justified legally infringed in the general interest, where there is a legitimate justification.* In other words, the rights under A1P1 appear to be qualified to a certain extent with a margin of appreciation left for state parties in areas such as implementation as discussed in detail below. A1P1 also makes reference to principles of international law. For example, UDHR[249] under article 17, states that everyone has the right to own property alone or in association with others and that no one shall be arbitrarily deprived of his property.

---

[245] R (on the application of Ashley) Secretary of state for communities and local government

[246] (*Kay and Others v. the United Kingdom*, § 74)

[247] Referred to here as A1P1

[248] Possession, law, property and human rights, Landmark chambers

[249] https://www.un.org/en/universal-declaration-human-rights/index.html

But even in the absence of explicit reference to property rights, under specific international law instruments, it can be forcefully and persuasively argued that such interference, especially when associated with the confiscation or demolition of one's home, creates a spiral effect which could potentially breach international human rights law collectively referred to as the international bill of human rights,[250] comprised of the *Universal Declaration of Human Rights, International Covenant on Economic, Social and Cultural Rights, International Covenant on Civil and Political Rights.* The focus here is on the relevant provisions that could be applicable to CPOs under estate regeneration.

General Scope of A1P1

As cited above, A1P1 protects against deprivation of possessions and unjustifiable intrusion in the peaceful enjoyment of one's possessions. This could be through practices that amount to s expropriation of property, planning restrictions or even temporary property seizures. A case in point is *Pressos Compani Naviera and others v Belgium*, where the state was held liable for extinguishing the applicants unresolved claims by retroactively passing legislation which extinguished the applicants' property rights.[251] In pursuing protection under A1P1, an important distinction should be made as to whether the alleged interference is deemed to be a deprivation or simply control of use the land or property, which could then determine subsequent qualification for compensation under A1P1.

A1P1,[252] is independent of national state definitions, covers all forms of property and does not limit ownership of possessions to physical goods. However, A1P1 does not cover prospective possessions or future possessions but emphasises current or existing possessions. This was an essential issue in the case of Marckx v Belgium[253] where a mother claimed breach of A1P1 because of the alleged impediments by the state authorities to prevent her from disposing off her property to what was described

---

[250] https://www.ohchr.org/Documents/Publications/FactSheet2Rev.1en.pdf

[251] Handbook no 10, the right to property under ECHR

[252] See Practical Law UK practice Note 8-385 5732

[253] CASE OF MARCKX v. BELGIUM. *Application no. 6833/74,* https://hudoc.echr.coe.int

as 'an illegimate child'. A term that is clearly unacceptable in contemporary times[254]. The court by a majority confirmed that A1P1 was relevant to the claims made by the mother and defined the scope of A1P1 as applying to existing possessions but not future possessions[255]. In another case, of *X v Germany*, where a determination of A1P1 right was an issue, the court held that a mere expectation by notaries that *'rates for their fees would not be reduced by law'* did not amount to a property right within the meaning of A1P1.[256]

However, it would appear that where there is a concrete legitimate expectation, future possessions could be considered. But as far as relevance to residents facing CPO effected home demolitions is concerned, the issue regarding future possessions would not affect them because this relates to homes in which they live or already own as opposed to a mere expectation of future occupation or possession for that matter.

Therefore, the issues directly relating to CPOs and Estate regeneration, under A1P1 include, inter alia, *what amounts to deprivation or legitimate expectation, whether the actions of the authorities were proportionate or justifiable, the margin of appreciation extended to states and the fairness of compensation.* These issues are discussed in detail below.

Legitimate expectation

One of the key issues considered under A1P1 is whether a landowner's legitimate expectation of enjoyment of property rights can be a basis for asserting A1P1. In Pine *Valley Developments*[257], the applicants had bought land under the expectation of planning permission being approved but was later annulled. The court ruled in the

---

[254] CASE OF MARCKX v. BELGIUM. *Application no. 6833/74*, https://hudoc.echr.coe.int

[255] Marckx and Marckx v Belgium, Merits and Just Satisfaction, App No 6833/74, [1979] ECHR 2, (1980) 2 EHRR 330, IHRL 22 (ECHR 1979), 13th June 1979, European Court of Human Rights [ECHR], https://opil.ouplaw.com

[256] Handbook no 10, the right to property under ECHR

[257] Pine Valley Developments Limited and ors v Ireland, Just satisfaction, App No 12742/87, A/246-B, (1993) 16 EHRR 379, [1993] ECHR 2, IHRL 3587 (ECHR 1993), 9th February 1993, Council of Europe; European Court of Human Rights [ECHR

applicants' favour holding that the applicants had been subjected to unlawful discrimination contrary to ART 14 in conjunction with A1P1.

The key point from this case, in relation to CPOs is that there is an obvious legitimate expectation of enjoyment of property rights and protection from discrimination under ECHR. Therefore potentially providing an avenue for challenging such activity, primarily due to the legitimate expectation of the legal security associated with their property interests. Manifested through leases or secure tenancies whose curtailment would engage A1P1.[258] This is illustrated in *Stretch*[259], where the court upheld a complaint alleging that the applicant 'had been unjustly denied extension of a further 21 year term lease'.[260]It was further noted that[261] because the option granted by the local authority had been ultra vires and therefore deemed to be a disproportionate interference with the applicant's peaceful enjoyment of his possessions, this was a violation of Article 1 of Protocol No. 1 to the Convention'. Therefore, under the principle of legitimate expectation is that it appears that even a potential legal claim under A1P1 could merit consideration as a possession or asset where a landowner has a legitimate expectation.[262] Especially that CPO affected parties have diametrically opposed legal interests, such as retention of their properties, which are threatened with expropriation by the acquiring authorities.

However, in *Plant v Lambeth (discussed in detail below), the high court* examined such a legitimate expectation, namely the alleged curtailment of the right to buy by a secure tenant that was not yet exercised. The court held that A1P1 had not been engaged in respect of secure tenants' rights to buy since he had not yet acted on it. This ruling is puzzling because Lambeth council had taken formal decisions to demolish the estate through use of a CPO. By doing that, the right to buy by the tenant had been or would be curtailed. The applicant sued to safeguard his right to

---

[258] Pine developments v Ireland(1992) 14 EHRR 319

[259] Stretch v UK *(Application no. 44277/98)*

[260] Practical Law UK practice Note 8-385 5732

[261] [2003] ECHR 320, (2004) 38 EHRR 12, [2003] NPC 125, [2004] 03 EG 100, [2003] 29 EG 118, [2004] 1 EGLR 11, *http://www.bailii.org/eu/cases/ECHR/2003/320.html*

[262] Pressos Compani Naviera v Belgium(1995) 2 EHHR 3010) , also see Practical Law UK practice note 8-385 5732

buy by citing among others A1P1. Therefore, the court's ruling in this specific regard appears contradictory. Furthermore, it would appear that the applicant was not allowed to appeal which curtailed any further opportunity to test that conclusion. Therefore, the successful nature of any such complaint by a CPO affected applicant appears uncertain in practice.

Deprivation

Deprivation is another important consideration under A1P1. A1P1 protects against unlawful deprivation of property, which includes curtailment of the legal rights of those affected. In examining the issue of deprivation, the court ascertains any de facto deprivation of A1P1 rights[263]as opposed mere control of use of property or possessions. For example in *Papamichalopoulous v Greece,*[264] the Navy had taken over the applicants' land to the extent that they could not make effective use of it and this was found to be a de facto expropriation. This is consistent with the circumstances faced by CPO affected parties who have their properties confiscated or unable to be used for their own enjoyment or utility, which could mean that they could be able to challenge such de-facto expropriation of their property in light of the rationale in the above case.

However, potential applicants affected by estate regeneration enforced through CPOs, should be cognizant of the fact that if the measures taken by the state amount to control of the use of the property or payment of taxes, the court could find that such an action did not amount to deprivation. A case in point is *Handyside V UK,*[265] where the temporary seizure of the applicant's books, which were alleged to contain obscene images, did not amount to deprivation since the seizure was temporary and

[263]The right to property under ECHR, A guide to the implementation of the right to property, Human rights hand book no 10

[264] CASE OF PAPAMICHALOPOULOS AND OTHERS v. GREECE (ARTICLE 50, Application no. 14556/89)

[265] CASE OF HANDYSIDE v. THE UNITED KINGDOM, (Application no. 5493/72)

was within the powers of the state under A1P1. The difference with CPO housing estate demolition affected parties and the facts or ruling in this case is that expropriation of estate regeneration homes is usually permanent as opposed to mere control. Therefore, this provision would not adversely affect any potential applicants faced with estate regeneration under CPOs. The overarching point here is that although there could be legitimate justifications for interference in an owner's property rights, under A1P1, depriving someone of their property can only be justified in exceptional circumstances as evident in *Lithgow et al,*[266]*where* deprivation of property was held to have happened under a CPO process. A similar ruling was held in *Sporrong and Lonnroth*, where the 'expropriation of building permits and building restrictions enforcement for specific durations was held to be interference in the applicants' enjoyment of their land amounting to deprivation of property.[267] These rulings affirm the protection under A1P1, for estate regeneration affected parties who are deprived of their property due to CPOs by local authorities.

However, it is important to emphasise that any potential applicants would need to prove that this was in fact deprivation not mere restrictions,[268] temporary deprivation or interference in the use or enjoyment of the property. Deprivation could be further proven where there is a partial loss of a significant or substantial part of a landowner's right, which amounts to deprivation without full expropriation. The rulings in *Sporrong and Lithgow* above appear to confirm the protection under ECHR the rights of those affected by CPOs where deprivation or even partial deprivation is found to have occurred by the court. CPO affected estate regeneration residents experience significant restrictions caused by CPOs, such as exposure to construction hazards like noise, fumes, vibration or contaminants or the restriction to sell to the open market as a willing buyer.[269]Residents could argue that this amounts to deprivation or partial deprivation under A1P1.

Deprivation could also be potentially established where there are two competing owners who already have rights in the property as opposed to the familiar practice of the acquiring authority taking over the property. This is illustrated in the case of *James v UK,*[270] where the court found that individuals with leases under the

[266] Lithgow v United Kingdom, Merits, App no 9006/80, App no 9262/81, App no 9263/81, App no 9265/81, App no 9266/81, App no 9313/81, App no 9405/81, A/102, (1986) 8 EHRR 329, [1986] ECHR 8, IHRL 59 (ECHR 1986), 8th July 1986, European Court of Human Rights [ECHR]

[267] Sporrong and Lonnroth(1982)5 EHHR 35

[268] See Practical Law UK practice Note 8-385 5732

[269] Imrie, R., & Thomas, H. (1997). Law, Legal Struggles and Urban Regeneration: Rethinking the Relationships. *Urban Studies*, *34*(9), 1401–1418. https://doi.org/10.1080/0042098975484

leasehold reform Act 1967, entitled to long leases, who could purchase freeholds of their leases, at a defined statutory price, deprived freeholders of their property, due to the inability to sell the property or set the sale price.[271]

Ironically such a principle laid down in *James v UK above,* could be utilised by CPO affected residents[272]to disentangle themselves from the acquiring authority, although the acquiring authority could still have significant statutory powers to initiate a CPO. The acquiring authority could do so by citing other grounds such as control, as highlighted in *Agosi V UK,*[273] where the main issue was seizure and forfeiture by customs of smuggled Kruegerrands and the court did not deem such an action by authorities to amount to deprivation.[274]

Therefore, CPO affected parties should be aware of claims of control as opposed to seizure by acquiring authorities. However, it is important to emphasise that although such a defence by the authorities could be entertained by the courts, there must be a clear need to balance community interests with the protection of the individual's right to peaceful enjoyment of his or her home, in order to justify controlling the use of property in the general interest. Otherwise, that would invite potential misuse of the significant latitude afforded to states under A1P1 as a defence against CPOs affected parties.[275] Therefore, a finding of deprivation under A1P1, is an important tool against authorities pursuing estate regeneration.

Proportionality

Another central tenet of A1P1 is the principle of proportionality, which emphasises a fair balance between the public interest and the property interests of the owners.[276] Simply put, if there is a valid legitimate and lawful interference then it has to be proportionate. However, such a need to demonstrate proportionality is arguably

---

[270] James V UK(1986) 8 EHRR 123

[271] See Practical Law UK practice Note 8-385 5732

[272] See Cressigham Gardens in Lambeth

[273] Agosi v UK(1987) 9 EHRR1

[274] Practical Law UK practice Note 8-385 5732

[275] See R Plant V LLBC(cite full)

[276] See James V UK App No 8793/79 (A/98) (Official Case No)

[1986] ECHR 2 (Neutral Citation) ; James and ors v United Kingdom, Decision on Merits, App no 8793/79, B/81, 11th May 1984, European Commission on Human Rights (historical) [ECHR]

undermined, in practice, by national authorities enjoying a wide margin of appreciation in determining the public or community interests within the law. [277]

There are several factors, which determine such a fair balance or proportionality. These include procedural safeguards of the owner's property rights, the nature of the penalty applied[278]the extent of interference, the duration or persistence of interference,[279] the actual fault of the owner with its consequential significance and the irrationality or arbitrary nature of the statute.[280]

However, even if a threshold that satisfies proportionality is met by those affected, the need for proportionality in control cases is not a basis for compensation but simply indicates a need for a fair balance to be found.[281]   Nevertheless, such interference may only be justified legally, if it's consistent with the public interest.[282]

As already mentioned, while the need to demonstrate the proportionality of the authorities' actions is a key protection measure for CPO affected residents, wider latitudes provided to the states arguably weaken those protections. Under A1P1 states are allowed a margin of appreciation in implementation of decisions associated with legitimate objectives of public interest [283]through proportionate measures designed to achieve greater social justice. While that appears to be a noble objective, in principle, such wide latitude leaves room for authorities to justify actions that are disproportionate to the affected residents whose homes are expropriated via schemes[284] like the wide scale demolition of homes with little[285] or no visible public interest.[286]

---

[277] Practical Law UK practice Note 8-835 57

[278] International Transport Roth v HS(2002) EWCA Civ 158

[279] Sporrong and Lonnroth

[280] R(Kensall) v SOS for Environment(2003) Admin 2003

[281] See Practical Law UK practice Note 8-385 5732

[282] In Tesco Stores Ltd v SOS

[283] James v UK above

[284] The Costs of Estate Regeneration: A Report by Architects for Social Housing, 7 SEPTEMBER 2018

[285] Knock it Down or Do it Up? The challenge of estate regeneration February 2015

[286] David Dewar, The implications of the SoS's rejection of an estate regeneration on grounds of social housing loss
https://www.planningresource.co.uk, regeneration-grounds-social-housing-loss ,January 2019

The wider powers afforded to the states under the margin of appreciation, are made even more difficult to challenge by potential applicants due to the inherent institutional impediments faced by any potential applicants. Simply explained, in order for affected parties to challenge the proportionality of actions that amount to interference of property rights, such actions should be foreseeable[287] and authorities need to be accessible and provide clear simple comprehensible communication of reasons for their actions. In the absence of such communication, accessibility and foreseeability, by an authority, it would be extremely cumbersome, almost an obstruction on part of the authority, for estate regeneration CPO affected parties to timely, fairly and justly secure their property and associated rights.

However, in practice, authorities delay, obfuscate, deduct and withhold information[288] from potential applicants which clearly disadvantages estate regeneration affected residents, as mentioned above in various reports and discussed in more detail under ART 6. For instance, campaigners like those on Westbury estate in Lambeth[289] among others cited in reports above, refer to the woeful inadequacy of social rent homes and the ubiquitous use of s106[290] between public authorities like Lambeth et al, as evidence of a potential manipulation of the margin of appreciation left to states under A1P1. This illustrates the almost vacuous nature of the protection under A1P1 when authorities appear to manipulate the margin of appreciation to suit their interests. The case of *Tesco Stores Ltd v SOS*[291] *for Environment and Transport,* concretises the public interest argument as well as the margin of appreciation highlighted above. In this case, Sullivan J emphasised the need for *a 'fair balance to be struck between the public interest such as redevelopment and the individual's right to a peaceful and quiet enjoyment of his possessions. Adding that such interference ought to be proportionate and necessary to meet the 'compelling case in the public interest' reflecting the necessary element of that balance'.*[292] The difficulty lies in determining what the clear public interest is and where the limits of its

[287] Hentrich V France(1994 18 EHRR 440 (1994)ECHR 29 Lithgow,

[288] LAMBETH COUNCIL REFUSE TO ANSWER FOI QUESTIONS MADE BY NEWS FROM CRYSTAL PALACE, https://newsfromcrystalpalace.wordpress.com/2018/11/26/lambeth-council-refuse-to-answer-foi-questions-made-by-news-from-crystal-palace

[289] https://en-gb.facebook.com/Save-Westbury-Estate-SW8-486344558188042/

[290] S106 and public interest requirements are discussed in detail under the chapter of the CPO process.

[291] J.P.L 2010,3 298-309

[292] Also see R (Clays Lane Housing cooperative ltd v Housing corp(2005),R (Pascoe v SOS(2007), R (Hall) v First SOS(2008) J.P.L 63 at 15

application end, especially in relation to taking or demolishing one's home with the spiral effect that follow as highlighted in numerous reports above.

The above comments by Sullivan J appear consistent with another observation made by the court in Chesterfield properties v Secretary of State, [293]that 'only another interest, a public interest, of greater force may override it'. In that CPO inspector's report,[294]objectors argued that as the Leaseholders' Article 1 and 8 rights have been breached, it is incumbent upon the Acquiring Authority to justify that breach in terms of proportionality. The objectors referred to, the case of R (Clays Lane) v Housing Corporation, where, Maurice Kay J stated that 'the appropriate test of proportionality requires a balancing exercise' between 'a decision which is justified on the basis of a compelling case in the public interest as being reasonably necessary' may not be 'obligatorily the least intrusive of Convention rights.' Adding that some leaseholders no longer have mortgages and many are no longer in employment, as a consequence of the CPO they will be separated from their family and friends and they will be unable to afford to return to the estate'.

During the stated CPO examination process the inspector agreed that, 'Paragraph 12 of the Guidance states that an acquiring authority should be sure that the purposes for which the compulsory purchase order is made justify interfering with the human rights of those with an interest in the land affected. They would need to invest considerable personal resources in addition to any compensation they would receive for their properties; the CPO would not only deprive them of their dwelling but also their financial security. If they chose not to pursue this option, they would inevitably need to leave the area and this would have implications for their family life, including the lives of that dependant on the.... together with the failure of the scheme to fully achieve the social, economic and environmental well-being. The interference with human rights would not be proportionate having regard to the level. The public benefits that the scheme would bring... a compelling case in the public interest has not been proved'.

These observations were reiterated in the Aylesbury estate case in Southwark, stated in the chapters above, where the inspector and subsequently the secretary of state found that the CPO backed estate regeneration was inconsistent with the

[293] Chesterfield Properties Plc v Secretary Of State For Environment & Ors [1997] EWHC Admin 709 (24th July, 1997), *http://www.bailii.org/ew/cases/EWHC/Admin/1997/709.html*
Cite as: 76 P & CR 117, (1997) 76 P & CR 117, [1997] EWHC Admin 709

[294] *CPO Report NPCU/CPO/A5840/74092 ,www.planningportal.gov.uk/planning inspectorate Page 73*

human rights of residents. Although it appears that the parties have since reached some sort of accommodation. The cases and comments above by both courts and the inspectors emphasise human rights as a fundamental consideration for CPO schemes not simply a peripheral matter.

How that is implemented on the ground to minimise or eliminate such human rights breaches appears to be almost impossible task. Therefore a finding of a breach A1P1 does not in effect protect applicants from dispossession. An approach that combines direct negotiations, political actions such as lobbying, and campaigns in parallel with any legal action appears to be more practically fruitful as opposed to relying on the protections of A1P1.

Justification

Despite the court rulings above, authorities could still potentially assert justification as a defence for the interference or deprivation of property rights. In other words, even if there was interference or a taking, the authorities could argue that they were within the law or legitimately justified to take the action they took.

Tax enforcement is one such route where that justification this could be applicable. As reiterated, a state has a right to enforce laws deemed necessary to control the use of property in accordance with the general interest to secure payment of taxes, penalties or lawful regulations, as long as the power is exercised rationally and proportionately, such as in the regulation of a sex shop.[295]

Nevertheless, despite such justification, the court could still find a breach where that justification is considered disproportionate or where there is a discretionary, unfair procedure creating an excessive burden born by the applicant and can further intervene in the absence of a reasonable justification for interference with property rights. Such an example is in *the case of Davie*s where the court held in the absence of fair compensation, there was a breach of the need to strike a fair balance between the public interest and the van owners confirming that therefore A1P1 had been engaged.[296] Which affirmed that natural or legal persons could only be deprived of property, such as contributory or non-contributory state benefits,[297] or other interests,[298]

[295] *Belfast CC v Miss Behavin' Ltd*,([2007] WLR 1420, [2007] 1 WLR 1420, [2007] 3 All ER 1007, [2007] UKHL 19, *http://www.bailii.org/uk/cases/UKHL/2007/19.html*

[296] R Mott v Environment Agency(2018) UKSC 10)

[297] Stec v UK (2005)41 EHRR SE18

subject to conditions provided by law and the general principles of international law. An affirmation that potential CPO effected estate regeneration residents could arguably rely on to enforce their legal rights. However, it is always important for CPO affected parties to bear in mind that it is possible to conclude that various actions fall under the margin of appreciation on part of the state, if there is a fair appeal system or if the interference is reasonable and proportionate as discussed above at length. It seems to be a high bar for often unrepresented, resource starved and distressed residents to overcome especially properly raised and if supported by evidence from the acquiring authorities.

Having explored in some detail the broader principles underpinning A1P1 namely, deprivation, legitimate expectation, proportionality, justification and the margin of appreciation, with relevant cases or examples, it is of paramount importance to discuss in detail some of the specific areas where estate demolition or confiscation supported by CPO processes, acutely affects those who occupy the homes or have interests in the properties. Such examples include issues like market rate, the right to buy, home environment/environment rehousing and compensation and the extent to which potential applicants under A1P1 both could pursue them de facto and de jure.

A1P1 fails to offer full protection and requires a margin of appreciation which arguably allows local authorities to effect property deprivations or interfere in peoples' enjoyment of their property. There is no clear limits of interpretations of the margin of appreciation and there is a concern that could be potentially used as a general defence by actions. Given the lack of resources and lack of parity between parties, those affected could simply give up an further challenges against the authorities because of the appearance of an arguably respectable explanation by the authorities without being fairly adjudicated in an impartial and fair tribunal process. The spiral effect of such an occurrence is that authorities get emboldened in pursuing CPOs in estate regeneration because there is no real meaningful challenges against them. Therefore, the margin of appreciation principle requires revisiting if not out right deletion from the A1P1 lest it becomes a default position even when its clear such a defence would not arise at all.

Chapter 8

---

[298] Beyeler v Italy (2001) 33 EHRR 52

Other specific *notable CPO estate regeneration issues under A1P1*

It should not be a contention that protection against interference in a home environment is among the most important protections under A1P1.[299]As discussed at some length above, such interference has to be consistent with the added imposition of a positive obligation on the contracting states to ensure that such interference is proportional to the stated aim. The home environment protection under A1P1 could intersect with Art 8, which asserts protection against the violation of the respect for one's home.[300] Among other issues that require attention is environmental pollution, which could seriously interfere with one's private or family life and deprive personal enjoyment of amenities associated with one's home such as[301] the case of *Moreno v Spain*[302] where the court concluded that noise pollution violated articles 8 and 13 of ECHR. Such interference may affect a person's wellbeing and prevent them from enjoying their homes, family life and adversely affect their health. CPO affected residents[303] have complained of noise, pollution and toxic hazards associated with construction hazards.[304]The courts appear to disregard apparent mere concerns about protection of healthy environment[305]and consider serious detriments to the persons concerned. If there is a nexus to the cause of such a serious effect, a complaint may arise under Art 8 to determine[306] state actions and the failure to effect measures necessary to prevent harmful activity.[307]

Emphasis is placed on the need for a causal link to be established as opposed to prospective harm depending on the repetitive nature of the negative activity.[308]Furthermore, it's not the general deterioration of the environment", per se, but harmful

---

[299] Hatton and others V UK,

[300] https://echr.coe.int/Documents/Convention_ENG.pdf

[301] CASE OF MORENO GÓMEZ v. SPAIN, *Application no. 4143/02*

[302] CASE OF MORENO GÓMEZ v. SPAIN (*Application no. 4143/02*)

[303] https://www.theguardian.com/uk-news/2019/jul/07/court-challenge-homes-southall-london-gasworks-brownfield-development

[304] https://www.theguardian.com/environment/2019/may/04/brownfield-site-new-homes-building-wrecking-health-southall,

[305] *Kyrtatos v Greece*

[306] (*Hatton and Others v. the United Kingdom* [GC], § 96; *Moreno Gómez v. Spain*, § 53)

[307] https://www.theguardian.com/environment/2019/may/04/brownfield-site-new-homes-building-wrecking-health-southall,

[308] *Fadeyeva v. Russia*, § 69.

effects that would be disproportionate to the accepted standards consistent with living in modern metropolitan areas.[309] For many affected residents or parties, it would be an obvious aim for prevention to be effected before any harm or interference in the peaceful enjoyment for affected faced with CPOs parties although in practice this is not always the case.[310] In reaching its decision regarding a breach under Art 8, associated with pollution, the courts consider process and substance.[311] Paying due regard to any vague or overbroad interference without reasoned decisions, processes, any shortcomings in a state's obligation or whether the right balance has been struck between the resident and other interested or parties.[312] Such state measures need not include extensive reports but could include professional assessments to determine the harmful consequences of construction activities. However, a decision may be made in the absence of such information[313] if a fair balance between parties exists.

Additionally, a failure to rehouse residents during demolition, excavation, redevelopment, could violate Art 8,[314] because in effect that would tantamount to a failure to protect their health and wellbeing.[315] Such protective measures should include regulatory and administrative mechanisms. Paradoxically, the court confines itself to respect for a home hence the wisdom of such a decision needs to be closely examined.[316] This was discussed in more detail under Art 8 respect for a home above. Despite a lack of clear blanket provision protecting the environment, per se, under A1P1, courts could be creative in dealing with decisions that had the effect of remedying environmental detriments associated with a home or home environment.[317] Such as in a case where transparency was required when residents living at a dangerous site with sodium cyanide or in proximity to hazardous effects were not

[309] . (*Asselbourg and Others v. Luxembourg* (Dec.)).

(*Martínez Martínez and Pino Manzano v. Spain*, § 42) (*Hardy and Maile v. the United Kingdom*

[310] https://www.theguardian.com/environment/2019/may/04/brownfield-site-new-homes-building-wrecking-health-southall

[311] (*Hatton and Others v. the United Kingdom* [GC], § 99).

[312] *Moreno Gómez v. Spain*, § 55). (*Fadeyeva v. Russia*, § 93; *Hardy and Maile v. the United Kingdom*, § 218

[313] *Hatton and Others v. the United Kingdom* [GC], § 128)

[314] *Fadeyeva v. Russia*, § 133

[315] *Tătar v. Romania*, § 88).

[316] (*Hatton and Others v. the United Kingdom* [GC], §§ 100 and 122),

[317] *López Ostra v. Spain*, §§ 56-58, *Moreno Gómez v. Spain*, § 61. *Di Sarno and Others v. Italy*, § 112).in (*Giacomelli v. Italy*, § 83),

provided access to information or conclusions of the study to permit such a scheme.[318] Which was similarly reiterated, in the case of *Giacomelli v. Italy*, the '*court found a violation in the absence of a prior environmental impact assessment and the failure to suspend the activities of a plant generating toxic emissions close to a residential area*'. Such a documented lack of transparency is consistent with the experiences of many residents living in CPO affected areas where there is a lack of independent impact environmental and equality impact assessments.[319]

A question arises whether authorities do not disclose such information because of the crucially potential benefit to affected residents because environmental impact damages may be linked to actual loss. A case in point, where such inference is raised, is where applicants, who lived near Heathrow,[320] were subjected to noise nuisance, which affected their property valuation, although it was concluded that there was no direct evidence to suggest that the value of the applicants' property was diminished or was unsalable.[321] The reasoning seems contradictory since such pollution could limit interest in the property and therefore drive down prices. Furthermore, apart from environmental pollution associated with construction hazards, bad housing conditions, disrepair or blight during CPOs related construction[322] may breach the quiet enjoyment and Art 8 in terms of respect for a home[323] which is intersectional with A1P1.

Although there are statutory obligations in the UK legal system to deal with such bad housing conditions, [324]there are doubts about local authorities' willingness to enforce their own statutory liability or potential culpability. Which therefore strengthens and necessitates the need for Art 8 intervention where there are unfit housing conditions but no adequate remedy.[325]

CPOs, right to buy and A1P1

---

[318] Hatton and Others v. the United Kingdom [GC] (§ 120),

[319] https://www.theguardian.com/environment/2019/may/04/brownfield-site-new-homes-building-wrecking-health-southall

[320] Hatton and Others v. the United Kingdom [GC] (§ 120),

[321] . However, a settlement was reached in one case in respect of Art 8, 13 and A1P1.

[322] Demolition or refurbishment of social housing?, https://www.ucl.ac.uk/engineering-exchange/research-projects, 2018

[323]https://www.echr.coe.int/Documents/Guide_Art_8_ENG.pdf

[324] Housing/repairs-in-rented-housing/disrepair-what-are-your-options-if-you-are-a-social-housing-tenant/disrepair-what-are-the-landlord-s-responsibilities, /https://www.citizensadvice.org.uk/

[325] HA1985 s604,

Another key area that needs consideration is the impact of CPOs on what is known as the right to buy for secure tenants and the protections under A1P1. The relevant context in this case is where estate regeneration can be argued to effectively interfere with the right to buy of the secure residents. Not the overall discussion of the advantages or disadvantages of the right to buy per se.

The case of R Plant v LLBC[326] highlights this issue, which affects secure tenants faced with a CPO and interference in their right to buy under A1P1. In this particular case, a central issue was whether A1P1 was engaged and breached by the council's decision to demolish the estate using CPOs. The claimant among other issues appears to have alleged breach of A1P1 due to interference with S118 of HA 1985, right to buy and S84 (1) rights, which prevent the court from issuing a possession order on such a property except on legal grounds in schedule 2 of the Act and other provisional requirements.[327] The court held that A1P1 was not applicable to the council's cabinet decision, concluding that, *'A1P1 was not engaged and was indistinguishable from other authorities.*[328] Noting that '*if engaged, it need only be considered in relation to the statutory right to buy when the authority commences County Court proceedings to obtain an order for possession of a particular home'.*

Notably, the court appeared to base its decision to the fact that the claimant had not already exercised his right to buy. However, it appears that the existence of that option and its removal clearly appeared to interfere in the claimant's property rights, hence engaging A1P1.

Nevertheless, it appears the court indirectly appeared to acknowledge that A1P1 was engaged but not breached, at least up to the point when steps would be taken to revoke it or a determination made as to whether it was breached. Stating that, *'If, contrary to the clear view I have reached, I had concluded that A1P1 was engaged in LLBC's decision, reached on 21 March 2016....the issue of whether it was breached would have been a matter for the Court to determine.'*[329] This Invites the question as to when the right time or forum would be for the claimant to enforce his rights under A1P1 if not at that specific court and that specific time. Moreover, If not why not?

---

[326] *R Plant v LLBC, [2016] EWHC 3324 (Admin)*

[327] *R Plant v LLB [2016] EWHC 3324 (Admin)*

[328] *Kay v Lambeth LBC [2005] QB 352 and Austin v Southwark LBC [2010] HLR 1'.*

[329] Citing *Belfast City Council v Miss Behavin' Ltd [2007] 1 WLR 1420 at paragraphs 13 to 15)'.*

However, questions remain after this ruling and it is not clear that those questions were adequately addressed by the court. Moreover, the unfortunate refusal to appeal closed down testing the *decision related to secure tenancy, CPOs and A1P1.*

However, a significant positive takeaway for CPO affected residents, especially with the right to buy, the court appears to have acknowledged their rights if they chose to move away. They would be secure tenants being provided with new secure tenancies if they decide to move elsewhere but not if they wish to be rehoused in a new home on their current location. In which case they would only be granted an assured tenancy.

Market Rate, CPOs and A1P1

Another extremely important issue for consideration by CPO affected estate regeneration residents that could be in violation of A1P1 is the inherent default prevention of applicants from selling their properties at market value. Such interference via CPOs therefore appears disproportionate since compensation should be reasonably related to the wider market value of the locality, taking into account the totality of the full circumstances associated with displacement and removal from a home or a locality. Furthermore, it would appear, A1P1 does not guarantee a right to full compensation in every situation since a margin of appreciation is allowed to the nation state in this respect.[330]

However, it must be emphasised that the issue, here is beyond market value per se. Market rate, in this context is disputed and is described as 'a euphemism for imposing compensation' on an unwilling seller.[331] Where owners are compelled to sell to a specific party, at a specific time, at a price largely determined by the same interested party usually the acquiring local authority also the arbiter of the planning decisions which appears to be a prima facie manifest conflict of interest.[332]

---

[330] See Lithgow and Practical Law UK Practice Note 8-385 5732

[331] Guy Roots et al, 2nd edition

[332] Neil Gray Libby Porter, By Any Means Necessary: Urban Regeneration and the "State of Exception" in Glasgow's Commonwealth Games 2014

The no scheme principle[333] and the equivalence principle[334] often cited in the government guidance regarding CPO compensation[335] appear woefully unrealistic since CPO affected areas face blight, crime, antisocial behaviour and disrepair which affect the market price.[336] Furthermore, those affected cannot simply move or sell to the open market due to the costs involved or the inability to sell in case of leaseholders. The compensation awarded does not often meet the prices or housing costs in the private sector within the locality. Not to mention the resulting severe emotional distress that affects the wellbeing, health, and avoidable psychological insecurity.

Additionally, residents largely buy or rent properties without any forthcoming knowledge of a CPO. In the case of Local authorities, leases can be for 125 years while life tenure with succession rights is routine for many local authority secure tenancies. Residents envisaged this as a safety net both as a home and for leaseholders as a potential long-term capital investment, which is crucial for social mobility.

Therefore, the reference to the so-called market price or apparent resemblance to market price does not reflect the necessary just, fair and equitable compensation for residents' families or other affected parties. There is a recognisable strong argument that compensation per se should be beyond statutory requirements and a central measure in assessing or the proportionate nature of the burden put on any CPO affected party.[337]

Chapter 9

Compensation and A1P1

---

[333] David Elvin, QC, the no scheme principle under s6a of LCA 1961, https://www.landmarkchambers.co.uk/wp-content/uploads/2018/08/CPO-Presentation-Seminar-25-Sept-2017-DEQC.pdf

[334] http://www.legislation.gov.uk/ukpga/Eliz2/9-10/33/section/5

[335] https://assets.publishing.service.gov.uk/government/uploads/system/uploads/attachment_data/file/817392/CPO_guidance_-_with_2019_update.pdf

[336] Loretta Lees, Mara Ferreri, Resisting gentrification on its final frontiers: Learning from the Heygate Estate in London (1974–2013),Cities, Volume 57,2016,Pages 14-24, https://doi.org/10.1016/j.cities.2015.12.005.(http://www.sciencedirect.com

[337] Deborah Rook, Property and Human Rights, 2001

As indicated above, compensation no doubt remains a contentious issue in CPO related matters and is set by statute as highlighted by the DCLG guidance.[338]The guidance cited above refers to market value plus home loss payments and disbursements,[339] apparently disregarding the value of the scheme on the value of the land in question. Instead, compensation assumes a willing seller without compulsion. This is via monetary payment at the open market value of the land, *'in so far as money can do it', to put one in the same position as land had not been taken from him…in so far as loss imposed on him in the public interest, but no greater'.*[340] However, this level of compensation does not cover the detrimental effects of being displaced from a settled community with the ensuing distress, fear and sense of powerlessness.[341] *Which would appear to resonate with A1P1 as reiterated In James v UK* and in *the former king of Greece et al v Greece*[342], where it was held that compensation that does not reasonably reflect the value of the property[343] could be deemed a disproportionate interference.[344]

A government review culminated into various law commission reports that were not implemented[345] leading to minimal changes.[346] DCLG guidance further explains this contentious and complex area'[347] stating that, *'compensation payable for the compulsory acquisition of an interest in land is based on the 'equivalence principle' (i.e. that the owner should be paid neither less nor more than their loss). The value*

---

[338]compulsory-purchase-process-and-the-crichel-down-rules-guidance

https://www.gov.uk/government/publications

[339]https://assets.publishing.service.gov.uk/government

[340] Lord justice Scott in Horn v Sunderland corporation

[341] Martine August, "It's all about power and you have none:" The marginalization of tenant resistance to mixed-income social housing redevelopment in Toronto, Canada,

Cities, Volume 57,2016, Pages 25-32, (http://www.sciencedirect.com

[342] Deborah Rook, Property Law and Human Rights, 2001

[343] Deborah Rook, Property Law and Human rights, 2001

[344] Holy Monasteries v Greece

[345] See urban renaissance report city university urban task force report, pg. 231,

[346] *Planning and Compulsory purchase Act 2004*

[347] DCLG guidance citing Part 1 Land compensation claims 1973

of land taken is the amount which it might be expected to realise if sold on the open market by a willing seller (Land Compensation Act 1961, section 5, rule 2), disregarding any effect on value of the scheme of the acquiring authority (known as the 'no scheme' principle); (see Land Compensation Act 1961, section 5, rule 5). Importantly, but unfortunate for those affected by CPOs, although it is implied under A1P1 that compensation will be paid,[348] the legitimate public interest may justify less than the financial equivalent to what the claimant lost based on the principle in *James*.[349] In addition, where rights to compensation are provided by statute, those provisions must be interpreted so as to be compatible with HRA 1998'.[350] Furthermore, A1P1 does not state how much compensation should be paid but states that *'the taking of property without any just compensation is justifiable only in exceptional circumstances'.* Compensation should be generous and proportionately beyond, market value or pecuniary loss given the spiral detriments including mental distress that befalls those affected by estate regeneration enforced by CPOs, as highlighted in the various reports above.

The compensation issue is best humorously articulated by John Pugh Smith,[351] who sums up the central concern for CPO affected landowners, as timely adequate compensation, *'especially for a welsh hill farmer'* as he put it.[352] This reference to the 'welsh farmer' could be arguably replicated to the majority of CPO affected parties or residents faced with the demolition of their homes under CPOs with the spiral affects which could be held as being in breach of A1P1. Therefore, it cannot be emphasised enough, the extent to which the expeditious nature and totality of compensation is central to the amicable resolutions of CPO related disputes or minimising the detrimental impact on residents. Acquiring authorities appear to seek to offer less compensation through a deliberately slow process, while livelihoods are on hold pending compensation.[353]

Rehousing

---

[348] Guy Roots et al, 2nd Edition

[349] James V UK, The Law of compulsory purchase, third edition, Guy Roots et al; *Thomas v Bridgend county council*,(2011), EWCA Civ 862, (2011) RVR 241

[350] Such as in *Thomas v Bridgend county council*,(2011), EWCA Civ 862, (2011) RVR 241, where the CA held that s19(3) of the Highway Act 1980, was incompatible with art 1 of the ECHR

[351] John Pugh –Smith, When is' enough ' legally enough, Encyclopaedia of Local government law bulletin,2015

[352] Saunders V Caerphilly CBC(2015)EWHC 1632 CH

[353] Alice Belotti, Estate regeneration and Community impact, LSE, 2016

S39 of the LCA 1973[354] sets out the grounds for rehousing which is summarised by the DCLG guidance[355]for many residents affected by estate regeneration enforced by CPOs, especially those with young children, finding secure and affordable accommodation is one of the most formidable barriers they face. Many are compelled either to live on potentially hazardous and dangerous protracted construction sites, such as asbestos contaminated land, move into temporary accommodation or move out of the locality entirely, which causes a series of detrimental impacts in all areas of their lives.[356]

The new properties tend to take many years[357]to build and are largely unaffordable. The new schemes such as shared ownerships, demote residents' property ownership interests, have stricter leases and diminish residents' equity, savings, home loss and disturbance. Residents who exercise any rights to stay as tenants are subjected to intrusive means testing or inquiries into unrelated areas of their lives despite the injustice of having one's home confiscated by the same acquiring authority.[358]

Additionally, the new housing may increase social divisions such as in a widely reported case, after estate demolition or regeneration, where children's playgrounds were segregated and there are familiar cases of 'poor doors'[359] depending on the housing tenure. Such division, it is strongly argued is incompatible with A1P1 in intersection with Art 14 of ECHR, which prohibits discrimination.[360] Primarily because

[354] http://www.legislation.gov.uk/ukpga/1973/26/contents

[355]https://assets.publishing.service.gov.uk/government/uploads/system/uploads/attachment_data/file/571453/booklet4.pdf

[356]PaulWatts,Its_not_for_us_Regeneration_the_2012_Olympics_and_the_gentrification_of_East_London_City_2013, http://www.academia.edu/6007431/;

Zoe Williams, the real cost of regeneration,http://www.execreview.com/2017/07/the-real-cost-of-regeneration/

[357] https://www.vice.com/en_uk/article/qkq4bx/every-flat-in-a-new-south-london-development-has-been-sold-to-foreign-investors

[358]PaulWatts,Its_not_for_us_Regeneration_the_2012_Olympics_and_the_gentrification_of_East_London_City_2013, http://www.academia.edu/6007431/;

Zoe Williams, the real cost of regenerationhttp://www.execreview.com

[359] https://www.newyorker.com/culture/cultural-comment/the-poor-door-and-the-glossy-reconfiguration-of-city-life

[360] /too-poor-to-play-children-in-social-housing-blocked-from-communal-playground

https://www.theguardian.com/cities/2019/mar/25

[361] Written by Jessica Perera, Institute of Race Relations, New IRR publication provides a fresh take on housing, policing and racism in London.

economic disadvantage tends to disproportionately affect women, racial minorities[361] and those with disabilities. All of which are protected characteristics under Art 14 of ECHR as well as EA2010 and HRA 98.

Therefore, taking into account of all the above issues, it is important that compensation should proportionately reflect the genuine or manifest public interest, [362] in individual circumstances and mirror the distinction between mere restrictions, which could amount to deprivation, and an actual taking of the physical property. Most CPO affected estate regeneration residents are affected by actual physical deprivation of property with associated emotional, social and financial detriments, both immediate and long-term. The statutory compensation does not appear to reflect the emotional or intangible but equally devastating detriments. Hence making the interference and deprivation acutely disproportionate and therefore in potential breach of A1P1 discussed in more detail above. Monetary compensation although helpful is not the panacea to displacement. It should be a package that includes mandatory adequate rehousing, take into account health implications, disruption to employment, education and support networks in balance with stated proven public interest for compulsory acquisition of one's home.

An issue that resonated with the US case of *Kelo,* [363] where the issue was a taking of a longstanding home by the local authorities. Justice Scalia noted that, 'yes you are paying for it, but you are giving the money to somebody, who does not want the money, who wants to live in the house that she's lived in her whole life. That counts for nothing? *'What this lady wants is not money. No amount of money is going to satisfy her. Living in this house her whole life. She does not want to move'*. That is the sense of deep injustice of the compulsory taking of homes, which are occupied especially in cases where residents have inculcated deep roots in the locality with a sense of cultural, economic and social attachments. That is not to minimise the more transient or temporary residents affected but there is no doubt that the impact is bound to be more damaging to those with entrenched roots in the community.

Chapter 10

---

[362] As stated in Trailer and Marina(leven) v Sec.of State 2004

[363] Kanner, Gideon. "Kelo v. New London: Bad Law, Bad Policy, and Bad Judgment." *The Urban Lawyer*, vol. 38, no. 2, 2006, pp. 201–235. *JSTOR*, www.jstor.org/stable/27895626.

Equal treatment under ART 14 and its convergence with A1P1

Equality[364] and fairness of treatment by those affected by CPOs, is critical to avoid breach of Art 14 in tandem with Art 8 and A1P1. Article 14 has no freestanding existence in absence of other rights. For Example in conjunction with Art 8, it was held that there was a breach of Art 14 where an 'occupant was prohibited from succeeding a tenancy after the death of his same-sex partner'.[365]

Therefore, CPO affected residents claiming art 14 protections could have to establish grounds for breach in other areas such as Art 8 or A1P1. The court appears to lay emphasis as to whether there are justiciable grounds within the scope of property rights. Such as in the case of *Marck v Belgium above,* where the court found in favour of a mother who alleged discrimination in relation to the freedom to dispose her property to so called illegitimate children although the court found no violation of A1P1 per se.

Similarly, in *Gaygusuz v Austria,* the court found a breach of Art 14 where there was a denial of assistance to an applicant who was not of Austrian Nationality.[366] Perhaps it could reflect the notably lower margin of appreciation in ART 14, which is very narrow, compared to A1P1. An applicant wishing to pursue a claim under ART 14 in relation to his or her property rights would have to prove elements of A1P1, such as possession but would not necessarily need to substantiate a violation of such rights to be able to make a claim of discrimination under Art 14. The applicant would be required to establish grounds under which his or rights under art 8 or A1P1 were breached and how such interference was different from other comparators in an unjustifiable manner.[367] Once the applicant establishes grounds for consideration of the claim under Art 14 and the associated Articles such as Art 8 or A1P1, the burden then falls on the state to justify the alleged discrimination in terms of its

---

[364] https://www.echr.coe.int/Documents/Convention_ENG.pdf

[365] (*Karner v. Austria*, §§ 41-43; *Kozak v. Poland*, § 99).

[366] The right to property, Human rights handbooks, No. 10

[367] Handbook No 10, property rights under ECHR

consistency with the law whether it is a legitimate aim and it is proportionate to that aim.

The interplay of art 14 and A1P1 also applies to Art 3[368] which is reiterated in the treaty of Rome as a free standing equal-treatment guarantee although the UK has not signed that treaty.

As far as Art 14 is specifically concerned, in terms of housing in general and estate demolition in particular, there are reports from bodies like the race audit and the Institute of race relations among others, [369]which cite disparity in housing and the disproportionate effects it has on racial minorities associated with estate regeneration.[370]

These have wider potentially intergenerational effects in terms of social mobility, access to opportunity and other social indicators where there are historical economic and social disadvantages among specific communities such as racial minorities, therefore national authorities have to pay close attention to the specific needs of minorities and those with protected characteristics which might require imposing certain conditions within certain limits.[371]

---

[368] Articles 2, 3 and 14, Equal access to justice in the case-law of the European Court of Human Rights on violence against women, https://www.echr.coe.int

[369] JESSICA PERERA,The London Clearances: Race, Housing and Policing, 2019

[370] https://www.ethnicity-facts-figures.service.gov.uk/

[371] (Connors v. the United Kingdom, § 84) Chapman v UK

United Kingdom [GC], § 96; Yordanova and Others v. Bulgaria, §§ 129-130 /(Codona v. the United Kingdom

[372] just-space-response-to-panel-note-7.3-20-may-2019.pdf, https://justspacelondon.files.wordpress.com/2019/04

[373]JESSICA PERERA, The London Clearances: Race, Housing and Policing, 2019

[374] CASE OF PINE VALLEY DEVELOPMENTS LTD AND OTHERS v. IRELAND, Application no. 12742/87

Specifically, in housing and estate regeneration, reports indicate that racial minorities[372] face a disproportionate detrimental impact.[373] This would appear to therefore be incompatible with the judgment In *Chapman,* for example, where the court affirmed that restricting the use of caravans, has an impact on the applicants' respect for their home. The applicant was notably from a racial minority group which is historically disadvantaged.

The ECHR has also held that there was discrimination and therefore a breach of Art 14 in the case of *Pine valley developments Ltd V Ireland[374],* where the applicants complained of discrimination due to a refusal of planning permission in respect of the applicant in comparison to other landowners. A similar ruling found in favour of the applicant in respect of Art 14 and A1P1 in the case of *Chassgnou and others V France[375],* where it was held that legislation appeared to favour large landowners, who could use their land as they wished which put smaller farmers in a discriminatory position. A ruling that was consistent with the case *Larkos v Cyprus[376]* where *'the court held that offering differential protection to tenants against eviction – according to whether they are renting state-owned property or renting from private landlords, entailed a violation of Article 14 taken in conjunction with Article 8, due to the unjustifiable difference of treatment'.*

This would be consistent with the residents affected by CPOs who have cultural links or may be disadvantaged by being forced to areas whey they face racial discrimination.[377]In addition the ruling above is consistent with the need to treat residents fairly and equally, especially in relation to issues such as valuations of properties, rehousing and compensation, where racial minorities face a disproportionate detrimental impact on their lives. Emphasis appears to be put on a positive obligation for a member state to cultivate appropriate safeguards to the extent even a lack of legal capacity leading to dispossession without meaningful participation in the process or access to the final determination by the courts was held to be a violation of art 8, by the court having considered protection measures and their inadequacy in the national state law.[378]

---

[375] CASE OF CHASSAGNOU AND OTHERS v. FRANCE. Applications nos. 25088/94, 28331/95 and 28443/95)

[376] App no 29515/95 (Application No) ECHR 1999-I (Official Citation)

[377] (*Chapman v. the United Kingdom* [GC], § 73).

A principle that appears to have been emphasised by the UK Supreme Court,[379] where the court asserted that the EA2010 provided further protection to a group of people who fall under the protected characteristics category.[380] The implication here for CPO affected parties, especially resident occupiers, is that where there is evidence of discrimination without a legitimate and proportionate aim, there are grounds upon which Art 14 in conjunction with A1P1 or other articles like art 8 could be upheld in their favour. Thereby protecting their property rights and other associated rights.

As already discussed above, beyond ECHR and the HRA 1998, international conventions bar discrimination and other human rights abuses.

This is an extensive area that will be covered in a separate chapter under international law especially how estate regeneration enforced by CPOs is consistent with international human rights law in light of the recent criticisms of the UK by the United Nations[381] and other interventions by the UN rapporteurs[382] cited above. Therefore, the discussion of international law is in a brief context covering the universal declaration of human rights which has moral authority [383] with given legal effect under the international convention on civil and political rights.[384] Applicable to housing are articles 23, 22, 3, 14 and 26[385], inter alia, ratified by the UK in 1976.[386]It appears that clear protections against discrimination exert moral or political

---

[378] *Zehentner v. Austria*, §§ 63 and 65) / (*A.-M.V. v. Finland*, §§ 82-84 and 90).

[379] In Akerman –Livingston v Aster Communities Ltd(UKSC) 15,

[380]https://justspacelondon.files.wordpress.com/2019/04/just-space-response-to-panel-note-7.3-20-may-2019.pdf; https://www.london.gov.uk/nlp_ex_33_cover_report.pdf

[381] https://www.ohchr.org/EN/Issues/Poverty/Pages/SRExtremePovertyIndex.aspx

[382] https://www.ohchr.org/en/issues/housing/pages/housingindex.aspx

[383] http://www.un.org/en/universal-declaration-human-rights/

[384] https://www.ohchr.org/en/professionalinterest/pages/ccpr.aspx

[385] https://www.ohchr.org/en/professionalinterest/pages/ccpr.aspx

[386] our-human-rights-work/monitoring-and-promoting-un-treaties, https://www.equalityhumanrights.com/en/

diplomatic pressure on states and encouragement to implement adequate protections.[387]

It is however important to examine the provisions of art 10 1nd 11 that are relevant to the topic t hand namely estate regeneration enforced through CPOs.

Chapter 11

Art 10 and 11 of ECHR

Another aspect of ECHR that appears to be relevant to property rights and estate regeneration enforced by CPOs is the freedom of association and expression, which are covered, by Articles 10 and 11. Art 10 and 11 of ECHR are considered together here since the protections they provide are intrinsically linked.

Art 10[388] states that ...

1   *Everyone has the right to freedom of expression. This right shall include freedom to hold opinions and to receive and impart information and ideas without interference by public authority and regardless of frontiers. This Article shall not prevent States from requiring the licensing of broadcasting, television or cinema enterprises.*

2.   *The exercise of these freedoms, since it carries with it duties and responsibilities, may be subject to such formalities, conditions, restrictions or penalties as are prescribed by law and are necessary in a democratic society, in the interests of national security, territorial integrity or public safety, for the prevention of*

---

[387] (*Stenegry and Adam v. France* (Dec.)).

[388] https://www.echr.coe.int/Documents/Convention_ENG.pdf

disorder or crime, for the protection of health or morals, for the protection of the reputation or rights of others, for preventing the disclosure of information received in confidence, or for maintaining the authority and impartiality of the judiciary.

Chapter 12

Art 11 and property rights

Article 11 – states that:

1. 'Everyone has the right to freedom of peaceful assembly and to freedom of association with others, including the right to form and to join trade unions for the protection of his interests.

2. No restrictions shall be placed on the exercise of these rights other than such as are prescribed by law and are necessary in a democratic society in the interests of national security or public safety, for the prevention of disorder or crime, for the protection of health or morals or for the protection of the rights and freedoms of others. This Article shall not prevent the imposition of lawful restrictions on the exercise of these rights by members of the armed forces, of the police or of the administration of the State'[389].

ECHR rights of expression or association although protected may be restricted by state authorities with certain qualifications within the law such as in the interest maintaining order or public safety. Hence any limitations on these freedoms is placed on these rights in balance with public policy grounds.[390]Authorities must ensure that the property rights, which are the issues here, are infringed or interfered with without lawful justification such as in the case of CPOs under A1P1 or Art 8.

---

[389] https://www.echr.coe.int/Documents/Convention_ENG.pdf

[390] Observer and the Guardian v the United Kingdom (1991)

The case of *Handy side v UK,*[391] mentioned above highlights the relevant issues associated with property rights, which may be applicable to CPOs. In this case, the authorities seized books published by the applicant on grounds that they contained lewd content. It was held that since state authorities have a margin of appreciation under art 10, there was no breach of either Art 10 or A1P1. The implication here in relation to CPOs is that as long as states can justify and prove their activity within the margin of appreciation accorded to states based on the facts of the case, the court could potentially hold in the respective states favour.

However, in the later case of *Ozturk v Turkey*[392], the court found that the confiscation and destruction of the applicant's book was apparently related to his prior conviction by the authorities and was therefore in breach of art 10. In addition, the court further concluded that it was therefore not necessary to consider A1P1 in the circumstances.

This later case above highlights the fact that where there is an unjustifiable and permanent expropriation of property, or infringement of another associated rights such as art 10, the court could find a breach of ECHR. Therefore, residents or parties who are faced with having their [393]property rights being expunged as well as having other rights breached may have a potential route to challenge such alleged transgressions by the state authorities.

The wider relevance to CPO affected parties is that local authorities influence and diminish the affected communities' ability to meet, organise and express themselves during the process of consultation or the entire process of acquisition.[394]

---

[391] App No 5493/72 (Application No)

A/24 (Official Citation), [1976] ECHR 5 (Other Reference)

[392] *Ozturk v Turkey*, application no. 22479/93 ,*https://hudoc.echr.coe.int/eng"Ozturk v Turkey"],"documentcollectionid2":["GRAND Chamber*

[394] https://www.socialhousingsoundarchive.com/westbury-estate

This reportedly happens when traditionally elected bodies known as TRAs or leaseholders forums are disbanded, [395]undermined[396] or singled out for lack of funding among other practices.[397] Such as in Lambeth council where residents' elected groups have been suspended which limits effective, representative association without influence or manipulation by the authorities concerned.

TRAs tend to be more effective and organised in challenging Local Authority decisions but there are examples where such associations have been either suspended or marginalised,[398] residents' advocates complained of being singled out, targeted or victimised.[399] Such actions are bound to have a chilling effect on residents' ability to scrutinise or challenge the decisions, actions of such public bodies, [400]therefore jeopardising residents' ability to safeguard their human rights.[401]

In many reported areas, there is no evidence to justify curtailment of those rights in the context of CPOs[402] Another issue that requires consideration is Art 2. Although not an obvious issue under CPO estate regeneration Art 2 is arguably linked to the CPO estate regeneration activities that affect the health and wellbeing of residents[403] especially the vulnerable, elderly and children. In the chapters above, reference was made to various reports that document the social, economic and racial impact on the community and individuals. Such as reports from the Runnymede trust, [404]the

---

[395] https://lambethleaseholders.wordpress.com/

[396] https://newsfromcrystalpalace.wordpress.com/2017/11/08/housing-scandal-one-council-to-choose-who-represents-tenants-and-leaseholders-on-new-residents-assembly/

[397] Tenants and Residents Associations

[398] https://lambethleaseholders.wordpress.com

[399] leaseholders-chairman-quits-amid-council-bullying-claims-green-party-councilor-says-siege-mentality-exists-in-lambeth/://newsfromcrystalpalace.wordpress.com

[400] http://lambeth.network

[401] https://www.equalityhumanrights.com/en/human-rights-act/article-11-freedom-assembly-and-association

[402] what-are-human-rights/human-rights-act/article-11-right-protest, https://www.libertyhumanrights.org.uk/human-rights/

[403] https://newsfromcrystalpalace.wordpress.com/2019/06/10/council-has-refused-us-air-monitoring-systems-tenants-chief-tells-committee-his-wife-had-to-visit-a-and-e-three-times-with-lung-inflammation

[404] Faraha Elahi and Omar Khan Ethnic inequality, Capital for all, https://www.runnymedetrust.org

institute of race relations[405] among others. Those paragraphs simply explain how that is related to Art 2 of the ECHR as discussed below.

Chapter 13

Art 2

Article 2 of ECHR[406]of state that

"1. Everyone's right to life shall be protected by law. No one shall be deprived of his life intentionally save in the execution of a sentence of a court following his conviction of a crime for which this penalty is provided by law.

Art 2 protects life with defences specified in Art 2(2)[407]. It asserts that governments should protect citizens from the excess, failures or illegalities of industry, which among other detriments may harm the public.[408] As highlighted in *Oneryildiz v Turkey, where violation of Art2 was found in respect of a lack of protection for citizens living near a garbage bin that led to an explosion, which caused loss of life.[409] Adding that Art 2 does not simply relate to use of force but in circumstances such as this, the authorities failed to do all they could were capable of doing to protect lives despite their knowledge of the danger to the victims. This is directly relevant to estate regeneration construction related activities where there is contamination and hazards elements, which authorities[410] are fully aware of but seem to be reluctant to take active measures to eliminate or minimise the risk to human health.[411].*

---

[405] Jessica, Pereira, The London clearances, http://www.irr.org.uk

[406] https://www.echr.coe.int/Documents/Convention_ENG.pdf

[407] https://www.echr.coe.int/Documents/Convention_ENG.pdf

[408] Dimitri Xenos, Asserting the Right to life (Article 2, ECHR) in the Context of Industry 8 German L.J. 231 (2007)

[409] Oneryildiz v. Turkey, 2004-XII Eur. Ct. HR 79, First, Do No Harm: Human Rights and Efforts to Combat Climate Change 38 Ga. J. Int'l & Comp. L. 593 (2009-2010

Art 2 is therefore relevant due to the reported adverse impact on residents' well-being, health[412] and public safety during protracted large scale construction projects[413] associated with universally known potentially harmful effects such as vibration, fumes, noise, asbestos contamination,[414] that residents are subjected to for prolonged periods[415] which is clearly incompatible with Art2. However, enforcement remains a formidable impediment due to lack of resources and imbalance of power between affected residents and local authorities in concert with developers as observed by Anna Minton.[416]

Chapter 14

Art 3

As indicated under Art 2,[417] a similar observation arguably applies to CPO estate regeneration under Art 3, if there is evidence of an arguable link between aspects of inhuman or degrading treatment under art 3 and CPO estate regeneration activities.

---

[410] https://www.theguardian.com/environment/2019/may/04/brownfield-site-new-homes-building-wrecking-health-southall

[411] https://www.theguardian.com/environment/2019/may/04/brownfield-site-new-homes-building-wrecking-health-southall

[412] https://www.annaminton.com/groundcontrol

[413] https://www.theguardian.com/environment/2019/may/04/brownfield-site-new-homes-building-wrecking-health-southall

[414] John L Adgate, Sook Ja Cho, Bruce H Alexander, Gurmurthy Ramachandran, Katherine K Raleigh

Jean Johnson,, Rita B Messing, A L Williams, James Kelly & Gregory C Pratt

Modelling community asbestos exposure near a vermiculite processing facility: Impact of human activities on cumulative exposure, Journal Of Exposure Science And Environmental Epidemiology

2011/02/23

[415] Brownfield-site-new-homes-building-wrecking-health-southallhttps://www.theguardian.com/environment/2019/may/04

[416] Anna Minton, 'Scaring the living daylights out of people': The local lobby and the failure of democracy

1 Feb 2013

[417] Marcia Gibson, Hilary Thomson, Ade Kearns & Mark Petticrew (2011) Understanding the Psychosocial Impacts of Housing Type: Qualitative Evidence from a Housing and Regeneration Intervention, Housing Studies, 26:04, 555-573, DOI: 10.1080/02673037.2011.559724

Art 3 states that No one shall be subjected to torture or to inhuman or degrading treatment or punishment.

Art 3 prohibits torture as well as inhuman and degrading treatment. Treatment *can be considered inhuman when it causes physical or mental pain or degrading when it debases or humiliates a person beyond that is usual from punishment*[418]

In property or estate regeneration related cases,[419] if there is evidence of sustained actions that amount to inhuman and degrading treatment, associated with CPO activity,[420] like hazardous elements, it is arguable that those affected could bring action under these grounds. However, it appears that the bar in property related terms is too high for potential applicants to cross the admissibility threshold. For example, in *Predojevic and others v Solvenia,* the court found as inadmissible claims that deprivation of pension amounted to inhuman and degrading treatment.

In spite of a high bar or threshold to satisfy Art 3 requirements in association with property rights, its arguable, therefore that if there are clear or identifiable facts from which the court can infer inhuman or degrading treatment art 3 could be engaged. Such an example could be where construction hazards[421] like industrial dust, noise, lead, asbestos or other contaminants, which cause or are linked to illness or severe emotional distress.[422]Therefore, although it is likely that the rights under art 3 associated with CPOs and estate regeneration could require more hard evidence, it would appear that if there is a nexus between inhuman and degrading treatment, associated with estate regeneration, there could be circumstances where potential applicants can make an arguable case.

---

[418] https://www.libertyhumanrights.org.uk/human-rights/what-are-human-rights/human-rights-act/article-3-no-torture

[419] Wellbeing and Regeneration, reflection from Carpenter estate, Alexandre Apsan Frediani, Stephanie Butcher and Paul Watt

[420] Regeneration and Well-Being in East-London: Stories from Carpenters Estate

[421] https://www.theguardian.com/environment/2019/may/04/brownfield-site-new-homes-building-wrecking-health-southall

[422]https://www.theguardian.com/uk-news/2019/jul/07/court-challenge-homes-southall-london-gasworks-brownfield-development

Conclusion

The above observations are a starting point in terms of laying the foundation to examine the impact of housing estate regeneration or expropriation enforced through CPOs on residents, and its compatibility with human rights law. This would create a basis upon which a plausible determination of the effectiveness human rights law in challenging estate regeneration related human rights abuses could be made.

From the initial analysis so far, there appears to be emerging evidence or existing evidence of incompatibility with human rights law. However, further analysis is necessary to obtain a more rounded understanding of the issue and the mechanisms needed for residents to fight back and protect their human rights violated by those pursuing estate regeneration through the CPO process.

The upcoming editions will look into greater detail international law highlighting, the lived or documented experiences of specific communities as documented, and the different methods that residents have deployed so far in challenging estate regeneration, an assessment of the, the effectiveness of current remedies and then consider suggestions for reform. To ensure that, human rights law in this area has real teeth. Otherwise, if there is a perception that human rights law or indeed courts cannot protect residents against the interests of the powerful or some local authorities in concert with private entities, as mentioned above, then there is a real danger that faith in the legal or judicial system could further evaporate. Which will leave the decades of progress in human rights law and the protection it offers in real peril.

Bibliography

1. MHCLG: Guidance on compulsory purchase process and the Crichel down Rules for the disposal of surplus land acquired by, or under the threat of, compulsion,

https://www.gov.uk/government/publications/compulsory-purchase-process-and-the-crichel-down-rules-guidance.

2. The Implications of Kilo in Land Use Law, Symposium Articles: Keynote Address - Kelo, Lingle, and San Remo Hotel, Santa Clara Law Review, Vol. 46, Issue 4 (2006), pp. 787-810 Curtin, Daniel J. Jr

3. Globalization, Communities and Human Rights: Community-Based Property Rights and Prior Informed Consent,2006 Sutton Colloquium Article, Denver Journal of International Law and Policy, Vol. 35, Issue 3 & 4 (Summer-Fall 2007),pp. 413 428 https://heinonline.org/419

4. Human Rights and Property Rights [article] United States Law Review, Vol. 64, Issue 11 (November 1930), pp. 581-594 Blume, Fred H.

5. Equating Human Rights and Property Rights--The Need for Moral Judgement in an Economic Analysis of Law and Social Policy, Ohio State Law Journal, Vol. 47, Issue 1 (1986), pp. 163-200 Malloy, Robin Paul

6. Douglas Maxwell, Journal of planning & Environmental Law, Article 1 of the First protocol: A paper tiger in the face of compulsory purchase orders for private profit?

7. Towards a Compulsory Purchase Code: https://www.lawcom.gov.uk/project/towards-a-compulsory-purchase-code/

8. Compulsory acquisition of land: Developers, by PLC Property https://uk.practicallaw.thomsonreuters.com

9. Planning Act 2016: http://www.housing.org.uk/resource-library/browse/the-housing-and- planning-act-2016/

10. Kept in the Dark; https://www.transparency.org.uk

11. The Law of compulsory purchase, third edition, Guy Roots et al

12. Estate-regeneration-why-people-power-is-forcing-london-to-rethink-housing; developers-alarmed-at-khans-plans-to-give-estate-residents-power; https://www.architectsjournal.co.uk/news

13. Mayor-and-conservatives-dispute-latest-London-housing-stats; https://www.insidehousing.co.uk/news/news/ https://www.bbc.co.uk

14. Phil Hubbard, Loretta Lees. (2018) the right to community? *City* 22:1, pages 8-25.

15. https://www.transparency.org.uk/faulty-towers

16. https://architectsforsocialhousing.wordpress.com/2016/03/24/the-doomsday-book/).

17. Towards a paradigm of Southern urbanism Seth Schindler City Volume 21, 2017 - Issue 1Published online: 6 Mar 2017

18. Reconstructing Berlin: Materiality and meaning in the symbolic politics of urban space

19. Dominik Bartmanski et al.City Volume 22, 2018 - Issue 2 Published online: 17 Apr 2018

20. Editorial Editor-in-Chief's note: What/whose order is to be asserted in the city?

21. Bob Catterall City Volume 22, 2018 - Issue 2

22. Published online: 7 Jun 2018

23. The right to community?: Legal geographies of resistance on London's gentrification frontiers

24. <u>Phil Hubbard</u> et al. City Volume 22, 2018 - Issue 1 Published online: 15 Mar 2018 editorial

25. <u>Editorial: The right to assert the order of things in the city</u> <u>Luke R. Barnesmoore</u> City

26. Volume 22, 2018 - Issue 2 Published online: 7 Jun 2018

27. Stuart Hodkinson, Chris Essen, (2015) "Grounding accumulation by dispossession in everyday life: The unjust geographies of urban regeneration under the Private Finance Initiative", International Journal of Law in the Built Environment, Vol. 7 Issue: 1, pp.72-91, https://doi.org/10.1108/IJLBE-01-2014-0007

28. <u>Towards a new perspective on the role of the city in social movements: Urban Policy after the 'Arab Spring'</u> <u>Raffael Beier</u> City Volume 22, 2018 - Issue 2 Published online: 17 Apr 2018

29. Adonis, A., and B. Davies, eds. 2015. City Villages: More Homes, Better Communities. London: IPPR. https://www.ippr.org/publications/city-villages-more-homes-better-communities

30. The London Borough of Southwark (Aylesbury Estate Site 1B-1C) Compulsory Purchase Order 2014 ('the Order': http://35percent.org/img/Decision_Letter_Final.pdf

31. Prime minister pledges to transform sink estates: https://www.gov.uk/government/news/prime-minister-pledges-to-transform-sink-estates: 10 January 2016

32. 'Cameron time to demolish sink estates': https://www.bbc.co.uk/news/av/uk-politics-35275516/cameron-time-to-demolish-worst-sink-housing-estates, 10 January 2016

33. Compulsory purchase and Compensation: An Overview of the system in England and Wales, By Frances Plimmer.

34. Paul Watt & Anna Minton (2016) London's housing crisis and its activisms, City, 20:2, 204-221, https://doi.org/10.1080/13604813.2016.1151707

35. Participation in the right of access to adequate housing, 14 Tulsa J Comp. & Intl L 269 2006 -2007, Hein online

36. Republic of SA v Grootboom & others 2000(11) BCLR 1169

37. Evadne Grant, Enforcing Social and Economic Rights: The right to adequate housing in south Africa, 15 Afr, J, intl & Comp,L 1 (2007), Hein online

38. The requirements for a compelling case in the public interest to justify a CPO (High Court) by Practical Law Planning: In Horada v Secretary of State for Communities and Local Government [2015] EWHC 2512 (Admin), Volume: 25 issue: 1, page(s): 115-135

39. The privatization of council housing, Norman Ginsburg, Issue published: February 1, 2005 https://doi.org/10.1177%2F0261018305048970

40. Haringey Council votes to cancel development vehicle despite Lendlease warning 18 July 2018:https://www.insidehousing.co.uk/news/news/haringey-council-votes-to-cancel-development-vehicle-despite-lendlease-warning-57250:

41. Watt, P. 2015. "The IMD as a WMD in the Regeneration of London Council Estates: Tackling Spatial Inequalities and Producing Socio-spatial Injustice." Paper at Tackling Spatial Inequalities Conference, Sheffield, September 10

42. Paul Watt (2009) Housing Stock Transfers, Regeneration and State-Led Gentrification in London, Urban Policy and Research, 27:3, 229-242, https://doi.org/10.1080/08111140903154147

43. Pam Douglas & Joanne Parkes (2016) 'Regeneration' and 'consultation' at a Lambeth council estate, City, 20:2, 287-291, https://doi.org/10.1080/13604813.2016.1143683

44. Bracking V Secretary of state for works and pensions [2013] EWCA Civ 1345, [2014] Eq LR 60

45. Knock it down or Do it UP? The challenge of estate regeneration https://www.london.gov.uk/about-us/london-assembly/london-assembly-publications/knock-it-down-or-do-it

46. HPA 2016 and how it affects housing associations: http://www.lag.org.uk/magazine/2016/07/a-devastating-blow-to-social-housing-in-england.aspx

47. EA2010Equality Act 2010 (Specific Duties and Public Authorities) Regulations 2017. PSED: specific duties in England, Practical Law UK Practice Note

48. CPA 1965: Compulsory Purchase Act 1965.

49. CP (VD) A 1981: Compulsory Purchase (Vesting Declarations) Act 1981.

50. LCA 1961: Land Compensation Act 1961.

51. LCA 1973: Land Compensation Act 1973.

52. TCPA 1990: Town and Country Planning Act 1990

53. https://www.libertyhumanrights.org.uk/

54. https://www.equalityhumanrights.com/en/about-us

55. https://www.ohchr.org/en/professionalinterest/pages/ccpr.aspx

56. https://echr.coe.int/

57. British Institute of human rights www.Bihr.org.uk

58. Chartered Institute of Housing www. Cih.org

59. DCLG www.coommunites.gov.uk

60. Housing Law practitioners Association www. Hipa.org.uk

61. The Law Society www.lawsociety.org

62. https://savecressingham.wordpress.com/

63. http://www.insidehousing.co.uk/cressingham-gardens-regeneration-approved-in-high-court/7018185.article

64. http://35percent.org/2013-06-08-the-heygate-diaspora/

65. https://www.southwarknews.co.uk/news/council-given-permission-take-aylesbury-estate-cpo-case-high-court-disappointing-blow-campaigners/

66. http://www.shelter.org.uk

67. http://www.axethehousingact.org.uk/page/2/ on

68. Localism Act 2011, https://uk.practicallaw.thomsonreuters.com/1-504-2706

69. Housing and equality law, By Robert Brown, Arden Chambers

    a. https://uk.practicallaw.thomsonreuters.com/w-012-0034

70. https://www.ashurst.com/en/news-and-insights/legal-updates/compulsory-purchase-life-after-aylesbury/

71. https://www.birketts.co.uk/insights/legal-updates/compulsory-purchase-and-what-to-do-about-it

72. https://assets.publishing.service.gov.uk/government/uploads/system/uploads/attachment_data/file/551698/ECHR_Memorandum.pdf

73. https://www.burges-salmon.com/news-and-insight/legal-updates/alternative-development-proposals-how-do-they-affect-cpo-validity/

74. Housing and Regeneration Act 2008, Housing and Regeneration Act 2008

    a. http://www.opsi.gov.uk/acts/acts2008/ukpga_20080017_en_1

75. Donnelly, Jack. Universal human rights in theory and practice. Cornell University Press, 2013.

76. Human rights Act 1998: https://uk.practicallaw.thomsonreuters.com/0-506-9287

77. Lexis   Nexis:
    https://www.lexisnexis.com/uk/lexispsl/publiclaw/document/413481/5DF5-Dealing_with_a_human_rights_challengehttps://www.lexisnexis.com/uk/lexispsl/publicl

78. New law journal: https://www.newlawjournal.co.uk/

79. Practicallaw:https://uk.practicallaw.thomsonreuters.com/Browse/Home/Practice/PublicLaw

80. Hansard- https://hansard.parliament.uk/

81. https://www.leighday.co.uk/News/2015/November-2015/Cressingham-Gardens-tenant-wins-High-Court-legal

82. https://www.theguardian.com/commentisfree/2017/oct/25/labour-council-regeneration-housing-crisis-high-court-judge

83. The Secretary of states' ruling re: Town and Country Planning Act 1990 Section 226(1) (a), Acquisition of Land Act 1981 The London Borough of Southwark (Aylesbury Estate Site 1B-1C) Compulsory Purchase Order 2014 ('

84. https://hsfnotes.com/realestatedevelopment/2016/09/28/a-new-right-to-a-community-decision-by-the-secretary-of-state-not-to-confirm-the-cpo-for-aylesbury-estate/

85. Compulsory_purchase_process_and_the_Crichel_Down_Rules_-_guidance_updated_180228;https://assets.publishing.service.gov.uk/government/uploads/system/uploads/attachment_data/file/684529/

86. http://www.legislation.gov.uk/ukpga/2010/15/

87. https://www.burges-salmon.com/news-and-insight/legal-updates/the-neighbourhood-planning-act-2017/

88. https://www.legislation.gov.uk/ukpga/2010/15/section/149

89. https://assets.publishing.service.gov.uk/government/uploads/system/uploads/attachment_data/file/475271/cpo_guidance.pdf

90. Knock   It   Down   Or   Do   It   Up; https://www.london.gov.uk/sites/default/files/gla_migrate_files_destination/

91. London's Housing Crisis Worse for Ethnic Minorities 22 March 2016;;https://www.runnymedetrust.org/news/638/272

92. Dispossession the great social housing swindle: https://www.dispossessionfilm.com/

93. City   Villages,   More   Homes,   Better   communities: https://www.ippr.org/files/publications/pdf/city-villages_Mar2015.pdf

94. Shelter. 2015. Homes for our Children. How much of the Housing Market is Affordable?,https://england.shelter.org.uk/Homes_for_our_Children.pdf

95. The-story-of-the-camberwell-submarine-4618, https://www.insidehousing.co.uk/insight/insight

96. Convention for the Protection of Individuals with regard to Automatic Processing of Personal Data Strasbourg, 28.I.1981 https://rm.coe.int/CoE

97. Legal Challenges to Implementing CPOs and Decisions under the Crichel down Rules by Tim Mould QC http://www.landmarkchambers.co.uk/userfiles/TM.pdf

98. The use of compulsory purchase powers for regeneration by Elvin QC, http://www.landmarkchambers.co.uk s. 149 of the Equality Act 2010

99. Land Compensation Claims: The Claimants Perspective by Simon Pickles Landmark Chambers http://www.landmarkchambers.co.uk/cases-compulsory_purchase_compensation.aspx

100. Compulsory purchase orders: stage 4, CPO compensation procedure: flowchart by Practical Law Planning, https://uk.practicallaw.thomsonreuters.com/2-629-7353

101. Twenty years later-Assessing the significance of the Human Rights Act 1998 to the residential possession proceedings, By Ian Loveland http://openaccess.city.ac.uk/17163/

102. Housing Act 1988 https://www.legislation.gov.uk/id/ukpga/1988/50

103. R on the application of Sainsbury's supermarket ltd) V Wolverhampton city Council (2010) UKSC

104. Waters v welsh development agency (2004)1WLR 1304

105. David Elvin QC paper, Use of compulsory purchase powers for regeneration, http://www.landmarkchambers.co.uk

106. Countryside Alliance v Attorney General [2007] UKHL 52

107. Article 1 of the first Protocol to the ECHR: protection of property, Practical Law UK Practice Note, https://uk.practicallaw.thomsonreuters.com/8-385-5732

108. Article 6 of the ECHR: right to a fair hearing Housing:

109. https://uk.practicallaw.thomsonreuters.com/2-385-8106

110. Part VII of the Housing Act 1996

111. Demolition or refurbishment of social housing? https://www.ucl.ac.uk/engineering-exchange/research-projects/2018/nov/demolition-or-refurbishment-social-housing

112. Stanton, J. (2014). The Big Society and Community Development: Neighbourhood Planning under the Localism Act. Environmental Law Review, 16(4), 262–276.

113. Murungaru v Home Secretary [2008] EWCA Civ 1015

114. Fazia Ali v The United Kingdom - 40378/10 Court (Fourth Section)) [2015] ECHR 924

115. Belfast City Council v Miss Behavin' Ltd [2007] UKHL 19

116. James V UK (A98 (1986 E.H.R.R 123 (ECHR)

117. Sporrong and Lönnroth [1982] 5 EHRR 35

118. Le Compte, Van Leuven and De Meyere v Belgium [1981] ECHR 3.

119. Bryan v United Kingdom [1995] ECHR 50, (1996) 21 EHRR 342

120. Begum v London Borough of Tower Hamlets [2003] UKHL 5

121. Lithgow and others v UK [1986] 8 EHRR 329)

122. Chapman v. the United Kingdom [GC], § 96;

123. Yordanova and Others v. Bulgaria, §§ 129-130

124. Zehentner v. Austria, §§ 63 and 65) / (A.-M.V. v. Finland, §§ 82-84 and 90).

125. Qazi v Harrow LBC (2003 UKHL 43: (2004) 1 AC 983 (HL)

126. Salvesen V Riddell(2013) UKSC 22: 2013 SC(U.K.S.C) 236(SC)

127. López Ostra v. Spain, §§ 56-58,

128. Moreno Gómez v. Spain, § 61.

129. Di Sarno and Others v. Italy, § 112).

130. Hatton and Others v. the United Kingdom [GC], § 96;

131. Moreno Gómez v. Spain, § 53)

132. Fadeyeva v. Russia, § 69.

133. (Asselbourg and Others v. Luxembourg (dec.)).

134. Martínez Martínez and Pino Manzano v. Spain,

135. (Hardy and Maile v. the United Kingdom

136. (Hatton and Others v. the United Kingdom [GC]

137. https://www.facebook.com/Savewestburysw8-804075296314550/

138. https://twitter.com/savewestburysw8

139. WestburySW8 a diary of Housing Estate Expropriation and Displacement-A lived experience.

HUMAN RIGHTS AND HOUSING ESTATES REGENERATION

By Shemi Esquire

Exclusively for JEB

This text analyses human rights under ECHR/ HRA 1998 in relation to Housing Estate regeneration enforced by CPOs. Although there are similarities with other UK devolved areas like Scotland, the acts here largely refer to England and wales.

Thanks to all those who made comments on the draft thesis chapter.[1]

---

[1] S Keenan -supervisor

Table of contents

Introduction

ECHR /HRA 98 Articles

Art 8

Art 6

A1P1

Art 2

Art 3

Art 10

Art 11

International legal issues

Conclusion

Bibliography

The aim of this text is to assess whether human rights law is an effective mechanism to challenge the harm caused by housing estate regeneration effected by the use of compulsory purchase orders in the United Kingdom.

The focus of this text relates to the actions of local authorities or public bodies that attract the jurisdiction of the ECHR and the applicable international human rights law.[2]

The book analyses any potential or existing human rights breaches associated with estate regeneration under the ECHR regime and briefly discusses the relevant international human rights law. International human rights law although discussed briefly below requires a separate chapter in terms of assessing how international human rights law safeguards against violations associated with CPO enforced estate regeneration. The ECHR rights examined here which are associated with the use of CPOs in housing estate demolition, include the right to a peaceful and quiet enjoyment of one's home, *respect for the home (Art 8), fairness, transparency and the expeditious nature of the whole process (Art 6), equality of treatment (Art 14), freedom of association, expression (Art 9 and 10), Art 13 dealing with Just compensation or the appropriate legal remedies, Art 2(right to life), Equal treatment, impact on children and applicable international law as indicated in detail below.*

The ECHR rights above are juxtaposed with the underlying practical policies, practices, decisions and impact on individuals or the wider community. Commencing with the initial decisions, consultation process, internal processes, viability reports, environmental issues, equality matters, planning permission and the eventual adverse impact on residents in the respective communities. The impact on communities is assessed by examining fundamental life indicators like employment, finances, culture, health, the disproportionate impact on racial minorities[3] and whether the statutory compensation is fair or equitable.[4]

By simple definition, compulsory purchase orders [5](CPOs) are a legal mechanism deployed by acquiring authorities to acquire land[6] which may be occupied or encumbered with competing property or legal interests through compulsion.[7]

---

[2] https://www.un.org/en/universal-declaration-human-rights

[3] 'It's not for us': Regeneration, the 2012 Olympics and the gentrification of East London, City, 2013

[4] Alice Belotti, Estate Regeneration and Community Impacts https://www.unicef.org/child-rights-conventionChallenges and lessons for social landlords, developers and local councils,2016

[5] Compulsory purchase orders , https://www.legislation.gov.uk/ukpga/1981/67/section/1

[6] /Knock It Down Or Do It Up pdf, https://www.london.gov.uk

[7] https://www.legislation.gov.uk/ukpga/1981/67/section/1

CPOs *'require approval of a confirming minister under the Acquisition of Land Act 198'.*[8] There are various enabling powers available and the determination to authorise will partly depend on the specific powers used. Such public bodies with statutory powers include 'local authorities, national parks, some executive agencies, the Homes and Communities Agency, health service bodies and government ministers. This is discussed in greater detail in other chapters.

There is a detailed process of CPO processes and various statutory requirements, discussed in other chapters. The focus of this book is not to discuss the detailed statutory CPO process but rather a detailed analysis of the detrimental impact on parties with interest in the land and whether such detrimental effects are compatible with human rights law.

Chapter 1

Overview of aspects of human rights law related to estate regeneration through the use of CPOs

Human rights[9] should be fundamental consideration in the authorisation process of compulsory purchase orders although this is not always the case in practice as discussed in greater detail below. Adherence to human rights law during the CPO process is emphasised in the government guidance, which states *that 'the purposes for which the compulsory purchase order is made',* should *'justify interfering with the human rights of those with an interest in the land affected.*[10] But the guidance also refers to a public sector duty requirement[11]   which by interpretation indicates that a failure to 'have proper regard to the public sector equality duty', related to affordable

---

[8] f-guidance-on-compulsory-purchase-and-the-crichel-down-rules-for-the-disposal-of-surplus-land-.

[9] See "Tesco Stores Limited v Secretary of State for the Environment and Others (Full Report)". *Journal of planning and environment law* (0307-4870), p. 581.

[10] Guidance-on-compulsory-purchase-and-the-crichel-down-rules-for-the-disposal-of-surplus-land-pdf

[11] In R (on the application of Reading BC v SoS DCL

housing, social infrastructure contributions and a vacancy credit policy[12] could be found to be unlawful.

The Government guidance further states that *'all public sector acquiring authorities are bound by the Public Sector Equality Duty as set out in section 149 of the Equality Act 2010. In exercising their compulsory purchase and related powers (e.g. powers of entry), these acquiring authorities must have regard to the effect of any differential impacts on groups with protected characteristics. For example, an important use of compulsory purchase powers is to help regenerate run down areas. Although low income is not a protected characteristic, it is not uncommon for people from ethnic minorities, the elderly or people with a disability to be overrepresented in low-income groups. As part of the Public Sector Equality Duty, acquiring authorities must have due regard to the need to promote equality of opportunity between persons who share a relevant protected characteristic and persons who do not share it.*

This might mean that the acquiring authority devises a process which promotes equality of opportunity by addressing particular problems that people with certain protected characteristics might have (e.g. making sure that documents are accessible for people with sight problems or learning difficulties and that people have access to advocates or advice.[13]

Despite the clear government, guidance above it appears that adherence to such guidance is often inadequate or arguably non-existent. To the extent that even a council lawyer expressed doubt or surprise, as to how the PSED[14] would apply to racial minorities.[15]

---

[12] Saira Kabir Sheikh QC, JPL, 2015

[13] CPO guidance, https://assets.publishing.service.gov.uk

[14] Nlp_ex_33b_appendix_2_legal_note.pdf , https://www.london.gov.uk/sites/default/files/

[15] Lambeth council lawyer, apart from disability, his client did not understand how THI applied to racial minorities; https://twitter.com/saveWestburySW8; https://www.facebook.com/Savewestburysw8-804075296314550/; Human Rights today blog

The CPO process in many respects is deemed to be unfair because the acquiring body or authority is also the main driver of the process as[16] documented by various reports highlighted above in detail, by entities like independent observers,[17] the Runnymede trust,[18] academics[19] among others.

In summary, the effects on residents include displacement,[20] financial disenfranchisement, dispossession,[21] environmental hazards,[22] disproportionate effect on racial minorities,[23] adverse health impact on residents, especially children, elderly and vulnerable adults. This is worsened by the unfair process, imbalance of resources and lack of adequate or meaningful access to an independent decision maker during the process, [24]which makes recourse to courts a complicated, cumbersome and expensive affair. From such observations, it would appear that there is at the very least prima facie evidence of possible incompatibility with human rights law, which is discussed in more detail below. The various aspects of the relevant human rights law are discussed below starting with ECHR which incorporates HRA 98.

---

[16]DCLG Guidance-on-compulsory-purchase-and-the-crichel-down-rules-for-the-disposal-of-surplus-land

[17] Anna Minton, GROUND CONTROL, Fear and Happiness in the Twenty-First Century City, by Anna Minton, Published by Penguin Books, paperback original, 26th June 2012; Anne Rendell (2017) 'Arry's Bar: condensing and displacing on the Aylesbury Estate, The Journal of Architecture, 22:3, 532-554, DOI: 10.1080/13602365.2017.1310125;

[18] UK NGOs' Alternative Report Submission to the UN Committee on the Elimination of Racial Discrimination with regard to the UK Government's 21st to 23rd Periodic Reports June 2016 Drafted by THE RUNNYMEDE TRUST

[19] Hubbard P and Lees L, "The Right to Community?" (2018) 22 City 8

Social exclusion, Paul Watt (2013) 'It's not for us', City; Paul Watt, Housing Stock Transfers, Regeneration and State-Led Gentrification in London Article in Urban Policy and Research.

Social exclusion, Paul Watt (2013) 'It's not for us', City; Paul Watt, Housing Stock Transfers, Regeneration and State-Led Gentrification in London Article in Urban Policy and Research.

[20] Alice Belotti, Challenges and lessons for social landlords, developers and local councils, 2016

[21] Demolition-watch-submission,http://www.demolitionwatchlondon.com, 14-march-2017,

[22] https://www.theguardian.com/environment/2019/may/04/brownfield-site-new-homes-building-wrecking-health-southall

[23] Jessica Perera, The-London-clearances-race-housing-and-policing, http://www.irr.org.uk

[24]Alice Belotti, Challenges and lessons for social landlords, developers and local councils, 2016;

Dispossession, The great social housing swindle, https://www.dispossessionfilm.com,

Chapter 2

ECHR Jurisdiction

The UK is a signatory to the ECHR,[25] which incorporated the Human Rights Act 1998 fundamental freedoms into UK domestic law. This therefore implies that the HRA 98 Act has to be read and given effect in compatibility with convention rights by public authorities, in terms of their processes, decisions, effect or impact thereof which by virtue of s3 of the HRA 1998.[26] Section 4 of the HRA 1998[27] refers to declaration of compatibility of local legislation with the HRA 98 while Section 6 of HRA 98 makes it unlawful for a public authority to act in a manner that is incompatible with convention rights and may apply to organisations which perform public functions.[28]

Furthermore, although UK courts do not have a requirement to make identical decisions to the ECHR, they have to take into account ECHR decisions.[29] Any person affected can bring a legal complaint but victims need to have standing under the CPO and the court can look at substance rather than form. A pressure group can be a victim if it shows that it is affected but it is for public authorities to show compatibility with ECHR rights. There is however a possibility of the complaint being rejected if it is raised too late.[30]

---

[25] The Law of compulsory purchase, third edition, Guy Roots et al

[26]http://www.legislation.gov.uk/ukpga/1998/42/section/3; Also See *nutshells, Human rights ;(state year?) See also HA1985-s7-Compulsory purchase/Human rights act guide to practitioners-Christopher Baker.*

[27] http://www.legislation.gov.uk/ukpga/1998/42/section/4

[28] http://www.legislation.gov.uk/ukpga/1998/42/section/6

[29] https://www.legislation.gov.uk/ukpga/1998/42/section/4

[30] https://www.legislation.gov.uk/ukpga/1998/42/contents

In dealing with the implementation of the ECHR incorporated rights or decisions, states possess a margin of appreciation in areas such as housing. It is argued that this is due to housing being part of the social economic policy of a state and this could require unique solutions unless there is a manifest unreasonable foundation.[31]

However, that assertion could be interpreted differently from the perspective of the international convention rights as highlighted by the UN Rapporteur on human rights.[32] The alternative argument would be that since housing is a basic human need, nothing warrants derogation from protection of that basic human need (shelter) especially in economies that have extensive resources such as the UK.[33]

Specific ECHR rights and relation to Estate regeneration

The rights protected by the ECHR are sixteen in total. These are categorised as absolute, limited or qualified as indicated by Andrew Drzemczewski.[34] From a strictly legal perspective, property rights fall in the qualified category but are human rights that are no lesser than any other human rights As already highlighted above, the most applicable human rights articles associated with CPOs include, *Art 2, Art 8, A1P1, Art 6, ART 14, Art 3, 10, 11, 13, 41 of the ECHR* incorporating the HRA 1998 and international convention on human rights.

 As a summary and as indicated above, Art 3[35] relates to inhuman and degrading treatment, Art 6 protects the right for a fair, expeditious and impartial process[36], Art 8 protects respect for a home and home environment,[37] while Article 1 of the first

---

[31] ECHR; https://www.echr.coe.int/Convention_ENG.pdf

[32] Special Rapporteur on extreme poverty and human rights; https://www.ohchr.orgExtremePoverty

[33] https://data.oecd.org/united-kingdom.htm

[34] https://scholarlycommons.law.wlu.edu/cgi/

[35] ECHR, https://www.echr.coe.int

[36] ECHR, https://www.echr.coe.int

[37] ECHR, https://www.echr.coe.int/Convention_ENG.pdf

protocol,[38] safeguards against unjustifiable, disproportionate interference in the peaceful and quite enjoyment of one's home and possessions[39].

Art 2 protects the right to life and by default health. In estate regeneration, the argument advanced here is that projects which threaten public health or public safety may trigger proceedings under article 2. ART 10 protects freedom of expression, Art 11 protects freedoms of association, ART13 deals with compensation and Art 41 specifies remedies. Article one of the first Protocol refers to principles of law and international law underlining the payment of compensation in as far as money can be compensation.[40] A1P1[41] refers to principles of international law by payment of compensation in as far as money can compensate the affected persons.

However, when considering compensation per se, under the official CPO guidance cited above, a distinction is made between a CPO where land is taken and where land is not taken. This is because a CPO could proceed through imposition of restrictions, which amount to a taking or interference with the use or enjoyment, or ownership of the land but no actual physical land is taken. Therefore, it is arguable that to maintain fairness, in terms of compensation, there is a need for balancing that distinction with the public interest, as highlighted by both statute[42] and human rights law.[43]

Other jurisdictions related to estate regeneration and human rights law

International law [44]

[38] Referred to as A1P1 for brevity

[39] ECHR, https://www.echr.coe.int/Convention_ENG.pdf

[40] ECHR, https://www.echr.coe.int/Convention_ENG.pdf

[41] ECHR, https://www.echr.coe.int/Documents/Guide_Art_1_Protocol_1_ENG.pdf

[42] ECHR, https://www.legislation.gov.uk/ukpga/1973/26/section/1

[43] ECHR, https://www.echr.coe.int/Documents/Guide_Art_1_Protocol_1_ENG.pdf

As mentioned above, among the key protections for those affected by estate regeneration mandated by CPOs, is A1P1, which makes an explicit reference to principles of international law.[45]   A1P1 states that, …'*every natural person or legal person is entitled to the peaceful enjoyment of his possessions and no one shall be deprived of his possessions except in the public interest and subject to the conditions provided for by law and by the general principles of international law'.*[46]

Such reference to international law therefore necessitates an examination of the wider international human rights law applicable to estate regeneration using CPOs. It is also important to point out that the UK is party to the Universal Declaration of Human rights[47]and other related conventions such as[48]the United Nations convention on economic, social and cultural rights which invoke 'the right of everyone to an adequate standard of living for himself and his family, including adequate housing.[49]

However, in notable cases[50] reference to principles[51] of international law, [52]was stated to be limited to persons who are not nationals. This restriction to non-nationals reflected in these cases requires further exploration. It would appear or it is possible part of the reasoning is that the architects of ECHR intended to allow non-nationals to secure their convention rights directly without the inbuilt disadvantages they would

---

[44] OHCHR, https://www.ohchr.org

[45] Egon Scweb, The Protection of the Right of Property of Nationals under the First Protocol to the European Convention on Human Rights, *The American Journal of Comparative Law*

Vol. 13, No. 4 (Autumn, 1964), pp. 518-541

[46] Guide on Article 1 of Protocol No. 1 to the European Convention on Human Rights Protection of property Updated on 31 August 2019, https://www.echr.coe.int/Documents/Guide_Art_1_Protocol_1_ENG.pdf

[47] http://www.un.org/en/universal-declaration-human-rights/

[48] incidentally I write this in the UN HW library in Geneva-7th1019

[49] OCHCHR, https://www.ohchr.org/Documents/ProfessionalInterest/ccpr.pdf

[50] in Lithgow v UK and James v UK

[51] Deborah Rook, Property Law and Human rights, 2001

[52] https://www.ohchr.org/en/professionalinterest/pages/internationallaw.aspx

face in the national legal system. Such disadvantages could include discrimination on the grounds of nationality, race or other grounds generally associated with being a non-national of a specific country, which would not necessarily apply to nationals. It could also be argued that nationals could be arguably protected by their local jurisdiction but this remains a very unclear rationale which needs further scrutiny.

Apart from the direct provisions of international law, there is also international scrutiny and domestic pressure to comply with international law[53] as evidenced by a report from the UNRA rapporteur on human rights, about issues that are arguably inextricably[54]linked to housing, socio-economic policies and therefore the wider issue of social housing. This has a direct policy link with large-scale CPO estate demolition,[55] which contributes to fuelling the housing problems in the UK[56]. It should not be read in isolation but in synthesis with the recognition of detrimental effects like dispossession, displacement and disenfranchisement that come with loss of a home, a sense of agency and support networks,[57]which is directly similar to the effects of CPO associated regeneration.[58]Therefore, any international scrutiny consistent with international law or public policy is a potential positive step in dealing with the detrimental social and economic impact that CPO affected residents face.

In his report, Professor Philip Alston observes that a wealthy country with the fifth largest economy in the world should not be 'patently unjust and contrary to British values that so many people are living in poverty'.[59] He quotes the Institute for Fiscal Studies which foresees, 'a 7% rise in child poverty between 2015 and 2022, and various sources predict child poverty rates of as high as 40%'. Professor Alston's

[53] UK NGOs' Alternative Report Submission to the UN Committee on the Elimination of Racial Discrimination with regard to the UK Government's 21st to 23rd Periodic Reports June 2016 Drafted by THE RUNNYMEDE TRUST

[54]Statement on visit to the United Kingdom, by Professor Philip Alston, United Nations Special Rapporteur on extreme poverty and human rights, https://www.ohchr.org/Documents/Issues/Poverty/EOM_GB_16Nov2018.pdf

[55] Anna Minton, Ground Control: Fear and Happiness in the Twenty-First-Century City; His-estates-10-year-wait-for-regeneration, https://www.insidehousing.co.uk

[56] Anna Minton, big capital who is London for

[57] Anna Minton, Ground control, fear and happiness in the 21st century

[58] https://haringeydefendcouncilhousingblog.wordpress.com/

[59] Professor Philip Alston, United Nations Special Rapporteur on extreme poverty and human rights

report further notes that 'almost one in every two children to be poor in twenty-first century Britain is not just a disgrace, but a social calamity and an economic disaster, all rolled into one'. He emphasises that, 'many of the recent changes to social support in the UK have a disparate impact on children'. Citing evidence from the Equality and Human Rights Commission which predicts that 'another 1.5 million more children will fall into poverty between 2010 and 2021/22 as a result of the changes to benefits and taxes, a 10% increase from 31% to 41%.' The report points to the legal aid cuts, 'in England and Wales since 2012 which overwhelmingly affected the poor and people with disabilities, many of whom cannot otherwise afford to challenge benefit denials or reductions and are thus effectively deprived of their human right to a remedy'. The report highlights ' the LASPO Act (Legal Aid, Sentencing and Punishment of Offenders Act) gutted the scope of cases that are handled, ratcheted up the level of means-tested eligibility criteria, and substituted telephonic for many previously face-to-face advice services'. According to Professor Philip Alston, the Social Metrics Commission, states that 'almost a third of children in the UK live in poverty. After years of progress, child poverty is rising again, and expected to continue increasing sharply in the coming years.'

As described above, this report has a direct policy link with large-scale CPO estate demolition,[60] which contributes to fuelling the housing problems in the UK.[61]

Prof. Alston concludes that 'It was a British philosopher, Thomas Hobbes, who memorably claimed that without a social contract; life outside society would be "solitary, poor, nasty, brutish, and short....many of the public places and institutions that previously brought communities together, such as libraries, community and recreation centres and public parks, have been steadily dismantled or undermined'.[62]

Arguably, Professor Philip Alston's report is acutely relevant to CPO affected residents in various respects. Such as the legal aid cuts in England and Wales since 2012, which overwhelmingly affected the poor or people with disabilities. A theme that is consistent with CPO affected residents who face a lack of access to legal aid

---

[60] Anna Minton, Ground Control: Fear and Happiness in the Twenty-First-Century City; His-estates-10-year-wait-for-regeneration, https://www.insidehousing.co.uk

[61] Anna Minton, big capital who is London for

[62] Report from UNRA rapporteur on human rights, by Professor Philip Alston, United Nations Special Rapporteur on extreme poverty and human rights https://www.ohchr.org/Documents/Issues/Poverty/EOM_GB_16Nov2018.pdf

which has a disproportionate impact on children, racial minorities, the disabled, elderly and historically disadvantaged communities. An issue that is highlighted by both the Institute on Racial relation[63] among others and would appear to be inconsistent with international conventions and international law. Such as the Universal Declaration of Human Rights[64], ICCPR (referred to1st generation rights)[65], ICESCR (referred to as second generation rights,)[66]CERD,ICE (in relation to racial discrimination)[67] and CROC (convention on the right of children 1989.[68]

These conventions aim to protect economic, social, political rights of individuals or groups, such a rights relating to protection for the home, family, health, racial minorities, access to justice and due process. The Universal Declaration on Human rights, specifically refers to a common understanding of a set of values applicable to the treatment of individual human beings, irrespective of their race, religion, gender or other protected characteristics. Furthermore, the European Social charter, protects health, family, property and against discrimination, among other rights.[69] Although enforceability and applicability and legal jurisdiction over member states remains a potent legal hurdle.[70]

Firstly, because such relief would require measures to be implemented by the faulting nation states through protracted legal and political mechanisms. Secondly, there is difficulty in terms of pursuing the international human rights law route due to the complexity of the law, lack of resources and technical support to those affected. Even at a national level, it remains a cumbersome, long and expensive process to pursue legal action against the acquiring authorities who often have access to extensive legal and financial resources. In comparison, residents or communities

[63]Jessica Perera, THE LONDON CLEARANCES A BACKGROUND PAPER ON RACE, HOUSING AND POLICING 2019, Institute of Race Relations

[64] Universal Declaration of Human rights, http://www.un.org/en/universal-declaration-human-rights/

[65]International convention on civil and political rights, https://www.ohchr.org/EN/ProfessionalInterest/Pages/CCPR.aspx

[66] International convention on social and economic rights,https://www.ohchr.org/en/professionalinterest/pages/cescr.aspx

[67] Committee on elimination of racial discrimination, https://www.ohchr.org/en/hrbodies/cerd

[68] Convention on the right of a Child, https://www.ohchr.org

[69] https://www.coe.int/european-social-charter

[70] https://www.un.org/en/universal-declaration-human-rights/

affected in some cases are litigants in person who use pro bono assistance, which therefore limits the degree of assistance available or other sources of funding just to initiate legal action. In addition to the many other day-to-day practical problems, they face due to compulsory acquisition of their homes.[71] Nevertheless, it is critical that there is a transnational approach and potential avenue for redress given that CPOs, eminent domains, forceful land acquisition or land grabbing in general, have wider long-lasting detrimental effects on particular communities and demographics, which are historically disadvantaged, marginalised, disenfranchised and oppressed. Therefore warranting an international redress mechanism and a degree of international legal intervention.[72]

Chapter 3

Individual ECHR Articles related to estate regeneration through the use of CPOs

As briefly discussed above, among the applicable articles of the ECHR, that are arguably directly triggered by CPOs, are Articles 8, A1P1 Art 6, Art 14, 2 and 3 and their relevance as a mechanism to challenge estate regeneration activities under human rights law. These will be discussed in the order highlighted above.

The subsequent chapters shall examine the statutory compensation regime, the adequacy of the current legal remedies to provide a more rounded understanding of the issue, suggested proposals for reform and a determination as to whether human rights law indeed is an effective mechanism for challenging CPOs.

Article 8 ECHR and estate regeneration through the use of CPOs

---

[71] Alice Belloti, Estate community regeneration and community impact, Case report 99, http://sticerd.lse.ac.uk/dps/case/cr/casereport99.pdf

[72] UK NGOs' Alternative Report Submission to the UN Committee on the Elimination of Racial Discrimination with regard to the UK Government's 21st to 23rd Periodic Reports June 2016 Drafted by THE RUNNYMEDE TRUST

Article 8 of ECHR,[73] states that:

1. 'Everyone has the right to respect for his private and family life, his home and his correspondence.

2. There shall be no interference by a public authority with the exercise of this right except such as is in accordance with the law and is necessary in a democratic society in the interests of national security, public safety or the economic well-being of the country, for the prevention of disorder or crime, for the protection of health or morals, or for the protection of the rights and freedoms of others'.

Before examining in depth the legal details or Art 8, it needs to be emphasised that just like other ECHR articles, there is a multitude of various areas of day-to-day life that could fall under the protections of Art 8. The focus here is on the relevant provisions that could be applicable to CPOs under estate regeneration.

Jurisdiction

Art 8 protects the respect for private and family life including one's home or correspondence[74] and could also be invoked in conjunction with A1P1. Observers, [75] point to a minute difference between these two articles in terms of the level of protection provided which may turn on particular facts of a specific applicant.

Scope of Art 8

---

[73] https://www.echr.coe.int/Documents/Guide_Art_8_ENG.pdf

[74] Aida Grigic, Zvonimir Mataga, Matija Longar and Ana Vilfan, The right to property under the ECHR, A guide to implementation of the ECHR, Human rights Hand Book no 10, https://rm.coe.int/168007ff55

[75] Aida Grigic, Zvonimir Mataga, Matija Longar and Ana Vilfan, The right to property under the ECHR, A guide to implementation of the ECHR, Human rights Hand Book no 10, https://rm.coe.int/168007ff55

Art 8[76] safeguards respect for a home and against deprivation of a home by way of access or occupation. It safeguards the right to live without interference and intrusion in one's family or private life and correspondence. Art 8 also refers to personal information being kept private or confidential and requires a positive step from a public authority.

Definition of a home

In brief and in this specific context of art 8, is a settled place where one lives, including a home one has the intention to move to,[77] described as an autonomous concept not based on domestic law categorisations.[78] In *Gillow V UK,* the court held that even though the applicants had not occupied the house for nineteen years[79] it was still their home. The applicants had not established domicile anywhere else and intended to live in the house.

To engage Art 8 protection, there has to be a determination on facts relating to continuous links and rights which cannot be interfered with, unless there is a reasonable justification.[80] Art 8 does not provide a general right to housing under HRA 98 or ECHR[81], except protection for respect for a home or unjustifiable interference of the peaceful and quiet enjoyment of one's home or possessions, under Art 8 and A1P1 respectively.

 Instead, Art 8 emphasises the need for the state to have a positive obligation to be proactive in regulating non-state interference and to provide remedies against

[76] ECHR

[77] Gillow v UK91986) ECHR 14

Donoghue V Poplar Housing association(2001)EWACA Civ 595

[78] https://www.echr.coe.int/Documents/Guide_Art_8_ENG.pdf

[79] CASE OF GILLOW v. THE UNITED KINGDOM (Application no. 9063/80)

[80] https://www.echr.coe.int/Documents/Guide_Art_8_ENG.pdf

[81] https://www.echr.coe.int/Documents/Guide_Art_8_ENG.pdf

harassment of individuals in and around their home as discussed in detail other chapters.[82]

The ECHR[83] further classifies a home as one that merits protection under the respect for a home legal principle. Which extends to property where the complainant is not an owner, a tenant, in long-term occupancy as well as a relative's house or a 'care' facility.[84] However, this may not apply to a home that one intends to build.[85]

Art 8[86] also appears to put emphasis on a home as being non-transient or exceedingly short term, like a hotel room. Although in *Buckley v UK,* [87]*which involved the retrospective denial of planning permission,* the notion of a home was not restricted to being lawfully established. Therefore, the designation or interpretation of what a home is or is not appears subjective.

In the context of a compulsory acquisition of social housing homes, such subjective academic notions of what is or is not a home per se, appears irrelevant for most residents due to the fact that they are actual physical owners and occupants of specific their homes either as secure tenants, leaseholders or freeholders. However, even for those that may not fall in those categories, there appears to be sufficient standing under Art 8 for them to assert their rights. Given that, they are non-transient accommodation or hotel rooms. Many live in these properties as their main homes with their families hence engaging Art 8. In terms of wider estate regeneration, conducted through the powers of CPOs, public authorities,[88] as social housing <u>providers attract the jurisdic</u>tion of HRA 1998 and Art 8 of ECHR.[89] Mainly because

[82] Marckx x Belgium(1979)ECHR 2

[83] https://www.echr.coe.int/Documents/Convention_ENG.pdf

[84] https://www.echr.coe.int/Documents/Guide_Art_8_ENG.pdf

[85] Louizdou V Turkey(1996)ECHR 70

[86] https://www.echr.coe.int/Documents/Convention_ENG.pdf

[87] https://minelres.lv/coe/court/Buckley.htm

[88] Connors V UK(2005) 40 EHRR 9 'gypsies' removal from a locality was violation of art8

[89] R (weaver v London & Quadrant Housing Trust(2009) EWCA Civ 587

the issue here involves home and family life which must be only interfered with in 'accordance with the law'.[90]

Therefore, residents affected by CPOs, could rely on Art 8(1) in asserting their human rights if the public authorities do so in contravention of the law as held in the case of Malone, where it was affirmed that the 'exercise of powers must be in accordance with the law'.[91] The issue in *Malone* involved determination of infringement of rights by surveillance and the court held that although this was consistent with domestic law, discretionary use or application by officers was arbitrary. Therefore being incompatible with Art 8 of ECHR, although in this case the issue involved a tangential issue of surveillance not necessarily confiscation of a home.

Nevertheless, it falls within the remit of Art 8 and it also highlights the principle of a requirement of public authorities acting in accordance with the law, which is applicable to CPO affected parties. The wider point that must be further emphasised here is that planning and public authorities possess opaque, extensive discretionary powers[92], which are susceptible to arbitrary use.[93] Such abuse could be detrimental to individuals affected by decisions arising from CPOs, such as the demolition of housing estate homes, inadequate compensation, environmental hazards, displacement, dislocation, low or disputed valuations and the need for rehousing. Hence, raising potential incompatibility with Art 8, if CPOs are applied unlawfully or where there are illegitimate aims and disproportionate actions.[94] Furthermore, there are implied positive obligations where environmental factors directly and seriously affect private and family life. For example in estate regenerated areas like Southall, Westbury in Lambeth and other areas like Hackney there are increased complaints of environmental pollution especially in areas where the developers are building on contaminated land such as in Southall and the Westbury estate in Lambeth, South

---

[90] https://swarb.co.uk/malone-v-the-united-kingdom-echr-2-aug-1984/

[91] Malone v UK (1984) ECHR 10

[92] Greg Brown & Sean Yeong Wei Chin (2013) Assessing the Effectiveness of Public Participation in Neighbourhood Planning, Planning Practice & Research, 28:5, 563-588, DOI: 10.1080/02697459.2013.820037

[93] Too-poor-to-play-children-in-social-housing-blocked-from-communal-playground, https://www.theguardian.com/cities/2019/mar/25/

[94] Lustig-Prean and Beckett v UK(1999)ECHR 71 relating to UK military ban on LBGT due to 'operational' issues

London[95]. Although there is protection against interference within Art 8 in tandem A1P1, such a provision does not guarantee peaceful enjoyment of property.

The rationale under A1P1, which appears to offer qualified guarantees, appears both outdated and puzzling. Given that environmental or construction hazards associated with CPOs, pose serious and sometimes an existential threat to the health of residents or those exposed to such exposure. Such construction hazards include asbestos, lead, co2, benzene, industrial noise, dust, and fumes among other toxins. So the question has to be asked if those hazards exist how can it be that those affected are not guaranteed a peaceful and quiet enjoyment of their homes or home environment?

Is it possible to completely separate the two aspects of environmental protections with the interference in the peaceful and quite enjoyment of one's life? It is possible that given the current ubiquitous and front stage environmental campaigns, the facts and impact on those affected by estate regeneration construction or demolition could have potential challenges that could force a revisit of the courts approach or conclusions on environmental protection under Art8 and A1P1. It therefore appears that under the current ECHR Art 8 regime, save in exceptionally serious cases, environmental protections for CPO construction affected parties remains uncertain under Art 8 and A1P1 OF ECHR.

Chapter 4

Other Associated rights under Art 8 during CPOs in Estate regeneration

Among other potential safeguards provided under Art 8, discussed in detail below, are associated with issues such as succession, contracts of parties and the protection of a positive duty for the integration of children since family law matters relate to a family home.[96] This protection under Art 8 extends to state benefits or

---

[95] https://www.theguardian.com/environment/2019/may/04/brownfield-site-new-homes-building-wrecking-health-southall

allowances emphasising respect for family life[97]but is not applicable to fiancées. This is critically relevant to residents facing CPOs, which could determine re-housing, compensation or succession rights, not just for individuals, but for those they share their homes with or their relatives.

Tenancies and Art 8 in CPOS

Among other issues, the impact on the various types of tenancies is one of the areas that may engage protection under Art 8 including CPO affected estate regeneration residents or affected parties. There may be preconditions imposed on residents under CPO schemes, [98]whose occupation rights had ceased or those who are short-term occupants after displacing secure tenants[99]during the so-called callously named decanting process.[100]

The relevance here is that due to welfare cuts, high rents, low pay and job insecurity, short or informal arrangements such as sub renting or sharing homes is the most affordable way to live[101] or work in some cities[102]. It is arguable that such homes need a level of protection beyond the narrow confines of statutory or contractual arrangements.[103] This was highlighted in *Chapman V UK,[104] where* the concept of a home was expanded to cabins, bungalows stationed on land irrespective of the lawfulness under national law as well as second homes.[105] A principle that could be

---

[96] https://www.echr.coe.int/Documents/Convention_ENG.pdf

[97] https://www.echr.coe.int/Documents/Guide_Art_8_ENG.pdf

[98] http://estateregeneration.lambeth.gov.uk/key_guarantees#homeowners

[99] Part IV of HA 1985, amended by HA1988 and HA 96.

[100] Alice Belotti LSE Housing & Communities, Estate Regeneration and Community Impacts Challenges and lessons for social landlords, developers and local councils, Case report 99, March 2016

[101] Fenton, Alex. "Housing benefit reform and the spatial segregation of low-income households in London." (2011).

[102] Hamnett, Chris. "Moving the poor out of central London? The implications of the coalition government 2010 cuts to Housing Benefits." *Environment and Planning A* 42.12 (2010): 2809-2819.

[103] Michael Edwards (2016) The housing crisis and London, City, 20:2, 222-237, DOI: 10.1080/13604813.2016.1145947

[104] Chapman-v-united-kingdom-application-no-2723895

asserted by CPO affected residents who may not be long-term occupants or have formal tenancies.

There may however be limitations where there has been minimal occupation or weak links to the property to the extent that they are expunged. Therefore, sufficient nexus or occupation is necessary for recognition of a right to a home. Hence a mere possibility of inheritance may not give rise to a connection to a home under Art 8[106]al though altering the terms of tenancy[107] was found to be an interference with Art 8.[108]

It is nevertheless, evident that on the face of it, CPO processes, interfere with the respect for a home. Despite the fact, that such interference can be qualified under A1P1[109] to allow a member state some latitude in implementation, [110]if certain criteria are attached to the measures.[111] However, if the right in point is critical to the individual's enjoyment of personal intimate rights, the courts minimise the margin of appreciation.[112] Such as where there is demolition of homes[113] leading to[114] compulsion to move and hence a clear interference in the respect to a home under Art 8.[115] This rationale was unambiguously emphasised in Connors v. UK[116] where the court held *inter alia*, 'that the loss of one's home is a most extreme form of interference with the right to respect for the home'. In addition, since there was no justification for such interference, such as what the court referred to as a *pressing*

---

[105] https://www.echr.coe.int/Guide_Art_8_ENG.pdf

[106] https://www.echr.coe.int/Guide_Art_8_ENG.pdf

[107] Loretta Lees,The Urban Injustices of New Labour's "New Urban Renewal": The Case of the Aylesbury Estate in London, 2013

[108] (*Berger-Krall and Others v. Slovenia*, § 264);

[109] (*Howard v. the United Kingdom*,

[110] Alec Samuels, The planning process and judicial control: the case for better judicial involvement and control,J.P.L 1570

[111] *Noack and Others v. Germany*

[112] (*Connors v. the United Kingdom*, § 82).

[113] (*Aboufadda v. France* (Dec.));

[114] *Selçuk and Asker v. Turkey*, § 86; *Akdivar and Others v. Turkey* [GC], § 88; *Menteş and Others v. Turkey*, § 73).

[115] *Noack and Others v. Germany* (Dec.));

[116] Application no. 66746/01

social need or a legitimate aim, the court concluded that there was a violation of Art 8 pf ECHR[117]. This judgement accurately reflects the predicament of CPO affected residents by housing estates regeneration and could potentially provide an avenue to challenge such interference.

Estate regeneration disrepair or blight and Art 8 associated with CPOs

Another issue to consider is that in areas where CPO processes are enacted or merely announced, disrepair or neglect is a common feature.[118] Observers believe this appears to be managed decline to hasten what is termed as the decanting process.[119] A term that reflects the inhumanity and sanitisation of the arguably inhumane process of home expropriation[120]. The use of language and other phrases like brownfield sites or opportunity area drain or minimise any human association or presence in the areas or homes being expropriated. Coupled with the disrepair, blight and the consequential anti-social behaviour, the communities become ripe for targeted added claims by the acquiring authorities of an urgent need for regeneration,[121] which then softens the CPO approval process.

Disrepair has been found to be an infringement of Art 8 even[122]after examining the existence of procedural guarantees to determine the margin of appreciation. Disrepair, neglect and blight are also associated with *nuisance in the legal context under the pollution act 1972 or a public nuisance which falls under criminal law. This*

---

[117] CASE OF CONNORS v. THE UNITED KINGDOM (Application no. 66746/01) JUDGMENT STRASBOURG, 27 May 2004,https://www.refworld.org/cases,ECHR

[118] Estate Regeneration and Community Impacts Challenges and lessons for social landlords, developers and local councils, Case report 99,Alice Belotti LSE Housing & Communities March 2016;

See also Save Cressingham gardens; Save Central Hill: @savewetburysw8

[119] (*Khamidov v. Russia,*

[120] States and real estate private equity firms questioned for compliance with human rights, https://www.ohchr.org

[121] Estate Regeneration and Community Impacts Challenges and lessons for social landlords, developers and local councils, Case report 99,Alice Belotti LSE Housing & Communities March 2016;

[122] *Novoseletskiy v. Ukraine*, §§ 84-88).

is therefore another aspect that could come under the remit of Art 8 where parties who may not possess direct proprietary interest may seek to pursue their property rights from that perspective under Art 8. This is especially during construction related to CPO enforced estate regeneration. Such as in a case where a tree was felled into a neighbour's garden.[123] This is applicable to parties affected by CPO construction nuisances, asbestos or other contaminants as sighted in the Westbury and Southall cases[124] above. As mentioned such a nuisance could attract criminal sanctions under the codes such as the Asbestos Code 2012[125], as well as arising to the standard that breaches the respect for a home or home environment, hence being in contravention of Art 8 of ECHR.

Although Art 8 does not offer an inherent protection of a clean environment per se, planning decisions interfere with people's home and family lives, therefore triggering Art 8 and A1P1.[126] Moreover, since the convention is considered a living instrument, [127] it should be interpreted to fit present day conditions[128]to balance the rights of residents affected with a CPO due to public authorities' actions, which fall under the purview of art 8.[129]

It is arguably due to such hazardous intrusion or exposure that heightens the sense of dangerous impact on communities[130], which compels them to move away from their locality, family and their support networks.[131] There by essentially destroying the '*essential ingredient of a family … the right to live together, enjoy each other's*

---

[123] *Lane V The Royal Borough of Kensington and Chelsea London Borough Council(2013)EWHC 1320(QB)*

[124] https://www.theguardian.com/environment/2019/may/04/brownfield-site-new-homes-building-wrecking-health-southall

[125] http://www.hse.gov.uk/asbestos/regulations.htm
[126] *J.P.L 2010,3 298-309*

[127] *Tyrer V UK*

[128] *J.P.L 2010, 3 298-309*

[129] https://www.echr.coe.int/Documents/Guide_Art_8_ENG.pdf

[130] Paul Watt (2013) 'It's not for us', City, 17:1, 99-118, DOI: 10.1080/13604813.2012.754190

[131] Tom Slater (2009) Missing Marcuse: On gentrification and displacement, City, 13:2-3, 292-311, DOI: 10.1080/13604810902982250

company[132] *and relationship development'*[133] consistent with the 'notion of family life being an autonomous concept'.[134]

Private life and Art 8 in CPOs

Under ECHR, private life is interpreted widely to include 'personal and physical integrity'.[135] The relevancy to CPOs is the excessive unjustifiable intrusion into people's lives culminating to eventual displacement[136]instigated and characterised by collection of personal data,[137] especially in circumstances where many residents could be vulnerable[138]with no access to independent advice or support. Furthermore, such intrusion and demand for disclosure requires justification to avoid contravention of Art 8[139] especially where the acquiring authority is the intruding party, which arguably gains competitive negotiating, commercial and legal advantage.

It appears that even providing information for census purposes may be an interference of rights under Art 8, including surveys, under the realm of Art 8 jurisdiction.[140]Furthermore, intrusion in private life also includes the loss of support networks in the locality, which disrupts employment and professional associations[141]

---

[132] Olson v Sweden

[133] Marckx v Belgium

[134] Marckx v Belgium; https://www.echr.coe.int /Guide_Art_8_ENG.pdf

[135] X and Y v the Netherlands(1985) ECHR 4

[136] Jane Rendell (2017) 'Arry's Bar: condensing and displacing on the Aylesbury Estate, The Journal of Architecture, 22:3, 532-554, DOI: 10.1080/13602365.2017.1310125

[137] http://newmanfrancis.org/projects/westbury-lambeth/

[138] https://www.ucl.ac.uk/engineering-exchange/sites/engineering-exchange/files/fact-sheet-health-and-wellbeing-social-housing.pdf

[139] As held in, Hilton V UK Application no,12015/86

[140] Z v Finland(1997) 25 EHHR 371

which appears to be an example where there seems to be a convergence of Art 8 with A1P1 where interference in one is private, personal, or family life could lead to a legitimate challenge under both Articles. As held, In *Niemietz v Germany[142]*, where the applicant's complaints of entry and seizure of the documents in the lawyer's office was found to be disproportionate and inconsistent with the expectation of confidentiality *'inherent in the lawyer's profession'[143]*, although in Niemietz, the court did not find any *'separate issue under A1P1.'[144]*

Moreover, as indicated above, circumstances that could potentially lead to breach of Art 8 are more extensive than just physical possessions per se since art 8 protects attributes that are consistent with the preservation of family life and associated human dignity. Consequently, the court has also found[145]the loss of employment for a *breach of oath* to trigger Art 8, due to the impact it has on *relationships, material well-being, fami*ly and reputation. This is applicable to CPO affected parties, in the sense that compulsion to move from one's home has spiral effects on access to employment, education, support networks, well-being, family life and consequently one's human dignity and reputation as mentioned in the reports above. The other consideration for potential breach of art 8 is the fairness of the associated process which is discussed in detail below under art 6 but briefly in the paragraphs below under art 8.

Fair process and Art 8 during CPOs in Estate regeneration

Public authorities often use bureaucratic and inscrutable language or opaque processes. CPO decisions and processes may not be understood or formalised during a disruptive protracted process for residents. Valuations, advance payment

---

[141] Volkov Ukraine(21722/11) 2013 IRLR 480(ECtHR),

[142] 13710/88, [1992] 16 EHRR 97, [1992] ECHR 80

[143] Guidance Note 10, The right to property under ECHR

[144] Guidance No 10, The Right to property under the ECHR, pg 21

[145] Practical Law UK practice Note 8 835 5732

and negotiations for compensation or rehousing require specialist technical advice or access to financial resources.[146] Specifically, valuations are determined largely by the acquiring authority with limited independent oversight and imposition of pre-conditions in case of a valuation dispute.[147]This is worsened by the seeming lack of clear reasoning or timely information provided to residents, especially those that face measures that lead to eviction, which attracts protection under Art 8.[148]

The process is characterised by a lack of transparency, imbalance of resources, state self-interests or conflicts of interest due to decision makers being the acquiring party.[149] Planning decisions leading to CPOs [150] are sometimes authorised by the same acquiring party, which would appear to be a manifest conflict of interest with devastating detrimental impact in some cases.[151] An issue highlighted by Anna Minton, in her report 'Scaring the living daylight', [152]a situation which is acutely relevant to victims of estate regeneration enforced through CPOs.[153] In a nutshell, CPO affected residents who are in effect removed and therefore evicted from their homes and community[154] are subjected to obscure, broad, arbitrary and vague language without access to independent legal advice.[155]

---

[146] Stuart Hodkinson, Chris Essen, (2015) "Grounding accumulation by dispossession in everyday life: The unjust geographies of urban regeneration under the Private Finance Initiative", International Journal of Law in the Built Environment, Vol. 7 Issue: 1, pp.72-91, https://doi.org/10.1108/IJLBE-01-2014-0007

[147] Estate Regeneration and Community Impacts Challenges and lessons for social landlords, developers and local councils, Case report 99,Alice Belotti LSE Housing & Communities March 2016; See also Save Cressingham gardens;

See inter alia Hackworth & Smith, 2001; Glynn, 2008; Lees et al., 2008; Shaw, 2008, argue that Stock transfer in London can be understood through the lens of state-led 'third-wave gentrification', a widespread phenomenon across British, North American and Australian cities.

[148] Donoghue, above

[149]See inter alia Hackworth & Smith, 2001; Glynn, 2008; Lees et al., 2008; Shaw, 2008, argue that Stock transfer in London can be understood through the lens of state-led 'third-wave gentrification', a widespread phenomenon across British, North American and Australian cities.

[150] Buckley v. the United Kingdom, § 60);

[151]Siobhan O'Sullivan, et al. "Hearing the Voices of Children and Youth in Housing Estate Regeneration." Children, Youth and Environments, vol. 27, no. 3, 2017, pp. 1–15. JSTOR, www.jstor.org/27.3.0001.

[152] http://spinwatch.org/images/Reports/Scaring_the_living_daylight_final_27_March_13.pdf

[153] Estate Regeneration and Community Impacts Challenges and lessons for social landlords, developers and local councils, Case report 99,Alice Belotti LSE Housing & Communities March 2016; See also Save Cressingham gardens;

[154] Jane Rendell (2017) 'Arry's Bar: condensing and displacing on the Aylesbury Estate, The Journal of Architecture, 22:3, 532-554, DOI: 10.1080/13602365.2017.1310125

The Kate Barker Report, regarding the use of land for planning[156] further highlights the problems associated with the procedural unfairness in the planning process. It refers to 'planning decisions as policy decisions or expediency decisions, conducted in an anomalous manner'. An observation or description that would be consistent with the view that CPOs are imbalanced, favour acquiring parties, lack transparency and there is no real independent scrutiny, as highlighted in the various reports above.

Although, there is a possibility of judicial review it characteristically, largely focuses on procedural flaws, requires extensive resources and is characterised with structural impediments, which are looked at in more detail, under Art 6 below. As an example of such impediments, challenging such arbitrary decisions through judicial review would require a duty to give reasons by a public authority, documentation of the facts and any associated detrimental impact. However, requested information is not always provided, often delayed, deducted when provided, vague or broad even when conducted through freedom of information requests under the FOI Act.[157] Specifically, in areas like Southwark[158], Lambeth[159]and others, [160]residents' demand for due process remains a distant or box ticking exercise.

Therefore, the importance for a public authority to provide reasons for its actions or decisions cannot be understated. Such importance, to give reasons, in matters such as CPOs is captured in the law gazette article, in dramatic language. The article

[155] Duty to give reasons, :*https://www.lawgazette.co.uk/legal-updates/local-government-duty-to-give-reasons*

[156] J.P.L 1570

[157] https://www.whatdotheyknow.com/request/quantity_of_freedom_of_informati#incoming-1055418; https://www.whatdotheyknow.com/request/information_related_to_the_impac#outgoing-950497; http://www.brixtonbuzz.com/2017/12/lambeth-council-refuses-to-admit-how-many-empty-homes-are-on-cressingham-gardens-estate/

[158] http://35percent.org/heygate-regeneration-faq/ https://www.theguardian.com/cities/2018/sep/12/london-council-aylesbury-estate-development-southwark-financial-risk

[159] https://www.socialhousingsoundarchive.com/westbury-estate, https://savewestburysw8.wordpress.com/2015/04/14/the-westbury-residents-main-concerns/

[160] https://haringeydefendcouncilhousingblog.wordpress.com/

points to *'Shakespeare's decadent, drunken and corpulently challenged knight, Falstaff, when pressed to give reasons to verify an obvious lie, robustly declined. He declared that if '... reasons were as plentiful as blackberries, I would give no man a reason upon compulsion. But although Falstaff as a private individual was presumably within his rights to deny reasons, public authorities cannot be so cavalier.*[161] Despite the Shakespearean dramatization, there is a very serious point about accountability, transparency, protection against abuse of office or at worst impunity especially where 'the decision-maker is disagreeing with a considered and reasoned recommendation', as Lewison LJ, observed in the Court of Appeal'.[162]

Such intrusive and detrimental actions necessitate a need for the estate regeneration process to be conducted in a manner that respects the human dignity of affected persons and gives respect to their home,[163] giving appropriate weight to individual circumstances.[164] A point that was highlighted in *Connors V UK*[165] where it was held that the so called *gypsies* removal from a locality was in violation of Art 8, since the authority in question, appeared to evade statutory issues by making the applicant's wife sign a notice to quit without due regard to respect for his home. These actions effectively evaded any proper, fair or adequate due process. The emphasis on proper due process appears to be also reflected in *McCann*, where it was reiterated that 'any person at risk of an interference of this magnitude should in principle be able to have the proportionality of the measure determined by an independent tribunal in the light of the relevant principles under Article 8.*[166]

Therefore, for many CPO affected parties facing loss of their homes and the spiral detrimental effects that follow such potential displacement or dispossession, [167]the need for a fair and expeditious due process is an issue that cannot be minimised as indicated above.[168] It is however important to point out that despite the inherent

---

[161] Local government, duty to give reasons, *https://www.lawgazette.co.uk*
[162] Local government, duty to give reasons, *https://www.lawgazette.co.uk*

[163] (*Rousk v. Sweden*, §§ 137-142).

[164] (*Gillow v. the United Kingdom*, §§ 56-58).

[165] (2005) 40 EHRR9

[166] *McCann v. the United Kingdom*, § 50

[167] Such as loss of employment, extraction from school, effect on wellbeing, financial hardship or disruption

unfairness of the process and decisions, in some cases, such as Horada,[169] the initial decisions were overruled. In *Horada,* the court stopped the plans to demolish shepherds bush market, which would displace and dispossess thousands of local small businesses. It is however noticeable that these were businesses as opposed to homes and it's not clear whether that contributed to the reasoning in the final decision, an issue that needs further scrutiny which will be discussed in further detail in the later chapters detailing CPOs on a case by case basis.

In nutshell, as discussed above, Art 8, both substantively and procedurally appears to at least in law, provide a potential mechanism for challenging housing estate expropriation by public authorities. But such further relief under Art 8 appears inextricably linked with other rights under Art 6 and A1P1, such as the guarantee of the peaceful enjoyment of possessions, safeguard for ownership and other property rights under A1P1, as long as certain criteria are met. However, it is important to emphasise that while these protections appear intersectional with procedural rights under art 6 or protections under A1P1, there appears to be no unfettered protection given the various qualifications or limitations.

Art 6

Art 6 (1) of the ECHR states that," In the determination of his civil rights and obligations or of any criminal charge against him, everyone is entitled to a fair and public hearing within a reasonable time by an independent and impartial tribunal established by law'.

Art 6(1) is applicable to property rights, privacy matters, internal hearings or processes in terms of procedural fairness, access to an independent tribunal or equality of arms. Although Art 6 is not absolute,[170] it refers to some procedural limits

---

[168] Dispossession, the great housing swindle, https://www.dispossessionfilm.com/

[169] [2016] WLR(D) 148, [2016] PTSR 1271, [2016] EWCA Civ 169

[170] Ashingdale v UK(1985) 7 EHRR 528

as acceptable without procedural guarantees at every stage and stresses access to a court with full jurisdiction.[171]

As mentioned above, the focus here is about the relevant provisions of art 6 and others that could be applicable to estate regeneration through the use of CPOs. In analysing such relevance, a key issue therefore is a determination as to whether a civil right in Art 6 is 'a private right as opposed to a public right'.[172] In the context of estate regeneration, which is a housing matter, there is no ambiguity that this is consistent with a civil right in the context of ECHR and international conventions.[173] It is therefore the civil arm of Art 6 that is applicable to estate regenerations which therefore requires an identifiable issue over rights that have jurisdiction in domestic law[174]and consideration of the application of those rights.[175] In estate regeneration, there is an array of issues that require an expeditious, fair and independent determination as under art 6 stipulations. Such issues include the various competing interests between CPO affected parties, a need for examination of the consultation process,[176] a fundamental need for fair hearings as well as expeditious just compensation and adequate rehousing.[177]

The civil arm of Art 6 provides procedural guarantees in resolving disputes concerning property and ensures access to a court as well as a fair independent tribunal to safeguard the rights of those affected, although it covers permissible

[171] Golder V UK (1975) EHRR 524

[172] Alec Samuels, The planning process and judicial control: the case for better judicial involvement and control,J.P.L 1570

[173] Kenna, P. (2008). Housing rights: positive duties and enforceable rights at the European Court of Human Rights. European Human Rights Law Review, 13(2), 193-208

[174] H V Belgium(1987) 8 EHH 123 and GEorgiadis V Greece

[175] Bentehm V Netherlands(1985 8 EHRR

[176] Bokrosova v LLB http://www.bailii.org/ew/cases/EWHC/Admin/2015/3386.html

[177] Begum v London Borough of Tower Hamlets(2003) UKHL 5

[178] Handbook n0 10, Property rights under ECHR

[179] CASE OF DRAON v. FRANCE, (Application no. 1513/03), https://hudoc.echr.coe.int

interferences. To be admissible under Art 6 any potential applicant needs to have an existing interest or legitimate expectation in terms of possession or property rights under A1P1. However, where the eventual outcome is final after determination, it appears that no such prior requirement is mandated under Art 6[178]. It would also appear that emphasis will be placed on A1P1 if there is an issue that calls for the finality or decisiveness of the domestic legal actions but will be placed on Art 6 If the issue is about process. For instance, In *Draon v France,*[179] the court found a breach of the applicant's right to property due to a law limiting compensation associated with disability prior to the conclusion of the proceedings. Similarly, in the case of *Canea Catholic Church v Greece,* the court found that denying the applicant's legal personality was in breach of Art 6 after refusing to entertain the church's contention that such a rejection would deprive the church of the possibility of taking part in legal proceedings.

A question that arises is whether this is a clear signal that the court will take a pragmatic view rather than a uniform approach, as to what strand of specific issues are entertained and how to channel such issues when considering property rights under its jurisdiction. Whatever the answer to this question is , a potential lesson for CPO estate regeneration potential applicants, in terms of strategic and timely positioning of any potential legal actions under Art 8, A1P1 and Art 6, is that applicants should be cognizant of the fact that although there might be a prima facie case of breach ECHR rights, a strategic positioning of specific issues to determine a specific legal principle would appear to have a chance of success than a wider claim of breach of property rights.

The difficulty for almost all potential CPO estate regeneration affected applicants is that their main and prime goal is to preserve their property, homes and associated rights or livelihoods. As opposed to setting legal principles under the ECHR, which is a costly, protracted and academic process.

Access and delays

As discussed above, briefly, the other aspect that estate regeneration CPO affected parties face during housing estate expropriation is a lack of access to an expeditious fair process and independent tribunal. This is made worse by high costs, extensive

time constraints and lack of parity between the competing parties. Furthermore, residents are faced with the prospect of proceedings such as valuation disputes not being determined by an independent tribunal.[180] A situation which is consistent with *Ali V UK*,[181] where it was held that an applicant should have been afforded access to a fair hearing before an independent and impartial tribunal.

Similarly, resolutions should be consistent with the individual circumstances of those concerned which is consistent with HRA/ECHR art 6 which a fair process part of which would require an expeditious process or remedies such as just compensation or suitable adequate rehousing. Otherwise CPO affected potential applicants could be successful in alleging a breach of art 6 rights due to a delayed process or decision such as in *Robins v UK, where* there was a breach of Art 6[182] due to an unreasonable delay. CPO processes characteristically take years to conclude, [183]with detrimental effect on residents on various areas of their lives. Yet acquiring authorities have extensive resources unlike individuals who are compelled to accept offers such as lower valuations that would otherwise be unacceptable.[184] The decision making process is characteristically structurally advantageously skewed in favour of or conducted by acquiring authorities' to secure their legal, financial and political interests.[185]

Even when those affected pursue successful legal action related to unfair procedural issues, the acquiring authorities could circumnavigate the ruling by essentially starting the process again. For example Lambeth council was held to have failed to follow lawful process in reaching its decisions. A decision that residents affected thought would cause the council to abandon the entire scheme. However, the council did not abandon the scheme although residents have since applied for the right to

[180] See DCLG guidance; https://www.gov.uk/government/publications/compulsory-purchase-process-and-the-crichel-down-rules-guidance

[181] Ali V UK(2016) 63 HRR 20,

[182] https://www.echr.coe.int/documents/guide_art_6_eng.pdf file:///T:/002-7866.pdf

[183] Dispossession the great social housing swindle : https://www.dispossessionfilm.com

[184] Stuart Hodkinson, Chris Essen, (2015) "Grounding accumulation by dispossession in everyday life: The unjust geographies of urban regeneration under the Private Finance Initiative", International Journal of Law in the Built Environment, Vol. 7 Issue: 1, pp.72-91, https://doi.org/10.1108/IJLBE-01-2014-0007

[185] Alice Belotti, Estate regeneration and community impact, http://sticerd.lse.ac.uk/dps/case/cr/casereport99.pdf

manage successfully[186]. Whether this will force the council to abandon the demolition f cressingham gardens[187] remains to be seen.

This was in the case of *Bokrosova V Lambeth,*[188] where it was held that Lambeth acted unlawfully due to a failure to observe procedural issues in reaching its decisions. The court stated that the process of consultation, '*must include sufficient reasons for the proposals to enable consultees to consider them, and respond to them intelligently; enough time must be given for that; and the consultation responses must be taken conscientiously into account when the decision is taken…. ensure public participation in the local authority's decision making process and … in order for consultation to achieve that objective, it must fulfil basic minimum requirements'.*[189]

However, despite the ruling, that essentially quashed their decisions, the council still pursued the regeneration by restarting the process.[190] The council's ability to do this raises questions about the effectiveness of judicial review as a mechanism to challenge CPOs. Since then the residents of Cressingham gardens have secured the right to manage as mentioned above[191] and it is interesting to see how Lambeth council will respond or how that affects the overall housing estate demolition programme[192] under Lambeth council.

As already highlighted above, part of a fair process requires access to an independent and impartial tribunal. Although pursuing legal action could theoretically attempt to meet the requirement of access to a fair and impartial hearing or tribunal, it is a costly and long process for CPO affected residents. Prohibitive costs bar aggrieved residents from instigating legal action especially in the case of leaseholders who risk cost orders,[193] even if they satisfy the impeding requirements

---

[186] Right-to-transfer-determination-cressingham-gardens-estate, https://www.gov.uk
[187] http://cressinghampeoplesplan.org.uk/
[188] (2015)EWHC 3386(ADMIN)

[189] Citing *'one aspect of the Coughlan test'*

[190] https://savecressingham.wordpress.com/2016/12/21/residents-vow-to-fight-on-after-high-court-decision/

[191] right-to-transfer-determination-cressingham-gardens-estate
[192] https://savecressingham.wordpress.com/

such as seeking leave to commence legal proceedings.[194] Parties with deep pockets such as public bodies or property developers may unreasonably delay or deny their rights without the opportunity for the full circumstances ought to be fairly, diligently and impartially determined to prevent abuse of process or punitive penalties.[195] Such tactics are often deployed by the acquiring authorities in concert with developers or interested parties.[196] Therefore, CPO affected residents could have Art 6 engaged if they were subjected to processes that amount to barring them from bringing civil actions against the acquiring authority as was the case in *Z and others V UK*, [197]where the court clarified that, *'the inability of applicants to sue the local authority flowed from the principles governing the substantive right of action in negligence`* and art 6 was therefore engaged. In other words rejecting the argument was being advanced to prevent the applicants from suing the authorities.

However, even when there is an avenue of access to an independent, fair and impartial process, there are other criteria necessary that CPO affected parties would have to satisfy due to the fact engagement of Art 6 requires a disputable implementation of national law in a specific matter.[198]

An issue that was considered in *Lithgow,* where the nationalisation of property, under a local Act,[199] was found to engage Art 6 after the applicants alleged a lack of statutory compensation.[200] In this case, there was an undisputable right of a property owners' claim to statutory compensation, legislated for under the s39 of the Land Compensation Act 1973,[201] which in this particular case appears not to have been

---

[193] part-44-general-rules-about-costs,www.justice.gov.uk/courts/procedure-rules/c

[194] H V UK, Application no 11559/85

[195] Osman V UK(2000) 29 EHRR 245 (1998) ECHR 101 (1999) 1 LGRT 431

[196] Anna Minton, Scaring the living day light of people, https://www.annaminton.com/single-post/2016/03/21/Scaring-The-Living-Daylights-Out-Of-People

[197] Z and others V UK(2001) ECHRR 333, (2002) 34 EHRR 9

[198] Lithgow v UK

[199] Aircraft and Shipbuilding industries ACT 1977

[200] Practical Law Practice note 835 5732

satisfactorily implemented by the state. Therefore, where the local authorities do not apply the relevant ECHR rights, such as art 6, it is plausible that there is a real possibility of a justiciable issue by the affected parties.

That could be in instances where there are unreasonable or disproportionate barriers to a person's rights, derived from state actions, or an issue of a decisive nature in relation to the rights of an affected party,[202] such as a home or business affected by a CPO, that could lead to life changing intergenerational detriments. As was the case in *Koning V Germany*[203], where a civil right, under ECHR, was considered to be of substantive character and defined autonomously irrespective of the characterisation under national law.[204] Similarly, in *Brugger V Austria*, it was held that the complainant was entitled to an oral hearing especially that judicial review was not available as remedy in the local jurisdiction. Therefore, it would appear that once there is a clear determination of a right at peril under Art 6, the courts are prepared to provide latitude or opportunity for such determination, which is a potential positive trend for CPO, affected parties due to estate regeneration, which ofcourse have direct effect on the UK as a signatory to the ECHR but also via the HRA 98 which incorporates the ECHR rights.

However, as indicated above, the recent curtailment of legal aid is an inherent disadvantage, which makes it almost impossible for disenfranchised residents to challenge detrimental decisions associated with CPO decisions. Particularly leaseholders who may have the value of their homes taken into account as capital and therefore could fall outside the threshold for legal aid eligibility hence risk substantial cost orders that would be attached to their homes. Despite the fact fundamental rights associated with home expropriation, are at issue here which make legal aid arguably necessary in such civil proceedings.[205]This also raises a legitimate question as to whether there is overall property ownership in light of state dispossession through the use of the law. This is a wider question that will be covered in detail in the chapters below.

---

[201] http://www.legislation.gov.uk/1973

[202] Practical Law Practice note 835 5732

[203] Koning V Germany(1978) 2 EHRR 170

[204] Practical law practice note,J.P.L, 2010,3, 298-309

[205] Stars and Chambers v Procurator-where appointment of a temporary sheriff was held to be incompatible with Art 6. One local authority proposed to appoint its own mechanisms of final arbitration

However, the central theme appears to be the manifest imbalance of power and appearance of conflicts of interest in planning processes characterised by a lack of fairness or equality of arms, procedural fairness or propriety or access to an independent adjudication.[206] An inherent imbalance which is arguably worsened, where local authorities' planning or cabinet decisions appear to favour the interests of the acquiring party which are usually the same Local Authority, in the case of estate demolitions, such as in Lambeth[207], Southwark[208] and Haringey[209] among others. For example, in documented cases, during the CPO related proceedings, residents are accorded less time to argue their case or rebuttal of disputable facts and refused access to information[210]. This seems to be inherently incompatible with Art 6, as was the case in *Borgers v Belgium*[211], where a defendant who could not hear or make responses to official arguments was said to have had his art 6 rights breached.[212] Even where it would be assumed that the process was fair, planning conditions are reportedly changed, breached after the process[213] or at least not implemented as issued.[214] A practice that raises pertinent questions about the integrity of the whole process and whose interests are being served.[215]

Lack of access to information by residents

---

[206] R v (Wright v SOS for health and another(2009) UKHL 3

[207] https://www.opendemocracy.net/en/shine-a-light/residents-challenge-lambeth-plans-to-demolish-homes/

[208] https://www.newstatesman.com/politics/2013/11/look-heygate-estate-whats-wrong-londons-housing

[209] https://www.theguardian.com/commentisfree/2017/jul/03/britain-power-contempt-grenfell-labour-haringey-social-housing

[210] https://newsfromcrystalpalace.wordpress.com/tag/campaign-for-freedom-of-information/

[211] Borgers v Belgium(1993) 15 EHRR 92

[212] Practical law practice note public sector.

[213] Council tenants win 'segregated' garden rule fight, https://www.bbc.com/news/uk-england-london-

[214] https://www.theguardian.com/cities/2019/mar/25/ too-poor-to-play-children-in-social-housing-blocked-from-communal-playground

[215] Anna Minton, Big Capital, who is London For

Another common complaint by CPO affected residents is the lack of access[216] to material information and the need to be heard which is critical to the equality of arms.[217] In any process of challenging or asserting one's rights from public authorities or such entities, information from such public authorities is critical. However, freedom of information requests are protracted affairs and substantial information is either not timely provided[218] denied, [219]deducted or is in vague broad language whilst access to hearings in public is not always guaranteed.[220]

Lack of independent review

Another common feature is the fact that the unfairness of the process is heightened by the fact that there appears to be no genuinely independent review mechanisms, save for the court system whose encumbrances, such as cost or complexity have been documented above. This is not assisted by the increasing perception that planning functions and permission granting processes conducted by local authorities [221] appear to be more political, are not always based on statutory grounds[222] and objections do not lead to a hearing per se as part of due process.[223] This makes the need for a fair balance between the rights of the community or potential applicants to be presided over by an independent and impartial decision maker, from the beginning more urgent than ever. Especially when faced with the most intrusive action of all the loss or demolition of one's home.

The imbalance and the lack of impartiality is highlighted in *Tsfayo v UK (2007) ECHR 656*, where the issue involved an applicants' renewal for housing and council tax, which was rejected by the review board. The ECHR found that the board was not an

---

[216] https://newsfromcrystalpalace.wordpress.com/2018/11/26/lambeth-council-refuse-to-answer-foi-questions-made-by-news-from-crystal-palace/

[217] Feldbrugge V Netherlands(1986) 8 EHRR 425, see practice note above

[218]https://www.whatdotheyknow.com/request/asbestos_enquiry#incoming-1327131

[219]https://www.whatdotheyknow.com/request/somerleyton_road_steering_group_2321`11

[220] https://www.dailymail.co.uk/news/article-4656656/Kensington-councillor-DEFENDS-decision-meet-secret.html

[221] Bryan V UK(1995) 21 EHRR 342

[222] DCLG guidance

[223] R (Adlard V SOS for environment(2002) EWCA

independent tribunal and the possibility of judicial review was not a reprieve from the lack of independence and included councillors. Since public authorities review, their decisions by committees often staffed by councillors, such as in the CPO process, the lack of a fair and impartial consideration would appear to engage Art 6 given that the imminent loss of a home, such as that associated with a CPO, *ought to be a serious consideration.*[224]There should be procedural measures and safeguards to protect parties' convention rights,[225] with scrutiny placed on the protection of the residents' legitimate interests.[226] The court appeared to agree with the view that the vesting of land subject to a CPO *'cannot comply with Art.6 of the Convention, unless the courts have a jurisdiction to examine that decision on broad public law grounds'.*[227] Therefore, a similar decision by a public body, associated with a CPO could be *'unlawful if it were made for a purpose not recognised in the compulsory purchase order*[228]*or unconnected with the reason for the grant of those powers.'*[229]

Furthermore, where environmental or nuisance complaints are raised, during demolition or construction, some local authorities with confidential s106 agreements explained above, as agreements which essentially enable a scheme that would not be approved to proceed[230] or other agreements with developers[231] may have their impartiality or practical ability to enforce any planning regulations compromised. Therefore, potentially leading to planning conditions being ignored or breached[232] during and after grant of planning permission.[233] For example, on the Westbury Estate,[234] residents' repeated formal and informal requests or demands to have the HSE investigate the safety measures in place to protect residents from exposure to

---

[224] (*Ivanova and Cherkezov v. Bulgaria*)

[225] (*Irina Smirnova v. Ukraine*, § 94).

[226] (*Orlić v. Croatia*, § 64; *Gladysheva v. Russia*, §§ 94-95; *Kryvitska and Kryvitskyy v. Ukraine*, § 50; *Andrey Medvedev v. Russia*, § 55)

[227] Jonathan Ferris, 2010, Journal of Planning & Environment Law Compulsory purchase: is there a general right to judicial review to challenge the decision to vest land the subject of a confirmed compulsory purchase order?

[228] (*Grice v Dudley*8; *Capital Investments Ltd v Wednesfield Urban DC*9).

[229] *Congreve v Home Office*11; and *R. v Birmingham Licensing Committee Ex p. Kennedy*12).

[230] See www.Lambeth.gov.uk Westbury estate

[231] Council tenants win 'segregated' garden rule fight,https://www.london.gov.uk/sites/default/files/berkley_group.pdf

[232] https://www.bbc.com/news/uk-england-london-

[233] https://www.theguardian.com/cities/2019/mar/25/too-poor-to-play-children-in-social-housing-blocked-from-communal-playground

[234] Westbury-a-year-after-Grenfell, http://housingactivists.co.uk/grenfell

asbestos were reportedly routinely ignored[235] and were often referred to the developers themselves namely the Berkeley group.[236] Residents' concerns[237] appear to be supported by the findings of the HSE report[238]after concerted pressure from the local M[239]P and other parties. The HSE report found that procedures like using water suppression, covering dust, storage of asbestos[240] were not satisfactory or acceptable despite the initial claims by Lambeth Council.

Overall, the inherent impediments associated with instigating legal challenges to the planning process or decisions made by the local authorities. This adds to the manifest imbalance and inherent unfairness experienced by CPO affected parties. Planning policies, such as a CPO process infringe the rights of enjoyment of one's home and property . CPO processes under estate regeneration may further reduce market value because arguably buyers would avoid buying CPO affected properties and worse the planning process is regarded as favourable to developers intent on maximising profits by raising the prices of the new properties while minimising the values of the existing properties owned by residents.[241] The process is characterised with disputed valuation processes[242] without fair appeal processes, which prejudice residents' rights without the proportionality of the measures in question being determined by an independent tribunal. Cumulatively, this creates a hindrance for CPO challengers[243]and objectors from having a fair crack of the whip through a transparent, independent process as well as timely access to any requested related material.[244] Therefore creating a prejudicial effect to the probative value of such material at a later stage in the process, [245]which could be a potential breach of Art 6

[235] Families hit out at London gasworks redevelopment, Brownfield-site-new-homes-building-wrecking-health-southall, https://www.theguardian.com/environment/2019/may/04/

[236] The Lambeth and London 'estate clearances: PRESENCE of still uncovered believed to be hazardous construction soil , https://humanlawyerist.blogspot.com/2019/04/the-lambeth-and-london-estate;

[237] Homes for Lambeth Review, https://moderngov.lambeth.gov.uk

[238] Agenda and draft minutes, Cabinet Monday 4 March 2019 5.00 , https://moderngov.lambeth.gov.uk

[239] Kate Hoey(MP) for Vauxhall
[240] https://humanlawyerist.blogspot.com/2019/04/the-lambeth-and-london-estate.html

[241] https://www.theguardian.com/cities/2015/jun/25/london-developers-viability-planning-affordable-social-housing-regeneration-oliver-wainwright

[242] Westbury-a-year-after-Grenfell, http://housingactivists.co.uk/grenfell

[243] Peter Harrison Qc, Glimpsed views of the legal land scape,

[244] R (on the application of Vieira) v Camden LBC

and an infringement of Article 8.[246] Hence providing a potential avenue for estate regeneration affected residents to assert their human rights once they overcome the hurdles associates with instigating legal action.

Chapter 7

Article 1 of the first protocol of the ECHR[247] and CPOs

Overview

A1P1 states that, *'every natural person or legal person is entitled to the peaceful enjoyment of his possessions and no one shall be deprived of his possessions except in the public interest and subject to the conditions provided for by law and by the general principles of international law. The preceding provisions shall not, however, in any way, impair the right of a state to enforce such laws, as it deems necessary to control the use of property in accordance with the general interest or to secure the payment of taxes or other contributions or penalties'*.

The three main rules which describe the degree of interference[248] under A1P1 include *non-interference with possession, no deprivation of property except in the public interest and that state control may only be justified legally infringed in the general interest, where there is a legitimate justification.* In other words, the rights under A1P1 appear to be qualified to a certain extent with a margin of appreciation left for state parties in areas such as implementation as discussed in detail below. A1P1 also makes reference to principles of international law. For example, UDHR[249] under article 17, states that everyone has the right to own property alone or in association with others and that no one shall be arbitrarily deprived of his property.

---

[245] R (on the application of Ashley) Secretary of state for communities and local government

[246] (*Kay and Others v. the United Kingdom*, § 74)

[247] Referred to here as A1P1

[248] Possession, law, property and human rights, Landmark chambers

[249] https://www.un.org/en/universal-declaration-human-rights/index.html

But even in the absence of explicit reference to property rights, under specific international law instruments, it can be forcefully and persuasively argued that such interference, especially when associated with the confiscation or demolition of one's home, creates a spiral effect which could potentially breach international human rights law collectively referred to as the international bill of human rights,[250] comprised of the *Universal Declaration of Human Rights, International Covenant on Economic, Social and Cultural Rights, International Covenant on Civil and Political Rights.* The focus here is on the relevant provisions that could be applicable to CPOs under estate regeneration.

General Scope of A1P1

As cited above, A1P1 protects against deprivation of possessions and unjustifiable intrusion in the peaceful enjoyment of one's possessions. This could be through practices that amount to s expropriation of property, planning restrictions or even temporary property seizures. A case in point is *Pressos Compani Naviera and others v Belgium*, where the state was held liable for extinguishing the applicants unresolved claims by retroactively passing legislation which extinguished the applicants' property rights.[251] In pursuing protection under A1P1, an important distinction should be made as to whether the alleged interference is deemed to be a deprivation or simply control of use the land or property, which could then determine subsequent qualification for compensation under A1P1.

A1P1,[252] is independent of national state definitions, covers all forms of property and does not limit ownership of possessions to physical goods. However, A1P1 does not cover prospective possessions or future possessions but emphasises current or existing possessions. This was an essential issue in the case of Marckx v Belgium[253] where a mother claimed breach of A1P1 because of the alleged impediments by the state authorities to prevent her from disposing off her property to what was described

---

[250] https://www.ohchr.org/Documents/Publications/FactSheet2Rev.1en.pdf

[251] Handbook no 10, the right to property under ECHR

[252] See Practical Law UK practice Note 8-385 5732

[253] CASE OF MARCKX v. BELGIUM. *Application no. 6833/74*, https://hudoc.echr.coe.int

as 'an illegimate child'. A term that is clearly unacceptable in contemporary times[254]. The court by a majority confirmed that A1P1 was relevant to the claims made by the mother and defined the scope of A1P1 as applying to existing possessions but not future possessions[255]. In another case, of *X v Germany*, where a determination of A1P1 right was an issue, the court held that a mere expectation by notaries that *'rates for their fees would not be reduced by law'* did not amount to a property right within the meaning of A1P1.[256]

However, it would appear that where there is a concrete legitimate expectation, future possessions could be considered. But as far as relevance to residents facing CPO effected home demolitions is concerned, the issue regarding future possessions would not affect them because this relates to homes in which they live or already own as opposed to a mere expectation of future occupation or possession for that matter.

Therefore, the issues directly relating to CPOs and Estate regeneration, under A1P1 include, inter alia, *what amounts to deprivation or legitimate expectation, whether the actions of the authorities were proportionate or justifiable, the margin of appreciation extended to states and the fairness of compensation.* These issues are discussed in detail below.

Legitimate expectation

One of the key issues considered under A1P1 is whether a landowner's legitimate expectation of enjoyment of property rights can be a basis for asserting A1P1. In Pine *Valley Developments*[257], the applicants had bought land under the expectation of planning permission being approved but was later annulled. The court ruled in the

---

[254] CASE OF MARCKX v. BELGIUM. *Application no. 6833/74*, https://hudoc.echr.coe.int

[255] Marckx and Marckx v Belgium, Merits and Just Satisfaction, App No 6833/74, [1979] ECHR 2, (1980) 2 EHRR 330, IHRL 22 (ECHR 1979), 13th June 1979, European Court of Human Rights [ECHR], https://opil.ouplaw.com

[256] Handbook no 10, the right to property under ECHR

[257] Pine Valley Developments Limited and ors v Ireland, Just satisfaction, App No 12742/87, A/246-B, (1993) 16 EHRR 379, [1993] ECHR 2, IHRL 3587 (ECHR 1993), 9th February 1993, Council of Europe; European Court of Human Rights [ECHR

applicants' favour holding that the applicants had been subjected to unlawful discrimination contrary to ART 14 in conjunction with A1P1.

The key point from this case, in relation to CPOs is that there is an obvious legitimate expectation of enjoyment of property rights and protection from discrimination under ECHR. Therefore potentially providing an avenue for challenging such activity, primarily due to the legitimate expectation of the legal security associated with their property interests. Manifested through leases or secure tenancies whose curtailment would engage A1P1.[258] This is illustrated in *Stretch*[259], where the court upheld a complaint alleging that the applicant 'had been unjustly denied extension of a further 21 year term lease'.[260]It was further noted that[261] because the option granted by the local authority had been ultra vires and therefore deemed to be a disproportionate interference with the applicant's peaceful enjoyment of his possessions, this was a violation of Article 1 of Protocol No. 1 to the Convention'. Therefore, under the principle of legitimate expectation is that it appears that even a potential legal claim under A1P1 could merit consideration as a possession or asset where a landowner has a legitimate expectation.[262] Especially that CPO affected parties have diametrically opposed legal interests, such as retention of their properties, which are threatened with expropriation by the acquiring authorities.

However, in *Plant v Lambeth (discussed in detail below), the high court* examined such a legitimate expectation, namely the alleged curtailment of the right to buy by a secure tenant that was not yet exercised. The court held that A1P1 had not been engaged in respect of secure tenants' rights to buy since he had not yet acted on it. This ruling is puzzling because Lambeth council had taken formal decisions to demolish the estate through use of a CPO. By doing that, the right to buy by the tenant had been or would be curtailed. The applicant sued to safeguard his right to

---

[258] Pine developments v Ireland(1992) 14 EHRR 319

[259] Stretch v UK *(Application no. 44277/98)*

[260] Practical Law UK practice Note 8-385 5732

[261] [2003] ECHR 320, (2004) 38 EHRR 12, [2003] NPC 125, [2004] 03 EG 100, [2003] 29 EG 118, [2004] 1 EGLR 11, *http://www.bailii.org/eu/cases/ECHR/2003/320.html*

[262] Pressos Compani Naviera v Belgium(1995) 2 EHHR 3010) , also see Practical Law UK practice note 8-385 5732

buy by citing among others A1P1. Therefore, the court's ruling in this specific regard appears contradictory. Furthermore, it would appear that the applicant was not allowed to appeal which curtailed any further opportunity to test that conclusion. Therefore, the successful nature of any such complaint by a CPO affected applicant appears uncertain in practice.

Deprivation

Deprivation is another important consideration under A1P1. A1P1 protects against unlawful deprivation of property, which includes curtailment of the legal rights of those affected. In examining the issue of deprivation, the court ascertains any de facto deprivation of A1P1 rights[263]as opposed mere control of use of property or possessions. For example in *Papamichalopoulous v Greece,*[264] the Navy had taken over the applicants' land to the extent that they could not make effective use of it and this was found to be a de facto expropriation. This is consistent with the circumstances faced by CPO affected parties who have their properties confiscated or unable to be used for their own enjoyment or utility, which could mean that they could be able to challenge such de-facto expropriation of their property in light of the rationale in the above case.

However, potential applicants affected by estate regeneration enforced through CPOs, should be cognizant of the fact that if the measures taken by the state amount to control of the use of the property or payment of taxes, the court could find that such an action did not amount to deprivation. A case in point is *Handyside V UK,*[265] where the temporary seizure of the applicant's books, which were alleged to contain obscene images, did not amount to deprivation since the seizure was temporary and

---

[263]The right to property under ECHR, A guide to the implementation of the right to property, Human rights hand book no 10

[264] CASE OF PAPAMICHALOPOULOS AND OTHERS v. GREECE (ARTICLE 50, Application no. 14556/89)

[265] CASE OF HANDYSIDE v. THE UNITED KINGDOM, (Application no. 5493/72)

was within the powers of the state under A1P1. The difference with CPO housing estate demolition affected parties and the facts or ruling in this case is that expropriation of estate regeneration homes is usually permanent as opposed to mere control. Therefore, this provision would not adversely affect any potential applicants faced with estate regeneration under CPOs. The overarching point here is that although there could be legitimate justifications for interference in an owner's property rights, under A1P1, depriving someone of their property can only be justified in exceptional circumstances as evident in *Lithgow et al,*[266]where deprivation of property was held to have happened under a CPO process. A similar ruling was held in *Sporrong and Lonnroth*, where the 'expropriation of building permits and building restrictions enforcement for specific durations was held to be interference in the applicants' enjoyment of their land amounting to deprivation of property.[267] These rulings affirm the protection under A1P1, for estate regeneration affected parties who are deprived of their property due to CPOs by local authorities.

However, it is important to emphasise that any potential applicants would need to prove that this was in fact deprivation not mere restrictions,[268] temporary deprivation or interference in the use or enjoyment of the property. Deprivation could be further proven where there is a partial loss of a significant or substantial part of a landowner's right, which amounts to deprivation without full expropriation. The rulings in *Sporrong and Lithgow* above appear to confirm the protection under ECHR the rights of those affected by CPOs where deprivation or even partial deprivation is found to have occurred by the court. CPO affected estate regeneration residents experience significant restrictions caused by CPOs, such as exposure to construction hazards like noise, fumes, vibration or contaminants or the restriction to sell to the open market as a willing buyer.[269]Residents could argue that this amounts to deprivation or partial deprivation under A1P1.

Deprivation could also be potentially established where there are two competing owners who already have rights in the property as opposed to the familiar practice of the acquiring authority taking over the property. This is illustrated in the case of *James v UK,*[270] where the court found that individuals with leases under the

---

[266] Lithgow v United Kingdom, Merits, App no 9006/80, App no 9262/81, App no 9263/81, App no 9265/81, App no 9266/81, App no 9313/81, App no 9405/81, A/102, (1986) 8 EHRR 329, [1986] ECHR 8, IHRL 59 (ECHR 1986), 8th July 1986, European Court of Human Rights [ECHR]

[267] Sporrong and Lonnroth(1982)5 EHHR 35

[268] See Practical Law UK practice Note 8-385 5732

[269] Imrie, R., & Thomas, H. (1997). Law, Legal Struggles and Urban Regeneration: Rethinking the Relationships. *Urban Studies*, *34*(9), 1401–1418. https://doi.org/10.1080/0042098975484

leasehold reform Act 1967, entitled to long leases, who could purchase freeholds of their leases, at a defined statutory price, deprived freeholders of their property, due to the inability to sell the property or set the sale price.[271]

Ironically such a principle laid down in *James v UK above,* could be utilised by CPO affected residents[272]to disentangle themselves from the acquiring authority, although the acquiring authority could still have significant statutory powers to initiate a CPO. The acquiring authority could do so by citing other grounds such as control, as highlighted in *Agosi V UK,[273]* where the main issue was seizure and forfeiture by customs of smuggled Kruegerrands and the court did not deem such an action by authorities to amount to deprivation.[274]

Therefore, CPO affected parties should be aware of claims of control as opposed to seizure by acquiring authorities. However, it is important to emphasise that although such a defence by the authorities could be entertained by the courts, there must be a clear need to balance community interests with the protection of the individual's right to peaceful enjoyment of his or her home, in order to justify controlling the use of property in the general interest. Otherwise, that would invite potential misuse of the significant latitude afforded to states under A1P1 as a defence against CPOs affected parties.[275] Therefore, a finding of deprivation under A1P1, is an important tool against authorities pursuing estate regeneration.

Proportionality

Another central tenet of A1P1 is the principle of proportionality, which emphasises a fair balance between the public interest and the property interests of the owners.[276] Simply put, if there is a valid legitimate and lawful interference then it has to be proportionate. However, such a need to demonstrate proportionality is arguably

---

[270] James V UK(1986) 8 EHRR 123

[271] See Practical Law UK practice Note 8-385 5732

[272] See Cressigham Gardens in Lambeth

[273] Agosi v UK(1987) 9 EHRR1

[274] Practical Law UK practice Note 8-385 5732

[275] See R Plant V LLBC(cite full)

[276] See James V UK App No 8793/79 (A/98) (Official Case No)

[1986] ECHR 2 (Neutral Citation) ; James and ors v United Kingdom, Decision on Merits, App no 8793/79, B/81, 11th May 1984, European Commission on Human Rights (historical) [ECHR]

undermined, in practice, by national authorities enjoying a wide margin of appreciation in determining the public or community interests within the law. [277]

There are several factors, which determine such a fair balance or proportionality. These include procedural safeguards of the owner's property rights, the nature of the penalty applied[278]the extent of interference, the duration or persistence of interference,[279] the actual fault of the owner with its consequential significance and the irrationality or arbitrary nature of the statute.[280]

However, even if a threshold that satisfies proportionality is met by those affected, the need for proportionality in control cases is not a basis for compensation but simply indicates a need for a fair balance to be found.[281] Nevertheless, such interference may only be justified legally, if it's consistent with the public interest.[282]

As already mentioned, while the need to demonstrate the proportionality of the authorities' actions is a key protection measure for CPO affected residents, wider latitudes provided to the states arguably weaken those protections. Under A1P1 states are allowed a margin of appreciation in implementation of decisions associated with legitimate objectives of public interest [283]through proportionate measures designed to achieve greater social justice. While that appears to be a noble objective, in principle, such wide latitude leaves room for authorities to justify actions that are disproportionate to the affected residents whose homes are expropriated via schemes[284] like the wide scale demolition of homes with little[285] or no visible public interest.[286]

---

[277] Practical Law UK practice Note 8-835 57

[278] International Transport Roth v HS(2002) EWCA Civ 158

[279] Sporrong and Lonnroth

[280] R(Kensall) v SOS for Environment(2003) Admin 2003

[281] See Practical Law UK practice Note 8-385 5732

[282] *In Tesco Stores Ltd v SOS*

[283] James v UK above

[284] The Costs of Estate Regeneration: A Report by Architects for Social Housing, 7 SEPTEMBER 2018

[285] Knock it Down or Do it Up? The challenge of estate regeneration February 2015

[286] David Dewar, The implications of the SoS's rejection of an estate regeneration on grounds of social housing loss
https://www.planningresource.co.uk, regeneration-grounds-social-housing-loss ,January 2019

The wider powers afforded to the states under the margin of appreciation, are made even more difficult to challenge by potential applicants due to the inherent institutional impediments faced by any potential applicants. Simply explained, in order for affected parties to challenge the proportionality of actions that amount to interference of property rights, such actions should be foreseeable[287] and authorities need to be accessible and provide clear simple comprehensible communication of reasons for their actions. In the absence of such communication, accessibility and foreseeability, by an authority, it would be extremely cumbersome, almost an obstruction on part of the authority, for estate regeneration CPO affected parties to timely, fairly and justly secure their property and associated rights.

However, in practice, authorities delay, obfuscate, deduct and withhold information[288] from potential applicants which clearly disadvantages estate regeneration affected residents, as mentioned above in various reports and discussed in more detail under ART 6. For instance, campaigners like those on Westbury estate in Lambeth[289] among others cited in reports above, refer to the woeful inadequacy of social rent homes and the ubiquitous use of s106[290] between public authorities like Lambeth et al, as evidence of a potential manipulation of the margin of appreciation left to states under A1P1. This illustrates the almost vacuous nature of the protection under A1P1 when authorities appear to manipulate the margin of appreciation to suit their interests. The case of *Tesco Stores Ltd v SOS*[291] *for Environment and Transport,* concretises the public interest argument as well as the margin of appreciation highlighted above. In this case, Sullivan J emphasised the need for *a 'fair balance to be struck between the public interest such as redevelopment and the individual's right to a peaceful and quiet enjoyment of his possessions. Adding that such interference ought to be proportionate and necessary to meet the 'compelling case in the public interest' reflecting the necessary element of that balance'.*[292] The difficulty lies in determining what the clear public interest is and where the limits of its

---

[287] Hentrich V France(1994 18 EHRR 440 (1994)ECHR 29 Lithgow,

[288] LAMBETH COUNCIL REFUSE TO ANSWER FOI QUESTIONS MADE BY NEWS FROM CRYSTAL PALACE, https://newsfromcrystalpalace.wordpress.com/2018/11/26/lambeth-council-refuse-to-answer-foi-questions-made-by-news-from-crystal-palace

[289] https://en-gb.facebook.com/Save-Westbury-Estate-SW8-486344558188042/

[290] S106 and public interest requirements are discussed in detail under the chapter of the CPO process.

[291] J.P.L 2010,3 298-309

[292] Also see R (Clays Lane Housing cooperative ltd v Housing corp(2005),R (Pascoe v SOS(2007), R (Hall) v First SOS(2008) J.P.L 63 at 15

application end, especially in relation to taking or demolishing one's home with the spiral effect that follow as highlighted in numerous reports above.

The above comments by Sullivan J appear consistent with another observation made by the court in Chesterfield properties v Secretary of State, [293]that 'only another interest, a public interest, of greater force may override it'. In that CPO inspector's report,[294]objectors argued that as the Leaseholders' Article 1 and 8 rights have been breached, it is incumbent upon the Acquiring Authority to justify that breach in terms of proportionality. The objectors referred to, the case of R (Clays Lane) v Housing Corporation, where, Maurice Kay J stated that 'the appropriate test of proportionality requires a balancing exercise' between 'a decision which is justified on the basis of a compelling case in the public interest as being reasonably necessary' may not be 'obligatorily the least intrusive of Convention rights.' Adding that some leaseholders no longer have mortgages and many are no longer in employment, as a consequence of the CPO they will be separated from their family and friends and they will be unable to afford to return to the estate'.

During the stated CPO examination process the inspector agreed that, 'Paragraph 12 of the Guidance states that an acquiring authority should be sure that the purposes for which the compulsory purchase order is made justify interfering with the human rights of those with an interest in the land affected. They would need to invest considerable personal resources in addition to any compensation they would receive for their properties; the CPO would not only deprive them of their dwelling but also their financial security. If they chose not to pursue this option, they would inevitably need to leave the area and this would have implications for their family life, including the lives of that dependant on the…. together with the failure of the scheme to fully achieve the social, economic and environmental well-being. The interference with human rights would not be proportionate having regard to the level. The public benefits that the scheme would bring… a compelling case in the public interest has not been proved'.

These observations were reiterated in the Aylesbury estate case in Southwark, stated in the chapters above, where the inspector and subsequently the secretary of state found that the CPO backed estate regeneration was inconsistent with the

[293] Chesterfield Properties Plc v Secretary Of State For Environment & Ors [1997] EWHC Admin 709 (24th July, 1997), http://www.bailii.org/ew/cases/EWHC/Admin/1997/709.html
Cite as: 76 P & CR 117, (1997) 76 P & CR 117, [1997] EWHC Admin 709

[294] CPO Report NPCU/CPO/A5840/74092 ,www.planningportal.gov.uk/planning inspectorate Page 73

human rights of residents. Although it appears that the parties have since reached some sort of accommodation. The cases and comments above by both courts and the inspectors emphasise human rights as a fundamental consideration for CPO schemes not simply a peripheral matter.

How that is implemented on the ground to minimise or eliminate such human rights breaches appears to be almost impossible task. Therefore a finding of a breach A1P1 does not in effect protect applicants from dispossession. An approach that combines direct negotiations, political actions such as lobbying, and campaigns in parallel with any legal action appears to be more practically fruitful as opposed to relying on the protections of A1P1.

Justification

Despite the court rulings above, authorities could still potentially assert justification as a defence for the interference or deprivation of property rights. In other words, even if there was interference or a taking, the authorities could argue that they were within the law or legitimately justified to take the action they took.

Tax enforcement is one such route where that justification this could be applicable. As reiterated, a state has a right to enforce laws deemed necessary to control the use of property in accordance with the general interest to secure payment of taxes, penalties or lawful regulations, as long as the power is exercised rationally and proportionately, such as in the regulation of a sex shop.[295]

Nevertheless, despite such justification, the court could still find a breach where that justification is considered disproportionate or where there is a discretionary, unfair procedure creating an excessive burden born by the applicant and can further intervene in the absence of a reasonable justification for interference with property rights. Such an example is in *the case of Davie*s where the court held in the absence of fair compensation, there was a breach of the need to strike a fair balance between the public interest and the van owners confirming that therefore A1P1 had been engaged.[296] Which affirmed that natural or legal persons could only be deprived of property, such as contributory or non-contributory state benefits,[297] or other interests,[298]

[295] *Belfast CC v Miss Behavin' Ltd*,([2007] WLR 1420, [2007] 1 WLR 1420, [2007] 3 All ER 1007, [2007] UKHL 19, *http://www.bailii.org/uk/cases/UKHL/2007/19.html*

[296] R Mott v Environment Agency(2018) UKSC 10)

[297] Stec v UK (2005)41 EHRR SE18

subject to conditions provided by law and the general principles of international law. An affirmation that potential CPO effected estate regeneration residents could arguably rely on to enforce their legal rights. However, it is always important for CPO affected parties to bear in mind that it is possible to conclude that various actions fall under the margin of appreciation on part of the state, if there is a fair appeal system or if the interference is reasonable and proportionate as discussed above at length. It seems to be a high bar for often unrepresented, resource starved and distressed residents to overcome especially properly raised and if supported by evidence from the acquiring authorities.

Having explored in some detail the broader principles underpinning A1P1 namely, deprivation, legitimate expectation, proportionality, justification and the margin of appreciation, with relevant cases or examples, it is of paramount importance to discuss in detail some of the specific areas where estate demolition or confiscation supported by CPO processes, acutely affects those who occupy the homes or have interests in the properties. Such examples include issues like market rate, the right to buy, home environment/environment rehousing and compensation and the extent to which potential applicants under A1P1 both could pursue them de facto and de jure.

A1P1 fails to offer full protection and requires a margin of appreciation which arguably allows local authorities to effect property deprivations or interfere in peoples' enjoyment of their property. There is no clear limits of interpretations of the margin of appreciation and there is a concern that could be potentially used as a general defence by actions. Given the lack of resources and lack of parity between parties, those affected could simply give up an further challenges against the authorities because of the appearance of an arguably respectable explanation by the authorities without being fairly adjudicated in an impartial and fair tribunal process. The spiral effect of such an occurrence is that authorities get emboldened in pursuing CPOs in estate regeneration because there is no real meaningful challenges against them. Therefore, the margin of appreciation principle requires revisiting if not out right deletion from the A1P1 lest it becomes a default position even when its clear such a defence would not arise at all.

Chapter 8

---

[298] Beyeler v Italy (2001) 33 EHRR 52

Other specific *notable CPO estate regeneration issues under A1P1*

It should not be a contention that protection against interference in a home environment is among the most important protections under A1P1.[299]As discussed at some length above, such interference has to be consistent with the added imposition of a positive obligation on the contracting states to ensure that such interference is proportional to the stated aim. The home environment protection under A1P1 could intersect with Art 8, which asserts protection against the violation of the respect for one's home.[300] Among other issues that require attention is environmental pollution, which could seriously interfere with one's private or family life and deprive personal enjoyment of amenities associated with one's home such as[301] the case of *Moreno v Spain*[302] where the court concluded that noise pollution violated articles 8 and 13 of ECHR. Such interference may affect a person's wellbeing and prevent them from enjoying their homes, family life and adversely affect their health. CPO affected residents[303] have complained of noise, pollution and toxic hazards associated with construction hazards.[304]The courts appear to disregard apparent mere concerns about protection of healthy environment[305]and consider serious detriments to the persons concerned. If there is a nexus to the cause of such a serious effect, a complaint may arise under Art 8 to determine[306] state actions and the failure to effect measures necessary to prevent harmful activity.[307]

Emphasis is placed on the need for a causal link to be established as opposed to prospective harm depending on the repetitive nature of the negative activity.[308]Furthe rmore, it's not the general deterioration of the environment", per se, but harmful

---

[299] Hatton and others V UK,

[300] https://echr.coe.int/Documents/Convention_ENG.pdf

[301] CASE OF MORENO GÓMEZ v. SPAIN, *Application no. 4143/02*

[302] CASE OF MORENO GÓMEZ v. SPAIN *(Application no. 4143/02)*

[303] https://www.theguardian.com/uk-news/2019/jul/07/court-challenge-homes-southall-london-gasworks-brownfield-development

[304] https://www.theguardian.com/environment/2019/may/04/brownfield-site-new-homes-building-wrecking-health-southall,

[305] *Kyrtatos v Greece*

[306] *(Hatton and Others v. the United Kingdom* [GC], § 96; *Moreno Gómez v. Spain*, § 53)

[307] https://www.theguardian.com/environment/2019/may/04/brownfield-site-new-homes-building-wrecking-health-southall,

[308] *Fadeyeva v. Russia*, § 69.

effects that would be disproportionate to the accepted standards consistent with living in modern metropolitan areas.[309] For many affected residents or parties, it would be an obvious aim for prevention to be effected before any harm or interference in the peaceful enjoyment for affected faced with CPOs parties although in practice this is not always the case.[310] In reaching its decision regarding a breach under Art 8, associated with pollution, the courts consider process and substance.[311] Paying due regard to any vague or overbroad interference without reasoned decisions, processes, any shortcomings in a state's obligation or whether the right balance has been struck between the resident and other interested or parties.[312] Such state measures need not include extensive reports but could include professional assessments to determine the harmful consequences of construction activities. However, a decision may be made in the absence of such information[313] if a fair balance between parties exists.

Additionally, a failure to rehouse residents during demolition, excavation, redevelopment, could violate Art 8,[314] because in effect that would tantamount to a failure to protect their health and wellbeing.[315] Such protective measures should include regulatory and administrative mechanisms. Paradoxically, the court confines itself to respect for a home hence the wisdom of such a decision needs to be closely examined.[316] This was discussed in more detail under Art 8 respect for a home above. Despite a lack of clear blanket provision protecting the environment, per se, under A1P1, courts could be creative in dealing with decisions that had the effect of remedying environmental detriments associated with a home or home environment.[317] Such as in a case where transparency was required when residents living at a <u>dangerous site with sodium</u> cyanide or in proximity to hazardous effects were not

[309] . (*Asselbourg and Others v. Luxembourg* (Dec.)).

(*Martínez Martínez and Pino Manzano v. Spain*, § 42) (*Hardy and Maile v. the United Kingdom*

[310] https://www.theguardian.com/environment/2019/may/04/brownfield-site-new-homes-building-wrecking-health-southall

[311] (*Hatton and Others v. the United Kingdom* [GC], § 99).

[312] *Moreno Gómez v. Spain*, § 55). (*Fadeyeva v. Russia*, § 93; *Hardy and Maile v. the United Kingdom*, § 218

[313] *Hatton and Others v. the United Kingdom* [GC], § 128)

[314] *Fadeyeva v. Russia*, § 133

[315] *Tătar v. Romania*, § 88).

[316] (*Hatton and Others v. the United Kingdom* [GC], §§ 100 and 122),

[317] *López Ostra v. Spain*, §§ 56-58, *Moreno Gómez v. Spain*, § 61. *Di Sarno and Others v. Italy*, § 112).in (Giacomelli v. Italy, § 83),

provided access to information or conclusions of the study to permit such a scheme.[318] Which was similarly reiterated, in the case of *Giacomelli v. Italy,* the *'court found a violation in the absence of a prior environmental impact assessment and the failure to suspend the activities of a plant generating toxic emissions close to a residential area'.* Such a documented lack of transparency is consistent with the experiences of many residents living in CPO affected areas where there is a lack of independent impact environmental and equality impact assessments.[319]

A question arises whether authorities do not disclose such information because of the crucially potential benefit to affected residents because environmental impact damages may be linked to actual loss. A case in point, where such inference is raised, is where applicants, who lived near Heathrow,[320] were subjected to noise nuisance, which affected their property valuation, although it was concluded that there was no direct evidence to suggest that the value of the applicants' property was diminished or was unsalable.[321] The reasoning seems contradictory since such pollution could limit interest in the property and therefore drive down prices. Furthermore, apart from environmental pollution associated with construction hazards, bad housing conditions, disrepair or blight during CPOs related construction[322] may breach the quiet enjoyment and Art 8 in terms of respect for a home[323] which is intersectional with A1P1.

Although there are statutory obligations in the UK legal system to deal with such bad housing conditions, [324]there are doubts about local authorities' willingness to enforce their own statutory liability or potential culpability. Which therefore strengthens and necessitates the need for Art 8 intervention where there are unfit housing conditions but no adequate remedy.[325]

CPOs, right to buy and A1P1

[318] Hatton and Others v. the United Kingdom [GC] (§ 120),

[319] https://www.theguardian.com/environment/2019/may/04/brownfield-site-new-homes-building-wrecking-health-southall

[320] Hatton and Others v. the United Kingdom [GC] (§ 120),

[321] . However, a settlement was reached in one case in respect of Art 8, 13 and A1P1.

[322] Demolition or refurbishment of social housing?, https://www.ucl.ac.uk/engineering-exchange/research-projects, 2018

[323]https://www.echr.coe.int/Documents/Guide_Art_8_ENG.pdf

[324] Housing/repairs-in-rented-housing/disrepair-what-are-your-options-if-you-are-a-social-housing-tenant/disrepair-what-are-the-landlord-s-responsibilities, /https://www.citizensadvice.org.uk/

[325] HA1985 s604,

Another key area that needs consideration is the impact of CPOs on what is known as the right to buy for secure tenants and the protections under A1P1. The relevant context in this case is where estate regeneration can be argued to effectively interfere with the right to buy of the secure residents. Not the overall discussion of the advantages or disadvantages of the right to buy per se.

The case of R Plant v LLBC[326] highlights this issue, which affects secure tenants faced with a CPO and interference in their right to buy under A1P1. In this particular case, a central issue was whether A1P1 was engaged and breached by the council's decision to demolish the estate using CPOs. The claimant among other issues appears to have alleged breach of A1P1 due to interference with S118 of HA 1985, right to buy and S84 (1) rights, which prevent the court from issuing a possession order on such a property except on legal grounds in schedule 2 of the Act and other provisional requirements.[327] The court held that A1P1 was not applicable to the council's cabinet decision, concluding that, *'A1P1 was not engaged and was indistinguishable from other authorities.*[328] Noting that 'if *engaged, it need only be considered in relation to the statutory right to buy when the authority commences County Court proceedings to obtain an order for possession of a particular home'*.

Notably, the court appeared to base its decision to the fact that the claimant had not already exercised his right to buy. However, it appears that the existence of that option and its removal clearly appeared to interfere in the claimant's property rights, hence engaging A1P1.

Nevertheless, it appears the court indirectly appeared to acknowledge that A1P1 was engaged but not breached, at least up to the point when steps would be taken to revoke it or a determination made as to whether it was breached. Stating that, *'If, contrary to the clear view I have reached, I had concluded that A1P1 was engaged in LLBC's decision, reached on 21 March 2016....the issue of whether it was breached would have been a matter for the Court to determine.'*[329] This Invites the question as to when the right time or forum would be for the claimant to enforce his rights under A1P1 if not at that specific court and that specific time. Moreover, If not why not?

---

[326] *R Plant v LLBC, [2016] EWHC 3324 (Admin)*

[327] *R Plant v LLB [2016] EWHC 3324 (Admin)*

[328] *Kay v Lambeth LBC [2005] QB 352 and Austin v Southwark LBC [2010] HLR 1'.*

[329] Citing *Belfast City Council v Miss Behavin' Ltd [2007] 1 WLR 1420 at paragraphs 13 to 15)'.*

However, questions remain after this ruling and it is not clear that those questions were adequately addressed by the court. Moreover, the unfortunate refusal to appeal closed down testing the *decision related to secure tenancy, CPOs and A1P1.*

However, a significant positive takeaway for CPO affected residents, especially with the right to buy, the court appears to have acknowledged their rights if they chose to move away. They would be secure tenants being provided with new secure tenancies if they decide to move elsewhere but not if they wish to be rehoused in a new home on their current location. In which case they would only be granted an assured tenancy.

Market Rate, CPOs and A1P1

Another extremely important issue for consideration by CPO affected estate regeneration residents that could be in violation of A1P1 is the inherent default prevention of applicants from selling their properties at market value. Such interference via CPOs therefore appears disproportionate since compensation should be reasonably related to the wider market value of the locality, taking into account the totality of the full circumstances associated with displacement and removal from a home or a locality. Furthermore, it would appear, A1P1 does not guarantee a right to full compensation in every situation since a margin of appreciation is allowed to the nation state in this respect.[330]

However, it must be emphasised that the issue, here is beyond market value per se. Market rate, in this context is disputed and is described as 'a euphemism for imposing compensation' on an unwilling seller.[331]Where owners are compelled to sell to a specific party, at a specific time, at a price largely determined by the same interested party usually the acquiring local authority also the arbiter of the planning decisions which appears to be a prima facie manifest conflict of interest.[332]

---

[330] See Lithgow and Practical Law UK Practice Note 8-385 5732

[331] Guy Roots et al, 2nd edition

[332]Neil Gray Libby Porter, By Any Means Necessary: Urban Regeneration and the "State of Exception" in Glasgow's Commonwealth Games 2014

The no scheme principle[333] and the equivalence principle[334] often cited in the government guidance regarding CPO compensation[335] appear woefully unrealistic since CPO affected areas face blight, crime, antisocial behaviour and disrepair which affect the market price.[336] Furthermore, those affected cannot simply move or sell to the open market due to the costs involved or the inability to sell in case of leaseholders. The compensation awarded does not often meet the prices or housing costs in the private sector within the locality. Not to mention the resulting severe emotional distress that affects the wellbeing, health, and avoidable psychological insecurity.

Additionally, residents largely buy or rent properties without any forthcoming knowledge of a CPO. In the case of Local authorities, leases can be for 125 years while life tenure with succession rights is routine for many local authority secure tenancies. Residents envisaged this as a safety net both as a home and for leaseholders as a potential long-term capital investment, which is crucial for social mobility.

Therefore, the reference to the so-called market price or apparent resemblance to market price does not reflect the necessary just, fair and equitable compensation for residents' families or other affected parties. There is a recognisable strong argument that compensation per se should be beyond statutory requirements and a central measure in assessing or the proportionate nature of the burden put on any CPO affected party.[337]

Chapter 9

Compensation and A1P1

---

[333] David Elvin, QC, the no scheme principle under s6a of LCA 1961, https://www.landmarkchambers.co.uk/wp-content/uploads/2018/08/CPO-Presentation-Seminar-25-Sept-2017-DEQC.pdf

[334] http://www.legislation.gov.uk/ukpga/Eliz2/9-10/33/section/5

[335] https://assets.publishing.service.gov.uk/government/uploads/system/uploads/attachment_data/file/817392/CPO_guidance_-_with_2019_update.pdf

[336] Loretta Lees, Mara Ferreri, Resisting gentrification on its final frontiers: Learning from the Heygate Estate in London (1974–2013),Cities, Volume 57,2016,Pages 14-24, https://doi.org/10.1016/j.cities.2015.12.005.(http://www.sciencedirect.com

[337] Deborah Rook, Property and Human Rights, 2001

As indicated above, compensation no doubt remains a contentious issue in CPO related matters and is set by statute as highlighted by the DCLG guidance.[338]The guidance cited above refers to market value plus home loss payments and disbursements,[339] apparently disregarding the value of the scheme on the value of the land in question. Instead, compensation assumes a willing seller without compulsion. This is via monetary payment at the open market value of the land, *'in so far as money can do it', to put one in the same position as land had not been taken from him…in so far as loss imposed on him in the public interest, but no greater'.[340]* However, this level of compensation does not cover the detrimental effects of being displaced from a settled community with the ensuing distress, fear and sense of powerlessness.[341] *Which would appear to resonate with A1P1 as reiterated In James v UK and in the former king of Greece et al v Greece[342]*, where it was held that compensation that does not reasonably reflect the value of the property[343] could be deemed a disproportionate interference.[344]

A government review culminated into various law commission reports that were not implemented[345] leading to minimal changes.[346] DCLG guidance further explains this contentious and complex area'[347] stating that, *'compensation payable for the compulsory acquisition of an interest in land is based on the 'equivalence principle' (i.e. that the owner should be paid neither less nor more than their loss). The value*

---

[338]compulsory-purchase-process-and-the-crichel-down-rules-guidance

https://www.gov.uk/government/publications

[339]https://assets.publishing.service.gov.uk/government

[340] Lord justice Scott in Horn v Sunderland corporation

[341] Martine August, "It's all about power and you have none:" The marginalization of tenant resistance to mixed-income social housing redevelopment in Toronto, Canada,

Cities, Volume 57,2016, Pages 25-32, (http://www.sciencedirect.com

[342] Deborah Rook, Property Law and Human Rights, 2001

[343] Deborah Rook, Property Law and Human rights, 2001

[344] Holy Monasteries v Greece

[345] See urban renaissance report city university urban task force report, pg. 231,

[346] *Planning and Compulsory purchase Act 2004*

[347] DCLG guidance citing Part 1 Land compensation claims 1973

of land taken is the amount which it might be expected to realise if sold on the open market by a willing seller (Land Compensation Act 1961, section 5, rule 2), disregarding any effect on value of the scheme of the acquiring authority (known as the 'no scheme' principle); (see Land Compensation Act 1961, section 5, rule 5). Importantly, but unfortunate for those affected by CPOs, although it is implied under A1P1 that compensation will be paid,[348] the legitimate public interest may justify less than the financial equivalent to what the claimant lost based on the principle in *James*.[349] In addition, where rights to compensation are provided by statute, those provisions must be interpreted so as to be compatible with HRA 1998'.[350] Furthermore, A1P1 does not state how much compensation should be paid but states that *'the taking of property without any just compensation is justifiable only in exceptional circumstances'*. Compensation should be generous and proportionately beyond, market value or pecuniary loss given the spiral detriments including mental distress that befalls those affected by estate regeneration enforced by CPOs, as highlighted in the various reports above.

The compensation issue is best humorously articulated by John Pugh Smith,[351] who sums up the central concern for CPO affected landowners, as timely adequate compensation, *'especially for a welsh hill farmer'* as he put it.[352] This reference to the 'welsh farmer' could be arguably replicated to the majority of CPO affected parties or residents faced with the demolition of their homes under CPOs with the spiral affects which could be held as being in breach of A1P1. Therefore, it cannot be emphasised enough, the extent to which the expeditious nature and totality of compensation is central to the amicable resolutions of CPO related disputes or minimising the detrimental impact on residents. Acquiring authorities appear to seek to offer less compensation through a deliberately slow process, while livelihoods are on hold pending compensation.[353]

Rehousing

---

[348] Guy Roots et al, 2nd Edition

[349] James V UK, The Law of compulsory purchase, third edition, Guy Roots et al; *Thomas v Bridgend county council*,(2011), EWCA Civ 862, (2011) RVR 241

[350] Such as in *Thomas v Bridgend county council*,(2011), EWCA Civ 862, (2011) RVR 241, where the CA held that s19(3) of the Highway Act 1980, was incompatible with art 1 of the ECHR

[351] John Pugh –Smith, When is' enough ' legally enough, Encyclopaedia of Local government law bulletin,2015

[352] Saunders V Caerphilly CBC(2015)EWHC 1632 CH

[353] Alice Belotti, Estate regeneration and Community impact, LSE, 2016

S39 of the LCA 1973[354] sets out the grounds for rehousing which is summarised by the DCLG guidance[355]for many residents affected by estate regeneration enforced by CPOs, especially those with young children, finding secure and affordable accommodation is one of the most formidable barriers they face. Many are compelled either to live on potentially hazardous and dangerous protracted construction sites, such as asbestos contaminated land, move into temporary accommodation or move out of the locality entirely, which causes a series of detrimental impacts in all areas of their lives.[356]

The new properties tend to take many years[357]to build and are largely unaffordable. The new schemes such as shared ownerships, demote residents' property ownership interests, have stricter leases and diminish residents' equity, savings, home loss and disturbance. Residents who exercise any rights to stay as tenants are subjected to intrusive means testing or inquiries into unrelated areas of their lives despite the injustice of having one's home confiscated by the same acquiring authority.[358]

Additionally, the new housing may increase social divisions such as in a widely reported case, after estate demolition or regeneration, where children's playgrounds were segregated and there are familiar cases of 'poor doors'[359] depending on the housing tenure. Such division, it is strongly argued is incompatible with A1P1 in intersection with Art 14 of ECHR, which prohibits discrimination.[360] Primarily because

[354] http://www.legislation.gov.uk/ukpga/1973/26/contents

[355]https://assets.publishing.service.gov.uk/government/uploads/system/uploads/attachment_data/file/571453/booklet4.pdf

[356]*PaulWatts,Its_not_for_us_Regeneration_the_2012_Olympics_and_the_gentrification_of_East_London_City_2013, http://www.academia.edu/6007431/;*

Zoe Williams, the real cost of regeneration,http://www.execreview.com/2017/07/the-real-cost-of-regeneration/

[357] https://www.vice.com/en_uk/article/qkq4bx/every-flat-in-a-new-south-london-development-has-been-sold-to-foreign-investors

[358]*PaulWatts,Its_not_for_us_Regeneration_the_2012_Olympics_and_the_gentrification_of_East_London_City_2013, http://www.academia.edu/6007431/;*

Zoe Williams, the real cost of regenerationhttp://www.execreview.com

[359] https://www.newyorker.com/culture/cultural-comment/the-poor-door-and-the-glossy-reconfiguration-of-city-life

[360] /too-poor-to-play-children-in-social-housing-blocked-from-communal-playground

https://www.theguardian.com/cities/2019/mar/25

[361] Written by Jessica Perera, Institute of Race Relations, New IRR publication provides a fresh take on housing, policing and racism in London.

economic disadvantage tends to disproportionately affect women, racial minorities[361] and those with disabilities. All of which are protected characteristics under Art 14 of ECHR as well as EA2010 and HRA 98.

Therefore, taking into account of all the above issues, it is important that compensation should proportionately reflect the genuine or manifest public interest, [362] in individual circumstances and mirror the distinction between mere restrictions, which could amount to deprivation, and an actual taking of the physical property. Most CPO affected estate regeneration residents are affected by actual physical deprivation of property with associated emotional, social and financial detriments, both immediate and long-term. The statutory compensation does not appear to reflect the emotional or intangible but equally devastating detriments. Hence making the interference and deprivation acutely disproportionate and therefore in potential breach of A1P1 discussed in more detail above. Monetary compensation although helpful is not the panacea to displacement. It should be a package that includes mandatory adequate rehousing, take into account health implications, disruption to employment, education and support networks in balance with stated proven public interest for compulsory acquisition of one's home.

An issue that resonated with the US case of *Kelo,* [363]where the issue was a taking of a longstanding home by the local authorities. Justice Scalia noted that, 'yes you are paying for it, but you are giving the money to somebody, who does not want the money, who wants to live in the house that she's lived in her whole life. That counts for nothing? *'What this lady wants is not money. No amount of money is going to satisfy her. Living in this house her whole life. She does not want to move'.* That is the sense of deep injustice of the compulsory taking of homes, which are occupied especially in cases where residents have inculcated deep roots in the locality with a sense of cultural, economic and social attachments. That is not to minimise the more transient or temporary residents affected but there is no doubt that the impact is bound to be more damaging to those with entrenched roots in the community.

Chapter 10

---

[362] As stated in Trailer and Marina(leven) v Sec.of State 2004

[363] Kanner, Gideon. "Kelo v. New London: Bad Law, Bad Policy, and Bad Judgment." *The Urban Lawyer*, vol. 38, no. 2, 2006, pp. 201–235. *JSTOR*, www.jstor.org/stable/27895626.

Equal treatment under ART 14 and its convergence with A1P1

Equality[364] and fairness of treatment by those affected by CPOs, is critical to avoid breach of Art 14 in tandem with Art 8 and A1P1. Article 14 has no freestanding existence in absence of other rights. For Example in conjunction with Art 8, it was held that there was a breach of Art 14 where an 'occupant was prohibited from succeeding a tenancy after the death of his same-sex partner'.[365]

Therefore, CPO affected residents claiming art 14 protections could have to establish grounds for breach in other areas such as Art 8 or A1P1. The court appears to lay emphasis as to whether there are justiciable grounds within the scope of property rights. Such as in the case of *Marck v Belgium above,* where the court found in favour of a mother who alleged discrimination in relation to the freedom to dispose her property to so called illegitimate children although the court found no violation of A1P1 per se.

Similarly, in *Gaygusuz v Austria,* the court found a breach of Art 14 where there was a denial of assistance to an applicant who was not of Austrian Nationality.[366] Perhaps it could reflect the notably lower margin of appreciation in ART 14, which is very narrow, compared to A1P1. An applicant wishing to pursue a claim under ART 14 in relation to his or her property rights would have to prove elements of A1P1, such as possession but would not necessarily need to substantiate a violation of such rights to be able to make a claim of discrimination under Art 14. The applicant would be required to establish grounds under which his or rights under art 8 or A1P1 were breached and how such interference was different from other comparators in an unjustifiable manner.[367] Once the applicant establishes grounds for consideration of the claim under Art 14 and the associated Articles such as Art 8 or A1P1, the burden then falls on the state to justify the alleged discrimination in terms of its

---

[364] https://www.echr.coe.int/Documents/Convention_ENG.pdf

[365] (*Karner v. Austria,* §§ 41-43; *Kozak v. Poland,* § 99).

[366] The right to property, Human rights handbooks, No. 10

[367] Handbook No 10, property rights under ECHR

consistency with the law whether it is a legitimate aim and it is proportionate to that aim.

The interplay of art 14 and A1P1 also applies to Art 3[368] which is reiterated in the treaty of Rome as a free standing equal-treatment guarantee although the UK has not signed that treaty.

As far as Art 14 is specifically concerned, in terms of housing in general and estate demolition in particular, there are reports from bodies like the race audit and the Institute of race relations among others, [369]which cite disparity in housing and the disproportionate effects it has on racial minorities associated with estate regeneration.[370]

These have wider potentially intergenerational effects in terms of social mobility, access to opportunity and other social indicators where there are historical economic and social disadvantages among specific communities such as racial minorities, therefore national authorities have to pay close attention to the specific needs of minorities and those with protected characteristics which might require imposing certain conditions within certain limits.[371]

---

[368] Articles 2, 3 and 14, Equal access to justice in the case-law of the European Court of Human Rights on violence against women, https://www.echr.coe.int

[369] JESSICA PERERA,The London Clearances: Race, Housing and Policing, 2019

[370] https://www.ethnicity-facts-figures.service.gov.uk/

[371] (Connors v. the United Kingdom, § 84) Chapman v UK

United Kingdom [GC], § 96; Yordanova and Others v. Bulgaria, §§ 129-130 /(Codona v. the United Kingdom

[372] just-space-response-to-panel-note-7.3-20-may-2019.pdf, https://justspacelondon.files.wordpress.com/2019/04

[373]JESSICA PERERA, The London Clearances: Race, Housing and Policing, 2019

[374] CASE OF PINE VALLEY DEVELOPMENTS LTD AND OTHERS v. IRELAND, Application no. 12742/87

Specifically, in housing and estate regeneration, reports indicate that racial minorities[372] face a disproportionate detrimental impact.[373] This would appear to therefore be incompatible with the judgment In *Chapman,* for example, where the court affirmed that restricting the use of caravans, has an impact on the applicants' respect for their home. The applicant was notably from a racial minority group which is historically disadvantaged.

The ECHR has also held that there was discrimination and therefore a breach of Art 14 in the case of *Pine valley developments Ltd V Ireland*[374], where the applicants complained of discrimination due to a refusal of planning permission in respect of the applicant in comparison to other landowners. A similar ruling found in favour of the applicant in respect of Art 14 and A1P1 in the case of *Chassgnou and others V France*[375], where it was held that legislation appeared to favour large landowners, who could use their land as they wished which put smaller farmers in a discriminatory position. A ruling that was consistent with the case *Larkos v Cyprus*[376] where *'the court held that offering differential protection to tenants against eviction – according to whether they are renting state-owned property or renting from private landlords, entailed a violation of Article 14 taken in conjunction with Article 8, due to the unjustifiable difference of treatment'.*

This would be consistent with the residents affected by CPOs who have cultural links or may be disadvantaged by being forced to areas whey they face racial discrimination.[377]In addition the ruling above is consistent with the need to treat residents fairly and equally, especially in relation to issues such as valuations of properties, rehousing and compensation, where racial minorities face a disproportionate detrimental impact on their lives. Emphasis appears to be put on a positive obligation for a member state to cultivate appropriate safeguards to the extent even a lack of legal capacity leading to dispossession without meaningful participation in the process or access to the final determination by the courts was held to be a violation of art 8, by the court having considered protection measures and their inadequacy in the national state law.[378]

---

[375] CASE OF CHASSAGNOU AND OTHERS v. FRANCE. Applications nos. 25088/94, 28331/95 and 28443/95)

[376] App no 29515/95 (Application No) ECHR 1999-I (Official Citation)

[377] (*Chapman v. the United Kingdom* [GC], § 73).

A principle that appears to have been emphasised by the UK Supreme Court,[379] where the court asserted that the EA2010 provided further protection to a group of people who fall under the protected characteristics category.[380] The implication here for CPO affected parties, especially resident occupiers, is that where there is evidence of discrimination without a legitimate and proportionate aim, there are grounds upon which Art 14 in conjunction with A1P1 or other articles like art 8 could be upheld in their favour. Thereby protecting their property rights and other associated rights.

As already discussed above, beyond ECHR and the HRA 1998, international conventions bar discrimination and other human rights abuses.

This is an extensive area that will be covered in a separate chapter under international law especially how estate regeneration enforced by CPOs is consistent with international human rights law in light of the recent criticisms of the UK by the United Nations[381] and other interventions by the UN rapporteurs[382] cited above. Therefore, the discussion of international law is in a brief context covering the universal declaration of human rights which has moral authority [383] with given legal effect under the international convention on civil and political rights.[384] Applicable to housing are articles 23, 22, 3, 14 and 26[385], inter alia, ratified by the UK in 1976.[386]It appears that clear protections against discrimination exert moral or political

---

[378] *Zehentner v. Austria*, §§ 63 and 65) / (*A.-M.V. v. Finland*, §§ 82-84 and 90).

[379] In Akerman –Livingston v Aster Communities Ltd(UKSC) 15,

[380]https://justspacelondon.files.wordpress.com/2019/04/just-space-response-to-panel-note-7.3-20-may-2019.pdf; https://www.london.gov.uk/nlp_ex_33_cover_report.pdf

[381] https://www.ohchr.org/EN/Issues/Poverty/Pages/SRExtremePovertyIndex.aspx

[382] https://www.ohchr.org/en/issues/housing/pages/housingindex.aspx

[383] http://www.un.org/en/universal-declaration-human-rights/

[384] https://www.ohchr.org/en/professionalinterest/pages/ccpr.aspx

[385] https://www.ohchr.org/en/professionalinterest/pages/ccpr.aspx

[386] our-human-rights-work/monitoring-and-promoting-un-treaties, https://www.equalityhumanrights.com/en/

diplomatic pressure on states and encouragement to implement adequate protections.[387]

It is however important to examine the provisions of art 10 1nd 11 that are relevant to the topic t hand namely estate regeneration enforced through CPOs.

Chapter 11

Art 10 and 11 of ECHR

Another aspect of ECHR that appears to be relevant to property rights and estate regeneration enforced by CPOs is the freedom of association and expression, which are covered, by Articles 10 and 11. Art 10 and 11 of ECHR are considered together here since the protections they provide are intrinsically linked.

Art 10[388] states that …

1   *Everyone has the right to freedom of expression. This right shall include freedom to hold opinions and to receive and impart information and ideas without interference by public authority and regardless of frontiers. This Article shall not prevent States from requiring the licensing of broadcasting, television or cinema enterprises.*

2.   *The exercise of these freedoms, since it carries with it duties and responsibilities, may be subject to such formalities, conditions, restrictions or penalties as are prescribed by law and are necessary in a democratic society, in the interests of national security, territorial integrity or public safety, for the prevention of*

---

[387] (*Stenegry and Adam v. France* (Dec.)).

[388] https://www.echr.coe.int/Documents/Convention_ENG.pdf

disorder or crime, for the protection of health or morals, for the protection of the reputation or rights of others, for preventing the disclosure of information received in confidence, or for maintaining the authority and impartiality of the judiciary.

Chapter 12

Art 11 and property rights

Article 11 – states that:

1. 'Everyone has the right to freedom of peaceful assembly and to freedom of association with others, including the right to form and to join trade unions for the protection of his interests.

2. No restrictions shall be placed on the exercise of these rights other than such as are prescribed by law and are necessary in a democratic society in the interests of national security or public safety, for the prevention of disorder or crime, for the protection of health or morals or for the protection of the rights and freedoms of others. This Article shall not prevent the imposition of lawful restrictions on the exercise of these rights by members of the armed forces, of the police or of the administration of the State'[389].

ECHR rights of expression or association although protected may be restricted by state authorities with certain qualifications within the law such as in the interest maintaining order or public safety. Hence any limitations on these freedoms is placed on these rights in balance with public policy grounds.[390]Authorities must ensure that the property rights, which are the issues here, are infringed or interfered with without lawful justification such as in the case of CPOs under A1P1 or Art 8.

---

[389] https://www.echr.coe.int/Documents/Convention_ENG.pdf

[390] Observer and the Guardian v the United Kingdom (1991)

The case of *Handy side v UK*,[391] mentioned above highlights the relevant issues associated with property rights, which may be applicable to CPOs. In this case, the authorities seized books published by the applicant on grounds that they contained lewd content. It was held that since state authorities have a margin of appreciation under art 10, there was no breach of either Art 10 or A1P1. The implication here in relation to CPOs is that as long as states can justify and prove their activity within the margin of appreciation accorded to states based on the facts of the case, the court could potentially hold in the respective states favour.

However, in the later case of *Ozturk v Turkey*[392], the court found that the confiscation and destruction of the applicant's book was apparently related to his prior conviction by the authorities and was therefore in breach of art 10. In addition, the court further concluded that it was therefore not necessary to consider A1P1 in the circumstances.

This later case above highlights the fact that where there is an unjustifiable and permanent expropriation of property, or infringement of another associated rights such as art 10, the court could find a breach of ECHR. Therefore, residents or parties who are faced with having their [393]property rights being expunged as well as having other rights breached may have a potential route to challenge such alleged transgressions by the state authorities.

The wider relevance to CPO affected parties is that local authorities influence and diminish the affected communities' ability to meet, organise and express themselves during the process of consultation or the entire process of acquisition.[394]

---

[391] App No 5493/72 (Application No)

A/24 (Official Citation), [1976] ECHR 5 (Other Reference)

[392] *Ozturk v Turkey*, application no. 22479/93 ,*https://hudoc.echr.coe.int/eng"Ozturk v Turkey"],"documentcollectionid2":["GRAND Chamber*

[394] https://www.socialhousingsoundarchive.com/westbury-estate

This reportedly happens when traditionally elected bodies known as TRAs or leaseholders forums are disbanded, [395]undermined[396] or singled out for lack of funding among other practices.[397] Such as in Lambeth council where residents' elected groups have been suspended which limits effective, representative association without influence or manipulation by the authorities concerned.

TRAs tend to be more effective and organised in challenging Local Authority decisions but there are examples where such associations have been either suspended or marginalised,[398] residents' advocates complained of being singled out, targeted or victimised.[399] Such actions are bound to have a chilling effect on residents' ability to scrutinise or challenge the decisions, actions of such public bodies, [400]therefore jeopardising residents' ability to safeguard their human rights.[401]

In many reported areas, there is no evidence to justify curtailment of those rights in the context of CPOs[402] Another issue that requires consideration is Art 2. Although not an obvious issue under CPO estate regeneration Art 2 is arguably linked to the CPO estate regeneration activities that affect the health and wellbeing of residents[403] especially the vulnerable, elderly and children. In the chapters above, reference was made to various reports that document the social, economic and racial impact on the community and individuals. Such as reports from the Runnymede trust, [404]the

---

[395] https://lambethleaseholders.wordpress.com/

[396] https://newsfromcrystalpalace.wordpress.com/2017/11/08/housing-scandal-one-council-to-choose-who-represents-tenants-and-leaseholders-on-new-residents-assembly/

[397] Tenants and Residents Associations

[398] https://lambethleaseholders.wordpress.com

[399] leaseholders-chairman-quits-amid-council-bullying-claims-green-party-councilor-says-siege-mentality-exists-in-lambeth/://newsfromcrystalpalace.wordpress.com

[400] http://lambeth.network

[401] https://www.equalityhumanrights.com/en/human-rights-act/article-11-freedom-assembly-and-association

[402] what-are-human-rights/human-rights-act/article-11-right-protest, https://www.libertyhumanrights.org.uk/human-rights/

[403] https://newsfromcrystalpalace.wordpress.com/2019/06/10/council-has-refused-us-air-monitoring-systems-tenants-chief-tells-committee-his-wife-had-to-visit-a-and-e-three-times-with-lung-inflammation

[404] Faraha Elahi and Omar Khan Ethnic inequality, Capital for all, https://www.runnymedetrust.org

institute of race relations[405] among others. Those paragraphs simply explain how that is related to Art 2 of the ECHR as discussed below.

Chapter 13

Art 2

Article 2 of ECHR[406]of state that

"1. *Everyone's right to life shall be protected by law. No one shall be deprived of his life intentionally save in the execution of a sentence of a court following his conviction of a crime for which this penalty is provided by law.*

Art 2 protects life with defences specified in Art 2(2)[407]. It asserts that governments should protect citizens from the excess, failures or illegalities of industry, which among other detriments may harm the public.[408] As highlighted in *Oneryildiz v Turkey, where violation of Art2 was found in respect of a lack of protection for citizens living near a garbage bin that led to an explosion, which caused loss of life.[409] Adding that Art 2 does not simply relate to use of force but in circumstances such as this, the authorities failed to do all they could were capable of doing to protect lives despite their knowledge of the danger to the victims. This is directly relevant to estate regeneration construction related activities where there is contamination and hazards elements, which authorities[410] are fully aware of but seem to be reluctant to take active measures to eliminate or minimise the risk to human health.[411].*

---

[405] Jessica, Pereira, The London clearances, http://www.irr.org.uk

[406] https://www.echr.coe.int/Documents/Convention_ENG.pdf

[407] https://www.echr.coe.int/Documents/Convention_ENG.pdf

[408] Dimitri Xenos, Asserting the Right to life (Article 2, ECHR) in the Context of Industry 8 German L.J. 231 (2007)

[409] Oneryildiz v. Turkey, 2004-XII Eur. Ct. HR 79, First, Do No Harm: Human Rights and Efforts to Combat Climate Change 38 Ga. J. Int'l & Comp. L. 593 (2009-2010

Art 2 is therefore relevant due to the reported adverse impact on residents' well-being, health[412] and public safety during protracted large scale construction projects[413] associated with universally known potentially harmful effects such as vibration, fumes, noise, asbestos contamination,[414] that residents are subjected to for prolonged periods[415] which is clearly incompatible with Art2. However, enforcement remains a formidable impediment due to lack of resources and imbalance of power between affected residents and local authorities in concert with developers as observed by Anna Minton.[416]

Chapter 14

Art 3

As indicated under Art 2,[417] a similar observation arguably applies to CPO estate regeneration under Art 3, if there is evidence of an arguable link between aspects of inhuman or degrading treatment under art 3 and CPO estate regeneration activities.

---

[410] https://www.theguardian.com/environment/2019/may/04/brownfield-site-new-homes-building-wrecking-health-southall

[411] https://www.theguardian.com/environment/2019/may/04/brownfield-site-new-homes-building-wrecking-health-southall

[412] https://www.annaminton.com/groundcontrol

[413] https://www.theguardian.com/environment/2019/may/04/brownfield-site-new-homes-building-wrecking-health-southall

[414] John L Adgate, Sook Ja Cho, Bruce H Alexander, Gurmurthy Ramachandran, Katherine K Raleigh

Jean Johnson,, Rita B Messing, A L Williams, James Kelly & Gregory C Pratt

Modelling community asbestos exposure near a vermiculite processing facility: Impact of human activities on cumulative exposure, Journal Of Exposure Science And Environmental Epidemiology

2011/02/23

[415] Brownfield-site-new-homes-building-wrecking-health-southallhttps://www.theguardian.com/environment/2019/may/04

[416] Anna Minton, 'Scaring the living daylights out of people': The local lobby and the failure of democracy

1 Feb 2013

[417] Marcia Gibson, Hilary Thomson, Ade Kearns & Mark Petticrew (2011) Understanding the Psychosocial Impacts of Housing Type: Qualitative Evidence from a Housing and Regeneration Intervention, Housing Studies, 26:04, 555-573, DOI: 10.1080/02673037.2011.559724

Art 3 states that No one shall be subjected to torture or to inhuman or degrading treatment or punishment.

Art 3 prohibits torture as well as inhuman and degrading treatment. Treatment *can be considered inhuman when it causes physical or mental pain or degrading when it debases or humiliates a person beyond that is usual from punishment*[418]

In property or estate regeneration related cases,[419] if there is evidence of sustained actions that amount to inhuman and degrading treatment, associated with CPO activity,[420] like hazardous elements, it is arguable that those affected could bring action under these grounds. However, it appears that the bar in property related terms is too high for potential applicants to cross the admissibility threshold. For example, in *Predojevic and others v Solvenia,* the court found as inadmissible claims that deprivation of pension amounted to inhuman and degrading treatment.

In spite of a high bar or threshold to satisfy Art 3 requirements in association with property rights, its arguable, therefore that if there are clear or identifiable facts from which the court can infer inhuman or degrading treatment art 3 could be engaged. Such an example could be where construction hazards[421] like industrial dust, noise, lead, asbestos or other contaminants, which cause or are linked to illness or severe emotional distress.[422]Therefore, although it is likely that the rights under art 3 associated with CPOs and estate regeneration could require more hard evidence, it would appear that if there is a nexus between inhuman and degrading treatment, associated with estate regeneration, there could be circumstances where potential applicants can make an arguable case.

---

[418] https://www.libertyhumanrights.org.uk/human-rights/what-are-human-rights/human-rights-act/article-3-no-torture

[419] Wellbeing and Regeneration, reflection from Carpenter estate, Alexandre Apsan Frediani, Stephanie Butcher and Paul Watt

[420] Regeneration and Well-Being in East-London: Stories from Carpenters Estate

[421] https://www.theguardian.com/environment/2019/may/04/brownfield-site-new-homes-building-wrecking-health-southall

[422]https://www.theguardian.com/uk-news/2019/jul/07/court-challenge-homes-southall-london-gasworks-brownfield-development

Conclusion

The above observations are a starting point in terms of laying the foundation to examine the impact of housing estate regeneration or expropriation enforced through CPOs on residents, and its compatibility with human rights law. This would create a basis upon which a plausible determination of the effectiveness human rights law in challenging estate regeneration related human rights abuses could be made.

From the initial analysis so far, there appears to be emerging evidence or existing evidence of incompatibility with human rights law. However, further analysis is necessary to obtain a more rounded understanding of the issue and the mechanisms needed for residents to fight back and protect their human rights violated by those pursuing estate regeneration through the CPO process.

The upcoming editions will look into greater detail international law highlighting, the lived or documented experiences of specific communities as documented, and the different methods that residents have deployed so far in challenging estate regeneration, an assessment of the, the effectiveness of current remedies and then consider suggestions for reform. To ensure that, human rights law in this area has real teeth. Otherwise, if there is a perception that human rights law or indeed courts cannot protect residents against the interests of the powerful or some local authorities in concert with private entities, as mentioned above, then there is a real danger that faith in the legal or judicial system could further evaporate. Which will leave the decades of progress in human rights law and the protection it offers in real peril.

Bibliography

1. MHCLG: Guidance on compulsory purchase process and the Crichel down Rules for the disposal of surplus land acquired by, or under the threat of, compulsion,

https://www.gov.uk/government/publications/compulsory-purchase-process-and-the-crichel-down-rules-guidance.

2. The Implications of Kilo in Land Use Law, Symposium Articles: Keynote Address - Kelo, Lingle, and San Remo Hotel, Santa Clara Law Review, Vol. 46, Issue 4 (2006), pp. 787-810 Curtin, Daniel J. Jr

3. Globalization, Communities and Human Rights: Community-Based Property Rights and Prior Informed Consent,2006 Sutton Colloquium Article, Denver Journal of International Law and Policy, Vol. 35, Issue 3 & 4 (Summer-Fall 2007),pp. 413 428 https://heinonline.org/419

4. Human Rights and Property Rights [article] United States Law Review, Vol. 64, Issue 11 (November 1930), pp. 581-594 Blume, Fred H.

5. Equating Human Rights and Property Rights--The Need for Moral Judgement in an Economic Analysis of Law and Social Policy, Ohio State Law Journal, Vol. 47, Issue 1 (1986), pp. 163-200 Malloy, Robin Paul

6. Douglas Maxwell, Journal of planning & Environmental Law, Article 1 of the First protocol: A paper tiger in the face of compulsory purchase orders for private profit?

7. Towards a Compulsory Purchase Code: https://www.lawcom.gov.uk/project/towards-a-compulsory-purchase-code/

8. Compulsory acquisition of land: Developers, by PLC Property https://uk.practicallaw.thomsonreuters.com

9. Planning Act 2016: http://www.housing.org.uk/resource-library/browse/the-housing-
    and- planning-act-2016/

10. Kept in the Dark; https://www.transparency.org.uk

11. The Law of compulsory purchase, third edition, Guy Roots et al

12. Estate-regeneration-why-people-power-is-forcing-london-to-rethink-housing;
    developers-alarmed-at-khans-plans-to-give-estate-residents-power;
    https://www.architectsjournal.co.uk/news

13. Mayor-and-conservatives-dispute-latest-London-housing-stats;
    https://www.insidehousing.co.uk/news/news/ https://www.bbc.co.uk

14. Phil Hubbard, Loretta Lees. (2018) the right to community? *City* 22:1, pages 8-25.

15. https://www.transparency.org.uk/faulty-towers

16. https://architectsforsocialhousing.wordpress.com/2016/03/24/the-doomsday-book/).

17. Towards a paradigm of Southern urbanism Seth Schindler City Volume 21, 2017 -
    Issue 1Published online: 6 Mar 2017

18. Reconstructing Berlin: Materiality and meaning in the symbolic politics of urban
    space

19. Dominik Bartmanski et al.City Volume 22, 2018 - Issue 2 Published online: 17 Apr
    2018

20. Editorial Editor-in-Chief's note: What/whose order is to be asserted in the city?

21. Bob Catterall City Volume 22, 2018 - Issue 2

22. Published online: 7 Jun 2018

23. The right to community?: Legal geographies of resistance on London's gentrification
    frontiers

24. Phil Hubbard et al. City Volume 22, 2018 - Issue 1 Published online: 15 Mar 2018 editorial

25. Editorial: The right to assert the order of things in the city Luke R. Barnesmoore City

26. Volume 22, 2018 - Issue 2 Published online: 7 Jun 2018

27. Stuart Hodkinson, Chris Essen, (2015) "Grounding accumulation by dispossession in everyday life: The unjust geographies of urban regeneration under the Private Finance Initiative", International Journal of Law in the Built Environment, Vol. 7 Issue: 1, pp.72-91, https://doi.org/10.1108/IJLBE-01-2014-0007

28. Towards a new perspective on the role of the city in social movements: Urban Policy after the 'Arab Spring' Raffael Beier City Volume 22, 2018 - Issue 2 Published online: 17 Apr 2018

29. Adonis, A., and B. Davies, eds. 2015. City Villages: More Homes, Better Communities. London: IPPR. https://www.ippr.org/publications/city-villages-more-homes-better-communities

30. The London Borough of Southwark (Aylesbury Estate Site 1B-1C) Compulsory Purchase Order 2014 ('the Order': http://35percent.org/img/Decision_Letter_Final.pdf

31. Prime minister pledges to transform sink estates: https://www.gov.uk/government/news/prime-minister-pledges-to-transform-sink-estates: 10 January 2016

32. 'Cameron time to demolish sink estates': https://www.bbc.co.uk/news/av/uk-politics-35275516/cameron-time-to-demolish-worst-sink-housing-estates, 10 January 2016

33. Compulsory purchase and Compensation: An Overview of the system in England and Wales, By Frances Plimmer.

34. Paul Watt & Anna Minton (2016) London's housing crisis and its activisms, City, 20:2, 204-221, https://doi.org/10.1080/13604813.2016.1151707

35. Participation in the right of access to adequate housing, 14 Tulsa J Comp. & Intl L 269 2006 -2007, Hein online

36. Republic of SA v Grootboom & others 2000(11) BCLR 1169

37. Evadne Grant, Enforcing Social and Economic Rights: The right to adequate housing in south Africa, 15 Afr, J, intl & Comp,L 1 (2007), Hein online

38. The requirements for a compelling case in the public interest to justify a CPO (High Court) by Practical Law Planning: In Horada v Secretary of State for Communities and Local Government [2015] EWHC 2512 (Admin), Volume: 25 issue: 1, page(s): 115-135

39. The privatization of council housing, Norman Ginsburg, Issue published: February 1, 2005 https://doi.org/10.1177%2F0261018305048970

40. Haringey Council votes to cancel development vehicle despite Lendlease warning 18 July 2018:https://www.insidehousing.co.uk/news/news/haringey-council-votes-to-cancel-development-vehicle-despite-lendlease-warning-57250:

41. Watt, P. 2015. "The IMD as a WMD in the Regeneration of London Council Estates: Tackling Spatial Inequalities and Producing Socio-spatial Injustice." Paper at Tackling Spatial Inequalities Conference, Sheffield, September 10

42. Paul Watt (2009) Housing Stock Transfers, Regeneration and State-Led Gentrification in London, Urban Policy and Research, 27:3, 229-242, https://doi.org/10.1080/08111140903154147

43. Pam Douglas & Joanne Parkes (2016) 'Regeneration' and 'consultation' at a Lambeth council estate, City, 20:2, 287-291, https://doi.org/10.1080/13604813.2016.1143683

44. Bracking V Secretary of state for works and pensions [2013] EWCA Civ 1345, [2014] Eq LR 60

45. Knock it down or Do it UP? The challenge of estate regeneration https://www.london.gov.uk/about-us/london-assembly/london-assembly-publications/knock-it-down-or-do-it

46. HPA 2016 and how it affects housing associations: http://www.lag.org.uk/magazine/2016/07/a-devastating-blow-to-social-housing-in-england.aspx

47. EA2010Equality Act 2010 (Specific Duties and Public Authorities) Regulations 2017. PSED: specific duties in England, Practical Law UK Practice Note

48. CPA 1965: Compulsory Purchase Act 1965.

49. CP (VD) A 1981: Compulsory Purchase (Vesting Declarations) Act 1981.

50. LCA 1961: Land Compensation Act 1961.

51. LCA 1973: Land Compensation Act 1973.

52. TCPA 1990: Town and Country Planning Act 1990

53. https://www.libertyhumanrights.org.uk/

54. https://www.equalityhumanrights.com/en/about-us

55. https://www.ohchr.org/en/professionalinterest/pages/ccpr.aspx

56. https://echr.coe.int/

57. British Institute of human rights www.Bihr.org.uk

58. Chartered Institute of Housing www. Cih.org

59. DCLG www.coommunites.gov.uk

60. Housing Law practitioners Association www. Hipa.org.uk

61. The Law Society www.lawsociety.org

62. https://savecressingham.wordpress.com/

63. http://www.insidehousing.co.uk/cressingham-gardens-regeneration-approved-in-high-court/7018185.article

64. http://35percent.org/2013-06-08-the-heygate-diaspora/

65. https://www.southwarknews.co.uk/news/council-given-permission-take-aylesbury-estate-cpo-case-high-court-disappointing-blow-campaigners/

66. http://www.shelter.org.uk

67. http://www.axethehousingact.org.uk/page/2/ on

68. Localism Act 2011, https://uk.practicallaw.thomsonreuters.com/1-504-2706

69. Housing and equality law, By Robert Brown, Arden Chambers

    a. https://uk.practicallaw.thomsonreuters.com/w-012-0034

70. https://www.ashurst.com/en/news-and-insights/legal-updates/compulsory-purchase-life-after-aylesbury/

71. https://www.birketts.co.uk/insights/legal-updates/compulsory-purchase-and-what-to-do-about-it

72. https://assets.publishing.service.gov.uk/government/uploads/system/uploads/attachment_data/file/551698/ECHR_Memorandum.pdf

73. https://www.burges-salmon.com/news-and-insight/legal-updates/alternative-development-proposals-how-do-they-affect-cpo-validity/

74. Housing and Regeneration Act 2008, Housing and Regeneration Act 2008

    a. http://www.opsi.gov.uk/acts/acts2008/ukpga_20080017_en_1

75. Donnelly, Jack. Universal human rights in theory and practice. Cornell University Press, 2013.

76. Human rights Act 1998: https://uk.practicallaw.thomsonreuters.com/0-506-9287

77. Lexis   Nexis:
    https://www.lexisnexis.com/uk/lexispsl/publiclaw/document/413481/5DF5-Dealing_with_a_human_rights_challengehttps://www.lexisnexis.com/uk/lexispsl/publicl

78. New law journal: https://www.newlawjournal.co.uk/

79. Practicallaw:https://uk.practicallaw.thomsonreuters.com/Browse/Home/Practice/PublicLaw

80. Hansard- https://hansard.parliament.uk/

81. https://www.leighday.co.uk/News/2015/November-2015/Cressingham-Gardens-tenant-wins-High-Court-legal

82. https://www.theguardian.com/commentisfree/2017/oct/25/labour-council-regeneration-housing-crisis-high-court-judge

83. The Secretary of states' ruling re: Town and Country Planning Act 1990 Section 226(1) (a), Acquisition of Land Act 1981 The London Borough of Southwark (Aylesbury Estate Site 1B-1C) Compulsory Purchase Order 2014 ('

84. https://hsfnotes.com/realestatedevelopment/2016/09/28/a-new-right-to-a-community-decision-by-the-secretary-of-state-not-to-confirm-the-cpo-for-aylesbury-estate/

85. Compulsory_purchase_process_and_the_Crichel_Down_Rules_-_guidance_updated_180228;https://assets.publishing.service.gov.uk/government/uploads/system/uploads/attachment_data/file/684529/

86. http://www.legislation.gov.uk/ukpga/2010/15/

87. https://www.burges-salmon.com/news-and-insight/legal-updates/the-neighbourhood-planning-act-2017/

88. https://www.legislation.gov.uk/ukpga/2010/15/section/149

89. https://assets.publishing.service.gov.uk/government/uploads/system/uploads/attachment_data/file/475271/cpo_guidance.pdf

90. Knock It Down Or Do It Up; https://www.london.gov.uk/sites/default/files/gla_migrate_files_destination/

91. London's Housing Crisis Worse for Ethnic Minorities 22 March 2016;;https://www.runnymedetrust.org/news/638/272

92. Dispossession the great social housing swindle: https://www.dispossessionfilm.com/

93. City Villages, More Homes, Better communities: https://www.ippr.org/files/publications/pdf/city-villages_Mar2015.pdf

94. Shelter. 2015. Homes for our Children. How much of the Housing Market is Affordable?,https://england.shelter.org.uk/Homes_for_our_Children.pdf

95. The-story-of-the-camberwell-submarine-4618, https://www.insidehousing.co.uk/insight/insight

96. Convention for the Protection of Individuals with regard to Automatic Processing of Personal Data Strasbourg, 28.I.1981 https://rm.coe.int/CoE

97. Legal Challenges to Implementing CPOs and Decisions under the Crichel down Rules by Tim Mould QC http://www.landmarkchambers.co.uk/userfiles/TM.pdf

98. The use of compulsory purchase powers for regeneration by Elvin QC, http://www.landmarkchambers.co.uk s. 149 of the Equality Act 2010

99. Land Compensation Claims: The Claimants Perspective by Simon Pickles Landmark Chambers http://www.landmarkchambers.co.uk/cases-compulsory_purchase_compensation.aspx

100. Compulsory purchase orders: stage 4, CPO compensation procedure: flowchart by Practical Law Planning, https://uk.practicallaw.thomsonreuters.com/2-629-7353

101. Twenty years later-Assessing the significance of the Human Rights Act 1998 to the residential possession proceedings, By Ian Loveland http://openaccess.city.ac.uk/17163/

102. Housing Act 1988 https://www.legislation.gov.uk/id/ukpga/1988/50

103. R on the application of Sainsbury's supermarket ltd) V Wolverhampton city Council (2010) UKSC

104. Waters v welsh development agency (2004)1WLR 1304

105.   David Elvin QC paper, Use of compulsory purchase powers for regeneration, http://www.landmarkchambers.co.uk

106.   Countryside Alliance v Attorney General [2007] UKHL 52

107.   Article 1 of the first Protocol to the ECHR: protection of property, Practical Law UK Practice Note, https://uk.practicallaw.thomsonreuters.com/8-385-5732

108.   Article 6 of the ECHR: right to a fair hearing Housing:

109.   https://uk.practicallaw.thomsonreuters.com/2-385-8106

110.   Part VII of the Housing Act 1996

111.   Demolition or refurbishment of social housing? https://www.ucl.ac.uk/engineering-exchange/research-projects/2018/nov/demolition-or-refurbishment-social-housing

112.   Stanton, J. (2014). The Big Society and Community Development: Neighbourhood Planning under the Localism Act. Environmental Law Review, 16(4), 262–276.

113.   Murungaru v Home Secretary [2008] EWCA Civ 1015

114.   Fazia Ali v The United Kingdom - 40378/10 Court (Fourth Section)) [2015] ECHR 924

115.   Belfast City Council v Miss Behavin' Ltd [2007] UKHL 19

116.   James V UK (A98 (1986 E.H.R.R 123 (ECHR)

117.   Sporrong and Lönnroth [1982] 5 EHRR 35

118.   Le Compte, Van Leuven and De Meyere v Belgium [1981] ECHR 3.

119.   Bryan v United Kingdom [1995] ECHR 50, (1996) 21 EHRR 342

120.   Begum v London Borough of Tower Hamlets [2003] UKHL 5

121.   Lithgow and others v UK [1986] 8 EHRR 329)

122.   Chapman v. the United Kingdom [GC], § 96;

123.   Yordanova and Others v. Bulgaria, §§ 129-130

124.   Zehentner v. Austria, §§ 63 and 65) / (A.-M.V. v. Finland, §§ 82-84 and 90).

125.   Qazi v Harrow LBC (2003 UKHL 43: (2004) 1 AC 983 (HL)

126.   Salvesen V Riddell(2013) UKSC 22: 2013 SC(U.K.S.C) 236(SC)

127.   López Ostra v. Spain, §§ 56-58,

128.   Moreno Gómez v. Spain, § 61.

129.   Di Sarno and Others v. Italy, § 112).

130.   Hatton and Others v. the United Kingdom [GC], § 96;

131.   Moreno Gómez v. Spain, § 53)

132.   Fadeyeva v. Russia, § 69.

133.   (Asselbourg and Others v. Luxembourg (dec.)).

134.   Martínez Martínez and Pino Manzano v. Spain,

135.   (Hardy and Maile v. the United Kingdom

136.   (Hatton and Others v. the United Kingdom [GC]

137.   https://www.facebook.com/Savewestburysw8-804075296314550/

138.   https://twitter.com/savewestburysw8

139.   WestburySW8 a diary of Housing Estate Expropriation and Displacement-A lived experience.

HUMAN RIGHTS AND HOUSING ESTATES REGENERATION

This text is analyses human rights under ECHR/ HRA 1998 in relation to Housing Estate regeneration enforced by CPOs. Although there are similarities with other UK devolved areas like Scotland, the acts here largely refer to England and wales.

By Shemi Esquire

Exclusively for JEB

Table of contents

Introduction

ECHR /HRA 98 Articles

Art 8

Art 6

A1P1

Art 2

Art 3

Art 10

Art 11

International legal issues

Conclusion

Bibliography

The aim of this text is to assess whether human rights law is an effective mechanism to challenge the harm caused by housing estate regeneration effected by the use of compulsory purchase orders in the United Kingdom. The immediate focus of this thesis relates to the actions of local authorities or public bodies that attract the jurisdiction of the ECHR and the applicable international human rights law.[1]

The book analyses any potential or existing human rights breaches associated with estate regeneration under the ECHR regime and briefly discusses the relevant international human rights law. International human rights law although discussed briefly below requires a separate chapter in terms of assessing how international human rights law safeguards against violations associated with CPO enforced estate regeneration. The ECHR rights examined here which are associated with the use of CPOs in housing estate demolition, include the right to a peaceful and quiet enjoyment of one's home, *respect for the home (Art 8), fairness, transparency and the expeditious nature of the whole process (Art 6), equality of treatment (Art 14), freedom of association, expression (Art 9 and 10), Art 13 dealing with Just compensation or the appropriate legal remedies, Art 2(right to life), Equal treatment, impact on children and applicable international law as indicated in detail below.*

The ECHR rights above are juxtaposed with the underlying practical policies, practices, decisions and impact on individuals or the wider community. Commencing with the initial decisions, consultation process, internal processes, viability reports, environmental issues, equality matters, planning permission and the eventual adverse impact on residents in the respective communities. The impact on communities is assessed by examining fundamental life indicators like employment, finances, culture, health, the disproportionate impact on racial minorities[2] and whether the statutory compensation is fair or equitable.[3]

By simple definition, compulsory purchase orders [4](CPOs) are a legal mechanism deployed by acquiring authorities to acquire land[5] which may be occupied or encumbered with competing property or legal interests through compulsion.[6]

---

[1] https://www.un.org/en/universal-declaration-human-rights

[2] 'It's not for us': Regeneration, the 2012 Olympics and the gentrification of East London, City, 2013

[3] Alice Belotti, Estate Regeneration and Community Impacts https://www.unicef.org/child-rights-conventionChallenges and lessons for social landlords, developers and local councils,2016

[4] Compulsory purchase orders , https://www.legislation.gov.uk/ukpga/1981/67/section/1

[5] /Knock It Down Or Do It Up pdf, https://www.london.gov.uk

[6] https://www.legislation.gov.uk/ukpga/1981/67/section/1

CPOs 'require approval of a confirming minister under the Acquisition of Land Act 198'.[7] There are various enabling powers available and the determination to authorise will partly depend on the specific powers used. Such public bodies with statutory powers include 'local authorities, national parks, some executive agencies, the Homes and Communities Agency, health service bodies and government ministers. This is discussed in greater detail in other chapters.

There is a detailed process of CPO processes and various statutory requirements, discussed in other chapters. The focus of this book is not to discuss the detailed statutory CPO process but rather a detailed analysis of the detrimental impact on parties with interest in the land and whether such detrimental effects are compatible with human rights law.

Chapter 1

Overview of aspects of human rights law related to estate regeneration through the use of CPOs

Human rights[8] should be fundamental consideration in the authorisation process of compulsory purchase orders although this is not always the case in practice as discussed in greater detail below. Adherence to human rights law during the CPO process is emphasised in the government guidance, which states *that 'the purposes for which the compulsory purchase order is made',* should *'justify interfering with the human rights of those with an interest in the land affected.[9]* But the guidance also refers to a public sector duty requirement[10] which by interpretation indicates that a failure to 'have proper regard to the public sector equality duty', related to affordable

---

[7] f-guidance-on-compulsory-purchase-and-the-crichel-down-rules-for-the-disposal-of-surplus-land-.

[8] See "Tesco Stores Limited v Secretary of State for the Environment and Others (Full Report)". *Journal of planning and environment law* (0307-4870), p. 581.

[9] Guidance-on-compulsory-purchase-and-the-crichel-down-rules-for-the-disposal-of-surplus-land-pdf

[10] In R (on the application of Reading BC v SoS DCL

housing, social infrastructure contributions and a vacancy credit policy[11] could be found to be unlawful.

The Government guidance further states that *'all public sector acquiring authorities are bound by the Public Sector Equality Duty as set out in section 149 of the Equality Act 2010. In exercising their compulsory purchase and related powers (e.g. powers of entry), these acquiring authorities must have regard to the effect of any differential impacts on groups with protected characteristics. For example, an important use of compulsory purchase powers is to help regenerate run down areas. Although low income is not a protected characteristic, it is not uncommon for people from ethnic minorities, the elderly or people with a disability to be overrepresented in low-income groups. As part of the Public Sector Equality Duty, acquiring authorities must have due regard to the need to promote equality of opportunity between persons who share a relevant protected characteristic and persons who do not share it.*

This might mean that the acquiring authority devises a process which promotes equality of opportunity by addressing particular problems that people with certain protected characteristics might have (e.g. making sure that documents are accessible for people with sight problems or learning difficulties and that people have access to advocates or advice.[12]

Despite the clear government, guidance above it appears that adherence to such guidance is often inadequate or arguably non-existent. To the extent that even a council lawyer expressed doubt or surprise, as to how the PSED[13] would apply to racial minorities.[14]

---

[11] Saira Kabir Sheikh QC, JPL, 2015

[12] CPO guidance, https://assets.publishing.service.gov.uk

[13] Nlp_ex_33b_appendix_2_legal_note.pdf , https://www.london.gov.uk/sites/default/files/

[14] Lambeth council lawyer, apart from disability, his client did not understand how THI applied to racial minorities; https://twitter.com/saveWestburySW8; https://www.facebook.com/Savewestburysw8-804075296314550/; Human Rights today blog

The CPO process in many respects is deemed to be unfair because the acquiring body or authority is also the main driver of the process as[15] documented by various reports highlighted above in detail, by entities like independent observers,[16] the Runnymede trust,[17] academics[18] among others.

In summary, the effects on residents include displacement,[19] financial disenfranchisement, dispossession,[20] environmental hazards,[21] disproportionate effect on racial minorities,[22] adverse health impact on residents, especially children, elderly and vulnerable adults. This is worsened by the unfair process, imbalance of resources and lack of adequate or meaningful access to an independent decision maker during the process, [23]which makes recourse to courts a complicated, cumbersome and expensive affair. From such observations, it would appear that there is at the very least prima facie evidence of possible incompatibility with human rights law, which is discussed in more detail below. The various aspects of the relevant human rights law are discussed below starting with ECHR which incorporates HRA 98.

---

[15]DCLG Guidance-on-compulsory-purchase-and-the-crichel-down-rules-for-the-disposal-of-surplus-land

[16] Anna Minton, GROUND CONTROL, Fear and Happiness in the Twenty-First Century City, by Anna Minton, Published by Penguin Books, paperback original, 26th June 2012; Anne Rendell (2017) 'Arry's Bar: condensing and displacing on the Aylesbury Estate, The Journal of Architecture, 22:3, 532-554, DOI: 10.1080/13602365.2017.1310125;

[17] UK NGOs' Alternative Report Submission to the UN Committee on the Elimination of Racial Discrimination with regard to the UK Government's 21st to 23rd Periodic Reports June 2016 Drafted by THE RUNNYMEDE TRUST

[18] Hubbard P and Lees L, "The Right to Community?" (2018) 22 City 8

Social exclusion, Paul Watt (2013) 'It's not for us', City; Paul Watt, Housing Stock Transfers, Regeneration and State-Led Gentrification in London Article in Urban Policy and Research.

Social exclusion, Paul Watt (2013) 'It's not for us', City; Paul Watt, Housing Stock Transfers, Regeneration and State-Led Gentrification in London Article in Urban Policy and Research.

[19] Alice Belotti, Challenges and lessons for social landlords, developers and local councils, 2016

[20] Demolition-watch-submission,http://www.demolitionwatchlondon.com, 14-march-2017,

[21] https://www.theguardian.com/environment/2019/may/04/brownfield-site-new-homes-building-wrecking-health-southall

[22] Jessica Perera, The-London-clearances-race-housing-and-policing, http://www.irr.org.uk

[23]Alice Belotti, Challenges and lessons for social landlords, developers and local councils, 2016;

Dispossession, The great social housing swindle, https://www.dispossessionfilm.com,

Chapter 2

ECHR Jurisdiction

The UK is a signatory to the ECHR,[24] which incorporated the Human Rights Act 1998 fundamental freedoms into UK domestic law. This therefore implies that the HRA 98 Act has to be read and given effect in compatibility with convention rights by public authorities, in terms of their processes, decisions, effect or impact thereof which by virtue of s3 of the HRA 1998.[25] Section 4 of the HRA 1998[26] refers to declaration of compatibility of local legislation with the HRA 98 while Section 6 of HRA 98 makes it unlawful for a public authority to act in a manner that is incompatible with convention rights and may apply to organisations which perform public functions.[27]

Furthermore, although UK courts do not have a requirement to make identical decisions to the ECHR, they have to take into account ECHR decisions.[28] Any person affected can bring a legal complaint but victims need to have standing under the CPO and the court can look at substance rather than form. A pressure group can be a victim if it shows that it is affected but it is for public authorities to show compatibility with ECHR rights. There is however a possibility of the complaint being rejected if it is raised too late.[29]

---

[24] The Law of compulsory purchase, third edition, Guy Roots et al

[25] http://www.legislation.gov.uk/ukpga/1998/42/section/3; Also See *nutshells, Human rights ;(state year?) See also HA1985-s7-*

Compulsory purchase/Human rights act guide to practitioners-Christopher Baker.

[26] http://www.legislation.gov.uk/ukpga/1998/42/section/4

[27] http://www.legislation.gov.uk/ukpga/1998/42/section/6

[28] https://www.legislation.gov.uk/ukpga/1998/42/section/4

[29] https://www.legislation.gov.uk/ukpga/1998/42/contents

In dealing with the implementation of the ECHR incorporated rights or decisions, states possess a margin of appreciation in areas such as housing. It is argued that this is due to housing being part of the social economic policy of a state and this could require unique solutions unless there is a manifest unreasonable foundation.[30]

However, that assertion could be interpreted differently from the perspective of the international convention rights as highlighted by the UN Rapporteur on human rights.[31] The alternative argument would be that since housing is a basic human need, nothing warrants derogation from protection of that basic human need (shelter) especially in economies that have extensive resources such as the UK.[32]

Specific ECHR rights and relation to Estate regeneration

The rights protected by the ECHR are sixteen in total. These are categorised as absolute, limited or qualified as indicated by Andrew Drzemczewski.[33] From a strictly legal perspective, property rights fall in the qualified category but are human rights that are no lesser than any other human rights As already highlighted above, the most applicable human rights articles associated with CPOs include, *Art 2, Art 8, A1P1, Art 6, ART 14, Art 3, 10, 11, 13, 41 of the ECHR* incorporating the HRA 1998 and international convention on human rights.

As a summary and as indicated above, Art 3[34] relates to inhuman and degrading treatment, Art 6 protects the right for a fair, expeditious and impartial process[35], Art 8 protects respect for a home and home environment,[36] while Article 1 of the first

---

[30] ECHR; https://www.echr.coe.int/Convention_ENG.pdf

[31] Special Rapporteur on extreme poverty and human rights; https://www.ohchr.orgExtremePoverty

[32] https://data.oecd.org/united-kingdom.htm

[33] https://scholarlycommons.law.wlu.edu/cgi/

[34] ECHR, https://www.echr.coe.int

[35] ECHR, https://www.echr.coe.int

[36] ECHR, https://www.echr.coe.int/Convention_ENG.pdf

protocol,[37] safeguards against unjustifiable, disproportionate interference in the peaceful and quite enjoyment of one's home and possessions[38].

Art 2 protects the right to life and by default health. In estate regeneration, the argument advanced here is that projects which threaten public health or public safety may trigger proceedings under article 2. ART 10 protects freedom of expression, Art 11 protects freedoms of association, ART13 deals with compensation and Art 41 specifies remedies. Article one of the first Protocol refers to principles of law and international law underlining the payment of compensation in as far as money can be compensation.[39] A1P1[40] refers to principles of international law by payment of compensation in as far as money can compensate the affected persons.

However, when considering compensation per se, under the official CPO guidance cited above, a distinction is made between a CPO where land is taken and where land is not taken. This is because a CPO could proceed through imposition of restrictions, which amount to a taking or interference with the use or enjoyment, or ownership of the land but no actual physical land is taken. Therefore, it is arguable that to maintain fairness, in terms of compensation, there is a need for balancing that distinction with the public interest, as highlighted by both statute[41] and human rights law.[42]

Other jurisdictions related to estate regeneration and human rights law

International law [43]

[37] Referred to as A1P1 for brevity

[38] ECHR, https://www.echr.coe.int/Convention_ENG.pdf

[39] ECHR, https://www.echr.coe.int/Convention_ENG.pdf

[40] ECHR, https://www.echr.coe.int/Documents/Guide_Art_1_Protocol_1_ENG.pdf

[41]ECHR, https://www.legislation.gov.uk/ukpga/1973/26/section/1

[42] ECHR, https://www.echr.coe.int/Documents/Guide_Art_1_Protocol_1_ENG.pdf

As mentioned above, among the key protections for those affected by estate regeneration mandated by CPOs, is A1P1, which makes an explicit reference to principles of international law.[44] A1P1 states that, ...'*every natural person or legal person is entitled to the peaceful enjoyment of his possessions and no one shall be deprived of his possessions except in the public interest and subject to the conditions provided for by law and by the general principles of international law*'.[45]

Such reference to international law therefore necessitates an examination of the wider international human rights law applicable to estate regeneration using CPOs. It is also important to point out that the UK is party to the Universal Declaration of Human rights[46]and other related conventions such as[47]the United Nations convention on economic, social and cultural rights which invoke 'the right of everyone to an adequate standard of living for himself and his family, including adequate housing.[48]

However, in notable cases[49] reference to principles[50] of international law, [51]was stated to be limited to persons who are not nationals. This restriction to non-nationals reflected in these cases requires further exploration. It would appear or it is possible part of the reasoning is that the architects of ECHR intended to allow non-nationals to secure their convention rights directly without the inbuilt disadvantages they would

---

[43] OHCHR, https://www.ohchr.org

[44] Egon Scweb, The Protection of the Right of Property of Nationals under the First Protocol to the European Convention on Human Rights, *The American Journal of Comparative Law*

Vol. 13, No. 4 (Autumn, 1964), pp. 518-541

[45] Guide on Article 1 of Protocol No. 1 to the European Convention on Human Rights Protection of property Updated on 31 August 2019, https://www.echr.coe.int/Documents/Guide_Art_1_Protocol_1_ENG.pdf

[46] http://www.un.org/en/universal-declaration-human-rights/

[47] incidentally I write this in the UN HW library in Geneva-7th1019

[48] OCHCHR, https://www.ohchr.org/Documents/ProfessionalInterest/ccpr.pdf

[49] in Lithgow v UK and James v UK

[50] Deborah Rook, Property Law and Human rights, 2001

[51] https://www.ohchr.org/en/professionalinterest/pages/internationallaw.aspx

face in the national legal system. Such disadvantages could include discrimination on the grounds of nationality, race or other grounds generally associated with being a non-national of a specific country, which would not necessarily apply to nationals. It could also be argued that nationals could be arguably protected by their local jurisdiction but this remains a very unclear rationale which needs further scrutiny.

Apart from the direct provisions of international law, there is also international scrutiny and domestic pressure to comply with international law[52] as evidenced by a report from the UNRA rapporteur on human rights, about issues that are arguably inextricably[53]linked to housing, socio-economic policies and therefore the wider issue of social housing. This has a direct policy link with large-scale CPO estate demolition,[54] which contributes to fuelling the housing problems in the UK[55]. It should not be read in isolation but in synthesis with the recognition of detrimental effects like dispossession, displacement and disenfranchisement that come with loss of a home, a sense of agency and support networks,[56]which is directly similar to the effects of CPO associated regeneration.[57]Therefore, any international scrutiny consistent with international law or public policy is a potential positive step in dealing with the detrimental social and economic impact that CPO affected residents face.

In his report, Professor Philip Alston observes that a wealthy country with the fifth largest economy in the world should not be 'patently unjust and contrary to British values that so many people are living in poverty'.[58] He quotes the Institute for Fiscal Studies which foresees, 'a 7% rise in child poverty between 2015 and 2022, and various sources predict child poverty rates of as high as 40%'. Professor Alston's

---

[52] UK NGOs' Alternative Report Submission to the UN Committee on the Elimination of Racial Discrimination with regard to the UK Government's 21st to 23rd Periodic Reports June 2016 Drafted by THE RUNNYMEDE TRUST

[53]Statement on visit to the United Kingdom, by Professor Philip Alston, United Nations Special Rapporteur on extreme poverty and human rights, https://www.ohchr.org/Documents/Issues/Poverty/EOM_GB_16Nov2018.pdf

[54] Anna Minton, Ground Control: Fear and Happiness in the Twenty-First-Century City; His-estates-10-year-wait-for-regeneration, https://www.insidehousing.co.uk

[55] Anna Minton, big capital who is London for

[56] Anna Minton, Ground control, fear and happiness in the 21st century

[57] https://haringeydefendcouncilhousingblog.wordpress.com/

[58] Professor Philip Alston, United Nations Special Rapporteur on extreme poverty and human rights

report further notes that 'almost one in every two children to be poor in twenty-first century Britain is not just a disgrace, but a social calamity and an economic disaster, all rolled into one'. He emphasises that, 'many of the recent changes to social support in the UK have a disparate impact on children'. Citing evidence from the Equality and Human Rights Commission which predicts that 'another 1.5 million more children will fall into poverty between 2010 and 2021/22 as a result of the changes to benefits and taxes, a 10% increase from 31% to 41%.' The report points to the legal aid cuts, 'in England and Wales since 2012 which overwhelmingly affected the poor and people with disabilities, many of whom cannot otherwise afford to challenge benefit denials or reductions and are thus effectively deprived of their human right to a remedy'. The report highlights ' the LASPO Act (Legal Aid, Sentencing and Punishment of Offenders Act) gutted the scope of cases that are handled, ratcheted up the level of means-tested eligibility criteria, and substituted telephonic for many previously face-to-face advice services'. According to Professor Philip Alston, the Social Metrics Commission, states that 'almost a third of children in the UK live in poverty. After years of progress, child poverty is rising again, and expected to continue increasing sharply in the coming years.'

As described above, this report has a direct policy link with large-scale CPO estate demolition,[59] which contributes to fuelling the housing problems in the UK.[60]

Prof. Alston concludes that 'It was a British philosopher, Thomas Hobbes, who memorably claimed that without a social contract; life outside society would be "solitary, poor, nasty, brutish, and short....many of the public places and institutions that previously brought communities together, such as libraries, community and recreation centres and public parks, have been steadily dismantled or undermined'.[61]

Arguably, Professor Philip Alston's report is acutely relevant to CPO affected residents in various respects. Such as the legal aid cuts in England and Wales since 2012, which overwhelmingly affected the poor or people with disabilities. A theme that is consistent with CPO affected residents who face a lack of access to legal aid

---

[59] Anna Minton, Ground Control: Fear and Happiness in the Twenty-First-Century City; His-estates-10-year-wait-for-regeneration, https://www.insidehousing.co.uk

[60] Anna Minton, big capital who is London for

[61] Report from UNRA rapporteur on human rights, by Professor Philip Alston, United Nations Special Rapporteur on extreme poverty and human rights https://www.ohchr.org/Documents/Issues/Poverty/EOM_GB_16Nov2018.pdf

which has a disproportionate impact on children, racial minorities, the disabled, elderly and historically disadvantaged communities. An issue that is highlighted by both the Institute on Racial relation[62] among others and would appear to be inconsistent with international conventions and international law. Such as the Universal Declaration of Human Rights[63], ICCPR (referred to1st generation rights)[64], ICESCR (referred to as second generation rights,)[65]CERD,ICE (in relation to racial discrimination)[66] and CROC (convention on the right of children 1989.[67]

These conventions aim to protect economic, social, political rights of individuals or groups, such a rights relating to protection for the home, family, health, racial minorities, access to justice and due process. The Universal Declaration on Human rights, specifically refers to a common understanding of a set of values applicable to the treatment of individual human beings, irrespective of their race, religion, gender or other protected characteristics. Furthermore, the European Social charter, protects health, family, property and against discrimination, among other rights.[68] Although enforceability and applicability and legal jurisdiction over member states remains a potent legal hurdle.[69]

Firstly, because such relief would require measures to be implemented by the faulting nation states through protracted legal and political mechanisms. Secondly, there is difficulty in terms of pursuing the international human rights law route due to the complexity of the law, lack of resources and technical support to those affected. Even at a national level, it remains a cumbersome, long and expensive process to pursue legal action against the acquiring authorities who often have access to extensive legal and financial resources. In comparison, residents or communities

[62]Jessica Perera, THE LONDON CLEARANCES A BACKGROUND PAPER ON RACE, HOUSING AND POLICING 2019, Institute of Race Relations

[63] Universal Declaration of Human rights, http://www.un.org/en/universal-declaration-human-rights/

[64]International convention on civil and political rights, https://www.ohchr.org/EN/ProfessionalInterest/Pages/CCPR.aspx

[65] International convention on social and economic rights,https://www.ohchr.org/en/professionalinterest/pages/cescr.aspx

[66] Committee on elimination of racial discrimination, https://www.ohchr.org/en/hrbodies/cerd

[67] Convention on the right of a Child, https://www.ohchr.org

[68] https://www.coe.int/european-social-charter

[69] https://www.un.org/en/universal-declaration-human-rights/

affected in some cases are litigants in person who use pro bono assistance, which therefore limits the degree of assistance available or other sources of funding just to initiate legal action. In addition to the many other day-to-day practical problems, they face due to compulsory acquisition of their homes.[70] Nevertheless, it is critical that there is a transnational approach and potential avenue for redress given that CPOs, eminent domains, forceful land acquisition or land grabbing in general, have wider long-lasting detrimental effects on particular communities and demographics, which are historically disadvantaged, marginalised, disenfranchised and oppressed. Therefore warranting an international redress mechanism and a degree of international legal intervention.[71]

Chapter 3

Individual ECHR Articles related to estate regeneration through the use of CPOs

As briefly discussed above, among the applicable articles of the ECHR, that are arguably directly triggered by CPOs, are Articles 8, A1P1 Art 6, Art 14, 2 and 3 and their relevance as a mechanism to challenge estate regeneration activities under human rights law. These will be discussed in the order highlighted above.

The subsequent chapters shall examine the statutory compensation regime, the adequacy of the current legal remedies to provide a more rounded understanding of the issue, suggested proposals for reform and a determination as to whether human rights law indeed is an effective mechanism for challenging CPOs.

Article 8 ECHR and estate regeneration through the use of CPOs

---

[70] Alice Belloti, Estate community regeneration and community impact, Case report 99,
http://sticerd.lse.ac.uk/dps/case/cr/casereport99.pdf

[71] UK NGOs' Alternative Report Submission to the UN Committee on the Elimination of Racial Discrimination with regard to the UK Government's 21st to 23rd Periodic Reports June 2016 Drafted by THE RUNNYMEDE TRUST

Article 8 of ECHR,[72] states that:

1. 'Everyone has the right to respect for his private and family life, his home and his correspondence.

2. There shall be no interference by a public authority with the exercise of this right except such as is in accordance with the law and is necessary in a democratic society in the interests of national security, public safety or the economic well-being of the country, for the prevention of disorder or crime, for the protection of health or morals, or for the protection of the rights and freedoms of others'.

Before examining in depth the legal details or Art 8, it needs to be emphasised that just like other ECHR articles, there is a multitude of various areas of day-to-day life that could fall under the protections of Art 8. The focus here is on the relevant provisions that could be applicable to CPOs under estate regeneration.

Jurisdiction

Art 8 protects the respect for private and family life including one's home or correspondence[73] and could also be invoked in conjunction with A1P1. Observers, [74] point to a minute difference between these two articles in terms of the level of protection provided which may turn on particular facts of a specific applicant.

Scope of Art 8

---

[72] https://www.echr.coe.int/Documents/Guide_Art_8_ENG.pdf

[73] Aida Grigic, Zvonimir Mataga, Matija Longar and Ana Vilfan, The right to property under the ECHR, A guide to implementation of the ECHR, Human rights Hand Book no 10, https://rm.coe.int/168007ff55

[74] Aida Grigic, Zvonimir Mataga, Matija Longar and Ana Vilfan, The right to property under the ECHR, A guide to implementation of the ECHR, Human rights Hand Book no 10, https://rm.coe.int/168007ff55

Art 8[75] safeguards respect for a home and against deprivation of a home by way of access or occupation. It safeguards the right to live without interference and intrusion in one's family or private life and correspondence. Art 8 also refers to personal information being kept private or confidential and requires a positive step from a public authority.

Definition of a home

In brief and in this specific context of art 8, is a settled place where one lives, including a home one has the intention to move to,[76] described as an autonomous concept not based on domestic law categorisations.[77] In *Gillow V UK,* the court held that even though the applicants had not occupied the house for nineteen years[78] it was still their home. The applicants had not established domicile anywhere else and intended to live in the house.

To engage Art 8 protection, there has to be a determination on facts relating to continuous links and rights which cannot be interfered with, unless there is a reasonable justification.[79] Art 8 does not provide a general right to housing under HRA 98 or ECHR[80], except protection for respect for a home or unjustifiable interference of the peaceful and quiet enjoyment of one's home or possessions, under Art 8 and A1P1 respectively.

 Instead, Art 8 emphasises the need for the state to have a positive obligation to be proactive in regulating non-state interference and to provide remedies against

[75] ECHR

[76] Gillow v UK91986) ECHR 14

Donoghue V Poplar Housing association(2001)EWACA Civ 595

[77] https://www.echr.coe.int/Documents/Guide_Art_8_ENG.pdf

[78] CASE OF GILLOW v. THE UNITED KINGDOM (Application no. 9063/80)

[79] https://www.echr.coe.int/Documents/Guide_Art_8_ENG.pdf

[80] https://www.echr.coe.int/Documents/Guide_Art_8_ENG.pdf

harassment of individuals in and around their home as discussed in detail other chapters.[81]

The ECHR[82] further classifies a home as one that merits protection under the respect for a home legal principle. Which extends to property where the complainant is not an owner, a tenant, in long-term occupancy as well as a relative's house or a 'care' facility.[83] However, this may not apply to a home that one intends to build.[84]

Art 8[85] also appears to put emphasis on a home as being non-transient or exceedingly short term, like a hotel room. Although in *Buckley v UK,* [86]*which involved the retrospective denial of planning permission,* the notion of a home was not restricted to being lawfully established. Therefore, the designation or interpretation of what a home is or is not appears subjective.

In the context of a compulsory acquisition of social housing homes, such subjective academic notions of what is or is not a home per se, appears irrelevant for most residents due to the fact that they are actual physical owners and occupants of specific their homes either as secure tenants, leaseholders or freeholders. However, even for those that may not fall in those categories, there appears to be sufficient standing under Art 8 for them to assert their rights. Given that, they are non-transient accommodation or hotel rooms. Many live in these properties as their main homes with their families hence engaging Art 8. In terms of wider estate regeneration, conducted through the powers of CPOs, public authorities,[87] as social housing providers attract the jurisdiction of HRA 1998 and Art 8 of ECHR.[88] Mainly because

---

[81] Marckx x Belgium(1979)ECHR 2

[82] https://www.echr.coe.int/Documents/Convention_ENG.pdf

[83] https://www.echr.coe.int/Documents/Guide_Art_8_ENG.pdf

[84] Louizdou V Turkey(1996)ECHR 70

[85] https://www.echr.coe.int/Documents/Convention_ENG.pdf

[86] https://minelres.lv/coe/court/Buckley.htm

[87] Connors V UK(2005) 40 EHRR 9 'gypsies' removal from a locality was violation of art8

[88] R (weaver v London & Quadrant Housing Trust(2009) EWCA Civ 587

the issue here involves home and family life which must be only interfered with in 'accordance with the law'.[89]

Therefore, residents affected by CPOs, could rely on Art 8(1) in asserting their human rights if the public authorities do so in contravention of the law as held in the case of Malone, where it was affirmed that the 'exercise of powers must be in accordance with the law'.[90] The issue in *Malone* involved determination of infringement of rights by surveillance and the court held that although this was consistent with domestic law, discretionary use or application by officers was arbitrary. Therefore being incompatible with Art 8 of ECHR, although in this case the issue involved a tangential issue of surveillance not necessarily confiscation of a home.

Nevertheless, it falls within the remit of Art 8 and it also highlights the principle of a requirement of public authorities acting in accordance with the law, which is applicable to CPO affected parties. The wider point that must be further emphasised here is that planning and public authorities possess opaque, extensive discretionary powers[91], which are susceptible to arbitrary use.[92] Such abuse could be detrimental to individuals affected by decisions arising from CPOs, such as the demolition of housing estate homes, inadequate compensation, environmental hazards, displacement, dislocation, low or disputed valuations and the need for rehousing. Hence, raising potential incompatibility with Art 8, if CPOs are applied unlawfully or where there are illegitimate aims and disproportionate actions.[93] Furthermore, there are implied positive obligations where environmental factors directly and seriously affect private and family life. For example in estate regenerated areas like Southall, Westbury in Lambeth and other areas like Hackney there are increased complaints of environmental pollution especially in areas where the developers are building on contaminated land such as in Southall and the Westbury estate in Lambeth, South

---

[89] https://swarb.co.uk/malone-v-the-united-kingdom-echr-2-aug-1984/

[90] Malone v UK (1984) ECHR 10

[91] Greg Brown & Sean Yeong Wei Chin (2013) Assessing the Effectiveness of Public Participation in Neighbourhood Planning, Planning Practice & Research, 28:5, 563-588, DOI: 10.1080/02697459.2013.820037

[92] Too-poor-to-play-children-in-social-housing-blocked-from-communal-playground, https://www.theguardian.com/cities/2019/mar/25/

[93] Lustig-Prean and Beckett v UK(1999)ECHR 71 relating to UK military ban on LBGT due to 'operational' issues

London[94]. Although there is protection against interference within Art 8 in tandem A1P1, such a provision does not guarantee peaceful enjoyment of property.

The rationale under A1P1, which appears to offer qualified guarantees, appears both outdated and puzzling. Given that environmental or construction hazards associated with CPOs, pose serious and sometimes an existential threat to the health of residents or those exposed to such exposure. Such construction hazards include asbestos, lead, co2, benzene, industrial noise, dust, and fumes among other toxins. So the question has to be asked if those hazards exist how can it be that those affected are not guaranteed a peaceful and quiet enjoyment of their homes or home environment?

Is it possible to completely separate the two aspects of environmental protections with the interference in the peaceful and quite enjoyment of one's life? It is possible that given the current ubiquitous and front stage environmental campaigns, the facts and impact on those affected by estate regeneration construction or demolition could have potential challenges that could force a revisit of the courts approach or conclusions on environmental protection under Art8 and A1P1. It therefore appears that under the current ECHR Art 8 regime, save in exceptionally serious cases, environmental protections for CPO construction affected parties remains uncertain under Art 8 and A1P1 OF ECHR.

Chapter 4

Other Associated rights under Art 8 during CPOs in Estate regeneration

Among other potential safeguards provided under Art 8, discussed in detail below, are associated with issues such as succession, contracts of parties and the protection of a positive duty for the integration of children since family law matters relate to a family home.[95] This protection under Art 8 extends to state benefits or

---

[94] https://www.theguardian.com/environment/2019/may/04/brownfield-site-new-homes-building-wrecking-health-southall

allowances emphasising respect for family life[96]but is not applicable to fiancées. This is critically relevant to residents facing CPOs, which could determine re-housing, compensation or succession rights, not just for individuals, but for those they share their homes with or their relatives.

Tenancies and Art 8 in CPOS

Among other issues, the impact on the various types of tenancies is one of the areas that may engage protection under Art 8 including CPO affected estate regeneration residents or affected parties. There may be preconditions imposed on residents under CPO schemes, [97]whose occupation rights had ceased or those who are short-term occupants after displacing secure tenants[98]during the so-called callously named decanting process.[99]

The relevance here is that due to welfare cuts, high rents, low pay and job insecurity, short or informal arrangements such as sub renting or sharing homes is the most affordable way to live[100] or work in some cities[101]. It is arguable that such homes need a level of protection beyond the narrow confines of statutory or contractual arrangements.[102] This was highlighted in *Chapman V UK,*[103] *where* the concept of a home was expanded to cabins, bungalows stationed on land irrespective of the lawfulness under national law as well as second homes.[104] A principle that could be

---

[95] https://www.echr.coe.int/Documents/Convention_ENG.pdf

[96] https://www.echr.coe.int/Documents/Guide_Art_8_ENG.pdf

[97] http://estateregeneration.lambeth.gov.uk/key_guarantees#homeowners

[98] Part IV of HA 1985, amended by HA1988 and HA 96.

[99] Alice Belotti LSE Housing & Communities, Estate Regeneration and Community Impacts Challenges and lessons for social landlords, developers and local councils, Case report 99, March 2016

[100] Fenton, Alex. "Housing benefit reform and the spatial segregation of low-income households in London." (2011).

[101] Hamnett, Chris. "Moving the poor out of central London? The implications of the coalition government 2010 cuts to Housing Benefits." *Environment and Planning A* 42.12 (2010): 2809-2819.

[102] Michael Edwards (2016) The housing crisis and London, City, 20:2, 222-237, DOI: 10.1080/13604813.2016.1145947

[103] Chapman-v-united-kingdom-application-no-2723895

asserted by CPO affected residents who may not be long-term occupants or have formal tenancies.

There may however be limitations where there has been minimal occupation or weak links to the property to the extent that they are expunged. Therefore, sufficient nexus or occupation is necessary for recognition of a right to a home. Hence a mere possibility of inheritance may not give rise to a connection to a home under Art 8[105]al though altering the terms of tenancy[106] was found to be an interference with Art 8.[107]

It is nevertheless, evident that on the face of it, CPO processes, interfere with the respect for a home. Despite the fact, that such interference can be qualified under A1P1[108] to allow a member state some latitude in implementation, [109]if certain criteria are attached to the measures.[110] However, if the right in point is critical to the individual's enjoyment of personal intimate rights, the courts minimise the margin of appreciation.[111] Such as where there is demolition of homes[112] leading to[113] compulsion to move and hence a clear interference in the respect to a home under Art 8.[114] This rationale was unambiguously emphasised in Connors v. UK[115] where the court held *inter alia*, 'that the loss of one's home is a most extreme form of interference with the right to respect for the home'. In addition, since there was no justification for such interference, such as what the court referred to as a *pressing*

---

[104] https://www.echr.coe.int/Guide_Art_8_ENG.pdf

[105] https://www.echr.coe.int/Guide_Art_8_ENG.pdf

[106] Loretta Lees,The Urban Injustices of New Labour's "New Urban Renewal": The Case of the Aylesbury Estate in London, 2013

[107] (*Berger-Krall and Others v. Slovenia*, § 264);

[108] (*Howard v. the United Kingdom*,

[109] Alec Samuels, The planning process and judicial control: the case for better judicial involvement and control,J.P.L 1570

[110] *Noack and Others v. Germany*

[111] (*Connors v. the United Kingdom*, § 82).

[112] (*Aboufadda v. France* (Dec.));

[113] *Selçuk and Asker v. Turkey*, § 86; *Akdivar and Others v. Turkey* [GC], § 88; *Menteş and Others v. Turkey*, § 73).

[114] *Noack and Others v. Germany* (Dec.));

[115] Application no. 66746/01

social need or a legitimate aim, the court concluded that there was a violation of Art 8 pf ECHR[116].   This judgement accurately reflects the predicament of CPO affected residents by housing estates regeneration and could potentially provide an avenue to challenge such interference.

Estate regeneration disrepair or blight and Art 8 associated with CPOs

Another issue to consider is that in areas where CPO processes are enacted or merely announced, disrepair or neglect is a common feature.[117] Observers believe this appears to be managed decline to hasten what is termed as the decanting process.[118] A term that reflects the inhumanity and sanitisation of the arguably inhumane process of home expropriation[119]. The use of language and other phrases like brownfield sites or opportunity area drain or minimise any human association or presence in the areas or homes being expropriated. Coupled with the disrepair, blight and the consequential anti-social behaviour, the communities become ripe for targeted added claims by the acquiring authorities of an urgent need for regeneration,[120] which then softens the CPO approval process.

Disrepair has been found to be an infringement of Art 8 even[121]after examining the existence of procedural guarantees to determine the margin of appreciation. Disrepair, neglect and blight are also associated with *nuisance in the legal context under the pollution act 1972 or a public nuisance which falls under criminal law. This*

---

[116] CASE OF CONNORS v. THE UNITED KINGDOM (Application no. 66746/01) JUDGMENT STRASBOURG, 27 May 2004,https://www.refworld.org/cases,ECHR

[117] Estate Regeneration and Community Impacts Challenges and lessons for social landlords, developers and local councils, Case report 99,Alice Belotti LSE Housing & Communities March 2016;

See also Save Cressingham gardens; Save Central Hill: @savewetburysw8

[118] (*Khamidov v. Russia,*

[119] States and real estate private equity firms questioned for compliance with human rights, https://www.ohchr.org

[120] Estate Regeneration and Community Impacts Challenges and lessons for social landlords, developers and local councils, Case report 99,Alice Belotti LSE Housing & Communities March 2016;

[121] *Novoseletskiy v. Ukraine*, §§ 84-88).

is therefore another aspect that could come under the remit of Art 8 where parties who may not possess direct proprietary interest may seek to pursue their property rights from that perspective under Art 8. This is especially during construction related to CPO enforced estate regeneration. Such as in a case where a tree was felled into a neighbour's garden.[122] This is applicable to parties affected by CPO construction nuisances, asbestos or other contaminants as sighted in the Westbury and Southall cases[123] above. As mentioned such a nuisance could attract criminal sanctions under the codes such as the Asbestos Code 2012[124], as well as arising to the standard that breaches the respect for a home or home environment, hence being in contravention of Art 8 of ECHR.

Although Art 8 does not offer an inherent protection of a clean environment per se, planning decisions interfere with people's home and family lives, therefore triggering Art 8 and A1P1.[125] Moreover, since the convention is considered a living instrument, [126] it should be interpreted to fit present day conditions[127] to balance the rights of residents affected with a CPO due to public authorities' actions, which fall under the purview of art 8.[128]

It is arguably due to such hazardous intrusion or exposure that heightens the sense of dangerous impact on communities[129], which compels them to move away from their locality, family and their support networks.[130] There by essentially destroying the '*essential ingredient of a family … the right to live together, enjoy each other's*

---

[122] *Lane V The Royal Borough of Kensington and Chelsea London Borough Council(2013)EWHC 1320(QB)*

[123] https://www.theguardian.com/environment/2019/may/04/brownfield-site-new-homes-building-wrecking-health-southall

[124] http://www.hse.gov.uk/asbestos/regulations.htm
[125] *J.P.L 2010,3 298-309*

[126] *Tyrer V UK*

[127] *J.P.L 2010, 3 298-309*

[128] https://www.echr.coe.int/Documents/Guide_Art_8_ENG.pdf

[129] Paul Watt (2013) 'It's not for us', City, 17:1, 99-118, DOI: 10.1080/13604813.2012.754190

[130] Tom Slater (2009) Missing Marcuse: On gentrification and displacement, City, 13:2-3, 292-311, DOI: 10.1080/13604810902982250

company[131] and relationship development'[132] consistent with the 'notion of family life being an autonomous concept'.[133]

Private life and Art 8 in CPOs

Under ECHR, private life is interpreted widely to include 'personal and physical integrity'.[134] The relevancy to CPOs is the excessive unjustifiable intrusion into people's lives culminating to eventual displacement[135]instigated and characterised by collection of personal data,[136] especially in circumstances where many residents could be vulnerable[137]with no access to independent advice or support. Furthermore, such intrusion and demand for disclosure requires justification to avoid contravention of Art 8[138] especially where the acquiring authority is the intruding party, which arguably gains competitive negotiating, commercial and legal advantage.

It appears that even providing information for census purposes may be an interference of rights under Art 8, including surveys, under the realm of Art 8 jurisdiction.[139]Furthermore, intrusion in private life also includes the loss of support networks in the locality, which disrupts employment and professional associations[140]

---

[131] Olson v Sweden

[132] Marckx v Belgium

[133] Marckx v Belgium; https://www.echr.coe.int /Guide_Art_8_ENG.pdf

[134] X and Y v the Netherlands(1985) ECHR 4

[135] Jane Rendell (2017) 'Arry's Bar: condensing and displacing on the Aylesbury Estate, The Journal of Architecture, 22:3, 532-554, DOI: 10.1080/13602365.2017.1310125

[136] *http://newmanfrancis.org/projects/westbury-lambeth/*

[137] https://www.ucl.ac.uk/engineering-exchange/sites/engineering-exchange/files/fact-sheet-health-and-wellbeing-social-housing.pdf

[138] As held in, Hilton V UK Application no,12015/86

[139] Z v Finland(1997) 25 EHHR 371

which appears to be an example where there seems to be a convergence of Art 8 with A1P1 where interference in one is private, personal, or family life could lead to a legitimate challenge under both Articles. As held, In *Niemietz v Germany*[141], where the applicant's complaints of entry and seizure of the documents in the lawyer's office was found to be disproportionate and inconsistent with the expectation of confidentiality *'inherent in the lawyer's profession'*[142], although in *Niemietz*, the court did not find any *'separate issue under A1P1.'*[143]

Moreover, as indicated above, circumstances that could potentially lead to breach of Art 8 are more extensive than just physical possessions per se since art 8 protects attributes that are consistent with the preservation of family life and associated human dignity. Consequently, the court has also found[144]the loss of employment for a *breach of oath* to trigger Art 8, due to the impact it has on *relationships, material well-being, fami*ly and reputation. This is applicable to CPO affected parties, in the sense that compulsion to move from one's home has spiral effects on access to employment, education, support networks, well-being, family life and consequently one's human dignity and reputation as mentioned in the reports above. The other consideration for potential breach of art 8 is the fairness of the associated process which is discussed in detail below under art 6 but briefly in the paragraphs below under art 8.

Fair process and Art 8 during CPOs in Estate regeneration

Public authorities often use bureaucratic and inscrutable language or opaque processes. CPO decisions and processes may not be understood or formalised during a disruptive protracted process for residents. Valuations, advance payment

---

[140] Volkov Ukraine(21722/11) 2013 IRLR 480(ECtHR),

[141] 13710/88, [1992] 16 EHRR 97, [1992] ECHR 80

[142] Guidance Note 10, The right to property under ECHR

[143] Guidance No 10, The Right to property under the ECHR, pg 21

[144] Practical Law UK practice Note 8 835 5732

and negotiations for compensation or rehousing require specialist technical advice or access to financial resources.[145] Specifically, valuations are determined largely by the acquiring authority with limited independent oversight and imposition of pre-conditions in case of a valuation dispute.[146]This is worsened by the seeming lack of clear reasoning or timely information provided to residents, especially those that face measures that lead to eviction, which attracts protection under Art 8.[147]

The process is characterised by a lack of transparency, imbalance of resources, state self-interests or conflicts of interest due to decision makers being the acquiring party.[148] Planning decisions leading to CPOs [149] are sometimes authorised by the same acquiring party, which would appear to be a manifest conflict of interest with devastating detrimental impact in some cases.[150] An issue highlighted by Anna Minton, in her report 'Scaring the living daylight', [151]a situation which is acutely relevant to victims of estate regeneration enforced through CPOs.[152] In a nutshell, CPO affected residents who are in effect removed and therefore evicted from their homes and community[153] are subjected to obscure, broad, arbitrary and vague language without access to independent legal advice.[154]

[145] Stuart Hodkinson, Chris Essen, (2015) "Grounding accumulation by dispossession in everyday life: The unjust geographies of urban regeneration under the Private Finance Initiative", International Journal of Law in the Built Environment, Vol. 7 Issue: 1, pp.72-91, https://doi.org/10.1108/IJLBE-01-2014-0007

[146] Estate Regeneration and Community Impacts Challenges and lessons for social landlords, developers and local councils, Case report 99,Alice Belotti LSE Housing & Communities March 2016; See also Save Cressingham gardens;

See inter alia Hackworth & Smith, 2001; Glynn, 2008; Lees et al., 2008; Shaw, 2008, argue that Stock transfer in London can be understood through the lens of state-led 'third-wave gentrification', a widespread phenomenon across British, North American and Australian cities.

[147] Donoghue, above

[148]See inter alia Hackworth & Smith, 2001; Glynn, 2008; Lees et al., 2008; Shaw, 2008, argue that Stock transfer in London can be understood through the lens of state-led 'third-wave gentrification', a widespread phenomenon across British, North American and Australian cities.

[149] Buckley v. the United Kingdom, § 60);

[150]Siobhan O'Sullivan, et al. "Hearing the Voices of Children and Youth in Housing Estate Regeneration." Children, Youth and Environments, vol. 27, no. 3, 2017, pp. 1–15. JSTOR, www.jstor.org/27.3.0001.

[151] http://spinwatch.org/images/Reports/Scaring_the_living_daylight_final_27_March_13.pdf

[152] Estate Regeneration and Community Impacts Challenges and lessons for social landlords, developers and local councils, Case report 99,Alice Belotti LSE Housing & Communities March 2016; See also Save Cressingham gardens;

[153] Jane Rendell (2017) 'Arry's Bar: condensing and displacing on the Aylesbury Estate, The Journal of Architecture, 22:3, 532-554, DOI: 10.1080/13602365.2017.1310125

The Kate Barker Report, regarding the use of land for planning[155] further highlights the problems associated with the procedural unfairness in the planning process. It refers to 'planning decisions as policy decisions or expediency decisions, conducted in an anomalous manner'. An observation or description that would be consistent with the view that CPOs are imbalanced, favour acquiring parties, lack transparency and there is no real independent scrutiny, as highlighted in the various reports above.

Although, there is a possibility of judicial review it characteristically, largely focuses on procedural flaws, requires extensive resources and is characterised with structural impediments, which are looked at in more detail, under Art 6 below. As an example of such impediments, challenging such arbitrary decisions through judicial review would require a duty to give reasons by a public authority, documentation of the facts and any associated detrimental impact. However, requested information is not always provided, often delayed, deducted when provided, vague or broad even when conducted through freedom of information requests under the FOI Act.[156] Specifically, in areas like Southwark[157], Lambeth[158] and others, [159]residents' demand for due process remains a distant or box ticking exercise.

Therefore, the importance for a public authority to provide reasons for its actions or decisions cannot be understated. Such importance, to give reasons, in matters such as CPOs is captured in the law gazette article, in dramatic language. The article

---

[154] Duty to give reasons, :*https://www.lawgazette.co.uk/legal-updates/local-government-duty-to-give-reasons*

[155] J.P.L 1570

[156] https://www.whatdotheyknow.com/request/quantity_of_freedom_of_informati#incoming-1055418; https://www.whatdotheyknow.com/request/information_related_to_the_impac#outgoing-950497; http://www.brixtonbuzz.com/2017/12/lambeth-council-refuses-to-admit-how-many-empty-homes-are-on-cressingham-gardens-estate/

[157] http://35percent.org/heygate-regeneration-faq/ https://www.theguardian.com/cities/2018/sep/12/london-council-aylesbury-estate-development-southwark-financial-risk

[158] https://www.socialhousingsoundarchive.com/westbury-estate, https://savewestburysw8.wordpress.com/2015/04/14/the-westbury-residents-main-concerns/

[159] https://haringeydefendcouncilhousingblog.wordpress.com/

points to *'Shakespeare's decadent, drunken and corpulently challenged knight, Falstaff, when pressed to give reasons to verify an obvious lie, robustly declined. He declared that if '... reasons were as plentiful as blackberries, I would give no man a reason upon compulsion. But although Falstaff as a private individual was presumably within his rights to deny reasons, public authorities cannot be so cavalier.*[160] Despite the Shakespearean dramatization, there is a very serious point about accountability, transparency, protection against abuse of office or at worst impunity especially where 'the decision-maker is disagreeing with a considered and reasoned recommendation', as Lewison LJ, observed in the Court of Appeal'.[161]

Such intrusive and detrimental actions necessitate a need for the estate regeneration process to be conducted in a manner that respects the human dignity of affected persons and gives respect to their home,[162] giving appropriate weight to individual circumstances.[163] A point that was highlighted in *Connors V UK*[164] where it was held that the so called *gypsies* removal from a locality was in violation of Art 8, since the authority in question, appeared to evade statutory issues by making the applicant's wife sign a notice to quit without due regard to respect for his home. These actions effectively evaded any proper, fair or adequate due process. The emphasis on proper due process appears to be also reflected in *McCann*, where it was reiterated that 'any person at risk of an interference of this magnitude should in principle be able to have the proportionality of the measure determined by an independent tribunal in the light of the relevant principles under Article 8.*[165]

Therefore, for many CPO affected parties facing loss of their homes and the spiral detrimental effects that follow such potential displacement or dispossession, [166]the need for a fair and expeditious due process is an issue that cannot be minimised as indicated above.[167] It is however important to point out that despite the inherent

---

[160] Local government, duty to give reasons, *https://www.lawgazette.co.uk*
[161] Local government, duty to give reasons, *https://www.lawgazette.co.uk*

[162] (*Rousk v. Sweden*, §§ 137-142).

[163] (*Gillow v. the United Kingdom*, §§ 56-58).

[164] (2005) 40 EHRR9

[165] *McCann v. the United Kingdom, § 50*

[166] Such as loss of employment, extraction from school, effect on wellbeing, financial hardship or disruption

unfairness of the process and decisions, in some cases, such as Horada,[168] the initial decisions were overruled. In *Horada,* the court stopped the plans to demolish shepherds bush market, which would displace and dispossess thousands of local small businesses. It is however noticeable that these were businesses as opposed to homes and it's not clear whether that contributed to the reasoning in the final decision, an issue that needs further scrutiny which will be discussed in further detail in the later chapters detailing CPOs on a case by case basis.

In nutshell, as discussed above, Art 8, both substantively and procedurally appears to at least in law, provide a potential mechanism for challenging housing estate expropriation by public authorities. But such further relief under Art 8 appears inextricably linked with other rights under Art 6 and A1P1, such as the guarantee of the peaceful enjoyment of possessions, safeguard for ownership and other property rights under A1P1, as long as certain criteria are met. However, it is important to emphasise that while these protections appear intersectional with procedural rights under art 6 or protections under A1P1, there appears to be no unfettered protection given the various qualifications or limitations.

Art 6

Art 6 (1) of the ECHR states that," In the determination of his civil rights and obligations or of any criminal charge against him, everyone is entitled to a fair and public hearing within a reasonable time by an independent and impartial tribunal established by law'.

Art 6(1) is applicable to property rights, privacy matters, internal hearings or processes in terms of procedural fairness, access to an independent tribunal or equality of arms. Although Art 6 is not absolute,[169] it refers to some procedural limits

---

[167] Dispossession, the great housing swindle, https://www.dispossessionfilm.com/

[168] [2016] WLR(D) 148, [2016] PTSR 1271, [2016] EWCA Civ 169

[169] Ashingdale v UK(1985) 7 EHRR 528

as acceptable without procedural guarantees at every stage and stresses access to a court with full jurisdiction.[170]

As mentioned above, the focus here is about the relevant provisions of art 6 and others that could be applicable to estate regeneration through the use of CPOs. In analysing such relevance, a key issue therefore is a determination as to whether a civil right in Art 6 is 'a private right as opposed to a public right'.[171] In the context of estate regeneration, which is a housing matter, there is no ambiguity that this is consistent with a civil right in the context of ECHR and international conventions.[172] It is therefore the civil arm of Art 6 that is applicable to estate regenerations which therefore requires an identifiable issue over rights that have jurisdiction in domestic law[173]and consideration of the application of those rights.[174] In estate regeneration, there is an array of issues that require an expeditious, fair and independent determination as under art 6 stipulations. Such issues include the various competing interests between CPO affected parties, a need for examination of the consultation process,[175] a fundamental need for fair hearings as well as expeditious just compensation and adequate rehousing.[176]

The civil arm of Art 6 provides procedural guarantees in resolving disputes concerning property and ensures access to a court as well as a fair independent tribunal to safeguard the rights of those affected, although it covers permissible

[170] Golder V UK (1975) EHRR 524

[171] Alec Samuels, The planning process and judicial control: the case for better judicial involvement and control,J.P.L 1570

[172] Kenna, P. (2008). Housing rights: positive duties and enforceable rights at the European Court of Human Rights. European Human Rights Law Review, 13(2), 193-208

[173] H V Belgium(1987) 8 EHH 123 and GEorgiadis V Greece

[174] Bentehm V Netherlands(1985 8 EHRR

[175] Bokrosova v LLB http://www.bailii.org/ew/cases/EWHC/Admin/2015/3386.html

[176] Begum v London Borough of Tower Hamlets(2003) UKHL 5

[177] Handbook n0 10, Property rights under ECHR

[178] CASE OF DRAON v. FRANCE, (Application no. 1513/03), https://hudoc.echr.coe.int

interferences. To be admissible under Art 6 any potential applicant needs to have an existing interest or legitimate expectation in terms of possession or property rights under A1P1. However, where the eventual outcome is final after determination, it appears that no such prior requirement is mandated under Art 6[177]. It would also appear that emphasis will be placed on A1P1 if there is an issue that calls for the finality or decisiveness of the domestic legal actions but will be placed on Art 6 If the issue is about process. For instance, In *Draon v France,*[178] the court found a breach of the applicant's right to property due to a law limiting compensation associated with disability prior to the conclusion of the proceedings. Similarly, in the case of *Canea Catholic Church v Greece,* the court found that denying the applicant's legal personality was in breach of Art 6 after refusing to entertain the church's contention that such a rejection would deprive the church of the possibility of taking part in legal proceedings.

A question that arises is whether this is a clear signal that the court will take a pragmatic view rather than a uniform approach, as to what strand of specific issues are entertained and how to channel such issues when considering property rights under its jurisdiction. Whatever the answer to this question is , a potential lesson for CPO estate regeneration potential applicants, in terms of strategic and timely positioning of any potential legal actions under Art 8, A1P1 and Art 6, is that applicants should be cognizant of the fact that although there might be a prima facie case of breach ECHR rights, a strategic positioning of specific issues to determine a specific legal principle would appear to have a chance of success than a wider claim of breach of property rights.

The difficulty for almost all potential CPO estate regeneration affected applicants is that their main and prime goal is to preserve their property, homes and associated rights or livelihoods. As opposed to setting legal principles under the ECHR, which is a costly, protracted and academic process.

Access and delays

As discussed above, briefly, the other aspect that estate regeneration CPO affected parties face during housing estate expropriation is a lack of access to an expeditious fair process and independent tribunal. This is made worse by high costs, extensive

time constraints and lack of parity between the competing parties. Furthermore, residents are faced with the prospect of proceedings such as valuation disputes not being determined by an independent tribunal.[179] A situation which is consistent with *Ali V UK*,[180] where it was held that an applicant should have been afforded access to a fair hearing before an independent and impartial tribunal.

Similarly, resolutions should be consistent with the individual circumstances of those concerned which is consistent with HRA/ECHR art 6 which a fair process part of which would require an expeditious process or remedies such as just compensation or suitable adequate rehousing. Otherwise CPO affected potential applicants could be successful in alleging a breach of art 6 rights due to a delayed process or decision such as in *Robins v UK, where* there was a breach of Art 6[181] due to an unreasonable delay. CPO processes characteristically take years to conclude, [182]with h detrimental effect on residents on various areas of their lives. Yet acquiring authorities have extensive resources unlike individuals who are compelled to accept offers such as lower valuations that would otherwise be unacceptable.[183] The decision making process is characteristically structurally advantageously skewed in favour of or conducted by acquiring authorities' to secure their legal, financial and political interests.[184]

Even when those affected pursue successful legal action related to unfair procedural issues, the acquiring authorities could circumnavigate the ruling by essentially starting the process again. For example Lambeth council was held to have failed to follow lawful process in reaching its decisions. A decision that residents affected thought would cause the council to abandon the entire scheme. However, the council did not abandon the scheme although residents have since applied for the right to

---

[179] See DCLG guidance; https://www.gov.uk/government/publications/compulsory-purchase-process-and-the-crichel-down-rules-guidance

[180] Ali V UK(2016) 63 HRR 20,

[181] https://www.echr.coe.int/documents/guide_art_6_eng.pdf file:///T:/002-7866.pdf

[182] Dispossession the great social housing swindle : https://www.dispossessionfilm.com

[183] Stuart Hodkinson, Chris Essen, (2015) "Grounding accumulation by dispossession in everyday life: The unjust geographies of urban regeneration under the Private Finance Initiative", International Journal of Law in the Built Environment, Vol. 7 Issue: 1, pp.72-91, https://doi.org/10.1108/IJLBE-01-2014-0007

[184] Alice Belotti, Estate regeneration and community impact, http://sticerd.lse.ac.uk/dps/case/cr/casereport99.pdf

manage successfully[185]. Whether this will force the council to abandon the demolition f cressingham gardens[186] remains to be seen.

This was in the case of *Bokrosova V Lambeth,[187]* where it was held that Lambeth acted unlawfully due to a failure to observe procedural issues in reaching its decisions. The court stated that the process of consultation, '*must include sufficient reasons for the proposals to enable consultees to consider them, and respond to them intelligently; enough time must be given for that; and the consultation responses must be taken conscientiously into account when the decision is taken…. ensure public participation in the local authority's decision making process and … in order for consultation to achieve that objective, it must fulfil basic minimum requirements'.[188]*

However, despite the ruling, that essentially quashed their decisions, the council still pursued the regeneration by restarting the process.[189] The council's ability to do this raises questions about the effectiveness of judicial review as a mechanism to challenge CPOs. Since then the residents of Cressingham gardens have secured the right to manage as mentioned above[190] and it is interesting to see how Lambeth council will respond or how that affects the overall housing estate demolition programme[191] under Lambeth council.

As already highlighted above, part of a fair process requires access to an independent and impartial tribunal. Although pursuing legal action could theoretically attempt to meet the requirement of access to a fair and impartial hearing or tribunal, it is a costly and long process for CPO affected residents. Prohibitive costs bar aggrieved residents from instigating legal action especially in the case of leaseholders who risk cost orders,[192] even if they satisfy the impeding requirements

---

[185] Right-to-transfer-determination-cressingham-gardens-estate, https://www.gov.uk
[186] http://cressinghampeoplesplan.org.uk/
[187] (2015)EWHC 3386(ADMIN)

[188] Citing *'one aspect of the Coughlan test'*

[189] https://savecressingham.wordpress.com/2016/12/21/residents-vow-to-fight-on-after-high-court-decision/

[190] right-to-transfer-determination-cressingham-gardens-estate
[191] https://savecressingham.wordpress.com/

such as seeking leave to commence legal proceedings.[193] Parties with deep pockets such as public bodies or property developers may unreasonably delay or deny their rights without the opportunity for the full circumstances ought to be fairly, diligently and impartially   determined to prevent abuse of process or punitive penalties.[194] Such tactics are often deployed by the acquiring authorities in concert with developers or interested parties.[195] Therefore, CPO affected residents could have Art 6 engaged if they were subjected to processes that amount to barring them from bringing civil actions against the acquiring authority as was the case in *Z and others V UK*, [196]where the court clarified that, *'the inability of applicants to sue the local authority flowed from the principles governing the substantive right of action in negligence`* and art 6 was therefore engaged. In other words rejecting the argument was being advanced to prevent the applicants from suing the authorities.

However, even when there is an avenue of access to an independent, fair and impartial process, there are other criteria necessary that CPO affected parties would have to satisfy due to the fact engagement of Art 6 requires a disputable implementation of national law in a specific matter.[197]

An issue that was considered in *Lithgow,* where the nationalisation of property, under a local Act,[198] was found to engage Art 6 after the applicants alleged a lack of statutory compensation.[199] In this case, there was an undisputable right of a property owners' claim to statutory compensation, legislated for under the s39 of the Land Compensation Act 1973,[200] which in this particular case appears not to have been

[192] part-44-general-rules-about-costs,www.justice.gov.uk/courts/procedure-rules/c

[193] H V UK, Application no 11559/85

[194] Osman V UK(2000) 29 EHRR 245 (1998) ECHR 101 (1999) 1 LGRT 431

[195] Anna Minton, Scaring the living day light of people, https://www.annaminton.com/single-post/2016/03/21/Scaring-The-Living-Daylights-Out-Of-People

[196] Z and others V UK(2001) ECHRR 333, (2002) 34 EHRR 9

[197] Lithgow v UK

[198] Aircraft and Shipbuilding industries ACT 1977

[199] Practical Law Practice note 835 5732

satisfactorily implemented by the state. Therefore, where the local authorities do not apply the relevant ECHR rights, such as art 6, it is plausible that there is a real possibility of a justiciable issue by the affected parties.

That could be in instances where there are unreasonable or disproportionate barriers to a person's rights, derived from state actions, or an issue of a decisive nature in relation to the rights of an affected party,[201] such as a home or business affected by a CPO, that could lead to life changing intergenerational detriments. As was the case in *Koning V Germany*[202], where a civil right, under ECHR, was considered to be of substantive character and defined autonomously irrespective of the characterisation under national law.[203] Similarly, in *Brugger V Austria*, it was held that the complainant was entitled to an oral hearing especially that judicial review was not available as remedy in the local jurisdiction. Therefore, it would appear that once there is a clear determination of a right at peril under Art 6, the courts are prepared to provide latitude or opportunity for such determination, which is a potential positive trend for CPO, affected parties due to estate regeneration, which ofcourse have direct effect on the UK as a signatory to the ECHR but also via the HRA 98 which incorporates the ECHR rights.

However, as indicated above, the recent curtailment of legal aid is an inherent disadvantage, which makes it almost impossible for disenfranchised residents to challenge detrimental decisions associated with CPO decisions. Particularly leaseholders who may have the value of their homes taken into account as capital and therefore could fall outside the threshold for legal aid eligibility hence risk substantial cost orders that would be attached to their homes. Despite the fact fundamental rights associated with home expropriation, are at issue here which make legal aid arguably necessary in such civil proceedings.[204]This also raises a legitimate question as to whether there is overall property ownership in light of state dispossession through the use of the law. This is a wider question that will be covered in detail in the chapters below.

[200] http://www.legislation.gov.uk/1973

[201] Practical Law Practice note 835 5732

[202] Koning V Germany(1978) 2 EHRR 170

[203] Practical law practice note,J.P.L, 2010,3, 298-309

[204] Stars and Chambers v Procurator-where appointment of a temporary sheriff was held to be incompatible with Art 6. One local authority proposed to appoint its own mechanisms of final arbitration

However, the central theme appears to be the manifest imbalance of power and appearance of conflicts of interest in planning processes characterised by a lack of fairness or equality of arms, procedural fairness or propriety or access to an independent adjudication.[205] An inherent imbalance which is arguably worsened, where local authorities' planning or cabinet decisions appear to favour the interests of the acquiring party which are usually the same Local Authority, in the case of estate demolitions, such as in Lambeth[206], Southwark[207] and Haringey[208] among others. For example, in documented cases, during the CPO related proceedings, residents are accorded less time to argue their case or rebuttal of disputable facts and refused access to information[209]. This seems to be inherently incompatible with Art 6, as was the case in *Borgers v Belgium*[210], where a defendant who could not hear or make responses to official arguments was said to have had his art 6 rights breached.[211] Even where it would be assumed that the process was fair, planning conditions are reportedly changed, breached after the process[212] or at least not implemented as issued.[213] A practice that raises pertinent questions about the integrity of the whole process and whose interests are being served.[214]

Lack of access to information by residents

---

[205] R v (Wright v SOS for health and another(2009) UKHL 3

[206] https://www.opendemocracy.net/en/shine-a-light/residents-challenge-lambeth-plans-to-demolish-homes/

[207] https://www.newstatesman.com/politics/2013/11/look-heygate-estate-whats-wrong-londons-housing

[208] https://www.theguardian.com/commentisfree/2017/jul/03/britain-power-contempt-grenfell-labour-haringey-social-housing

[209] https://newsfromcrystalpalace.wordpress.com/tag/campaign-for-freedom-of-information/

[210] Borgers v Belgium(1993) 15 EHRR 92

[211] Practical law practice note public sector.

[212] Council tenants win 'segregated' garden rule fight, https://www.bbc.com/news/uk-england-london-

[213] https://www.theguardian.com/cities/2019/mar/25/ too-poor-to-play-children-in-social-housing-blocked-from-communal-playground

[214] Anna Minton, Big Capital, who is London For

Another common complaint by CPO affected residents is the lack of access[215] to material information and the need to be heard which is critical to the equality of arms.[216] In any process of challenging or asserting one's rights from public authorities or such entities, information from such public authorities is critical. However, freedom of information requests are protracted affairs and substantial information is either not timely provided[217] denied, [218]deducted or is in vague broad language whilst access to hearings in public is not always guaranteed.[219]

Lack of independent review

Another common feature is the fact that the unfairness of the process is heightened by the fact that there appears to be no genuinely independent review mechanisms, save for the court system whose encumbrances, such as cost or complexity have been documented above. This is not assisted by the increasing perception that planning functions and permission granting processes conducted by local authorities [220] appear to be more political, are not always based on statutory grounds[221] and objections do not lead to a hearing per se as part of due process.[222] This makes the need for a fair balance between the rights of the community or potential applicants to be presided over by an independent and impartial decision maker, from the beginning more urgent than ever. Especially when faced with the most intrusive action of all the loss or demolition of one's home.

The imbalance and the lack of impartiality is highlighted in *Tsfayo v UK (2007) ECHR 656*, where the issue involved an applicants' renewal for housing and council tax, which was rejected by the review board. The ECHR found that the board was not an

---

[215] https://newsfromcrystalpalace.wordpress.com/2018/11/26/lambeth-council-refuse-to-answer-foi-questions-made-by-news-from-crystal-palace/

[216] Feldbrugge V Netherlands(1986) 8 EHRR 425, see practice note above

[217] https://www.whatdotheyknow.com/request/asbestos_enquiry#incoming-1327131

[218] https://www.whatdotheyknow.com/request/somerleyton_road_steering_group_2321`11

[219] https://www.dailymail.co.uk/news/article-4656656/Kensington-councillor-DEFENDS-decision-meet-secret.html

[220] Bryan V UK(1995) 21 EHRR 342

[221] DCLG guidance

[222] R (Adlard V SOS for environment(2002) EWCA

independent tribunal and the possibility of judicial review was not a reprieve from the lack of independence and included councillors. Since public authorities review, their decisions by committees often staffed by councillors, such as in the CPO process, the lack of a fair and impartial consideration would appear to engage Art 6 given that the imminent loss of a home, such as that associated with a CPO, *ought to be a serious consideration.*[223] There should be procedural measures and safeguards to protect parties' convention rights,[224] with scrutiny placed on the protection of the residents' legitimate interests.[225] The court appeared to agree with the view that the vesting of land subject to a CPO *'cannot comply with Art.6 of the Convention, unless the courts have a jurisdiction to examine that decision on broad public law grounds'.*[226] Therefore, a similar decision by a public body, associated with a CPO could be *'unlawful if it were made for a purpose not recognised in the compulsory purchase order*[227]*or unconnected with the reason for the grant of those powers.'*[228]

Furthermore, where environmental or nuisance complaints are raised, during demolition or construction, some local authorities with confidential s106 agreements explained above, as agreements which essentially enable a scheme that would not be approved to proceed[229] or other agreements with developers[230] may have their impartiality or practical ability to enforce any planning regulations compromised. Therefore, potentially leading to planning conditions being ignored or breached[231] during and after grant of planning permission.[232] For example, on the Westbury Estate,[233] residents' repeated formal and informal requests or demands to have the HSE investigate the safety measures in place to protect residents from exposure to

---

[223] (*Ivanova and Cherkezov v. Bulgaria*)

[224] (*Irina Smirnova v. Ukraine*, § 94).

[225] (*Orlić v. Croatia*, § 64; *Gladysheva v. Russia*, §§ 94-95; *Kryvitska and Kryvitskyy v. Ukraine*, § 50; *Andrey Medvedev v. Russia*, § 55)

[226] Jonathan Ferris, 2010, Journal of Planning & Environment Law Compulsory purchase: is there a general right to judicial review to challenge the decision to vest land the subject of a confirmed compulsory purchase order?

[227] (*Grice v Dudley*8; *Capital Investments Ltd v Wednesfield Urban DC*9).

[228] *Congreve v Home Office*11; and *R. v Birmingham Licensing Committee Ex p. Kennedy*12).

[229] See www.Lambeth.gov.uk Westbury estate

[230] Council tenants win 'segregated' garden rule fight,https://www.london.gov.uk/sites/default/files/berkley_group.pdf

[231] https://www.bbc.com/news/uk-england-london-

[232] https://www.theguardian.com/cities/2019/mar/25/too-poor-to-play-children-in-social-housing-blocked-from-communal-playground

[233] Westbury-a-year-after-Grenfell, http://housingactivists.co.uk/grenfell

asbestos were reportedly routinely ignored[234] and were often referred to the developers themselves namely the Berkeley group.[235] Residents' concerns[236] appear to be supported by the findings of the HSE report[237]after concerted pressure from the local M[238]P and other parties. The HSE report found that procedures like using water suppression, covering dust, storage of asbestos[239] were not satisfactory or acceptable despite the initial claims by Lambeth Council.

Overall, the inherent impediments associated with instigating legal challenges to the planning process or decisions made by the local authorities. This adds to the manifest imbalance and inherent unfairness experienced by CPO affected parties. Planning policies, such as a CPO process infringe the rights of enjoyment of one's home and property . CPO processes under estate regeneration may further reduce market value because arguably buyers would avoid buying CPO affected properties and worse the planning process is regarded as favourable to developers intent on maximising profits by raising the prices of the new properties while minimising the values of the existing properties owned by residents.[240] The process is characterised with disputed valuation processes[241] without fair appeal processes, which prejudice residents' rights without the proportionality of the measures in question being determined by an independent tribunal. Cumulatively, this creates a hindrance for CPO challengers[242]and objectors from having a fair crack of the whip through a transparent, independent process as well as timely access to any requested related material.[243] Therefore creating a prejudicial effect to the probative value of such material at a later stage in the process, [244]which could be a potential breach of Art 6

[234] Families hit out at London gasworks redevelopment, Brownfield-site-new-homes-building-wrecking-health-southall, https://www.theguardian.com/environment/2019/may/04/

[235] The Lambeth and London 'estate clearances: PRESENCE of still uncovered believed to be hazardous construction soil , https://humanlawyerist.blogspot.com/2019/04/the-lambeth-and-london-estate;

[236] Homes for Lambeth Review, https://moderngov.lambeth.gov.uk

[237] Agenda and draft minutes, Cabinet Monday 4 March 2019 5.00 , https://moderngov.lambeth.gov.uk

[238] Kate Hoey(MP) for Vauxhall
[239] https://humanlawyerist.blogspot.com/2019/04/the-lambeth-and-london-estate.html

[240] https://www.theguardian.com/cities/2015/jun/25/london-developers-viability-planning-affordable-social-housing-regeneration-oliver-wainwright

[241] Westbury-a-year-after-Grenfell, http://housingactivists.co.uk/grenfell

[242] Peter Harrison Qc, Glimpsed views of the legal land scape,

[243] R (on the application of Vieira) v Camden LBC

and an infringement of Article 8.[245] Hence providing a potential avenue for estate regeneration affected residents to assert their human rights once they overcome the hurdles associates with instigating legal action.

Chapter 7

Article 1 of the first protocol of the ECHR[246] and CPOs

Overview

A1P1 states that, *'every natural person or legal person is entitled to the peaceful enjoyment of his possessions and no one shall be deprived of his possessions except in the public interest and subject to the conditions provided for by law and by the general principles of international law. The preceding provisions shall not, however, in any way, impair the right of a state to enforce such laws, as it deems necessary to control the use of property in accordance with the general interest or to secure the payment of taxes or other contributions or penalties'.*

The three main rules which describe the degree of interference[247] under A1P1 include *non-interference with possession, no deprivation of property except in the public interest and that state control may only be justified legally infringed in the general interest, where there is a legitimate justification.* In other words, the rights under A1P1 appear to be qualified to a certain extent with a margin of appreciation left for state parties in areas such as implementation as discussed in detail below. A1P1 also makes reference to principles of international law. For example, UDHR[248] under article 17, states that everyone has the right to own property alone or in association with others and that no one shall be arbitrarily deprived of his property.

---

[244] R (on the application of Ashley) Secretary of state for communities and local government

[245] (*Kay and Others v. the United Kingdom*, § 74)

[246] Referred to here as A1P1

[247] Possession, law, property and human rights, Landmark chambers

[248] https://www.un.org/en/universal-declaration-human-rights/index.html

But even in the absence of explicit reference to property rights, under specific international law instruments, it can be forcefully and persuasively argued that such interference, especially when associated with the confiscation or demolition of one's home, creates a spiral effect which could potentially breach international human rights law collectively referred to as the international bill of human rights,[249] comprised of the *Universal Declaration of Human Rights, International Covenant on Economic, Social and Cultural Rights, International Covenant on Civil and Political Rights.* The focus here is on the relevant provisions that could be applicable to CPOs under estate regeneration.

General Scope of A1P1

As cited above, A1P1 protects against deprivation of possessions and unjustifiable intrusion in the peaceful enjoyment of one's possessions. This could be through practices that amount to s expropriation of property, planning restrictions or even temporary property seizures. A case in point is *Pressos Compani Naviera and others v Belgium*, where the state was held liable for extinguishing the applicants unresolved claims by retroactively passing legislation which extinguished the applicants' property rights.[250] In pursuing protection under A1P1, an important distinction should be made as to whether the alleged interference is deemed to be a deprivation or simply control of use the land or property, which could then determine subsequent qualification for compensation under A1P1.

A1P1,[251] is independent of national state definitions, covers all forms of property and does not limit ownership of possessions to physical goods. However, A1P1 does not cover prospective possessions or future possessions but emphasises current or existing possessions. This was an essential issue in the case of Marckx v Belgium[252] where a mother claimed breach of A1P1 because of the alleged impediments by the state authorities to prevent her from disposing off her property to what was described

---

[249] https://www.ohchr.org/Documents/Publications/FactSheet2Rev.1en.pdf

[250] Handbook no 10, the right to property under ECHR

[251] See Practical Law UK practice Note 8-385 5732

[252] CASE OF MARCKX v. BELGIUM. *Application no. 6833/74*, https://hudoc.echr.coe.int

as 'an illegimate child'. A term that is clearly unacceptable in contemporary times[253]. The court by a majority confirmed that A1P1 was relevant to the claims made by the mother and defined the scope of A1P1 as applying to existing possessions but not future possessions[254]. In another case, of *X v Germany*, where a determination of A1P1 right was an issue, the court held that a mere expectation by notaries that *'rates for their fees would not be reduced by law'* did not amount to a property right within the meaning of A1P1.[255]

However, it would appear that where there is a concrete legitimate expectation, future possessions could be considered. But as far as relevance to residents facing CPO effected home demolitions is concerned, the issue regarding future possessions would not affect them because this relates to homes in which they live or already own as opposed to a mere expectation of future occupation or possession for that matter.

Therefore, the issues directly relating to CPOs and Estate regeneration, under A1P1 include, inter alia, *what amounts to deprivation or legitimate expectation, whether the actions of the authorities were proportionate or justifiable, the margin of appreciation extended to states and the fairness of compensation.* These issues are discussed in detail below.

Legitimate expectation

One of the key issues considered under A1P1 is whether a landowner's legitimate expectation of enjoyment of property rights can be a basis for asserting A1P1. In Pine *Valley Developments*[256], the applicants had bought land under the expectation of planning permission being approved but was later annulled. The court ruled in the

---

[253] CASE OF MARCKX v. BELGIUM. *Application no. 6833/74*, https://hudoc.echr.coe.int

[254] Marckx and Marckx v Belgium, Merits and Just Satisfaction, App No 6833/74, [1979] ECHR 2, (1980) 2 EHRR 330, IHRL 22 (ECHR 1979), 13th June 1979, European Court of Human Rights [ECHR], https://opil.ouplaw.com

[255] Handbook no 10, the right to property under ECHR

[256] Pine Valley Developments Limited and ors v Ireland, Just satisfaction, App No 12742/87, A/246-B, (1993) 16 EHRR 379, [1993] ECHR 2, IHRL 3587 (ECHR 1993), 9th February 1993, Council of Europe; European Court of Human Rights [ECHR

applicants' favour holding that the applicants had been subjected to unlawful discrimination contrary to ART 14 in conjunction with A1P1.

The key point from this case, in relation to CPOs is that there is an obvious legitimate expectation of enjoyment of property rights and protection from discrimination under ECHR. Therefore potentially providing an avenue for challenging such activity, primarily due to the legitimate expectation of the legal security associated with their property interests. Manifested through leases or secure tenancies whose curtailment would engage A1P1.[257] This is illustrated in *Stretch*[258], where the court upheld a complaint alleging that the applicant 'had been unjustly denied extension of a further 21 year term lease'.[259]It was further noted that[260] because the option granted by the local authority had been ultra vires and therefore deemed to be a disproportionate interference with the applicant's peaceful enjoyment of his possessions, this was a violation of Article 1 of Protocol No. 1 to the Convention'. Therefore, under the principle of legitimate expectation is that it appears that even a potential legal claim under A1P1 could merit consideration as a possession or asset where a landowner has a legitimate expectation.[261] Especially that CPO affected parties have diametrically opposed legal interests, such as retention of their properties, which are threatened with expropriation by the acquiring authorities.

However, in *Plant v Lambeth (discussed in detail below), the high court* examined such a legitimate expectation, namely the alleged curtailment of the right to buy by a secure tenant that was not yet exercised. The court held that A1P1 had not been engaged in respect of secure tenants' rights to buy since he had not yet acted on it. This ruling is puzzling because Lambeth council had taken formal decisions to demolish the estate through use of a CPO. By doing that, the right to buy by the tenant had been or would be curtailed. The applicant sued to safeguard his right to

---

[257] Pine developments v Ireland(1992) 14 EHRR 319

[258] Stretch v UK *(Application no. 44277/98)*

[259] Practical Law UK practice Note 8-385 5732

[260] [2003] ECHR 320, (2004) 38 EHRR 12, [2003] NPC 125, [2004] 03 EG 100, [2003] 29 EG 118, [2004] 1 EGLR 11, *http://www.bailii.org/eu/cases/ECHR/2003/320.html*

[261] Pressos Compani Naviera v Belgium(1995) 2 EHHR 3010) , also see Practical Law UK practice note 8-385 5732

buy by citing among others A1P1. Therefore, the court's ruling in this specific regard appears contradictory. Furthermore, it would appear that the applicant was not allowed to appeal which curtailed any further opportunity to test that conclusion. Therefore, the successful nature of any such complaint by a CPO affected applicant appears uncertain in practice.

Deprivation

Deprivation is another important consideration under A1P1. A1P1 protects against unlawful deprivation of property, which includes curtailment of the legal rights of those affected. In examining the issue of deprivation, the court ascertains any de facto deprivation of A1P1 rights[262]as opposed mere control of use of property or possessions. For example in *Papamichalopoulous v Greece,*[263] the Navy had taken over the applicants' land to the extent that they could not make effective use of it and this was found to be a de facto expropriation. This is consistent with the circumstances faced by CPO affected parties who have their properties confiscated or unable to be used for their own enjoyment or utility, which could mean that they could be able to challenge such de-facto expropriation of their property in light of the rationale in the above case.

However, potential applicants affected by estate regeneration enforced through CPOs, should be cognizant of the fact that if the measures taken by the state amount to control of the use of the property or payment of taxes, the court could find that such an action did not amount to deprivation. A case in point is *Handyside V UK,*[264] where the temporary seizure of the applicant's books, which were alleged to contain obscene images, did not amount to deprivation since the seizure was temporary and

---

[262]The right to property under ECHR, A guide to the implementation of the right to property, Human rights hand book no 10

[263] CASE OF PAPAMICHALOPOULOS AND OTHERS v. GREECE (ARTICLE 50, Application no. 14556/89)

[264] CASE OF HANDYSIDE v. THE UNITED KINGDOM, (Application no. 5493/72)

was within the powers of the state under A1P1. The difference with CPO housing estate demolition affected parties and the facts or ruling in this case is that expropriation of estate regeneration homes is usually permanent as opposed to mere control. Therefore, this provision would not adversely affect any potential applicants faced with estate regeneration under CPOs. The overarching point here is that although there could be legitimate justifications for interference in an owner's property rights, under A1P1, depriving someone of their property can only be justified in exceptional circumstances as evident in *Lithgow et al,*[265]*where* deprivation of property was held to have happened under a CPO process. A similar ruling was held in *Sporrong and Lonnroth,* where the 'expropriation of building permits and building restrictions enforcement for specific durations was held to be interference in the applicants' enjoyment of their land amounting to deprivation of property.[266] These rulings affirm the protection under A1P1, for estate regeneration affected parties who are deprived of their property due to CPOs by local authorities.

However, it is important to emphasise that any potential applicants would need to prove that this was in fact deprivation not mere restrictions,[267] temporary deprivation or interference in the use or enjoyment of the property. Deprivation could be further proven where there is a partial loss of a significant or substantial part of a landowner's right, which amounts to deprivation without full expropriation. The rulings in *Sporrong and Lithgow* above appear to confirm the protection under ECHR the rights of those affected by CPOs where deprivation or even partial deprivation is found to have occurred by the court. CPO affected estate regeneration residents experience significant restrictions caused by CPOs, such as exposure to construction hazards like noise, fumes, vibration or contaminants or the restriction to sell to the open market as a willing buyer.[268]Residents could argue that this amounts to deprivation or partial deprivation under A1P1.

Deprivation could also be potentially established where there are two competing owners who already have rights in the property as opposed to the familiar practice of the acquiring authority taking over the property. This is illustrated in the case of James *v UK,*[269] where the court found that individuals with leases under the

---

[265] Lithgow v United Kingdom, Merits, App no 9006/80, App no 9262/81, App no 9263/81, App no 9265/81, App no 9266/81, App no 9313/81, App no 9405/81, A/102, (1986) 8 EHRR 329, [1986] ECHR 8, IHRL 59 (ECHR 1986), 8th July 1986, European Court of Human Rights [ECHR]

[266] Sporrong and Lonnroth(1982)5 EHHR 35

[267] See Practical Law UK practice Note 8-385 5732

[268] Imrie, R., & Thomas, H. (1997). Law, Legal Struggles and Urban Regeneration: Rethinking the Relationships. *Urban Studies*, *34*(9), 1401–1418. https://doi.org/10.1080/0042098975484

leasehold reform Act 1967, entitled to long leases, who could purchase freeholds of their leases, at a defined statutory price, deprived freeholders of their property, due to the inability to sell the property or set the sale price.[270]

Ironically such a principle laid down in *James v UK above,* could be utilised by CPO affected residents[271]to disentangle themselves from the acquiring authority, although the acquiring authority could still have significant statutory powers to initiate a CPO. The acquiring authority could do so by citing other grounds such as control, as highlighted in *Agosi V UK,*[272] where the main issue was seizure and forfeiture by customs of smuggled Kruegerrands and the court did not deem such an action by authorities to amount to deprivation.[273]

Therefore, CPO affected parties should be aware of claims of control as opposed to seizure by acquiring authorities. However, it is important to emphasise that although such a defence by the authorities could be entertained by the courts, there must be a clear need to balance community interests with the protection of the individual's right to peaceful enjoyment of his or her home, in order to justify controlling the use of property in the general interest. Otherwise, that would invite potential misuse of the significant latitude afforded to states under A1P1 as a defence against CPOs affected parties.[274] Therefore, a finding of deprivation under A1P1, is an important tool against authorities pursuing estate regeneration.

Proportionality

Another central tenet of A1P1 is the principle of proportionality, which emphasises a fair balance between the public interest and the property interests of the owners.[275] Simply put, if there is a valid legitimate and lawful interference then it has to be proportionate. However, such a need to demonstrate proportionality is arguably

---

[269] James V UK(1986) 8 EHRR 123

[270] See Practical Law UK practice Note 8-385 5732

[271] See Cressigham Gardens in Lambeth

[272] Agosi v UK(1987) 9 EHRR1

[273] Practical Law UK practice Note 8-385 5732

[274] See R Plant V LLBC(cite full)

[275] See James V UK App No 8793/79 (A/98) (Official Case No)

[1986] ECHR 2 (Neutral Citation) ; James and ors v United Kingdom, Decision on Merits, App no 8793/79, B/81, 11th May 1984, European Commission on Human Rights (historical) [ECHR]

undermined, in practice, by national authorities enjoying a wide margin of appreciation in determining the public or community interests within the law. [276]

There are several factors, which determine such a fair balance or proportionality. These include procedural safeguards of the owner's property rights, the nature of the penalty applied[277]the extent of interference, the duration or persistence of interference,[278] the actual fault of the owner with its consequential significance and the irrationality or arbitrary nature of the statute.[279]

However, even if a threshold that satisfies proportionality is met by those affected, the need for proportionality in control cases is not a basis for compensation but simply indicates a need for a fair balance to be found.[280] Nevertheless, such interference may only be justified legally, if it's consistent with the public interest.[281]

As already mentioned, while the need to demonstrate the proportionality of the authorities' actions is a key protection measure for CPO affected residents, wider latitudes provided to the states arguably weaken those protections. Under A1P1 states are allowed a margin of appreciation in implementation of decisions associated with legitimate objectives of public interest [282]through proportionate measures designed to achieve greater social justice. While that appears to be a noble objective, in principle, such wide latitude leaves room for authorities to justify actions that are disproportionate to the affected residents whose homes are expropriated via schemes[283] like the wide scale demolition of homes with little[284] or no visible public interest.[285]

---

[276] Practical Law UK practice Note 8-835 57

[277] International Transport Roth v HS(2002) EWCA Civ 158

[278] Sporrong and Lonnroth

[279] R(Kensall) v SOS for Environment(2003) Admin 2003

[280] See Practical Law UK practice Note 8-385 5732

[281] In Tesco Stores Ltd v SOS

[282] James v UK above

[283] The Costs of Estate Regeneration: A Report by Architects for Social Housing, 7 SEPTEMBER 2018

[284] Knock it Down or Do it Up? The challenge of estate regeneration February 2015

[285] David Dewar, The implications of the SoS's rejection of an estate regeneration on grounds of social housing loss https://www.planningresource.co.uk, regeneration-grounds-social-housing-loss ,January 2019

The wider powers afforded to the states under the margin of appreciation, are made even more difficult to challenge by potential applicants due to the inherent institutional impediments faced by any potential applicants. Simply explained, in order for affected parties to challenge the proportionality of actions that amount to interference of property rights, such actions should be foreseeable[286]and authorities need to be accessible and provide clear simple comprehensible communication of reasons for their actions. In the absence of such communication, accessibility and foreseeability, by an authority, it would be extremely cumbersome, almost an obstruction on part of the authority, for estate regeneration CPO affected parties to timely, fairly and justly secure their property and associated rights.

However, in practice, authorities delay, obfuscate, deduct and withhold information[287] from potential applicants which clearly disadvantages estate regeneration affected residents, as mentioned above in various reports and discussed in more detail under ART 6. For instance, campaigners like those on Westbury estate in Lambeth[288] among others cited in reports above, refer to the woeful inadequacy of social rent homes and the ubiquitous use of s106[289] between public authorities like Lambeth et al, as evidence of a potential manipulation of the margin of appreciation left to states under A1P1. This illustrates the almost vacuous nature of the protection under A1P1 when authorities appear to manipulate the margin of appreciation to suit their interests. The case of *Tesco Stores Ltd v SOS*[290] *for Environment and Transport*, concretises the public interest argument as well as the margin of appreciation highlighted above. In this case, Sullivan J emphasised the need for *a 'fair balance to be struck between the public interest such as redevelopment and the individual's right to a peaceful and quiet enjoyment of his possessions. Adding that such interference ought to be proportionate and necessary to meet the 'compelling case in the public interest' reflecting the necessary element of that balance'.*[291] The difficulty lies in determining what the clear public interest is and where the limits of its

[286] Hentrich V France(1994 18 EHRR 440 (1994)ECHR 29 Lithgow,

[287] LAMBETH COUNCIL REFUSE TO ANSWER FOI QUESTIONS MADE BY NEWS FROM CRYSTAL PALACE, https://newsfromcrystalpalace.wordpress.com/2018/11/26/lambeth-council-refuse-to-answer-foi-questions-made-by-news-from-crystal-palace

[288] https://en-gb.facebook.com/Save-Westbury-Estate-SW8-486344558188042/

[289] S106 and public interest requirements are discussed in detail under the chapter of the CPO process.

[290] J.P.L 2010,3 298-309

[291] Also see R (Clays Lane Housing cooperative ltd v Housing corp(2005),R (Pascoe v SOS(2007), R (Hall) v First SOS(2008) J.P.L 63 at 15

application end, especially in relation to taking or demolishing one's home with the spiral effect that follow as highlighted in numerous reports above.

The above comments by Sullivan J appear consistent with another observation made by the court in Chesterfield properties v Secretary of State, [292]that 'only another interest, a public interest, of greater force may override it'. In that CPO inspector's report,[293]objectors argued that as the Leaseholders' Article 1 and 8 rights have been breached, it is incumbent upon the Acquiring Authority to justify that breach in terms of proportionality. The objectors referred to, the case of R (Clays Lane) v Housing Corporation, where, Maurice Kay J stated that 'the appropriate test of proportionality requires a balancing exercise' between 'a decision which is justified on the basis of a compelling case in the public interest as being reasonably necessary' may not be 'obligatorily the least intrusive of Convention rights.' Adding that some leaseholders no longer have mortgages and many are no longer in employment, as a consequence of the CPO they will be separated from their family and friends and they will be unable to afford to return to the estate'.

During the stated CPO examination process the inspector agreed that, 'Paragraph 12 of the Guidance states that an acquiring authority should be sure that the purposes for which the compulsory purchase order is made justify interfering with the human rights of those with an interest in the land affected. They would need to invest considerable personal resources in addition to any compensation they would receive for their properties; the CPO would not only deprive them of their dwelling but also their financial security. If they chose not to pursue this option, they would inevitably need to leave the area and this would have implications for their family life, including the lives of that dependant on the.... together with the failure of the scheme to fully achieve the social, economic and environmental well-being. The interference with human rights would not be proportionate having regard to the level. The public benefits that the scheme would bring... a compelling case in the public interest has not been proved'.

These observations were reiterated in the Aylesbury estate case in Southwark, stated in the chapters above, where the inspector and subsequently the secretary of state found that the CPO backed estate regeneration was inconsistent with the

[292] Chesterfield Properties Plc v Secretary Of State For Environment & Ors [1997] EWHC Admin 709 (24th July, 1997), *http://www.bailii.org/ew/cases/EWHC/Admin/1997/709.html* Cite as: 76 P & CR 117, (1997) 76 P & CR 117, [1997] EWHC Admin 709

[293] *CPO Report NPCU/CPO/A5840/74092 ,www.planningportal.gov.uk/planning inspectorate Page 73*

human rights of residents. Although it appears that the parties have since reached some sort of accommodation. The cases and comments above by both courts and the inspectors emphasise human rights as a fundamental consideration for CPO schemes not simply a peripheral matter.

How that is implemented on the ground to minimise or eliminate such human rights breaches appears to be almost impossible task. Therefore a finding of a breach A1P1 does not in effect protect applicants from dispossession. An approach that combines direct negotiations, political actions such as lobbying, and campaigns in parallel with any legal action appears to be more practically fruitful as opposed to relying on the protections of A1P1.

Justification

Despite the court rulings above, authorities could still potentially assert justification as a defence for the interference or deprivation of property rights. In other words, even if there was interference or a taking, the authorities could argue that they were within the law or legitimately justified to take the action they took.

Tax enforcement is one such route where that justification this could be applicable. As reiterated, a state has a right to enforce laws deemed necessary to control the use of property in accordance with the general interest to secure payment of taxes, penalties or lawful regulations, as long as the power is exercised rationally and proportionately, such as in the regulation of a sex shop.[294]

Nevertheless, despite such justification, the court could still find a breach where that justification is considered disproportionate or where there is a discretionary, unfair procedure creating an excessive burden born by the applicant and can further intervene in the absence of a reasonable justification for interference with property rights. Such an example is in *the case of Davies* where the court held in the absence of fair compensation, there was a breach of the need to strike a fair balance between the public interest and the van owners confirming that therefore A1P1 had been engaged.[295] Which affirmed that natural or legal persons could only be deprived of property, such as contributory or non-contributory state benefits,[296] or other interests,[297]

---

[294] *Belfast CC v Miss Behavin' Ltd,*([2007] WLR 1420, [2007] 1 WLR 1420, [2007] 3 All ER 1007, [2007] UKHL 19, *http://www.bailii.org/uk/cases/UKHL/2007/19.html*

[295] R Mott v Environment Agency(2018) UKSC 10)

[296] Stec v UK (2005)41 EHRR SE18

subject to conditions provided by law and the general principles of international law. An affirmation that potential CPO effected estate regeneration residents could arguably rely on to enforce their legal rights. However, it is always important for CPO affected parties to bear in mind that it is possible to conclude that various actions fall under the margin of appreciation on part of the state, if there is a fair appeal system or if the interference is reasonable and proportionate as discussed above at length. It seems to be a high bar for often unrepresented, resource starved and distressed residents to overcome especially properly raised and if supported by evidence from the acquiring authorities.

Having explored in some detail the broader principles underpinning A1P1 namely, deprivation, legitimate expectation, proportionality, justification and the margin of appreciation, with relevant cases or examples, it is of paramount importance to discuss in detail some of the specific areas where estate demolition or confiscation supported by CPO processes, acutely affects those who occupy the homes or have interests in the properties. Such examples include issues like market rate, the right to buy, home environment/environment rehousing and compensation and the extent to which potential applicants under A1P1 both could pursue them de facto and de jure.

A1P1 fails to offer full protection and requires a margin of appreciation which arguably allows local authorities to effect property deprivations or interfere in peoples' enjoyment of their property. There is no clear limits of interpretations of the margin of appreciation and there is a concern that could be potentially used as a general defence by actions. Given the lack of resources and lack of parity between parties, those affected could simply give up an further challenges against the authorities because of the appearance of an arguably respectable explanation by the authorities without being fairly adjudicated in an impartial and fair tribunal process. The spiral effect of such an occurrence is that authorities get emboldened in pursuing CPOs in estate regeneration because there is no real meaningful challenges against them. Therefore, the margin of appreciation principle requires revisiting if not out right deletion from the A1P1 lest it becomes a default position even when its clear such a defence would not arise at all.

Chapter 8

---

[297] Beyeler v Italy (2001) 33 EHRR 52

Other specific *notable CPO estate regeneration issues under A1P1*

It should not be a contention that protection against interference in a home environment is among the most important protections under A1P1.[298]As discussed at some length above, such interference has to be consistent with the added imposition of a positive obligation on the contracting states to ensure that such interference is proportional to the stated aim. The home environment protection under A1P1 could intersect with Art 8, which asserts protection against the violation of the respect for one's home.[299] Among other issues that require attention is environmental pollution, which could seriously interfere with one's private or family life and deprive personal enjoyment of amenities associated with one's home such as[300] the case of *Moreno v Spain*[301] where the court concluded that noise pollution violated articles 8 and 13 of ECHR. Such interference may affect a person's wellbeing and prevent them from enjoying their homes, family life and adversely affect their health. CPO affected residents[302] have complained of noise, pollution and toxic hazards associated with construction hazards.[303]The courts appear to disregard apparent mere concerns about protection of healthy environment[304]and consider serious detriments to the persons concerned. If there is a nexus to the cause of such a serious effect, a complaint may arise under Art 8 to determine[305] state actions and the failure to effect measures necessary to prevent harmful activity.[306]

Emphasis is placed on the need for a causal link to be established as opposed to prospective harm depending on the repetitive nature of the negative activity.[307]Furthe rmore, it's not the general deterioration of the environment", per se, but harmful

---

[298] Hatton and others V UK,

[299] https://echr.coe.int/Documents/Convention_ENG.pdf

[300] CASE OF MORENO GÓMEZ v. SPAIN, *Application no. 4143/02*

[301] CASE OF MORENO GÓMEZ v. SPAIN *(Application no. 4143/02)*

[302] https://www.theguardian.com/uk-news/2019/jul/07/court-challenge-homes-southall-london-gasworks-brownfield-development

[303] https://www.theguardian.com/environment/2019/may/04/brownfield-site-new-homes-building-wrecking-health-southall,

[304] *Kyrtatos v Greece*

[305] (*Hatton and Others v. the United Kingdom* [GC], § 96; *Moreno Gómez v. Spain*, § 53)

[306] https://www.theguardian.com/environment/2019/may/04/brownfield-site-new-homes-building-wrecking-health-southall,

[307] *Fadeyeva v. Russia*, § 69.

effects that would be disproportionate to the accepted standards consistent with living in modern metropolitan areas.[308] For many affected residents or parties, it would be an obvious aim for prevention to be effected before any harm or interference in the peaceful enjoyment for affected faced with CPOs parties although in practice this is not always the case.[309] In reaching its decision regarding a breach under Art 8, associated with pollution, the courts consider process and substance.[310] Paying due regard to any vague or overbroad interference without reasoned decisions, processes, any shortcomings in a state's obligation or whether the right balance has been struck between the resident and other interested or parties.[311] Such state measures need not include extensive reports but could include professional assessments to determine the harmful consequences of construction activities. However, a decision may be made in the absence of such information[312] if a fair balance between parties exists.

Additionally, a failure to rehouse residents during demolition, excavation, redevelopment, could violate Art 8,[313] because in effect that would tantamount to a failure to protect their health and wellbeing.[314] Such protective measures should include regulatory and administrative mechanisms. Paradoxically, the court confines itself to respect for a home hence the wisdom of such a decision needs to be closely examined.[315] This was discussed in more detail under Art 8 respect for a home above. Despite a lack of clear blanket provision protecting the environment, per se, under A1P1, courts could be creative in dealing with decisions that had the effect of remedying environmental detriments associated with a home or home environment.[316] Such as in a case where transparency was required when residents living at a dangerous site with sodium cyanide or in proximity to hazardous effects were not

---

[308] . (*Asselbourg and Others v. Luxembourg* (Dec.)).

(*Martínez Martínez and Pino Manzano v. Spain*, § 42) (*Hardy and Maile v. the United Kingdom*

[309] https://www.theguardian.com/environment/2019/may/04/brownfield-site-new-homes-building-wrecking-health-southall

[310] (*Hatton and Others v. the United Kingdom* [GC], § 99).

[311] *Moreno Gómez v. Spain*, § 55). (*Fadeyeva v. Russia*, § 93; *Hardy and Maile v. the United Kingdom*, § 218

[312] *Hatton and Others v. the United Kingdom* [GC], § 128)

[313] *Fadeyeva v. Russia*, § 133

[314] *Tătar v. Romania*, § 88).

[315] (*Hatton and Others v. the United Kingdom* [GC], §§ 100 and 122),

[316] *López Ostra v. Spain*, §§ 56-58, *Moreno Gómez v. Spain*, § 61. *Di Sarno and Others v. Italy*, § 112).in (*Giacomelli v. Italy*, § 83),

provided access to information or conclusions of the study to permit such a scheme.[317] Which was similarly reiterated, in the case of _Giacomelli v. Italy_, the *'court found a violation in the absence of a prior environmental impact assessment and the failure to suspend the activities of a plant generating toxic emissions close to a residential area'*. Such a documented lack of transparency is consistent with the experiences of many residents living in CPO affected areas where there is a lack of independent impact environmental and equality impact assessments.[318]

A question arises whether authorities do not disclose such information because of the crucially potential benefit to affected residents because environmental impact damages may be linked to actual loss. A case in point, where such inference is raised, is where applicants, who lived near Heathrow,[319] were subjected to noise nuisance, which affected their property valuation, although it was concluded that there was no direct evidence to suggest that the value of the applicants' property was diminished or was unsalable.[320] The reasoning seems contradictory since such pollution could limit interest in the property and therefore drive down prices. Furthermore, apart from environmental pollution associated with construction hazards, bad housing conditions, disrepair or blight during CPOs related construction[321] may breach the quiet enjoyment and Art 8 in terms of respect for a home[322] which is intersectional with A1P1.

Although there are statutory obligations in the UK legal system to deal with such bad housing conditions, [323]there are doubts about local authorities' willingness to enforce their own statutory liability or potential culpability. Which therefore strengthens and necessitates the need for Art 8 intervention where there are unfit housing conditions but no adequate remedy.[324]

CPOs, right to buy and A1P1

[317] Hatton and Others v. the United Kingdom [GC] (§ 120),

[318] https://www.theguardian.com/environment/2019/may/04/brownfield-site-new-homes-building-wrecking-health-southall

[319] Hatton and Others v. the United Kingdom [GC] (§ 120),

[320] . However, a settlement was reached in one case in respect of Art 8, 13 and A1P1.

[321] Demolition or refurbishment of social housing?, https://www.ucl.ac.uk/engineering-exchange/research-projects, 2018

[322]https://www.echr.coe.int/Documents/Guide_Art_8_ENG.pdf

[323] Housing/repairs-in-rented-housing/disrepair-what-are-your-options-if-you-are-a-social-housing-tenant/disrepair-what-are-the-landlord-s-responsibilities, /https://www.citizensadvice.org.uk/

[324] HA1985 s604,

Another key area that needs consideration is the impact of CPOs on what is known as the right to buy for secure tenants and the protections under A1P1. The relevant context in this case is where estate regeneration can be argued to effectively interfere with the right to buy of the secure residents. Not the overall discussion of the advantages or disadvantages of the right to buy per se.

The case of R Plant v LLBC[325] highlights this issue, which affects secure tenants faced with a CPO and interference in their right to buy under A1P1. In this particular case, a central issue was whether A1P1 was engaged and breached by the council's decision to demolish the estate using CPOs. The claimant among other issues appears to have alleged breach of A1P1 due to interference with S118 of HA 1985, right to buy and S84 (1) rights, which prevent the court from issuing a possession order on such a property except on legal grounds in schedule 2 of the Act and other provisional requirements.[326] The court held that A1P1 was not applicable to the council's cabinet decision, concluding that, *'A1P1 was not engaged and was indistinguishable from other authorities.[327]* Noting that 'if *engaged, it need only be considered in relation to the statutory right to buy when the authority commences County Court proceedings to obtain an order for possession of a particular home'.*

Notably, the court appeared to base its decision to the fact that the claimant had not already exercised his right to buy. However, it appears that the existence of that option and its removal clearly appeared to interfere in the claimant's property rights, hence engaging A1P1.

Nevertheless, it appears the court indirectly appeared to acknowledge that A1P1 was engaged but not breached, at least up to the point when steps would be taken to revoke it or a determination made as to whether it was breached. Stating that, *'If, contrary to the clear view I have reached, I had concluded that A1P1 was engaged in LLBC's decision, reached on 21 March 2016....the issue of whether it was breached would have been a matter for the Court to determine.'[328] This* Invites the question as to when the right time or forum would be for the claimant to enforce his rights under A1P1 if not at that specific court and that specific time. Moreover, If not why not?

---

[325] *R Plant v LLBC, [2016] EWHC 3324 (Admin)*

[326] *R Plant v LLB [2016] EWHC 3324 (Admin)*

[327] *Kay v Lambeth LBC [2005] QB 352 and Austin v Southwark LBC [2010] HLR 1'.*

[328] Citing *Belfast City Council v Miss Behavin' Ltd [2007] 1 WLR 1420 at paragraphs 13 to 15)'.*

However, questions remain after this ruling and it is not clear that those questions were adequately addressed by the court. Moreover, the unfortunate refusal to appeal closed down testing the *decision related to secure tenancy, CPOs and A1P1.*

However, a significant positive takeaway for CPO affected residents, especially with the right to buy, the court appears to have acknowledged their rights if they chose to move away. They would be secure tenants being provided with new secure tenancies if they decide to move elsewhere but not if they wish to be rehoused in a new home on their current location. In which case they would only be granted an assured tenancy.

Market Rate, CPOs and A1P1

Another extremely important issue for consideration by CPO affected estate regeneration residents that could be in violation of A1P1 is the inherent default prevention of applicants from selling their properties at market value. Such interference via CPOs therefore appears disproportionate since compensation should be reasonably related to the wider market value of the locality, taking into account the totality of the full circumstances associated with displacement and removal from a home or a locality. Furthermore, it would appear, A1P1 does not guarantee a right to full compensation in every situation since a margin of appreciation is allowed to the nation state in this respect.[329]

However, it must be emphasised that the issue, here is beyond market value per se. Market rate, in this context is disputed and is described as 'a euphemism for imposing compensation' on an unwilling seller.[330]Where owners are compelled to sell to a specific party, at a specific time, at a price largely determined by the same interested party usually the acquiring local authority also the arbiter of the planning decisions which appears to be a prima facie manifest conflict of interest.[331]

---

[329] See Lithgow and Practical Law UK Practice Note 8-385 5732

[330] Guy Roots et al, 2nd edition

[331]Neil Gray Libby Porter, By Any Means Necessary: Urban Regeneration and the "State of Exception" in Glasgow's Commonwealth Games 2014

The no scheme principle[332] and the equivalence principle[333] often cited in the government guidance regarding CPO compensation[334] appear woefully unrealistic since CPO affected areas face blight, crime, antisocial behaviour and disrepair which affect the market price.[335] Furthermore, those affected cannot simply move or sell to the open market due to the costs involved or the inability to sell in case of leaseholders. The compensation awarded does not often meet the prices or housing costs in the private sector within the locality. Not to mention the resulting severe emotional distress that affects the wellbeing, health, and avoidable psychological insecurity.

Additionally, residents largely buy or rent properties without any forthcoming knowledge of a CPO. In the case of Local authorities, leases can be for 125 years while life tenure with succession rights is routine for many local authority secure tenancies. Residents envisaged this as a safety net both as a home and for leaseholders as a potential long-term capital investment, which is crucial for social mobility.

Therefore, the reference to the so-called market price or apparent resemblance to market price does not reflect the necessary just, fair and equitable compensation for residents' families or other affected parties. There is a recognisable strong argument that compensation per se should be beyond statutory requirements and a central measure in assessing or the proportionate nature of the burden put on any CPO affected party.[336]

Chapter 9

Compensation and A1P1

---

[332] David Elvin, QC, the no scheme principle under s6a of LCA 1961, https://www.landmarkchambers.co.uk/wp-content/uploads/2018/08/CPO-Presentation-Seminar-25-Sept-2017-DEQC.pdf

[333] http://www.legislation.gov.uk/ukpga/Eliz2/9-10/33/section/5

[334] https://assets.publishing.service.gov.uk/government/uploads/system/uploads/attachment_data/file/817392/CPO_guidance_-_with_2019_update.pdf

[335] Loretta Lees, Mara Ferreri, Resisting gentrification on its final frontiers: Learning from the Heygate Estate in London (1974–2013),Cities, Volume 57,2016,Pages 14-24, https://doi.org/10.1016/j.cities.2015.12.005.(http://www.sciencedirect.com

[336] Deborah Rook, Property and Human Rights, 2001

As indicated above, compensation no doubt remains a contentious issue in CPO related matters and is set by statute as highlighted by the DCLG guidance.[337]The guidance cited above refers to market value plus home loss payments and disbursements,[338] apparently disregarding the value of the scheme on the value of the land in question. Instead, compensation assumes a willing seller without compulsion. This is via monetary payment at the open market value of the land, *'in so far as money can do it', to put one in the same position as land had not been taken from him…in so far as loss imposed on him in the public interest, but no greater'.[339]* However, this level of compensation does not cover the detrimental effects of being displaced from a settled community with the ensuing distress, fear and sense of powerlessness.[340] *Which would appear to resonate with A1P1 as reiterated In James v UK* and in *the former king of Greece et al v Greece[341]*, where it was held that compensation that does not reasonably reflect the value of the property[342] could be deemed a disproportionate interference.[343]

A government review culminated into various law commission reports that were not implemented[344] leading to minimal changes.[345] DCLG guidance further explains this contentious and complex area'[346] stating that, *'compensation payable for the compulsory acquisition of an interest in land is based on the 'equivalence principle' (i.e. that the owner should be paid neither less nor more than their loss). The value*

---

[337]compulsory-purchase-process-and-the-crichel-down-rules-guidance

https://www.gov.uk/government/publications

[338]https://assets.publishing.service.gov.uk/government

[339] Lord justice Scott in Horn v Sunderland corporation

[340] Martine August, "It's all about power and you have none:" The marginalization of tenant resistance to mixed-income social housing redevelopment in Toronto, Canada,

Cities, Volume 57,2016, Pages 25-32, (http://www.sciencedirect.com

[341] Deborah Rook, Property Law and Human Rights, 2001

[342] Deborah Rook, Property Law and Human rights, 2001

[343] Holy Monasteries v Greece

[344] See urban renaissance report city university urban task force report, pg. 231,

[345] *Planning and Compulsory purchase Act 2004*

[346] DCLG guidance citing Part 1 Land compensation claims 1973

of land taken is the amount which it might be expected to realise if sold on the open market by a willing seller (Land Compensation Act 1961, section 5, rule 2), disregarding any effect on value of the scheme of the acquiring authority (known as the 'no scheme' principle); (see Land Compensation Act 1961, section 5, rule 5). Importantly, but unfortunate for those affected by CPOs, although it is implied under A1P1 that compensation will be paid,[347] the legitimate public interest may justify less than the financial equivalent to what the claimant lost based on the principle in *James.*[348] In addition, where rights to compensation are provided by statute, those provisions must be interpreted so as to be compatible with HRA 1998'.[349] Furthermore, A1P1 does not state how much compensation should be paid but states that *'the taking of property without any just compensation is justifiable only in exceptional circumstances'.* Compensation should be generous and proportionately beyond, market value or pecuniary loss given the spiral detriments including mental distress that befalls those affected by estate regeneration enforced by CPOs, as highlighted in the various reports above.

The compensation issue is best humorously articulated by John Pugh Smith,[350] who sums up the central concern for CPO affected landowners, as timely adequate compensation, *'especially for a welsh hill farmer'* as he put it.[351] This reference to the 'welsh farmer' could be arguably replicated to the majority of CPO affected parties or residents faced with the demolition of their homes under CPOs with the spiral affects which could be held as being in breach of A1P1. Therefore, it cannot be emphasised enough, the extent to which the expeditious nature and totality of compensation is central to the amicable resolutions of CPO related disputes or minimising the detrimental impact on residents. Acquiring authorities appear to seek to offer less compensation through a deliberately slow process, while livelihoods are on hold pending compensation.[352]

Rehousing

---

[347] Guy Roots et al, 2nd Edition

[348] James V UK, The Law of compulsory purchase, third edition, Guy Roots et al; *Thomas v Bridgend county council,*(2011), EWCA Civ 862, (2011) RVR 241

[349] Such as in *Thomas v Bridgend county council,*(2011), EWCA Civ 862, (2011) RVR 241, where the CA held that s19(3) of the Highway Act 1980, was incompatible with art 1 of the ECHR

[350] John Pugh –Smith, When is' enough ' legally enough, Encyclopaedia of Local government law bulletin,2015

[351] Saunders V Caerphilly CBC(2015)EWHC 1632 CH

[352] Alice Belotti, Estate regeneration and Community impact, LSE, 2016

S39 of the LCA 1973[353] sets out the grounds for rehousing which is summarised by the DCLG guidance[354] for many residents affected by estate regeneration enforced by CPOs, especially those with young children, finding secure and affordable accommodation is one of the most formidable barriers they face. Many are compelled either to live on potentially hazardous and dangerous protracted construction sites, such as asbestos contaminated land, move into temporary accommodation or move out of the locality entirely, which causes a series of detrimental impacts in all areas of their lives.[355]

The new properties tend to take many years[356] to build and are largely unaffordable. The new schemes such as shared ownerships, demote residents' property ownership interests, have stricter leases and diminish residents' equity, savings, home loss and disturbance. Residents who exercise any rights to stay as tenants are subjected to intrusive means testing or inquiries into unrelated areas of their lives despite the injustice of having one's home confiscated by the same acquiring authority.[357]

Additionally, the new housing may increase social divisions such as in a widely reported case, after estate demolition or regeneration, where children's playgrounds were segregated and there are familiar cases of 'poor doors'[358] depending on the housing tenure. Such division, it is strongly argued is incompatible with A1P1 in ~~intersection with Art 14 of~~ ECHR, which prohibits discrimination.[359] Primarily because

[353] http://www.legislation.gov.uk/ukpga/1973/26/contents

[354] https://assets.publishing.service.gov.uk/government/uploads/system/uploads/attachment_data/file/571453/booklet4.pdf

[355] *PaulWatts,Its_not_for_us_Regeneration_the_2012_Olympics_and_the_gentrification_of_East_London_City_2013,* *http://www.academia.edu/6007431/;*

Zoe Williams, the real cost of regeneration,http://www.execreview.com/2017/07/the-real-cost-of-regeneration/

[356] https://www.vice.com/en_uk/article/qkq4bx/every-flat-in-a-new-south-london-development-has-been-sold-to-foreign-investors

[357] *PaulWatts,Its_not_for_us_Regeneration_the_2012_Olympics_and_the_gentrification_of_East_London_City_2013,* *http://www.academia.edu/6007431/;*

Zoe Williams, the real cost of regenerationhttp://www.execreview.com

[358] https://www.newyorker.com/culture/cultural-comment/the-poor-door-and-the-glossy-reconfiguration-of-city-life

[359] /too-poor-to-play-children-in-social-housing-blocked-from-communal-playground

https://www.theguardian.com/cities/2019/mar/25

[360] Written by Jessica Perera, Institute of Race Relations, New IRR publication provides a fresh take on housing, policing and racism in London.

economic disadvantage tends to disproportionately affect women, racial minorities[360] and those with disabilities. All of which are protected characteristics under Art 14 of ECHR as well as EA2010 and HRA 98.

Therefore, taking into account of all the above issues, it is important that compensation should proportionately reflect the genuine or manifest public interest, [361] in individual circumstances and mirror the distinction between mere restrictions, which could amount to deprivation, and an actual taking of the physical property. Most CPO affected estate regeneration residents are affected by actual physical deprivation of property with associated emotional, social and financial detriments, both immediate and long-term. The statutory compensation does not appear to reflect the emotional or intangible but equally devastating detriments. Hence making the interference and deprivation acutely disproportionate and therefore in potential breach of A1P1 discussed in more detail above. Monetary compensation although helpful is not the panacea to displacement. It should be a package that includes mandatory adequate rehousing, take into account health implications, disruption to employment, education and support networks in balance with stated proven public interest for compulsory acquisition of one's home.

An issue that resonated with the US case of *Kelo,* [362] where the issue was a taking of a longstanding home by the local authorities. Justice Scalia noted that, 'yes you are paying for it, but you are giving the money to somebody, who does not want the money, who wants to live in the house that she's lived in her whole life. That counts for nothing? *'What this lady wants is not money. No amount of money is going to satisfy her. Living in this house her whole life. She does not want to move'.* That is the sense of deep injustice of the compulsory taking of homes, which are occupied especially in cases where residents have inculcated deep roots in the locality with a sense of cultural, economic and social attachments. That is not to minimise the more transient or temporary residents affected but there is no doubt that the impact is bound to be more damaging to those with entrenched roots in the community.

Chapter 10

---

[361] As stated in Trailer and Marina(Ieven) v Sec.of State 2004

[362] Kanner, Gideon. "Kelo v. New London: Bad Law, Bad Policy, and Bad Judgment." *The Urban Lawyer*, vol. 38, no. 2, 2006, pp. 201–235. *JSTOR*, www.jstor.org/stable/27895626.

Equal treatment under ART 14 and its convergence with A1P1

Equality[363] and fairness of treatment by those affected by CPOs, is critical to avoid breach of Art 14 in tandem with Art 8 and A1P1. Article 14 has no freestanding existence in absence of other rights. For Example in conjunction with Art 8, it was held that there was a breach of Art 14 where an 'occupant was prohibited from succeeding a tenancy after the death of his same-sex partner'.[364]

Therefore, CPO affected residents claiming art 14 protections could have to establish grounds for breach in other areas such as Art 8 or A1P1. The court appears to lay emphasis as to whether there are justiciable grounds within the scope of property rights. Such as in the case of *Marck v Belgium above,* where the court found in favour of a mother who alleged discrimination in relation to the freedom to dispose her property to so called illegitimate children although the court found no violation of A1P1 per se.

Similarly, in *Gaygusuz v Austria,* the court found a breach of Art 14 where there was a denial of assistance to an applicant who was not of Austrian Nationality.[365] Perhaps it could reflect the notably lower margin of appreciation in ART 14, which is very narrow, compared to A1P1. An applicant wishing to pursue a claim under ART 14 in relation to his or her property rights would have to prove elements of A1P1, such as possession but would not necessarily need to substantiate a violation of such rights to be able to make a claim of discrimination under Art 14. The applicant would be required to establish grounds under which his or rights under art 8 or A1P1 were breached and how such interference was different from other comparators in an unjustifiable manner.[366] Once the applicant establishes grounds for consideration of the claim under Art 14 and the associated Articles such as Art 8 or A1P1, the burden then falls on the state to justify the alleged discrimination in terms of its

---

[363] https://www.echr.coe.int/Documents/Convention_ENG.pdf

[364] (*Karner v. Austria*, §§ 41-43; *Kozak v. Poland*, § 99).

[365] The right to property, Human rights handbooks, No. 10

[366] Handbook No 10, property rights under ECHR

consistency with the law whether it is a legitimate aim and it is proportionate to that aim.

The interplay of art 14 and A1P1 also applies to Art 3[367] which is reiterated in the treaty of Rome as a free standing equal-treatment guarantee although the UK has not signed that treaty.

As far as Art 14 is specifically concerned, in terms of housing in general and estate demolition in particular, there are reports from bodies like the race audit and the Institute of race relations among others, [368]which cite disparity in housing and the disproportionate effects it has on racial minorities associated with estate regeneration.[369]

These have wider potentially intergenerational effects in terms of social mobility, access to opportunity and other social indicators where there are historical economic and social disadvantages among specific communities such as racial minorities, therefore national authorities have to pay close attention to the specific needs of minorities and those with protected characteristics which might require imposing certain conditions within certain limits.[370]

---

[367] Articles 2, 3 and 14, Equal access to justice in the case-law of the European Court of Human Rights on violence against women, https://www.echr.coe.int

[368] JESSICA PERERA,The London Clearances: Race, Housing and Policing, 2019

[369] https://www.ethnicity-facts-figures.service.gov.uk/

[370] (Connors v. the United Kingdom, § 84) Chapman v UK

United Kingdom [GC], § 96; Yordanova and Others v. Bulgaria, §§ 129-130 /(Codona v. the United Kingdom

[371] just-space-response-to-panel-note-7.3-20-may-2019.pdf, https://justspacelondon.files.wordpress.com/2019/04

[372]JESSICA PERERA, The London Clearances: Race, Housing and Policing, 2019

[373] CASE OF PINE VALLEY DEVELOPMENTS LTD AND OTHERS v. IRELAND, Application no. 12742/87

Specifically, in housing and estate regeneration, reports indicate that racial minorities[371] face a disproportionate detrimental impact.[372] This would appear to therefore be incompatible with the judgment In *Chapman,* for example, where the court affirmed that restricting the use of caravans, has an impact on the applicants' respect for their home. The applicant was notably from a racial minority group which is historically disadvantaged.

The ECHR has also held that there was discrimination and therefore a breach of Art 14 in the case of *Pine valley developments Ltd V Ireland*[373], where the applicants complained of discrimination due to a refusal of planning permission in respect of the applicant in comparison to other landowners. A similar ruling found in favour of the applicant in respect of Art 14 and A1P1 in the case of *Chassgnou and others V France*[374], where it was held that legislation appeared to favour large landowners, who could use their land as they wished which put smaller farmers in a discriminatory position. A ruling that was consistent with the case *Larkos v Cyprus*[375] where *'the court held that offering differential protection to tenants against eviction – according to whether they are renting state-owned property or renting from private landlords, entailed a violation of Article 14 taken in conjunction with Article 8, due to the unjustifiable difference of treatment'.*

This would be consistent with the residents affected by CPOs who have cultural links or may be disadvantaged by being forced to areas whey they face racial discrimination.[376]In addition the ruling above is consistent with the need to treat residents fairly and equally, especially in relation to issues such as valuations of properties, rehousing and compensation, where racial minorities face a disproportionate detrimental impact on their lives. Emphasis appears to be put on a positive obligation for a member state to cultivate appropriate safeguards to the extent even a lack of legal capacity leading to dispossession without meaningful participation in the process or access to the final determination by the courts was held to be a violation of art 8, by the court having considered protection measures and their inadequacy in the national state law.[377]

---

[374] CASE OF CHASSAGNOU AND OTHERS v. FRANCE. Applications nos. 25088/94, 28331/95 and 28443/95)

[375] App no 29515/95 (Application No) ECHR 1999-I (Official Citation)

[376] (*Chapman v. the United Kingdom* [GC], § 73).

A principle that appears to have been emphasised by the UK Supreme Court,[378] where the court asserted that the EA2010 provided further protection to a group of people who fall under the protected characteristics category.[379] The implication here for CPO affected parties, especially resident occupiers, is that where there is evidence of discrimination without a legitimate and proportionate aim, there are grounds upon which Art 14 in conjunction with A1P1 or other articles like art 8 could be upheld in their favour. Thereby protecting their property rights and other associated rights.

As already discussed above, beyond ECHR and the HRA 1998, international conventions bar discrimination and other human rights abuses.

This is an extensive area that will be covered in a separate chapter under international law especially how estate regeneration enforced by CPOs is consistent with international human rights law in light of the recent criticisms of the UK by the United Nations[380] and other interventions by the UN rapporteurs[381] cited above. Therefore, the discussion of international law is in a brief context covering the universal declaration of human rights which has moral authority [382] with given legal effect under the international convention on civil and political rights.[383] Applicable to housing are articles 23, 22, 3, 14 and 26[384], inter alia, ratified by the UK in 1976.[385]It appears that clear protections against discrimination exert moral or political

---

[377] *Zehentner v. Austria*, §§ 63 and 65) / (*A.-M.V. v. Finland*, §§ 82-84 and 90).

[378] In Akerman –Livingston v Aster Communities Ltd(UKSC) 15,

[379]https://justspacelondon.files.wordpress.com/2019/04/just-space-response-to-panel-note-7.3-20-may-2019.pdf; https://www.london.gov.uk/nlp_ex_33_cover_report.pdf

[380] https://www.ohchr.org/EN/Issues/Poverty/Pages/SRExtremePovertyIndex.aspx

[381] https://www.ohchr.org/en/issues/housing/pages/housingindex.aspx

[382] http://www.un.org/en/universal-declaration-human-rights/

[383] https://www.ohchr.org/en/professionalinterest/pages/ccpr.aspx

[384] https://www.ohchr.org/en/professionalinterest/pages/ccpr.aspx

[385] our-human-rights-work/monitoring-and-promoting-un-treaties, https://www.equalityhumanrights.com/en/

diplomatic pressure on states and encouragement to implement adequate protections.[386]

It is however important to examine the provisions of art 10 1nd 11 that are relevant to the topic t hand namely estate regeneration enforced through CPOs.

Chapter 11

Art 10 and 11 of ECHR

Another aspect of ECHR that appears to be relevant to property rights and estate regeneration enforced by CPOs is the freedom of association and expression, which are covered, by Articles 10 and 11. Art 10 and 11 of ECHR are considered together here since the protections they provide are intrinsically linked.

Art 10[387] states that …

1   *Everyone has the right to freedom of expression. This right shall include freedom to hold opinions and to receive and impart information and ideas without interference by public authority and regardless of frontiers. This Article shall not prevent States from requiring the licensing of broadcasting, television or cinema enterprises.*

2.   *The exercise of these freedoms, since it carries with it duties and responsibilities, may be subject to such formalities, conditions, restrictions or penalties as are prescribed by law and are necessary in a democratic society, in the interests of national security, territorial integrity or public safety, for the prevention of*

---

[386] (*Stenegry and Adam v. France* (Dec.)).

[387] https://www.echr.coe.int/Documents/Convention_ENG.pdf

disorder or crime, for the protection of health or morals, for the protection of the reputation or rights of others, for preventing the disclosure of information received in confidence, or for maintaining the authority and impartiality of the judiciary.

Chapter 12

Art 11 and property rights

Article 11 – states that:

1. 'Everyone has the right to freedom of peaceful assembly and to freedom of association with others, including the right to form and to join trade unions for the protection of his interests.

2. No restrictions shall be placed on the exercise of these rights other than such as are prescribed by law and are necessary in a democratic society in the interests of national security or public safety, for the prevention of disorder or crime, for the protection of health or morals or for the protection of the rights and freedoms of others. This Article shall not prevent the imposition of lawful restrictions on the exercise of these rights by members of the armed forces, of the police or of the administration of the State'[388].

ECHR rights of expression or association although protected may be restricted by state authorities with certain qualifications within the law such as in the interest maintaining order or public safety. Hence any limitations on these freedoms is placed on these rights in balance with public policy grounds.[389]Authorities must ensure that the property rights, which are the issues here, are infringed or interfered with without lawful justification such as in the case of CPOs under A1P1 or Art 8.

---

[388] https://www.echr.coe.int/Documents/Convention_ENG.pdf

[389] Observer and the Guardian v the United Kingdom (1991)

The case of *Handy side v UK*,[390] mentioned above highlights the relevant issues associated with property rights, which may be applicable to CPOs. In this case, the authorities seized books published by the applicant on grounds that they contained lewd content. It was held that since state authorities have a margin of appreciation under art 10, there was no breach of either Art 10 or A1P1. The implication here in relation to CPOs is that as long as states can justify and prove their activity within the margin of appreciation accorded to states based on the facts of the case, the court could potentially hold in the respective states favour.

However, in the later case of *Ozturk v Turkey*[391], the court found that the confiscation and destruction of the applicant's book was apparently related to his prior conviction by the authorities and was therefore in breach of art 10. In addition, the court further concluded that it was therefore not necessary to consider A1P1 in the circumstances.

This later case above highlights the fact that where there is an unjustifiable and permanent expropriation of property, or infringement of another associated rights such as art 10, the court could find a breach of ECHR. Therefore, residents or parties who are faced with having their [392]property rights being expunged as well as having other rights breached may have a potential route to challenge such alleged transgressions by the state authorities.

The wider relevance to CPO affected parties is that local authorities influence and diminish the affected communities' ability to meet, organise and express themselves during the process of consultation or the entire process of acquisition.[393]

---

[390] App No 5493/72 (Application No)

A/24 (Official Citation), [1976] ECHR 5 (Other Reference)

[391] *Ozturk v Turkey*, application no. 22479/93 ,https://hudoc.echr.coe.int/eng"Ozturk v Turkey"],"documentcollectionid2":["GRAND Chamber

[393] https://www.socialhousingsoundarchive.com/westbury-estate

This reportedly happens when traditionally elected bodies known as TRAs or leaseholders forums are disbanded, [394]undermined[395] or singled out for lack of funding among other practices.[396] Such as in Lambeth council where residents' elected groups have been suspended which limits effective, representative association without influence or manipulation by the authorities concerned.

TRAs tend to be more effective and organised in challenging Local Authority decisions but there are examples where such associations have been either suspended or marginalised,[397] residents' advocates complained of being singled out, targeted or victimised.[398] Such actions are bound to have a chilling effect on residents' ability to scrutinise or challenge the decisions, actions of such public bodies, [399]therefore jeopardising residents' ability to safeguard their human rights.[400]

In many reported areas, there is no evidence to justify curtailment of those rights in the context of CPOs[401] Another issue that requires consideration is Art 2. Although not an obvious issue under CPO estate regeneration Art 2 is arguably linked to the CPO estate regeneration activities that affect the health and wellbeing of residents[402] especially the vulnerable, elderly and children. In the chapters above, reference was made to various reports that document the social, economic and racial impact on the community and individuals. Such as reports from the Runnymede trust, [403]the

---

[394] https://lambethleaseholders.wordpress.com/

[395] https://newsfromcrystalpalace.wordpress.com/2017/11/08/housing-scandal-one-council-to-choose-who-represents-tenants-and-leaseholders-on-new-residents-assembly/

[396] Tenants and Residents Associations

[397] https://lambethleaseholders.wordpress.com

[398] leaseholders-chairman-quits-amid-council-bullying-claims-green-party-councilor-says-siege-mentality-exists-in-lambeth/://newsfromcrystalpalace.wordpress.com

[399] http://lambeth.network

[400] https://www.equalityhumanrights.com/en/human-rights-act/article-11-freedom-assembly-and-association

[401] what-are-human-rights/human-rights-act/article-11-right-protest, https://www.libertyhumanrights.org.uk/human-rights/

[402] https://newsfromcrystalpalace.wordpress.com/2019/06/10/council-has-refused-us-air-monitoring-systems-tenants-chief-tells-committee-his-wife-had-to-visit-a-and-e-three-times-with-lung-inflammation

[403] Faraha Elahi and Omar Khan Ethnic inequality, Capital for all, https://www.runnymedetrust.org

institute of race relations[404] among others. Those paragraphs simply explain how that is related to Art 2 of the ECHR as discussed below.

Chapter 13

Art 2

Article 2 of ECHR[405]of state that

"1. *Everyone's right to life shall be protected by law. No one shall be deprived of his life intentionally save in the execution of a sentence of a court following his conviction of a crime for which this penalty is provided by law.*

Art 2 protects life with defences specified in Art 2(2)[406]. It asserts that governments should protect citizens from the excess, failures or illegalities of industry, which among other detriments may harm the public.[407] As highlighted in *Oneryildiz v Turkey, where violation of Art2 was found in respect of a lack of protection for citizens living near a garbage bin that led to an explosion, which caused loss of life.[408] Adding that Art 2 does not simply relate to use of force but in circumstances such as this, the authorities failed to do all they could were capable of doing to protect lives despite their knowledge of the danger to the victims. This is directly relevant to estate regeneration construction related activities where there is contamination and hazards elements, which authorities[409] are fully aware of but seem to be reluctant to take active measures to eliminate or minimise the risk to human health.[410]*.

---

[404] Jessica, Pereira, The London clearances, http://www.irr.org.uk

[405] https://www.echr.coe.int/Documents/Convention_ENG.pdf

[406] https://www.echr.coe.int/Documents/Convention_ENG.pdf

[407] Dimitri Xenos, Asserting the Right to life (Article 2, ECHR) in the Context of Industry 8 German L.J. 231 (2007)

[408] Oneryildiz v. Turkey, 2004-XII Eur. Ct. HR 79, First, Do No Harm: Human Rights and Efforts to Combat Climate Change 38 Ga. J. Int'l & Comp. L. 593 (2009-2010

Art 2 is therefore relevant due to the reported adverse impact on residents' well-being, health[411] and public safety during protracted large scale construction projects[412] associated with universally known potentially harmful effects such as vibration, fumes, noise, asbestos contamination,[413] that residents are subjected to for prolonged periods[414] which is clearly incompatible with Art2. However, enforcement remains a formidable impediment due to lack of resources and imbalance of power between affected residents and local authorities in concert with developers as observed by Anna Minton.[415]

Chapter 14

Art 3

As indicated under Art 2,[416] a similar observation arguably applies to CPO estate regeneration under Art 3, if there is evidence of an arguable link between aspects of inhuman or degrading treatment under art 3 and CPO estate regeneration activities.

---

[409] https://www.theguardian.com/environment/2019/may/04/brownfield-site-new-homes-building-wrecking-health-southall

[410] https://www.theguardian.com/environment/2019/may/04/brownfield-site-new-homes-building-wrecking-health-southall

[411] https://www.annaminton.com/groundcontrol

[412] https://www.theguardian.com/environment/2019/may/04/brownfield-site-new-homes-building-wrecking-health-southall

[413] John L Adgate, Sook Ja Cho, Bruce H Alexander, Gurmurthy Ramachandran, Katherine K Raleigh

Jean Johnson,, Rita B Messing, A L Williams, James Kelly & Gregory C Pratt

Modelling community asbestos exposure near a vermiculite processing facility: Impact of human activities on cumulative exposure, Journal Of Exposure Science And Environmental Epidemiology

2011/02/23

[414] Brownfield-site-new-homes-building-wrecking-health-southallhttps://www.theguardian.com/environment/2019/may/04

[415] Anna Minton, 'Scaring the living daylights out of people': The local lobby and the failure of democracy

1 Feb 2013

[416] Marcia Gibson, Hilary Thomson, Ade Kearns & Mark Petticrew (2011) Understanding the Psychosocial Impacts of Housing Type: Qualitative Evidence from a Housing and Regeneration Intervention, Housing Studies, 26:04, 555-573, DOI: 10.1080/02673037.2011.559724

Art 3 states that No one shall be subjected to torture or to inhuman or degrading treatment or punishment.

Art 3 prohibits torture as well as inhuman and degrading treatment. Treatment *can be considered inhuman when it causes physical or mental pain or degrading when it debases or humiliates a person beyond that is usual from punishment*[417]

In property or estate regeneration related cases,[418] if there is evidence of sustained actions that amount to inhuman and degrading treatment, associated with CPO activity,[419] like hazardous elements, it is arguable that those affected could bring action under these grounds. However, it appears that the bar in property related terms is too high for potential applicants to cross the admissibility threshold. For example, in *Predojevic and others v Solvenia,* the court found as inadmissible claims that deprivation of pension amounted to inhuman and degrading treatment.

In spite of a high bar or threshold to satisfy Art 3 requirements in association with property rights, its arguable, therefore that if there are clear or identifiable facts from which the court can infer inhuman or degrading treatment art 3 could be engaged. Such an example could be where construction hazards[420] like industrial dust, noise, lead, asbestos or other contaminants, which cause or are linked to illness or severe emotional distress.[421]Therefore, although it is likely that the rights under art 3 associated with CPOs and estate regeneration could require more hard evidence, it would appear that if there is a nexus between inhuman and degrading treatment, associated with estate regeneration, there could be circumstances where potential applicants can make an arguable case.

---

[417] https://www.libertyhumanrights.org.uk/human-rights/what-are-human-rights/human-rights-act/article-3-no-torture

[418] Wellbeing and Regeneration, reflection from Carpenter estate, Alexandre Apsan Frediani, Stephanie Butcher and Paul Watt

[419] Regeneration and Well-Being in East-London: Stories from Carpenters Estate

[420] https://www.theguardian.com/environment/2019/may/04/brownfield-site-new-homes-building-wrecking-health-southall

[421]https://www.theguardian.com/uk-news/2019/jul/07/court-challenge-homes-southall-london-gasworks-brownfield-development

Conclusion

The above observations are a starting point in terms of laying the foundation to examine the impact of housing estate regeneration or expropriation enforced through CPOs on residents, and its compatibility with human rights law. This would create a basis upon which a plausible determination of the effectiveness human rights law in challenging estate regeneration related human rights abuses could be made.

From the initial analysis so far, there appears to be emerging evidence or existing evidence of incompatibility with human rights law. However, further analysis is necessary to obtain a more rounded understanding of the issue and the mechanisms needed for residents to fight back and protect their human rights violated by those pursuing estate regeneration through the CPO process.

The upcoming editions will look into greater detail international law highlighting, the lived or documented experiences of specific communities as documented, and the different methods that residents have deployed so far in challenging estate regeneration, an assessment of the, the effectiveness of current remedies and then consider suggestions for reform. To ensure that, human rights law in this area has real teeth. Otherwise, if there is a perception that human rights law or indeed courts cannot protect residents against the interests of the powerful or some local authorities in concert with private entities, as mentioned above, then there is a real danger that faith in the legal or judicial system could further evaporate. Which will leave the decades of progress in human rights law and the protection it offers in real peril.

Bibliography

1.   MHCLG: Guidance on compulsory purchase process and the Crichel down Rules for the disposal of surplus land acquired by, or under the threat of, compulsion,

https://www.gov.uk/government/publications/compulsory-purchase-process-and-the-crichel-down-rules-guidance.

2. The Implications of Kilo in Land Use Law, Symposium Articles: Keynote Address - Kelo, Lingle, and San Remo Hotel, Santa Clara Law Review, Vol. 46, Issue 4 (2006), pp. 787-810 Curtin, Daniel J. Jr

3. Globalization, Communities and Human Rights: Community-Based Property Rights and Prior Informed Consent,2006 Sutton Colloquium Article, Denver Journal of International Law and Policy, Vol. 35, Issue 3 & 4 (Summer-Fall 2007),pp. 413 428 https://heinonline.org/419

4. Human Rights and Property Rights [article] United States Law Review, Vol. 64, Issue 11 (November 1930), pp. 581-594 Blume, Fred H.

5. Equating Human Rights and Property Rights--The Need for Moral Judgement in an Economic Analysis of Law and Social Policy, Ohio State Law Journal, Vol. 47, Issue 1 (1986), pp. 163-200 Malloy, Robin Paul

6. Douglas Maxwell, Journal of planning & Environmental Law, Article 1 of the First protocol: A paper tiger in the face of compulsory purchase orders for private profit?

7. Towards a Compulsory Purchase Code: https://www.lawcom.gov.uk/project/towards-a-compulsory-purchase-code/

8. Compulsory acquisition of land: Developers, by PLC Property https://uk.practicallaw.thomsonreuters.com

9.   Planning Act 2016: http://www.housing.org.uk/resource-library/browse/the-housing-and- planning-act-2016/

10.   Kept in the Dark; https://www.transparency.org.uk

11.   The Law of compulsory purchase, third edition, Guy Roots et al

12.   Estate-regeneration-why-people-power-is-forcing-london-to-rethink-housing; developers-alarmed-at-khans-plans-to-give-estate-residents-power; https://www.architectsjournal.co.uk/news

13.   Mayor-and-conservatives-dispute-latest-London-housing-stats; https://www.insidehousing.co.uk/news/news/ https://www.bbc.co.uk

14.   Phil Hubbard, Loretta Lees. (2018) the right to community? *City* 22:1, pages 8-25.

15.   https://www.transparency.org.uk/faulty-towers

16.   https://architectsforsocialhousing.wordpress.com/2016/03/24/the-doomsday-book/).

17.   Towards a paradigm of Southern urbanism Seth Schindler City Volume 21, 2017 - Issue 1Published online: 6 Mar 2017

18.   Reconstructing Berlin: Materiality and meaning in the symbolic politics of urban space

19.   Dominik Bartmanski et al.City Volume 22, 2018 - Issue 2 Published online: 17 Apr 2018

20.   Editorial Editor-in-Chief's note: What/whose order is to be asserted in the city?

21.   Bob Catterall City Volume 22, 2018 - Issue 2

22.   Published online: 7 Jun 2018

23.   The right to community?: Legal geographies of resistance on London's gentrification frontiers

24.   Phil Hubbard et al. City Volume 22, 2018 - Issue 1 Published online: 15 Mar 2018 editorial

25.   Editorial: The right to assert the order of things in the city Luke R. Barnesmoore City

26.   Volume 22, 2018 - Issue 2 Published online: 7 Jun 2018

27.   Stuart Hodkinson, Chris Essen, (2015) "Grounding accumulation by dispossession in everyday life: The unjust geographies of urban regeneration under the Private Finance Initiative", International Journal of Law in the Built Environment, Vol. 7 Issue: 1, pp.72-91, https://doi.org/10.1108/IJLBE-01-2014-0007

28.   Towards a new perspective on the role of the city in social movements: Urban Policy after the 'Arab Spring' Raffael Beier City Volume 22, 2018 - Issue 2 Published online: 17 Apr 2018

29.   Adonis, A., and B. Davies, eds. 2015. City Villages: More Homes, Better Communities. London: IPPR. https://www.ippr.org/publications/city-villages-more-homes-better-communities

30.   The London Borough of Southwark (Aylesbury Estate Site 1B-1C) Compulsory Purchase Order 2014 ('the Order': http://35percent.org/img/Decision_Letter_Final.pdf

31. Prime minister pledges to transform sink estates: https://www.gov.uk/government/news/prime-minister-pledges-to-transform-sink-estates: 10 January 2016

32. 'Cameron time to demolish sink estates': https://www.bbc.co.uk/news/av/uk-politics-35275516/cameron-time-to-demolish-worst-sink-housing-estates, 10 January 2016

33. Compulsory purchase and Compensation: An Overview of the system in England and Wales, By Frances Plimmer.

34. Paul Watt & Anna Minton (2016) London's housing crisis and its activisms, City, 20:2, 204-221, https://doi.org/10.1080/13604813.2016.1151707

35. Participation in the right of access to adequate housing, 14 Tulsa J Comp. & Intl L 269 2006 -2007, Hein online

36. Republic of SA v Grootboom & others 2000(11) BCLR 1169

37. Evadne Grant, Enforcing Social and Economic Rights: The right to adequate housing in south Africa, 15 Afr, J, intl & Comp,L 1 (2007), Hein online

38. The requirements for a compelling case in the public interest to justify a CPO (High Court) by Practical Law Planning: In Horada v Secretary of State for Communities and Local Government [2015] EWHC 2512 (Admin), Volume: 25 issue: 1, page(s): 115-135

39. The privatization of council housing, Norman Ginsburg, Issue published: February 1, 2005 https://doi.org/10.1177%2F0261018305048970

40. Haringey Council votes to cancel development vehicle despite Lendlease warning 18 July 2018:https://www.insidehousing.co.uk/news/news/haringey-council-votes-to-cancel-development-vehicle-despite-lendlease-warning-57250:

41. Watt, P. 2015. "The IMD as a WMD in the Regeneration of London Council Estates: Tackling Spatial Inequalities and Producing Socio-spatial Injustice." Paper at Tackling Spatial Inequalities Conference, Sheffield, September 10

42. Paul Watt (2009) Housing Stock Transfers, Regeneration and State-Led Gentrification in London, Urban Policy and Research, 27:3, 229-242, https://doi.org/10.1080/08111140903154147

43. Pam Douglas & Joanne Parkes (2016) 'Regeneration' and 'consultation' at a Lambeth council estate, City, 20:2, 287-291, https://doi.org/10.1080/13604813.2016.1143683

44. Bracking V Secretary of state for works and pensions [2013] EWCA Civ 1345, [2014] Eq LR 60

45. Knock it down or Do it UP? The challenge of estate regeneration https://www.london.gov.uk/about-us/london-assembly/london-assembly-publications/knock-it-down-or-do-it

46. HPA 2016 and how it affects housing associations: http://www.lag.org.uk/magazine/2016/07/a-devastating-blow-to-social-housing-in-england.aspx

47. EA2010Equality Act 2010 (Specific Duties and Public Authorities) Regulations 2017. PSED: specific duties in England, Practical Law UK Practice Note

48.   CPA 1965: Compulsory Purchase Act 1965.

49.   CP (VD) A 1981: Compulsory Purchase (Vesting Declarations) Act 1981.

50.   LCA 1961: Land Compensation Act 1961.

51.   LCA 1973: Land Compensation Act 1973.

52.   TCPA 1990: Town and Country Planning Act 1990

53.   https://www.libertyhumanrights.org.uk/

54.   https://www.equalityhumanrights.com/en/about-us

55.   https://www.ohchr.org/en/professionalinterest/pages/ccpr.aspx

56.   https://echr.coe.int/

57.   British Institute of human rights www.Bihr.org.uk

58.   Chartered Institute of Housing www. Cih.org

59.   DCLG www.coommunites.gov.uk

60.   Housing Law practitioners Association www. Hipa.org.uk

61.   The Law Society www.lawsociety.org

62.   https://savecressingham.wordpress.com/

63.   http://www.insidehousing.co.uk/cressingham-gardens-regeneration-approved-in-high-court/7018185.article

64.   http://35percent.org/2013-06-08-the-heygate-diaspora/

65.   https://www.southwarknews.co.uk/news/council-given-permission-take-aylesbury-estate-cpo-case-high-court-disappointing-blow-campaigners/

66.   http://www.shelter.org.uk

67.   http://www.axethehousingact.org.uk/page/2/ on

68. Localism Act 2011, https://uk.practicallaw.thomsonreuters.com/1-504-2706

69. Housing and equality law, By Robert Brown, Arden Chambers

    a. https://uk.practicallaw.thomsonreuters.com/w-012-0034

70. https://www.ashurst.com/en/news-and-insights/legal-updates/compulsory-purchase-life-after-aylesbury/

71. https://www.birketts.co.uk/insights/legal-updates/compulsory-purchase-and-what-to-do-about-it

72. https://assets.publishing.service.gov.uk/government/uploads/system/uploads/attachment_data/file/551698/ECHR_Memorandum.pdf

73. https://www.burges-salmon.com/news-and-insight/legal-updates/alternative-development-proposals-how-do-they-affect-cpo-validity/

74. Housing and Regeneration Act 2008, Housing and Regeneration Act 2008

    a. http://www.opsi.gov.uk/acts/acts2008/ukpga_20080017_en_1

75. Donnelly, Jack. Universal human rights in theory and practice. Cornell University Press, 2013.

76. Human rights Act 1998: https://uk.practicallaw.thomsonreuters.com/0-506-9287

77. Lexis   Nexis:
    https://www.lexisnexis.com/uk/lexispsl/publiclaw/document/413481/5DF5-Dealing_with_a_human_rights_challengehttps://www.lexisnexis.com/uk/lexispsl/publicl

78. New law journal: https://www.newlawjournal.co.uk/

79. Practicallaw:https://uk.practicallaw.thomsonreuters.com/Browse/Home/Practice/P
     ublicLaw

80. Hansard- https://hansard.parliament.uk/

81. https://www.leighday.co.uk/News/2015/November-2015/Cressingham-Gardens-
     tenant-wins-High-Court-legal

82. https://www.theguardian.com/commentisfree/2017/oct/25/labour-council-
     regeneration-housing-crisis-high-court-judge

83. The Secretary of states' ruling re: Town and Country Planning Act 1990 Section
     226(1) (a), Acquisition of Land Act 1981 The London Borough of Southwark
     (Aylesbury Estate Site 1B-1C) Compulsory Purchase Order 2014 ('

84. https://hsfnotes.com/realestatedevelopment/2016/09/28/a-new-right-to-a-
     community-decision-by-the-secretary-of-state-not-to-confirm-the-cpo-for-
     aylesbury-estate/

85. Compulsory_purchase_process_and_the_Crichel_Down_Rules_-
     _guidance_updated_180228;https://assets.publishing.service.gov.uk/government/u
     ploads/system/uploads/attachment_data/file/684529/

86. http://www.legislation.gov.uk/ukpga/2010/15/

87. https://www.burges-salmon.com/news-and-insight/legal-updates/the-
     neighbourhood-planning-act-2017/

88. https://www.legislation.gov.uk/ukpga/2010/15/section/149

89. https://assets.publishing.service.gov.uk/government/uploads/system/uploads/attac
     hment_data/file/475271/cpo_guidance.pdf

90.   Knock   It   Down   Or   Do   It   Up;
      https://www.london.gov.uk/sites/default/files/gla_migrate_files_destination/

91.   London's   Housing   Crisis   Worse   for   Ethnic   Minorities   22   March
      2016;;https://www.runnymedetrust.org/news/638/272

92.   Dispossession   the   great   social   housing   swindle:

      https://www.dispossessionfilm.com/

93.   City   Villages,   More   Homes,   Better   communities:

      https://www.ippr.org/files/publications/pdf/city-villages_Mar2015.pdf

94.   Shelter. 2015. Homes for our Children. How much of the Housing Market is

      Affordable?,https://england.shelter.org.uk/Homes_for_our_Children.pdf

95.   The-story-of-the-camberwell-submarine-4618,
      https://www.insidehousing.co.uk/insight/insight

96.   Convention for the Protection of Individuals with regard to Automatic Processing
      of Personal Data Strasbourg, 28.I.1981 https://rm.coe.int/CoE

97.   Legal Challenges to Implementing CPOs and Decisions under the Crichel down

      Rules by Tim Mould QC http://www.landmarkchambers.co.uk/userfiles/TM.pdf

98.   The use of compulsory purchase powers for regeneration by Elvin QC,

      http://www.landmarkchambers.co.uk s. 149 of the Equality Act 2010

99.   Land Compensation Claims: The Claimants Perspective by Simon Pickles

      Landmark   Chambers   http://www.landmarkchambers.co.uk/cases-

      compulsory_purchase_compensation.aspx

100. Compulsory purchase orders: stage 4, CPO compensation procedure: flowchart by

      Practical Law Planning, https://uk.practicallaw.thomsonreuters.com/2-629-7353

101. Twenty years later-Assessing the significance of the Human Rights Act 1998 to the residential possession proceedings, By Ian Loveland http://openaccess.city.ac.uk/17163/

102. Housing Act 1988 https://www.legislation.gov.uk/id/ukpga/1988/50

103. R on the application of Sainsbury's supermarket ltd) V Wolverhampton city Council (2010) UKSC

104. Waters v welsh development agency (2004)1WLR 1304

105. David Elvin QC paper, Use of compulsory purchase powers for regeneration, http://www.landmarkchambers.co.uk

106. Countryside Alliance v Attorney General [2007] UKHL 52

107. Article 1 of the first Protocol to the ECHR: protection of property, Practical Law UK Practice Note, https://uk.practicallaw.thomsonreuters.com/8-385-5732

108. Article 6 of the ECHR: right to a fair hearing Housing:

109. https://uk.practicallaw.thomsonreuters.com/2-385-8106

110. Part VII of the Housing Act 1996

111. Demolition or refurbishment of social housing? https://www.ucl.ac.uk/engineering-exchange/research-projects/2018/nov/demolition-or-refurbishment-social-housing

112. Stanton, J. (2014). The Big Society and Community Development: Neighbourhood Planning under the Localism Act. Environmental Law Review, 16(4), 262–276.

113. Murungaru v Home Secretary [2008] EWCA Civ 1015

114. Fazia Ali v The United Kingdom - 40378/10 Court (Fourth Section)) [2015] ECHR 924

115. Belfast City Council v Miss Behavin' Ltd [2007] UKHL 19

116. James V UK (A98 (1986 E.H.R.R 123 (ECHR)

117. Sporrong and Lönnroth [1982] 5 EHRR 35

118. Le Compte, Van Leuven and De Meyere v Belgium [1981] ECHR 3.

119. Bryan v United Kingdom [1995] ECHR 50, (1996) 21 EHRR 342

120. Begum v London Borough of Tower Hamlets [2003] UKHL 5

121. Lithgow and others v UK [1986] 8 EHRR 329)

122. Chapman v. the United Kingdom [GC], § 96;

123. Yordanova and Others v. Bulgaria, §§ 129-130

124. Zehentner v. Austria, §§ 63 and 65) / (A.-M.V. v. Finland, §§ 82-84 and 90).

125. Qazi v Harrow LBC (2003 UKHL 43: (2004) 1 AC 983 (HL)

126. Salvesen V Riddell(2013) UKSC 22: 2013 SC(U.K.S.C) 236(SC)

127. López Ostra v. Spain, §§ 56-58,

128. Moreno Gómez v. Spain, § 61.

129. Di Sarno and Others v. Italy, § 112).

130. Hatton and Others v. the United Kingdom [GC], § 96;

131. Moreno Gómez v. Spain, § 53)

132. Fadeyeva v. Russia, § 69.

133.   (Asselbourg and Others v. Luxembourg (dec.)).

134.   Martínez Martínez and Pino Manzano v. Spain,

135.   (Hardy and Maile v. the United Kingdom

136.   (Hatton and Others v. the United Kingdom [GC]

137.   https://www.facebook.com/Savewestburysw8-804075296314550/

138.   https://twitter.com/savewestburysw8

139.   WestburySW8 a diary of Housing Estate Expropriation and Displacement-A lived experience.

HUMAN RIGHTS AND HOUSING ESTATES REGENERATION

By Shemi Esquire

Exclusively for JEB

This text analyses human rights under ECHR/ HRA 1998 in relation to Housing Estate regeneration enforced by CPOs. Although there are similarities with other UK devolved areas like Scotland, the acts here largely refer to England and wales.

Thanks to all those who made comments on the draft thesis chapter.[1]

---

[1] S Keenan -supervisor

Table of contents

Introduction

ECHR /HRA 98 Articles

Art 8

Art 6

A1P1

Art 2

Art 3

Art 10

Art 11

International legal issues

Conclusion

Bibliography

The aim of this text is to assess whether human rights law is an effective mechanism to challenge the harm caused by housing estate regeneration effected by the use of compulsory purchase orders in the United Kingdom.

The focus of this text relates to the actions of local authorities or public bodies that attract the jurisdiction of the ECHR and the applicable international human rights law.[2]

The book analyses any potential or existing human rights breaches associated with estate regeneration under the ECHR regime and briefly discusses the relevant international human rights law. International human rights law although discussed briefly below requires a separate chapter in terms of assessing how international human rights law safeguards against violations associated with CPO enforced estate regeneration. The ECHR rights examined here which are associated with the use of CPOs in housing estate demolition, include the right to a peaceful and quiet enjoyment of one's home, *respect for the home (Art 8), fairness, transparency and the expeditious nature of the whole process (Art 6), equality of treatment (Art 14), freedom of association, expression (Art 9 and 10), Art 13 dealing with Just compensation or the appropriate legal remedies, Art 2(right to life), Equal treatment, impact on children and applicable international law as indicated in detail below.*

The ECHR rights above are juxtaposed with the underlying practical policies, practices, decisions and impact on individuals or the wider community. Commencing with the initial decisions, consultation process, internal processes, viability reports, environmental issues, equality matters, planning permission and the eventual adverse impact on residents in the respective communities. The impact on communities is assessed by examining fundamental life indicators like employment, finances, culture, health, the disproportionate impact on racial minorities[3] and whether the statutory compensation is fair or equitable.[4]

By simple definition, compulsory purchase orders [5](CPOs) are a legal mechanism deployed by acquiring authorities to acquire land[6] which may be occupied or encumbered with competing property or legal interests through compulsion.[7]

---

[2] https://www.un.org/en/universal-declaration-human-rights

[3] 'It's not for us': Regeneration, the 2012 Olympics and the gentrification of East London, City, 2013

[4] Alice Belotti, Estate Regeneration and Community Impacts https://www.unicef.org/child-rights-conventionChallenges and lessons for social landlords, developers and local councils,2016

[5] Compulsory purchase orders , https://www.legislation.gov.uk/ukpga/1981/67/section/1

[6] /Knock It Down Or Do It Up pdf, https://www.london.gov.uk

[7] https://www.legislation.gov.uk/ukpga/1981/67/section/1

CPOs *'require approval of a confirming minister under the Acquisition of Land Act 198'.*[8]   There are various enabling powers available and the determination to authorise will partly depend on the specific powers used.   Such public' bodies with statutory powers include 'local authorities, national parks, some executive agencies, the Homes and Communities Agency, health service bodies and government ministers. This is discussed in greater detail in other chapters.

There is a detailed process of CPO processes and various statutory requirements, discussed in other chapters. The focus of this book is not to discuss the detailed statutory CPO process but rather a detailed analysis of the detrimental impact on parties with interest in the land and whether such detrimental effects are compatible with human rights law.

Chapter 1

Overview of aspects of human rights law related to estate regeneration through the use of CPOs

Human rights[9] should be fundamental consideration in the authorisation process of compulsory purchase orders although this is not always the case in practice as discussed in greater detail below. Adherence to human rights law during the CPO process is emphasised in the government guidance, which states *that 'the purposes for which the compulsory purchase order is made',* should *'justify interfering with the human rights of those with an interest in the land affected.*[10]   But the guidance also refers to a public sector duty requirement[11]   which by interpretation indicates that a failure to 'have proper regard to the public sector equality duty', related to affordable

[8] f-guidance-on-compulsory-purchase-and-the-crichel-down-rules-for-the-disposal-of-surplus-land-.

[9] See "Tesco Stores Limited v Secretary of State for the Environment and Others (Full Report)". *Journal of planning and environment law* (0307-4870), p. 581.

[10] Guidance-on-compulsory-purchase-and-the-crichel-down-rules-for-the-disposal-of-surplus-land-pdf

[11] In R (on the application of Reading BC v SoS DCL

housing, social infrastructure contributions and a vacancy credit policy[12] could be found to be unlawful.

The Government guidance further states that *'all public sector acquiring authorities are bound by the Public Sector Equality Duty as set out in section 149 of the Equality Act 2010. In exercising their compulsory purchase and related powers (e.g. powers of entry), these acquiring authorities must have regard to the effect of any differential impacts on groups with protected characteristics. For example, an important use of compulsory purchase powers is to help regenerate run down areas. Although low income is not a protected characteristic, it is not uncommon for people from ethnic minorities, the elderly or people with a disability to be overrepresented in low-income groups. As part of the Public Sector Equality Duty, acquiring authorities must have due regard to the need to promote equality of opportunity between persons who share a relevant protected characteristic and persons who do not share it.*

This might mean that the acquiring authority devises a process which promotes equality of opportunity by addressing particular problems that people with certain protected characteristics might have (e.g. making sure that documents are accessible for people with sight problems or learning difficulties and that people have access to advocates or advice.[13]

Despite the clear government, guidance above it appears that adherence to such guidance is often inadequate or arguably non-existent. To the extent that even a council lawyer expressed doubt or surprise, as to how the PSED[14] would apply to racial minorities.[15]

---

[12] Saira Kabir Sheikh QC, JPL, 2015

[13] CPO guidance, https://assets.publishing.service.gov.uk

[14] Nlp_ex_33b_appendix_2_legal_note.pdf , https://www.london.gov.uk/sites/default/files/

[15] Lambeth council lawyer, apart from disability, his client did not understand how THI applied to racial minorities; https://twitter.com/saveWestburySW8; https://www.facebook.com/Savewestburysw8-804075296314550/; Human Rights today blog

The CPO process in many respects is deemed to be unfair because the acquiring body or authority is also the main driver of the process as[16] documented by various reports highlighted above in detail, by entities like independent observers,[17] the Runnymede trust,[18] academics[19] among others.

In summary, the effects on residents include displacement,[20] financial disenfranchisement, dispossession,[21] environmental hazards,[22] disproportionate effect on racial minorities,[23] adverse health impact on residents, especially children, elderly and vulnerable adults. This is worsened by the unfair process, imbalance of resources and lack of adequate or meaningful access to an independent decision maker during the process, [24]which makes recourse to courts a complicated, cumbersome and expensive affair. From such observations, it would appear that there is at the very least prima facie evidence of possible incompatibility with human rights law, which is discussed in more detail below. The various aspects of the relevant human rights law are discussed below starting with ECHR which incorporates HRA 98.

---

[16]DCLG Guidance-on-compulsory-purchase-and-the-crichel-down-rules-for-the-disposal-of-surplus-land

[17] Anna Minton, GROUND CONTROL, Fear and Happiness in the Twenty-First Century City, by Anna Minton, Published by Penguin Books, paperback original, 26th June 2012; Anne Rendell (2017) 'Arry's Bar: condensing and displacing on the Aylesbury Estate, The Journal of Architecture, 22:3, 532-554, DOI: 10.1080/13602365.2017.1310125;

[18] UK NGOs' Alternative Report Submission to the UN Committee on the Elimination of Racial Discrimination with regard to the UK Government's 21st to 23rd Periodic Reports June 2016 Drafted by THE RUNNYMEDE TRUST

[19] Hubbard P and Lees L, "The Right to Community?" (2018) 22 City 8

Social exclusion, Paul Watt (2013) 'It's not for us', City; Paul Watt, Housing Stock Transfers, Regeneration and State-Led Gentrification in London Article in Urban Policy and Research.

Social exclusion, Paul Watt (2013) 'It's not for us', City; Paul Watt, Housing Stock Transfers, Regeneration and State-Led Gentrification in London Article in Urban Policy and Research.

[20] Alice Belotti, Challenges and lessons for social landlords, developers and local councils, 2016

[21] Demolition-watch-submission,http://www.demolitionwatchlondon.com, 14-march-2017,

[22] https://www.theguardian.com/environment/2019/may/04/brownfield-site-new-homes-building-wrecking-health-southall

[23] Jessica Perera, The-London-clearances-race-housing-and-policing, http://www.irr.org.uk

[24]Alice Belotti, Challenges and lessons for social landlords, developers and local councils, 2016;

Dispossession, The great social housing swindle, https://www.dispossessionfilm.com,

Chapter 2

ECHR Jurisdiction

The UK is a signatory to the ECHR,[25] which incorporated the Human Rights Act 1998 fundamental freedoms into UK domestic law. This therefore implies that the HRA 98 Act has to be read and given effect in compatibility with convention rights by public authorities, in terms of their processes, decisions, effect or impact thereof which by virtue of s3 of the HRA 1998.[26] Section 4 of the HRA 1998[27] refers to declaration of compatibility of local legislation with the HRA 98 while Section 6 of HRA 98 makes it unlawful for a public authority to act in a manner that is incompatible with convention rights and may apply to organisations which perform public functions.[28]

Furthermore, although UK courts do not have a requirement to make identical decisions to the ECHR, they have to take into account ECHR decisions.[29] Any person affected can bring a legal complaint but victims need to have standing under the CPO and the court can look at substance rather than form. A pressure group can be a victim if it shows that it is affected but it is for public authorities to show compatibility with ECHR rights. There is however a possibility of the complaint being rejected if it is raised too late.[30]

---

[25] The Law of compulsory purchase, third edition, Guy Roots et al

[26] http://www.legislation.gov.uk/ukpga/1998/42/section/3; Also See *nutshells, Human rights ;(state year?) See also HA1985-s7-Compulsory purchase/Human rights act guide to practitioners-Christopher Baker.*

[27] http://www.legislation.gov.uk/ukpga/1998/42/section/4

[28] http://www.legislation.gov.uk/ukpga/1998/42/section/6

[29] https://www.legislation.gov.uk/ukpga/1998/42/section/4

[30] https://www.legislation.gov.uk/ukpga/1998/42/contents

In dealing with the implementation of the ECHR incorporated rights or decisions, states possess a margin of appreciation in areas such as housing. It is argued that this is due to housing being part of the social economic policy of a state and this could require unique solutions unless there is a manifest unreasonable foundation.[31]

However, that assertion could be interpreted differently from the perspective of the international convention rights as highlighted by the UN Rapporteur on human rights.[32] The alternative argument would be that since housing is a basic human need, nothing warrants derogation from protection of that basic human need (shelter) especially in economies that have extensive resources such as the UK.[33]

Specific ECHR rights and relation to Estate regeneration

The rights protected by the ECHR are sixteen in total. These are categorised as absolute, limited or qualified as indicated by Andrew Drzemczewski.[34] From a strictly legal perspective, property rights fall in the qualified category but are human rights that are no lesser than any other human rights As already highlighted above, the most applicable human rights articles associated with CPOs include, *Art 2, Art 8, A1P1, Art 6, ART 14, Art 3, 10, 11, 13, 41 of the ECHR* incorporating the HRA 1998 and international convention on human rights.

As a summary and as indicated above, Art 3[35] relates to inhuman and degrading treatment, Art 6 protects the right for a fair, expeditious and impartial process[36], Art 8 protects respect for a home and home environment,[37] while Article 1 of the first

---

[31] ECHR; https://www.echr.coe.int/Convention_ENG.pdf

[32] Special Rapporteur on extreme poverty and human rights; https://www.ohchr.orgExtremePoverty

[33] https://data.oecd.org/united-kingdom.htm

[34] https://scholarlycommons.law.wlu.edu/cgi/

[35] ECHR, https://www.echr.coe.int

[36] ECHR, https://www.echr.coe.int

[37] ECHR, https://www.echr.coe.int/Convention_ENG.pdf

protocol,[38] safeguards against unjustifiable, disproportionate interference in the peaceful and quite enjoyment of one's home and possessions[39].

Art 2 protects the right to life and by default health. In estate regeneration, the argument advanced here is that projects which threaten public health or public safety may trigger proceedings under article 2. ART 10 protects freedom of expression, Art 11 protects freedoms of association, ART13 deals with compensation and Art 41 specifies remedies. Article one of the first Protocol refers to principles of law and international law underlining the payment of compensation in as far as money can be compensation.[40] A1P1[41] refers to principles of international law by payment of compensation in as far as money can compensate the affected persons.

However, when considering compensation per se, under the official CPO guidance cited above, a distinction is made between a CPO where land is taken and where land is not taken. This is because a CPO could proceed through imposition of restrictions, which amount to a taking or interference with the use or enjoyment, or ownership of the land but no actual physical land is taken. Therefore, it is arguable that to maintain fairness, in terms of compensation, there is a need for balancing that distinction with the public interest, as highlighted by both statute[42] and human rights law.[43]

Other jurisdictions related to estate regeneration and human rights law

International law [44]

[38] Referred to as A1P1 for brevity

[39] ECHR, https://www.echr.coe.int/Convention_ENG.pdf

[40] ECHR, https://www.echr.coe.int/Convention_ENG.pdf

[41] ECHR, https://www.echr.coe.int/Documents/Guide_Art_1_Protocol_1_ENG.pdf

[42]ECHR, https://www.legislation.gov.uk/ukpga/1973/26/section/1

[43] ECHR, https://www.echr.coe.int/Documents/Guide_Art_1_Protocol_1_ENG.pdf

As mentioned above, among the key protections for those affected by estate regeneration mandated by CPOs, is A1P1, which makes an explicit reference to principles of international law.[45] A1P1 states that, ...'*every natural person or legal person is entitled to the peaceful enjoyment of his possessions and no one shall be deprived of his possessions except in the public interest and subject to the conditions provided for by law and by the general principles of international law'.*[46]

Such reference to international law therefore necessitates an examination of the wider international human rights law applicable to estate regeneration using CPOs. It is also important to point out that the UK is party to the Universal Declaration of Human rights[47]and other related conventions such as[48]the United Nations convention on economic, social and cultural rights which invoke 'the right of everyone to an adequate standard of living for himself and his family, including adequate housing.[49]

However, in notable cases[50] reference to principles[51] of international law, [52]was stated to be limited to persons who are not nationals. This restriction to non-nationals reflected in these cases requires further exploration. It would appear or it is possible part of the reasoning is that the architects of ECHR intended to allow non-nationals to secure their convention rights directly without the inbuilt disadvantages they would

---

[44] OHCHR, https://www.ohchr.org

[45] Egon Scweb, The Protection of the Right of Property of Nationals under the First Protocol to the European Convention on Human Rights, *The American Journal of Comparative Law*

Vol. 13, No. 4 (Autumn, 1964), pp. 518-541

[46] Guide on Article 1 of Protocol No. 1 to the European Convention on Human Rights Protection of property Updated on 31 August 2019, https://www.echr.coe.int/Documents/Guide_Art_1_Protocol_1_ENG.pdf
[47] http://www.un.org/en/universal-declaration-human-rights/

[48] incidentally I write this in the UN HW library in Geneva-7th1019

[49] OCHCHR, https://www.ohchr.org/Documents/ProfessionalInterest/ccpr.pdf

[50] in Lithgow v UK and James v UK

[51] Deborah Rook, Property Law and Human rights, 2001

[52] https://www.ohchr.org/en/professionalinterest/pages/internationallaw.aspx

face in the national legal system. Such disadvantages could include discrimination on the grounds of nationality, race or other grounds generally associated with being a non-national of a specific country, which would not necessarily apply to nationals. It could also be argued that nationals could be arguably protected by their local jurisdiction but this remains a very unclear rationale which needs further scrutiny.

Apart from the direct provisions of international law, there is also international scrutiny and domestic pressure to comply with international law[53] as evidenced by a report from the UNRA rapporteur on human rights, about issues that are arguably inextricably[54]linked to housing, socio-economic policies and therefore the wider issue of social housing. This has a direct policy link with large-scale CPO estate demolition,[55] which contributes to fuelling the housing problems in the UK[56]. It should not be read in isolation but in synthesis with the recognition of detrimental effects like dispossession, displacement and disenfranchisement that come with loss of a home, a sense of agency and support networks,[57]which is directly similar to the effects of CPO associated regeneration.[58]Therefore, any international scrutiny consistent with international law or public policy is a potential positive step in dealing with the detrimental social and economic impact that CPO affected residents face.

In his report, Professor Philip Alston observes that a wealthy country with the fifth largest economy in the world should not be 'patently unjust and contrary to British values that so many people are living in poverty'.[59] He quotes the Institute for Fiscal Studies which foresees, 'a 7% rise in child poverty between 2015 and 2022, and various sources predict child poverty rates of as high as 40%'. Professor Alston's

---

[53] UK NGOs' Alternative Report Submission to the UN Committee on the Elimination of Racial Discrimination with regard to the UK Government's 21st to 23rd Periodic Reports June 2016 Drafted by THE RUNNYMEDE TRUST

[54]Statement on visit to the United Kingdom, by Professor Philip Alston, United Nations Special Rapporteur on extreme poverty and human rights, https://www.ohchr.org/Documents/Issues/Poverty/EOM_GB_16Nov2018.pdf

[55] Anna Minton, Ground Control: Fear and Happiness in the Twenty-First-Century City; His-estates-10-year-wait-for-regeneration, https://www.insidehousing.co.uk

[56] Anna Minton, big capital who is London for

[57] Anna Minton, Ground control, fear and happiness in the 21st century

[58] https://haringeydefendcouncilhousingblog.wordpress.com/

[59] Professor Philip Alston, United Nations Special Rapporteur on extreme poverty and human rights

report further notes that 'almost one in every two children to be poor in twenty-first century Britain is not just a disgrace, but a social calamity and an economic disaster, all rolled into one'. He emphasises that, 'many of the recent changes to social support in the UK have a disparate impact on children'. Citing evidence from the Equality and Human Rights Commission which predicts that 'another 1.5 million more children will fall into poverty between 2010 and 2021/22 as a result of the changes to benefits and taxes, a 10% increase from 31% to 41%.' The report points to the legal aid cuts, 'in England and Wales since 2012 which overwhelmingly affected the poor and people with disabilities, many of whom cannot otherwise afford to challenge benefit denials or reductions and are thus effectively deprived of their human right to a remedy'. The report highlights ' the LASPO Act (Legal Aid, Sentencing and Punishment of Offenders Act) gutted the scope of cases that are handled, ratcheted up the level of means-tested eligibility criteria, and substituted telephonic for many previously face-to-face advice services'. According to Professor Philip Alston, the Social Metrics Commission, states that 'almost a third of children in the UK live in poverty. After years of progress, child poverty is rising again, and expected to continue increasing sharply in the coming years.'

As described above, this report has a direct policy link with large-scale CPO estate demolition,[60] which contributes to fuelling the housing problems in the UK.[61]

Prof. Alston concludes that 'It was a British philosopher, Thomas Hobbes, who memorably claimed that without a social contract; life outside society would be "solitary, poor, nasty, brutish, and short....many of the public places and institutions that previously brought communities together, such as libraries, community and recreation centres and public parks, have been steadily dismantled or undermined'.[62]

Arguably, Professor Philip Alston's report is acutely relevant to CPO affected residents in various respects. Such as the legal aid cuts in England and Wales since 2012, which overwhelmingly affected the poor or people with disabilities. A theme that is consistent with CPO affected residents who face a lack of access to legal aid

[60] Anna Minton, Ground Control: Fear and Happiness in the Twenty-First-Century City; His-estates-10-year-wait-for-regeneration, https://www.insidehousing.co.uk

[61] Anna Minton, big capital who is London for

[62] Report from UNRA rapporteur on human rights, by Professor Philip Alston, United Nations Special Rapporteur on extreme poverty and human rights https://www.ohchr.org/Documents/Issues/Poverty/EOM_GB_16Nov2018.pdf

which has a disproportionate impact on children, racial minorities, the disabled, elderly and historically disadvantaged communities. An issue that is highlighted by both the Institute on Racial relation[63] among others and would appear to be inconsistent with international conventions and international law. Such as the Universal Declaration of Human Rights[64], ICCPR (referred to1st generation rights)[65], ICESCR (referred to as second generation rights,)[66]CERD,ICE (in relation to racial discrimination)[67] and CROC (convention on the right of children 1989.[68]

These conventions aim to protect economic, social, political rights of individuals or groups, such a rights relating to protection for the home, family, health, racial minorities, access to justice and due process. The Universal Declaration on Human rights, specifically refers to a common understanding of a set of values applicable to the treatment of individual human beings, irrespective of their race, religion, gender or other protected characteristics. Furthermore, the European Social charter, protects health, family, property and against discrimination, among other rights.[69] Although enforceability and applicability and legal jurisdiction over member states remains a potent legal hurdle.[70]

Firstly, because such relief would require measures to be implemented by the faulting nation states through protracted legal and political mechanisms. Secondly, there is difficulty in terms of pursuing the international human rights law route due to the complexity of the law, lack of resources and technical support to those affected. Even at a national level, it remains a cumbersome, long and expensive process to pursue legal action against the acquiring authorities who often have access to extensive legal and financial resources. In comparison, residents or communities

[63]Jessica Perera, THE LONDON CLEARANCES A BACKGROUND PAPER ON RACE, HOUSING AND POLICING 2019, Institute of Race Relations

[64] Universal Declaration of Human rights, http://www.un.org/en/universal-declaration-human-rights/

[65]International convention on civil and political rights, https://www.ohchr.org/EN/ProfessionalInterest/Pages/CCPR.aspx

[66] International convention on social and economic rights,https://www.ohchr.org/en/professionalinterest/pages/cescr.aspx

[67] Committee on elimination of racial discrimination, https://www.ohchr.org/en/hrbodies/cerd

[68] Convention on the right of a Child, https://www.ohchr.org

[69] https://www.coe.int/european-social-charter

[70] https://www.un.org/en/universal-declaration-human-rights/

affected in some cases are litigants in person who use pro bono assistance, which therefore limits the degree of assistance available or other sources of funding just to initiate legal action. In addition to the many other day-to-day practical problems, they face due to compulsory acquisition of their homes.[71] Nevertheless, it is critical that there is a transnational approach and potential avenue for redress given that CPOs, eminent domains, forceful land acquisition or land grabbing in general, have wider long-lasting detrimental effects on particular communities and demographics, which are historically disadvantaged, marginalised, disenfranchised and oppressed. Therefore warranting an international redress mechanism and a degree of international legal intervention.[72]

Chapter 3

Individual ECHR Articles related to estate regeneration through the use of CPOs

As briefly discussed above, among the applicable articles of the ECHR, that are arguably directly triggered by CPOs, are Articles 8, A1P1 Art 6, Art 14, 2 and 3 and their relevance as a mechanism to challenge estate regeneration activities under human rights law. These will be discussed in the order highlighted above.

The subsequent chapters shall examine the statutory compensation regime, the adequacy of the current legal remedies to provide a more rounded understanding of the issue, suggested proposals for reform and a determination as to whether human rights law indeed is an effective mechanism for challenging CPOs.

Article 8 ECHR and estate regeneration through the use of CPOs

---

[71] Alice Belloti, Estate community regeneration and community impact, Case report 99, http://sticerd.lse.ac.uk/dps/case/cr/casereport99.pdf

[72] UK NGOs' Alternative Report Submission to the UN Committee on the Elimination of Racial Discrimination with regard to the UK Government's 21st to 23rd Periodic Reports June 2016 Drafted by THE RUNNYMEDE TRUST

Article 8 of ECHR,[73] states that:

1. 'Everyone has the right to respect for his private and family life, his home and his correspondence.

2. There shall be no interference by a public authority with the exercise of this right except such as is in accordance with the law and is necessary in a democratic society in the interests of national security, public safety or the economic well-being of the country, for the prevention of disorder or crime, for the protection of health or morals, or for the protection of the rights and freedoms of others'.

Before examining in depth the legal details or Art 8, it needs to be emphasised that just like other ECHR articles, there is a multitude of various areas of day-to-day life that could fall under the protections of Art 8. The focus here is on the relevant provisions that could be applicable to CPOs under estate regeneration.

Jurisdiction

Art 8 protects the respect for private and family life including one's home or correspondence[74] and could also be invoked in conjunction with A1P1. Observers, [75] point to a minute difference between these two articles in terms of the level of protection provided which may turn on particular facts of a specific applicant.

Scope of Art 8

---

[73] https://www.echr.coe.int/Documents/Guide_Art_8_ENG.pdf

[74] Aida Grigic, Zvonimir Mataga, Matija Longar and Ana Vilfan, The right to property under the ECHR, A guide to implementation of the ECHR, Human rights Hand Book no 10, https://rm.coe.int/168007ff55

[75] Aida Grigic, Zvonimir Mataga, Matija Longar and Ana Vilfan, The right to property under the ECHR, A guide to implementation of the ECHR, Human rights Hand Book no 10, https://rm.coe.int/168007ff55

Art 8[76] safeguards respect for a home and against deprivation of a home by way of access or occupation. It safeguards the right to live without interference and intrusion in one's family or private life and correspondence. Art 8 also refers to personal information being kept private or confidential and requires a positive step from a public authority.

Definition of a home

In brief and in this specific context of art 8, is a settled place where one lives, including a home one has the intention to move to,[77] described as an autonomous concept not based on domestic law categorisations.[78] In *Gillow V UK,* the court held that even though the applicants had not occupied the house for nineteen years[79] it was still their home. The applicants had not established domicile anywhere else and intended to live in the house.

To engage Art 8 protection, there has to be a determination on facts relating to continuous links and rights which cannot be interfered with, unless there is a reasonable justification.[80] Art 8 does not provide a general right to housing under HRA 98 or ECHR[81], except protection for respect for a home or unjustifiable interference of the peaceful and quiet enjoyment of one's home or possessions, under Art 8 and A1P1 respectively.

 Instead, Art 8 emphasises the need for the state to have a positive obligation to be <u>proactive in regulating</u> non-state interference and to provide remedies against

[76] ECHR

[77] Gillow v UK91986) ECHR 14

Donoghue V Poplar Housing association(2001)EWACA Civ 595

[78] https://www.echr.coe.int/Documents/Guide_Art_8_ENG.pdf

[79] CASE OF GILLOW v. THE UNITED KINGDOM (Application no. 9063/80)

[80] https://www.echr.coe.int/Documents/Guide_Art_8_ENG.pdf

[81] https://www.echr.coe.int/Documents/Guide_Art_8_ENG.pdf

harassment of individuals in and around their home as discussed in detail other chapters.[82]

The ECHR[83] further classifies a home as one that merits protection under the respect for a home legal principle. Which extends to property where the complainant is not an owner, a tenant, in long-term occupancy as well as a relative's house or a 'care' facility.[84] However, this may not apply to a home that one intends to build.[85]

Art 8[86] also appears to put emphasis on a home as being non-transient or exceedingly short term, like a hotel room. Although in *Buckley v UK, [87]which involved the retrospective denial of planning permission,* the notion of a home was not restricted to being lawfully established. Therefore, the designation or interpretation of what a home is or is not appears subjective.

In the context of a compulsory acquisition of social housing homes, such subjective academic notions of what is or is not a home per se, appears irrelevant for most residents due to the fact that they are actual physical owners and occupants of specific their homes either as secure tenants, leaseholders or freeholders. However, even for those that may not fall in those categories, there appears to be sufficient standing under Art 8 for them to assert their rights. Given that, they are non-transient accommodation or hotel rooms. Many live in these properties as their main homes with their families hence engaging Art 8. In terms of wider estate regeneration, conducted through the powers of CPOs, public authorities,[88] as social housing providers attract the jurisdiction of HRA 1998 and Art 8 of ECHR.[89] Mainly because

[82] Marckx x Belgium(1979)ECHR 2

[83] https://www.echr.coe.int/Documents/Convention_ENG.pdf

[84] https://www.echr.coe.int/Documents/Guide_Art_8_ENG.pdf

[85] Louizdou V Turkey(1996)ECHR 70

[86] https://www.echr.coe.int/Documents/Convention_ENG.pdf

[87] https://minelres.lv/coe/court/Buckley.htm

[88] Connors V UK(2005) 40 EHRR 9 'gypsies' removal from a locality was violation of art8

[89] R (weaver v London & Quadrant Housing Trust(2009) EWCA Civ 587

the issue here involves home and family life which must be only interfered with in 'accordance with the law'.[90]

Therefore, residents affected by CPOs, could rely on Art 8(1) in asserting their human rights if the public authorities do so in contravention of the law as held in the case of Malone, where it was affirmed that the 'exercise of powers must be in accordance with the law'.[91] The issue in *Malone* involved determination of infringement of rights by surveillance and the court held that although this was consistent with domestic law, discretionary use or application by officers was arbitrary. Therefore being incompatible with Art 8 of ECHR, although in this case the issue involved a tangential issue of surveillance not necessarily confiscation of a home.

Nevertheless, it falls within the remit of Art 8 and it also highlights the principle of a requirement of public authorities acting in accordance with the law, which is applicable to CPO affected parties. The wider point that must be further emphasised here is that planning and public authorities possess opaque, extensive discretionary powers[92], which are susceptible to arbitrary use.[93] Such abuse could be detrimental to individuals affected by decisions arising from CPOs, such as the demolition of housing estate homes, inadequate compensation, environmental hazards, displacement, dislocation, low or disputed valuations and the need for rehousing. Hence, raising potential incompatibility with Art 8, if CPOs are applied unlawfully or where there are illegitimate aims and disproportionate actions.[94] Furthermore, there are implied positive obligations where environmental factors directly and seriously affect private and family life. For example in estate regenerated areas like Southall, Westbury in Lambeth and other areas like Hackney there are increased complaints of environmental pollution especially in areas where the developers are building on contaminated land such as in Southall and the Westbury estate in Lambeth, South

---

[90] https://swarb.co.uk/malone-v-the-united-kingdom-echr-2-aug-1984/

[91] Malone v UK (1984) ECHR 10

[92] Greg Brown & Sean Yeong Wei Chin (2013) Assessing the Effectiveness of Public Participation in Neighbourhood Planning, Planning Practice & Research, 28:5, 563-588, DOI: 10.1080/02697459.2013.820037

[93] Too-poor-to-play-children-in-social-housing-blocked-from-communal-playground, https://www.theguardian.com/cities/2019/mar/25/

[94] Lustig-Prean and Beckett v UK(1999)ECHR 71 relating to UK military ban on LBGT due to 'operational' issues

London[95]. Although there is protection against interference within Art 8 in tandem A1P1, such a provision does not guarantee peaceful enjoyment of property.

The rationale under A1P1, which appears to offer qualified guarantees, appears both outdated and puzzling. Given that environmental or construction hazards associated with CPOs, pose serious and sometimes an existential threat to the health of residents or those exposed to such exposure. Such construction hazards include asbestos, lead, co2, benzene, industrial noise, dust, and fumes among other toxins. So the question has to be asked if those hazards exist how can it be that those affected are not guaranteed a peaceful and quiet enjoyment of their homes or home environment?

Is it possible to completely separate the two aspects of environmental protections with the interference in the peaceful and quite enjoyment of one's life? It is possible that given the current ubiquitous and front stage environmental campaigns, the facts and impact on those affected by estate regeneration construction or demolition could have potential challenges that could force a revisit of the courts approach or conclusions on environmental protection under Art8 and A1P1. It therefore appears that under the current ECHR Art 8 regime, save in exceptionally serious cases, environmental protections for CPO construction affected parties remains uncertain under Art 8 and A1P1 OF ECHR.

Chapter 4

Other Associated rights under Art 8 during CPOs in Estate regeneration

Among other potential safeguards provided under Art 8, discussed in detail below, are associated with issues such as succession, contracts of parties and the protection of a positive duty for the integration of children since family law matters relate to a family home.[96] This protection under Art 8 extends to state benefits or

---

95 https://www.theguardian.com/environment/2019/may/04/brownfield-site-new-homes-building-wrecking-health-southall

allowances emphasising respect for family life[97]but is not applicable to fiancées. This is critically relevant to residents facing CPOs, which could determine re-housing, compensation or succession rights, not just for individuals, but for those they share their homes with or their relatives.

Tenancies and Art 8 in CPOS

Among other issues, the impact on the various types of tenancies is one of the areas that may engage protection under Art 8 including CPO affected estate regeneration residents or affected parties. There may be preconditions imposed on residents under CPO schemes, [98]whose occupation rights had ceased or those who are short-term occupants after displacing secure tenants[99]during the so-called callously named decanting process.[100]

The relevance here is that due to welfare cuts, high rents, low pay and job insecurity, short or informal arrangements such as sub renting or sharing homes is the most affordable way to live[101] or work in some cities[102]. It is arguable that such homes need a level of protection beyond the narrow confines of statutory or contractual arrangements.[103] This was highlighted in *Chapman V UK,[104] where* the concept of a home was expanded to cabins, bungalows stationed on land irrespective of the lawfulness under national law as well as second homes.[105] A principle that could be

---

[96] https://www.echr.coe.int/Documents/Convention_ENG.pdf

[97] https://www.echr.coe.int/Documents/Guide_Art_8_ENG.pdf

[98] http://estateregeneration.lambeth.gov.uk/key_guarantees#homeowners

[99] Part IV of HA 1985, amended by HA1988 and HA 96.

[100] Alice Belotti LSE Housing & Communities, Estate Regeneration and Community Impacts Challenges and lessons for social landlords, developers and local councils, Case report 99, March 2016

[101] Fenton, Alex. "Housing benefit reform and the spatial segregation of low-income households in London." (2011).

[102] Hamnett, Chris. "Moving the poor out of central London? The implications of the coalition government 2010 cuts to Housing Benefits." *Environment and Planning A* 42.12 (2010): 2809-2819.

[103] Michael Edwards (2016) The housing crisis and London, City, 20:2, 222-237, DOI: 10.1080/13604813.2016.1145947

[104] Chapman-v-united-kingdom-application-no-2723895

asserted by CPO affected residents who may not be long-term occupants or have formal tenancies.

There may however be limitations where there has been minimal occupation or weak links to the property to the extent that they are expunged. Therefore, sufficient nexus or occupation is necessary for recognition of a right to a home. Hence a mere possibility of inheritance may not give rise to a connection to a home under Art 8[106]al though altering the terms of tenancy[107] was found to be an interference with Art 8.[108]

It is nevertheless, evident that on the face of it, CPO processes, interfere with the respect for a home. Despite the fact, that such interference can be qualified under A1P1[109] to allow a member state some latitude in implementation, [110]if certain criteria are attached to the measures.[111] However, if the right in point is critical to the individual's enjoyment of personal intimate rights, the courts minimise the margin of appreciation.[112] Such as where there is demolition of homes[113] leading to[114] compulsion to move and hence a clear interference in the respect to a home under Art 8.[115] This rationale was unambiguously emphasised in Connors v. UK[116] where the court held *inter alia*, 'that the loss of one's home is a most extreme form of interference with the right to respect for the home'. In addition, since there was no justification for such interference, such as what the court referred to as a *pressing*

[105] https://www.echr.coe.int/Guide_Art_8_ENG.pdf

[106] https://www.echr.coe.int/Guide_Art_8_ENG.pdf

[107] Loretta Lees,The Urban Injustices of New Labour's "New Urban Renewal": The Case of the Aylesbury Estate in London, 2013

[108] (*Berger-Krall and Others v. Slovenia*, § 264);

[109] (*Howard v. the United Kingdom*,

[110] Alec Samuels, The planning process and judicial control: the case for better judicial involvement and control,J.P.L 1570

[111] *Noack and Others v. Germany*

[112] (*Connors v. the United Kingdom*, § 82).

[113] (*Aboufadda v. France* (Dec.));

[114] *Selçuk and Asker v. Turkey*, § 86; *Akdivar and Others v. Turkey* [GC], § 88; *Menteş and Others v. Turkey*, § 73).

[115] *Noack and Others v. Germany* (Dec.));

[116] Application no. 66746/01

social need or a legitimate aim, the court concluded that there was a violation of Art 8 pf ECHR[117]. This judgement accurately reflects the predicament of CPO affected residents by housing estates regeneration and could potentially provide an avenue to challenge such interference.

Estate regeneration disrepair or blight and Art 8 associated with CPOs

Another issue to consider is that in areas where CPO processes are enacted or merely announced, disrepair or neglect is a common feature.[118] Observers believe this appears to be managed decline to hasten what is termed as the decanting process.[119] A term that reflects the inhumanity and sanitisation of the arguably inhumane process of home expropriation[120]. The use of language and other phrases like brownfield sites or opportunity area drain or minimise any human association or presence in the areas or homes being expropriated. Coupled with the disrepair, blight and the consequential anti-social behaviour, the communities become ripe for targeted added claims by the acquiring authorities of an urgent need for regeneration,[121] which then softens the CPO approval process.

Disrepair has been found to be an infringement of Art 8 even[122]after examining the existence of procedural guarantees to determine the margin of appreciation. Disrepair, neglect and blight are also associated with *nuisance in the legal context under the pollution act 1972 or a public nuisance which falls under criminal law. This*

---

[117] CASE OF CONNORS v. THE UNITED KINGDOM (Application no. 66746/01) JUDGMENT STRASBOURG, 27 May 2004,https://www.refworld.org/cases,ECHR

[118] Estate Regeneration and Community Impacts Challenges and lessons for social landlords, developers and local councils, Case report 99,Alice Belotti LSE Housing & Communities March 2016;

See also Save Cressingham gardens; Save Central Hill: @savewetburysw8

[119] (*Khamidov v. Russia*,

[120] States and real estate private equity firms questioned for compliance with human rights, https://www.ohchr.org

[121] Estate Regeneration and Community Impacts Challenges and lessons for social landlords, developers and local councils, Case report 99,Alice Belotti LSE Housing & Communities March 2016;

[122] *Novoseletskiy v. Ukraine*, §§ 84-88).

is therefore another aspect that could come under the remit of Art 8 where parties who may not possess direct proprietary interest may seek to pursue their property rights from that perspective under Art 8. This is especially during construction related to CPO enforced estate regeneration. Such as in a case where a tree was felled into a neighbour's garden.[123] This is applicable to parties affected by CPO construction nuisances, asbestos or other contaminants as sighted in the Westbury and Southall cases[124] above. As mentioned such a nuisance could attract criminal sanctions under the codes such as the Asbestos Code 2012[125], as well as arising to the standard that breaches the respect for a home or home environment, hence being in contravention of Art 8 of ECHR.

Although Art 8 does not offer an inherent protection of a clean environment per se, planning decisions interfere with people's home and family lives, therefore triggering Art 8 and A1P1.[126] Moreover, since the convention is considered a living instrument, [127] it should be interpreted to fit present day conditions[128]to balance the rights of residents affected with a CPO due to public authorities' actions, which fall under the purview of art 8.[129]

It is arguably due to such hazardous intrusion or exposure that heightens the sense of dangerous impact on communities[130], which compels them to move away from their locality, family and their support networks.[131] There by essentially destroying the '*essential ingredient of a family ... the right to live together, enjoy each other's*

---

[123] *Lane V The Royal Borough of Kensington and Chelsea London Borough Council(2013)EWHC 1320(QB)*

[124] https://www.theguardian.com/environment/2019/may/04/brownfield-site-new-homes-building-wrecking-health-southall

[125] http://www.hse.gov.uk/asbestos/regulations.htm
[126] *J.P.L 2010,3 298-309*

[127] *Tyrer V UK*

[128] *J.P.L 2010, 3 298-309*

[129] https://www.echr.coe.int/Documents/Guide_Art_8_ENG.pdf

[130] Paul Watt (2013) 'It's not for us', City, 17:1, 99-118, DOI: 10.1080/13604813.2012.754190

[131] Tom Slater (2009) Missing Marcuse: On gentrification and displacement, City, 13:2-3, 292-311, DOI: 10.1080/13604810902982250

company[132] *and relationship development'*[133] consistent with the 'notion of family life being an autonomous concept'.[134]

Private life and Art 8 in CPOs

Under ECHR, private life is interpreted widely to include 'personal and physical integrity'.[135] The relevancy to CPOs is the excessive unjustifiable intrusion into people's lives culminating to eventual displacement[136]instigated and characterised by collection of personal data,[137] especially in circumstances where many residents could be vulnerable[138]with no access to independent advice or support. Furthermore, such intrusion and demand for disclosure requires justification to avoid contravention of Art 8[139] especially where the acquiring authority is the intruding party, which arguably gains competitive negotiating, commercial and legal advantage.

It appears that even providing information for census purposes may be an interference of rights under Art 8, including surveys, under the realm of Art 8 jurisdiction.[140]Furthermore, intrusion in private life also includes the loss of support networks in the locality, which disrupts employment and professional associations[141]

---

[132] Olson v Sweden

[133] Marckx v Belgium

[134] Marckx v Belgium; https://www.echr.coe.int /Guide_Art_8_ENG.pdf

[135] X and Y v the Netherlands(1985) ECHR 4

[136] Jane Rendell (2017) 'Arry's Bar: condensing and displacing on the Aylesbury Estate, The Journal of Architecture, 22:3, 532-554, DOI: 10.1080/13602365.2017.1310125

[137] http://newmanfrancis.org/projects/westbury-lambeth/

[138] https://www.ucl.ac.uk/engineering-exchange/sites/engineering-exchange/files/fact-sheet-health-and-wellbeing-social-housing.pdf

[139] As held in, Hilton V UK Application no,12015/86

[140] Z v Finland(1997) 25 EHHR 371

which appears to be an example where there seems to be a convergence of Art 8 with A1P1 where interference in one is private, personal, or family life could lead to a legitimate challenge under both Articles. As held, In *Niemietz v Germany[142]*, where the applicant's complaints of entry and seizure of the documents in the lawyer's office was found to be disproportionate and inconsistent with the expectation of confidentiality *'inherent in the lawyer's profession'[143]*, although in *Niemietz, the court did not find any 'separate issue under A1P1.'[144]*

Moreover, as indicated above, circumstances that could potentially lead to breach of Art 8 are more extensive than just physical possessions per se since art 8 protects attributes that are consistent with the preservation of family life and associated human dignity. Consequently, the court has also found[145]the loss of employment for a *breach of oath* to trigger Art 8, due to the impact it has on *relationships, material well-being, fami*ly and reputation. This is applicable to CPO affected parties, in the sense that compulsion to move from one's home has spiral effects on access to employment, education, support networks, well-being, family life and consequently one's human dignity and reputation as mentioned in the reports above. The other consideration for potential breach of art 8 is the fairness of the associated process which is discussed in detail below under art 6 but briefly in the paragraphs below under art 8.

Fair process and Art 8 during CPOs in Estate regeneration

Public authorities often use bureaucratic and inscrutable language or opaque processes. CPO decisions and processes may not be understood or formalised during a disruptive protracted process for residents. Valuations, advance payment

---

[141] Volkov Ukraine(21722/11) 2013 IRLR 480(ECtHR),

[142] 13710/88, [1992] 16 EHRR 97, [1992] ECHR 80

[143] Guidance Note 10, The right to property under ECHR

[144] Guidance No 10, The Right to property under the ECHR, pg 21

[145] Practical Law UK practice Note 8 835 5732

and negotiations for compensation or rehousing require specialist technical advice or access to financial resources.[146] Specifically, valuations are determined largely by the acquiring authority with limited independent oversight and imposition of pre-conditions in case of a valuation dispute.[147]This is worsened by the seeming lack of clear reasoning or timely information provided to residents, especially those that face measures that lead to eviction, which attracts protection under Art 8.[148]

The process is characterised by a lack of transparency, imbalance of resources, state self-interests or conflicts of interest due to decision makers being the acquiring party.[149] Planning decisions leading to CPOs [150] are sometimes authorised by the same acquiring party, which would appear to be a manifest conflict of interest with devastating detrimental impact in some cases.[151] An issue highlighted by Anna Minton, in her report 'Scaring the living daylight', [152]a situation which is acutely relevant to victims of estate regeneration enforced through CPOs.[153] In a nutshell, CPO affected residents who are in effect removed and therefore evicted from their homes and community[154] are subjected to obscure, broad, arbitrary and vague language without access to independent legal advice. [155]

[146] Stuart Hodkinson, Chris Essen, (2015) "Grounding accumulation by dispossession in everyday life: The unjust geographies of urban regeneration under the Private Finance Initiative", International Journal of Law in the Built Environment, Vol. 7 Issue: 1, pp.72-91, https://doi.org/10.1108/IJLBE-01-2014-0007

[147] Estate Regeneration and Community Impacts Challenges and lessons for social landlords, developers and local councils, Case report 99,Alice Belotti LSE Housing & Communities March 2016; See also Save Cressingham gardens;

See inter alia Hackworth & Smith, 2001; Glynn, 2008; Lees et al., 2008; Shaw, 2008, argue that Stock transfer in London can be understood through the lens of state-led 'third-wave gentrification', a widespread phenomenon across British, North American and Australian cities.

[148] Donoghue, above

[149]See inter alia Hackworth & Smith, 2001; Glynn, 2008; Lees et al., 2008; Shaw, 2008, argue that Stock transfer in London can be understood through the lens of state-led 'third-wave gentrification', a widespread phenomenon across British, North American and Australian cities.

[150] Buckley v. the United Kingdom, § 60);

[151]Siobhan O'Sullivan, et al. "Hearing the Voices of Children and Youth in Housing Estate Regeneration." Children, Youth and Environments, vol. 27, no. 3, 2017, pp. 1–15. JSTOR, www.jstor.org/27.3.0001.

[152] http://spinwatch.org/images/Reports/Scaring_the_living_daylight_final_27_March_13.pdf

[153] Estate Regeneration and Community Impacts Challenges and lessons for social landlords, developers and local councils, Case report 99,Alice Belotti LSE Housing & Communities March 2016; See also Save Cressingham gardens;

[154] Jane Rendell (2017) 'Arry's Bar: condensing and displacing on the Aylesbury Estate, The Journal of Architecture, 22:3, 532-554, DOI: 10.1080/13602365.2017.1310125

The Kate Barker Report, regarding the use of land for planning[156] further highlights the problems associated with the procedural unfairness in the planning process. It refers to 'planning decisions as policy decisions or expediency decisions, conducted in an anomalous manner'. An observation or description that would be consistent with the view that CPOs are imbalanced, favour acquiring parties, lack transparency and there is no real independent scrutiny, as highlighted in the various reports above.

Although, there is a possibility of judicial review it characteristically, largely focuses on procedural flaws, requires extensive resources and is characterised with structural impediments, which are looked at in more detail, under Art 6 below. As an example of such impediments, challenging such arbitrary decisions through judicial review would require a duty to give reasons by a public authority, documentation of the facts and any associated detrimental impact. However, requested information is not always provided, often delayed, deducted when provided, vague or broad even when conducted through freedom of information requests under the FOI Act.[157] Specifically, in areas like Southwark[158], Lambeth[159] and others, [160]residents' demand for due process remains a distant or box ticking exercise.

Therefore, the importance for a public authority to provide reasons for its actions or decisions cannot be understated. Such importance, to give reasons, in matters such as CPOs is captured in the law gazette article, in dramatic language. The article

---

[155] Duty to give reasons, :*https://www.lawgazette.co.uk/legal-updates/local-government-duty-to-give-reasons*

[156] J.P.L 1570

[157] https://www.whatdotheyknow.com/request/quantity_of_freedom_of_informati#incoming-1055418; https://www.whatdotheyknow.com/request/information_related_to_the_impac#outgoing-950497; http://www.brixtonbuzz.com/2017/12/lambeth-council-refuses-to-admit-how-many-empty-homes-are-on-cressingham-gardens-estate/

[158] http://35percent.org/heygate-regeneration-faq/ https://www.theguardian.com/cities/2018/sep/12/london-council-aylesbury-estate-development-southwark-financial-risk

[159] https://www.socialhousingsoundarchive.com/westbury-estate, https://savewestburysw8.wordpress.com/2015/04/14/the-westbury-residents-main-concerns/

[160] https://haringeydefendcouncilhousingblog.wordpress.com/

points to *'Shakespeare's decadent, drunken and corpulently challenged knight, Falstaff, when pressed to give reasons to verify an obvious lie, robustly declined. He declared that if '... reasons were as plentiful as blackberries, I would give no man a reason upon compulsion. But although Falstaff as a private individual was presumably within his rights to deny reasons, public authorities cannot be so cavalier.*[161] Despite the Shakespearean dramatization, there is a very serious point about accountability, transparency, protection against abuse of office or at worst impunity especially where 'the decision-maker is disagreeing with a considered and reasoned recommendation', as Lewison LJ, observed in the Court of Appeal'.[162]

Such intrusive and detrimental actions necessitate a need for the estate regeneration process to be conducted in a manner that respects the human dignity of affected persons and gives respect to their home,[163] giving appropriate weight to individual circumstances.[164] A point that was highlighted in *Connors V UK*[165] where it was held that the so called *gypsies* removal from a locality was in violation of Art 8, since the authority in question, appeared to evade statutory issues by making the applicant's wife sign a notice to quit without due regard to respect for his home. These actions effectively evaded any proper, fair or adequate due process. The emphasis on proper due process appears to be also reflected in *McCann*, where it was reiterated that 'any person at risk of an interference of this magnitude should in principle be able to have the proportionality of the measure determined by an independent tribunal in the light of the relevant principles under Article 8.*[166]

Therefore, for many CPO affected parties facing loss of their homes and the spiral detrimental effects that follow such potential displacement or dispossession, [167]the need for a fair and expeditious due process is an issue that cannot be minimised as indicated above.[168] It is however important to point out that despite the inherent

---

[161] Local government, duty to give reasons, *https://www.lawgazette.co.uk*
[162] Local government, duty to give reasons, *https://www.lawgazette.co.uk*

[163] (*Rousk v. Sweden*, §§ 137-142).

[164] (*Gillow v. the United Kingdom*, §§ 56-58).

[165] (2005) 40 EHRR9

[166] *McCann v. the United Kingdom*, § 50

[167] Such as loss of employment, extraction from school, effect on wellbeing, financial hardship or disruption

unfairness of the process and decisions, in some cases, such as Horada,[169] the initial decisions were overruled. In *Horada,* the court stopped the plans to demolish shepherds bush market, which would displace and dispossess thousands of local small businesses. It is however noticeable that these were businesses as opposed to homes and it's not clear whether that contributed to the reasoning in the final decision, an issue that needs further scrutiny which will be discussed in further detail in the later chapters detailing CPOs on a case by case basis.

In nutshell, as discussed above, Art 8, both substantively and procedurally appears to at least in law, provide a potential mechanism for challenging housing estate expropriation by public authorities. But such further relief under Art 8 appears inextricably linked with other rights under Art 6 and A1P1, such as the guarantee of the peaceful enjoyment of possessions, safeguard for ownership and other property rights under A1P1, as long as certain criteria are met. However, it is important to emphasise that while these protections appear intersectional with procedural rights under art 6 or protections under A1P1, there appears to be no unfettered protection given the various qualifications or limitations.

Art 6

Art 6 (1) of the ECHR states that," In the determination of his civil rights and obligations or of any criminal charge against him, everyone is entitled to a fair and public hearing within a reasonable time by an independent and impartial tribunal established by law'.

Art 6(1) is applicable to property rights, privacy matters, internal hearings or processes in terms of procedural fairness, access to an independent tribunal or equality of arms. Although Art 6 is not absolute,[170] it refers to some procedural limits

---

[168] Dispossession, the great housing swindle, https://www.dispossessionfilm.com/

[169] [2016] WLR(D) 148, [2016] PTSR 1271, [2016] EWCA Civ 169

[170] Ashingdale v UK(1985) 7 EHRR 528

as acceptable without procedural guarantees at every stage and stresses access to a court with full jurisdiction.[171]

As mentioned above, the focus here is about the relevant provisions of art 6 and others that could be applicable to estate regeneration through the use of CPOs. In analysing such relevance, a key issue therefore is a determination as to whether a civil right in Art 6 is 'a private right as opposed to a public right'.[172] In the context of estate regeneration, which is a housing matter, there is no ambiguity that this is consistent with a civil right in the context of ECHR and international conventions.[173] It is therefore the civil arm of Art 6 that is applicable to estate regenerations which therefore requires an identifiable issue over rights that have jurisdiction in domestic law[174]and consideration of the application of those rights.[175] In estate regeneration, there is an array of issues that require an expeditious, fair and independent determination as under art 6 stipulations. Such issues include the various competing interests between CPO affected parties, a need for examination of the consultation process,[176] a fundamental need for fair hearings as well as expeditious just compensation and adequate rehousing.[177]

The civil arm of Art 6 provides procedural guarantees in resolving disputes concerning property and ensures access to a court as well as a fair independent tribunal to safeguard the rights of those affected, although it covers permissible

[171] Golder V UK (1975) EHRR 524

[172] Alec Samuels, The planning process and judicial control: the case for better judicial involvement and control,J.P.L 1570

[173] Kenna, P. (2008). Housing rights: positive duties and enforceable rights at the European Court of Human Rights. European Human Rights Law Review, 13(2), 193-208

[174] H V Belgium(1987) 8 EHH 123 and GEorgiadis V Greece

[175] Bentehm V Netherlands(1985 8 EHRR

[176] Bokrosova v LLB http://www.bailii.org/ew/cases/EWHC/Admin/2015/3386.html

[177] Begum v London Borough of Tower Hamlets(2003) UKHL 5

[178] Handbook n0 10, Property rights under ECHR

[179] CASE OF DRAON v. FRANCE, *(Application no. 1513/03)*, *https://hudoc.echr.coe.int*

interferences. To be admissible under Art 6 any potential applicant needs to have an existing interest or legitimate expectation in terms of possession or property rights under A1P1. However, where the eventual outcome is final after determination, it appears that no such prior requirement is mandated under Art 6[178]. It would also appear that emphasis will be placed on A1P1 if there is an issue that calls for the finality or decisiveness of the domestic legal actions but will be placed on Art 6 If the issue is about process. For instance, In *Draon v France,*[179] the court found a breach of the applicant's right to property due to a law limiting compensation associated with disability prior to the conclusion of the proceedings. Similarly, in the case of *Canea Catholic Church v Greece,* the court found that denying the applicant's legal personality was in breach of Art 6 after refusing to entertain the church's contention that such a rejection would deprive the church of the possibility of taking part in legal proceedings.

A question that arises is whether this is a clear signal that the court will take a pragmatic view rather than a uniform approach, as to what strand of specific issues are entertained and how to channel such issues when considering property rights under its jurisdiction. Whatever the answer to this question is , a potential lesson for CPO estate regeneration potential applicants, in terms of strategic and timely positioning of any potential legal actions under Art 8, A1P1 and Art 6, is that applicants should be cognizant of the fact that although there might be a prima facie case of breach ECHR rights, a strategic positioning of specific issues to determine a specific legal principle would appear to have a chance of success than a wider claim of breach of property rights.

The difficulty for almost all potential CPO estate regeneration affected applicants is that their main and prime goal is to preserve their property, homes and associated rights or livelihoods. As opposed to setting legal principles under the ECHR, which is a costly, protracted and academic process.

Access and delays

As discussed above, briefly, the other aspect that estate regeneration CPO affected parties face during housing estate expropriation is a lack of access to an expeditious fair process and independent tribunal. This is made worse by high costs, extensive

time constraints and lack of parity between the competing parties. Furthermore, residents are faced with the prospect of proceedings such as valuation disputes not being determined by an independent tribunal.[180] A situation which is consistent with *Ali V UK,*[181] where it was held that an applicant should have been afforded access to a fair hearing before an independent and impartial tribunal.

Similarly, resolutions should be consistent with the individual circumstances of those concerned which is consistent with HRA/ECHR art 6 which a fair process part of which would require an expeditious process or remedies such as just compensation or suitable adequate rehousing. Otherwise CPO affected potential applicants could be successful in alleging a breach of art 6 rights due to a delayed process or decision such as in *Robins v UK, where* there was a breach of Art 6[182] due to an unreasonable delay. CPO processes characteristically take years to conclude, [183]with detrimental effect on residents on various areas of their lives. Yet acquiring authorities have extensive resources unlike individuals who are compelled to accept offers such as lower valuations that would otherwise be unacceptable.[184] The decision making process is characteristically structurally advantageously skewed in favour of or conducted by acquiring authorities' to secure their legal, financial and political interests.[185]

Even when those affected pursue successful legal action related to unfair procedural issues, the acquiring authorities could circumnavigate the ruling by essentially starting the process again. For example Lambeth council was held to have failed to follow lawful process in reaching its decisions. A decision that residents affected thought would cause the council to abandon the entire scheme. However, the council did not abandon the scheme although residents have since applied for the right to

---

[180] See DCLG guidance; https://www.gov.uk/government/publications/compulsory-purchase-process-and-the-crichel-down-rules-guidance

[181] Ali V UK(2016) 63 HRR 20,

[182] https://www.echr.coe.int/documents/guide_art_6_eng.pdf file:///T:/002-7866.pdf

[183] Dispossession the great social housing swindle : https://www.dispossessionfilm.com

[184] Stuart Hodkinson, Chris Essen, (2015) "Grounding accumulation by dispossession in everyday life: The unjust geographies of urban regeneration under the Private Finance Initiative", International Journal of Law in the Built Environment, Vol. 7 Issue: 1, pp.72-91, https://doi.org/10.1108/IJLBE-01-2014-0007

[185] Alice Belotti, Estate regeneration and community impact, http://sticerd.lse.ac.uk/dps/case/cr/casereport99.pdf

manage successfully[186]. Whether this will force the council to abandon the demolition f cressingham gardens[187] remains to be seen.

This was in the case of *Bokrosova V Lambeth,*[188] where it was held that Lambeth acted unlawfully due to a failure to observe procedural issues in reaching its decisions. The court stated that the process of consultation, '*must include sufficient reasons for the proposals to enable consultees to consider them, and respond to them intelligently; enough time must be given for that; and the consultation responses must be taken conscientiously into account when the decision is taken.... ensure public participation in the local authority's decision making process and ... in order for consultation to achieve that objective, it must fulfil basic minimum requirements'.*[189]

However, despite the ruling, that essentially quashed their decisions, the council still pursued the regeneration by restarting the process.[190] The council's ability to do this raises questions about the effectiveness of judicial review as a mechanism to challenge CPOs. Since then the residents of Cressingham gardens have secured the right to manage as mentioned above[191] and it is interesting to see how Lambeth council will respond or how that affects the overall housing estate demolition programme[192] under Lambeth council.

As already highlighted above, part of a fair process requires access to an independent and impartial tribunal. Although pursuing legal action could theoretically attempt to meet the requirement of access to a fair and impartial hearing or tribunal, it is a costly and long process for CPO affected residents. Prohibitive costs bar aggrieved residents from instigating legal action especially in the case of leaseholders who risk cost orders,[193] even if they satisfy the impeding requirements

---

[186] Right-to-transfer-determination-cressingham-gardens-estate, https://www.gov.uk

[187] http://cressinghampeoplesplan.org.uk/

[188] (2015)EWHC 3386(ADMIN)

[189] Citing '*one aspect of the Coughlan test'*

[190] https://savecressingham.wordpress.com/2016/12/21/residents-vow-to-fight-on-after-high-court-decision/

[191] right-to-transfer-determination-cressingham-gardens-estate

[192] https://savecressingham.wordpress.com/

such as seeking leave to commence legal proceedings.[194] Parties with deep pockets such as public bodies or property developers may unreasonably delay or deny their rights without the opportunity for the full circumstances ought to be fairly, diligently and impartially   determined to prevent abuse of process or punitive penalties.[195] Such tactics are often deployed by the acquiring authorities in concert with developers or interested parties.[196] Therefore, CPO affected residents could have Art 6 engaged if they were subjected to processes that amount to barring them from bringing civil actions against the acquiring authority as was the case in *Z and others V UK,* [197]where the court clarified that, *'the inability of applicants to sue the local authority flowed from the principles governing the substantive right of action in negligence`* and art 6 was therefore engaged. In other words rejecting the argument was being advanced to prevent the applicants from suing the authorities.

However, even when there is an avenue of access to an independent, fair and impartial process, there are other criteria necessary that CPO affected parties would have to satisfy due to the fact engagement of Art 6 requires a disputable implementation of national law in a specific matter.[198]

An issue that was considered in *Lithgow,* where the nationalisation of property, under a local Act,[199] was found to engage Art 6 after the applicants alleged a lack of statutory compensation.[200] In this case, there was an undisputable right of a property owners' claim to statutory compensation, legislated for under the s39 of the Land Compensation Act 1973,[201] which in this particular case appears not to have been

[193] part-44-general-rules-about-costs,www.justice.gov.uk/courts/procedure-rules/c

[194] H V UK, Application no 11559/85

[195] Osman V UK(2000) 29 EHRR 245 (1998) ECHR 101 (1999) 1 LGRT 431

[196] Anna Minton, Scaring the living day light of people, https://www.annaminton.com/single-post/2016/03/21/Scaring-The-Living-Daylights-Out-Of-People

[197] Z and others V UK(2001) ECHRR 333, (2002) 34 EHRR 9

[198] Lithgow v UK

[199] Aircraft and Shipbuilding industries ACT 1977

[200] Practical Law Practice note 835 5732

satisfactorily implemented by the state. Therefore, where the local authorities do not apply the relevant ECHR rights, such as art 6, it is plausible that there is a real possibility of a justiciable issue by the affected parties.

That could be in instances where there are unreasonable or disproportionate barriers to a person's rights, derived from state actions, or an issue of a decisive nature in relation to the rights of an affected party,[202] such as a home or business affected by a CPO, that could lead to life changing intergenerational detriments. As was the case in *Koning V Germany*[203], where a civil right, under ECHR, was considered to be of substantive character and defined autonomously irrespective of the characterisation under national law.[204] Similarly, in *Brugger V Austria*, it was held that the complainant was entitled to an oral hearing especially that judicial review was not available as remedy in the local jurisdiction. Therefore, it would appear that once there is a clear determination of a right at peril under Art 6, the courts are prepared to provide latitude or opportunity for such determination, which is a potential positive trend for CPO, affected parties due to estate regeneration, which ofcourse have direct effect on the UK as a signatory to the ECHR but also via the HRA 98 which incorporates the ECHR rights.

However, as indicated above, the recent curtailment of legal aid is an inherent disadvantage, which makes it almost impossible for disenfranchised residents to challenge detrimental decisions associated with CPO decisions. Particularly leaseholders who may have the value of their homes taken into account as capital and therefore could fall outside the threshold for legal aid eligibility hence risk substantial cost orders that would be attached to their homes. Despite the fact fundamental rights associated with home expropriation, are at issue here which make legal aid arguably necessary in such civil proceedings.[205]This also raises a legitimate question as to whether there is overall property ownership in light of state dispossession through the use of the law. This is a wider question that will be covered in detail in the chapters below.

---

[201] http://www.legislation.gov.uk/1973

[202] Practical Law Practice note 835 5732

[203] Koning V Germany(1978) 2 EHRR 170

[204] Practical law practice note,J.P.L, 2010,3, 298-309

[205] Stars and Chambers v Procurator-where appointment of a temporary sheriff was held to be incompatible with Art 6. One local authority proposed to appoint its own mechanisms of final arbitration

However, the central theme appears to be the manifest imbalance of power and appearance of conflicts of interest in planning processes characterised by a lack of fairness or equality of arms, procedural fairness or propriety or access to an independent adjudication.[206] An inherent imbalance which is arguably worsened, where local authorities' planning or cabinet decisions appear to favour the interests of the acquiring party which are usually the same Local Authority, in the case of estate demolitions, such as in Lambeth[207], Southwark[208] and Haringey[209] among others. For example, in documented cases, during the CPO related proceedings, residents are accorded less time to argue their case or rebuttal of disputable facts and refused access to information[210]. This seems to be inherently incompatible with Art 6, as was the case in *Borgers v Belgium*[211], where a defendant who could not hear or make responses to official arguments was said to have had his art 6 rights breached.[212] Even where it would be assumed that the process was fair, planning conditions are reportedly changed, breached after the process[213] or at least not implemented as issued.[214] A practice that raises pertinent questions about the integrity of the whole process and whose interests are being served.[215]

Lack of access to information by residents

---

[206] R v (Wright v SOS for health and another(2009) UKHL 3

[207] https://www.opendemocracy.net/en/shine-a-light/residents-challenge-lambeth-plans-to-demolish-homes/

[208] https://www.newstatesman.com/politics/2013/11/look-heygate-estate-whats-wrong-londons-housing

[209] https://www.theguardian.com/commentisfree/2017/jul/03/britain-power-contempt-grenfell-labour-haringey-social-housing

[210] https://newsfromcrystalpalace.wordpress.com/tag/campaign-for-freedom-of-information/

[211] Borgers v Belgium(1993) 15 EHRR 92

[212] Practical law practice note public sector.

[213] Council tenants win 'segregated' garden rule fight, https://www.bbc.com/news/uk-england-london-

[214] https://www.theguardian.com/cities/2019/mar/25/ too-poor-to-play-children-in-social-housing-blocked-from-communal-playground

[215] Anna Minton, Big Capital, who is London For

Another common complaint by CPO affected residents is the lack of access[216] to material information and the need to be heard which is critical to the equality of arms.[217] In any process of challenging or asserting one's rights from public authorities or such entities, information from such public authorities is critical. However, freedom of information requests are protracted affairs and substantial information is either not timely provided[218] denied, [219]deducted or is in vague broad language whilst access to hearings in public is not always guaranteed.[220]

Lack of independent review

Another common feature is the fact that the unfairness of the process is heightened by the fact that there appears to be no genuinely independent review mechanisms, save for the court system whose encumbrances, such as cost or complexity have been documented above. This is not assisted by the increasing perception that planning functions and permission granting processes conducted by local authorities [221] appear to be more political, are not always based on statutory grounds[222] and objections do not lead to a hearing per se as part of due process.[223] This makes the need for a fair balance between the rights of the community or potential applicants to be presided over by an independent and impartial decision maker, from the beginning more urgent than ever. Especially when faced with the most intrusive action of all the loss or demolition of one's home.

The imbalance and the lack of impartiality is highlighted in *Tsfayo v UK (2007) ECHR 656*, where the issue involved an applicants' renewal for housing and council tax, which was rejected by the review board. The ECHR found that the board was not an

---

[216] https://newsfromcrystalpalace.wordpress.com/2018/11/26/lambeth-council-refuse-to-answer-foi-questions-made-by-news-from-crystal-palace/

[217] Feldbrugge V Netherlands(1986) 8 EHRR 425, see practice note above

[218]https://www.whatdotheyknow.com/request/asbestos_enquiry#incoming-1327131

[219]https://www.whatdotheyknow.com/request/somerleyton_road_steering_group_2321`11

[220] https://www.dailymail.co.uk/news/article-4656656/Kensington-councillor-DEFENDS-decision-meet-secret.html

[221] Bryan V UK(1995) 21 EHRR 342

[222] DCLG guidance

[223] R (Adlard V SOS for environment(2002) EWCA

independent tribunal and the possibility of judicial review was not a reprieve from the lack of independence and included councillors. Since public authorities review, their decisions by committees often staffed by councillors, such as in the CPO process, the lack of a fair and impartial consideration would appear to engage Art 6 given that the imminent loss of a home, such as that associated with a CPO, *ought to be a serious consideration.*[224]There should be procedural measures and safeguards to protect parties' convention rights,[225] with scrutiny placed on the protection of the residents' legitimate interests.[226] The court appeared to agree with the view that the vesting of land subject to a CPO *'cannot comply with Art.6 of the Convention, unless the courts have a jurisdiction to examine that decision on broad public law grounds'.*[227] Therefore, a similar decision by a public body, associated with a CPO could be *'unlawful if it were made for a purpose not recognised in the compulsory purchase order*[228]*or unconnected with the reason for the grant of those powers.'*[229]

Furthermore, where environmental or nuisance complaints are raised, during demolition or construction, some local authorities with confidential s106 agreements explained above, as agreements which essentially enable a scheme that would not be approved to proceed[230] or other agreements with developers[231] may have their impartiality or practical ability to enforce any planning regulations compromised. Therefore, potentially leading to planning conditions being ignored or breached[232] during and after grant of planning permission.[233] For example, on the Westbury Estate,[234] residents' repeated formal and informal requests or demands to have the HSE investigate the safety measures in place to protect residents from exposure to

---

[224] (*Ivanova and Cherkezov v. Bulgaria*)

[225] (*Irina Smirnova v. Ukraine*, § 94).

[226] (*Orlić v. Croatia*, § 64; *Gladysheva v. Russia*, §§ 94-95; *Kryvitska and Kryvitskyy v. Ukraine*, § 50; *Andrey Medvedev v. Russia*, § 55)

[227]Jonathan Ferris, 2010, Journal of Planning & Environment Law Compulsory purchase: is there a general right to judicial review to challenge the decision to vest land the subject of a confirmed compulsory purchase order?

[228] (*Grice v Dudley*8; *Capital Investments Ltd v Wednesfield Urban DC*9).

[229] *Congreve v Home Office*11; and *R. v Birmingham Licensing Committee Ex p. Kennedy*12).

[230] See www.Lambeth.gov.uk Westbury estate

[231] Council tenants win 'segregated' garden rule fight,https://www.london.gov.uk/sites/default/files/berkley_group.pdf

[232] https://www.bbc.com/news/uk-england-london-

[233] https://www.theguardian.com/cities/2019/mar/25/too-poor-to-play-children-in-social-housing-blocked-from-communal-playground

[234] Westbury-a-year-after-Grenfell, http://housingactivists.co.uk/grenfell

asbestos were reportedly routinely ignored[235] and were often referred to the developers themselves namely the Berkeley group.[236] Residents' concerns[237] appear to be supported by the findings of the HSE report[238]after concerted pressure from the local M[239]P and other parties. The HSE report found that procedures like using water suppression, covering dust, storage of asbestos[240] were not satisfactory or acceptable despite the initial claims by Lambeth Council.

Overall, the inherent impediments associated with instigating legal challenges to the planning process or decisions made by the local authorities. This adds to the manifest imbalance and inherent unfairness experienced by CPO affected parties. Planning policies, such as a CPO process infringe the rights of enjoyment of one's home and property . CPO processes under estate regeneration may further reduce market value because arguably buyers would avoid buying CPO affected properties and worse the planning process is regarded as favourable to developers intent on maximising profits by raising the prices of the new properties while minimising the values of the existing properties owned by residents.[241] The process is characterised with disputed valuation processes[242] without fair appeal processes, which prejudice residents' rights without the proportionality of the measures in question being determined by an independent tribunal. Cumulatively, this creates a hindrance for CPO challengers[243]and objectors from having a fair crack of the whip through a transparent, independent process as well as timely access to any requested related material.[244] Therefore creating a prejudicial effect to the probative value of such material at a later stage in the process, [245]which could be a potential breach of Art 6

---

[235] Families hit out at London gasworks redevelopment, Brownfield-site-new-homes-building-wrecking-health-southall, https://www.theguardian.com/environment/2019/may/04/

[236] The Lambeth and London 'estate clearances: PRESENCE of still uncovered believed to be hazardous construction soil , https://humanlawyerist.blogspot.com/2019/04/the-lambeth-and-london-estate;

[237] Homes for Lambeth Review, https://moderngov.lambeth.gov.uk

[238] Agenda and draft minutes, Cabinet Monday 4 March 2019 5.00 , https://moderngov.lambeth.gov.uk

[239] Kate Hoey(MP) for Vauxhall
[240] https://humanlawyerist.blogspot.com/2019/04/the-lambeth-and-london-estate.html

[241] https://www.theguardian.com/cities/2015/jun/25/london-developers-viability-planning-affordable-social-housing-regeneration-oliver-wainwright

[242] Westbury-a-year-after-Grenfell, http://housingactivists.co.uk/grenfell

[243] Peter Harrison Qc, Glimpsed views of the legal land scape,

[244] R (on the application of Vieira) v Camden LBC

and an infringement of Article 8.[246] Hence providing a potential avenue for estate regeneration affected residents to assert their human rights once they overcome the hurdles associates with instigating legal action.

Chapter 7

Article 1 of the first protocol of the ECHR[247] and CPOs

Overview

A1P1 states that, *'every natural person or legal person is entitled to the peaceful enjoyment of his possessions and no one shall be deprived of his possessions except in the public interest and subject to the conditions provided for by law and by the general principles of international law. The preceding provisions shall not, however, in any way, impair the right of a state to enforce such laws, as it deems necessary to control the use of property in accordance with the general interest or to secure the payment of taxes or other contributions or penalties'.*

The three main rules which describe the degree of interference[248] under A1P1 include *non-interference with possession, no deprivation of property except in the public interest and that state control may only be justified legally infringed in the general interest, where there is a legitimate justification.* In other words, the rights under A1P1 appear to be qualified to a certain extent with a margin of appreciation left for state parties in areas such as implementation as discussed in detail below. A1P1 also makes reference to principles of international law. For example, UDHR[249] under article 17, states that everyone has the right to own property alone or in association with others and that no one shall be arbitrarily deprived of his property.

---

[245] R (on the application of Ashley) Secretary of state for communities and local government

[246] (*Kay and Others v. the United Kingdom*, § 74)

[247] Referred to here as A1P1

[248] Possession, law, property and human rights, Landmark chambers

[249] https://www.un.org/en/universal-declaration-human-rights/index.html

But even in the absence of explicit reference to property rights, under specific international law instruments, it can be forcefully and persuasively argued that such interference, especially when associated with the confiscation or demolition of one's home, creates a spiral effect which could potentially breach international human rights law collectively referred to as the international bill of human rights,[250] comprised of the *Universal Declaration of Human Rights, International Covenant on Economic, Social and Cultural Rights, International Covenant on Civil and Political Rights.* The focus here is on the relevant provisions that could be applicable to CPOs under estate regeneration.

General Scope of A1P1

As cited above, A1P1 protects against deprivation of possessions and unjustifiable intrusion in the peaceful enjoyment of one's possessions. This could be through practices that amount to s expropriation of property, planning restrictions or even temporary property seizures. A case in point is *Pressos Compani Naviera and others v Belgium*, where the state was held liable for extinguishing the applicants unresolved claims by retroactively passing legislation which extinguished the applicants' property rights.[251] In pursuing protection under A1P1, an important distinction should be made as to whether the alleged interference is deemed to be a deprivation or simply control of use the land or property, which could then determine subsequent qualification for compensation under A1P1.

A1P1,[252] is independent of national state definitions, covers all forms of property and does not limit ownership of possessions to physical goods. However, A1P1 does not cover prospective possessions or future possessions but emphasises current or existing possessions. This was an essential issue in the case of Marckx v Belgium[253] where a mother claimed breach of A1P1 because of the alleged impediments by the state authorities to prevent her from disposing off her property to what was described

---

[250] https://www.ohchr.org/Documents/Publications/FactSheet2Rev.1en.pdf

[251] Handbook no 10, the right to property under ECHR

[252] See Practical Law UK practice Note 8-385 5732

[253] CASE OF MARCKX v. BELGIUM. *Application no. 6833/74*, https://hudoc.echr.coe.int

as 'an illegimate child'. A term that is clearly unacceptable in contemporary times[254]. The court by a majority confirmed that A1P1 was relevant to the claims made by the mother and defined the scope of A1P1 as applying to existing possessions but not future possessions[255]. In another case, of *X v Germany*, where a determination of A1P1 right was an issue, the court held that a mere expectation by notaries that *'rates for their fees would not be reduced by law'* did not amount to a property right within the meaning of A1P1.[256]

However, it would appear that where there is a concrete legitimate expectation, future possessions could be considered. But as far as relevance to residents facing CPO effected home demolitions is concerned, the issue regarding future possessions would not affect them because this relates to homes in which they live or already own as opposed to a mere expectation of future occupation or possession for that matter.

Therefore, the issues directly relating to CPOs and Estate regeneration, under A1P1 include, inter alia, *what amounts to deprivation or legitimate expectation, whether the actions of the authorities were proportionate or justifiable, the margin of appreciation extended to states and the fairness of compensation.* These issues are discussed in detail below.

Legitimate expectation

One of the key issues considered under A1P1 is whether a landowner's legitimate expectation of enjoyment of property rights can be a basis for asserting A1P1. In Pine *Valley Developments*[257], the applicants had bought land under the expectation of planning permission being approved but was later annulled. The court ruled in the

---

[254] CASE OF MARCKX v. BELGIUM. *Application no. 6833/74*, https://hudoc.echr.coe.int

[255] Marckx and Marckx v Belgium, Merits and Just Satisfaction, App No 6833/74, [1979] ECHR 2, (1980) 2 EHRR 330, IHRL 22 (ECHR 1979), 13th June 1979, European Court of Human Rights [ECHR], https://opil.ouplaw.com

[256] Handbook no 10, the right to property under ECHR

[257] Pine Valley Developments Limited and ors v Ireland, Just satisfaction, App No 12742/87, A/246-B, (1993) 16 EHRR 379, [1993] ECHR 2, IHRL 3587 (ECHR 1993), 9th February 1993, Council of Europe; European Court of Human Rights [ECHR

applicants' favour holding that the applicants had been subjected to unlawful discrimination contrary to ART 14 in conjunction with A1P1.

The key point from this case, in relation to CPOs is that there is an obvious legitimate expectation of enjoyment of property rights and protection from discrimination under ECHR. Therefore potentially providing an avenue for challenging such activity, primarily due to the legitimate expectation of the legal security associated with their property interests. Manifested through leases or secure tenancies whose curtailment would engage A1P1.[258] This is illustrated in *Stretch*[259], where the court upheld a complaint alleging that the applicant 'had been unjustly denied extension of a further 21 year term lease'.[260]It was further noted that[261] because the option granted by the local authority had been ultra vires and therefore deemed to be a disproportionate interference with the applicant's peaceful enjoyment of his possessions, this was a violation of Article 1 of Protocol No. 1 to the Convention'. Therefore, under the principle of legitimate expectation is that it appears that even a potential legal claim under A1P1 could merit consideration as a possession or asset where a landowner has a legitimate expectation.[262] Especially that CPO affected parties have diametrically opposed legal interests, such as retention of their properties, which are threatened with expropriation by the acquiring authorities.

However, in *Plant v Lambeth (discussed in detail below), the high court* examined such a legitimate expectation, namely the alleged curtailment of the right to buy by a secure tenant that was not yet exercised. The court held that A1P1 had not been engaged in respect of secure tenants' rights to buy since he had not yet acted on it. This ruling is puzzling because Lambeth council had taken formal decisions to demolish the estate through use of a CPO. By doing that, the right to buy by the tenant had been or would be curtailed. The applicant sued to safeguard his right to

---

[258] Pine developments v Ireland(1992) 14 EHRR 319

[259] Stretch v UK *(Application no. 44277/98)*

[260] Practical Law UK practice Note 8-385 5732

[261] [2003] ECHR 320, (2004) 38 EHRR 12, [2003] NPC 125, [2004] 03 EG 100, [2003] 29 EG 118, [2004] 1 EGLR 11, *http://www.bailii.org/eu/cases/ECHR/2003/320.html*

[262] Pressos Compani Naviera v Belgium(1995) 2 EHHR 3010) , also see Practical Law UK practice note 8-385 5732

buy by citing among others A1P1. Therefore, the court's ruling in this specific regard appears contradictory. Furthermore, it would appear that the applicant was not allowed to appeal which curtailed any further opportunity to test that conclusion. Therefore, the successful nature of any such complaint by a CPO affected applicant appears uncertain in practice.

Deprivation

Deprivation is another important consideration under A1P1. A1P1 protects against unlawful deprivation of property, which includes curtailment of the legal rights of those affected. In examining the issue of deprivation, the court ascertains any de facto deprivation of A1P1 rights[263]as opposed mere control of use of property or possessions. For example in *Papamichalopoulous v Greece,*[264] the Navy had taken over the applicants' land to the extent that they could not make effective use of it and this was found to be a de facto expropriation. This is consistent with the circumstances faced by CPO affected parties who have their properties confiscated or unable to be used for their own enjoyment or utility, which could mean that they could be able to challenge such de-facto expropriation of their property in light of the rationale in the above case.

However, potential applicants affected by estate regeneration enforced through CPOs, should be cognizant of the fact that if the measures taken by the state amount to control of the use of the property or payment of taxes, the court could find that such an action did not amount to deprivation. A case in point is *Handyside V UK,*[265] where the temporary seizure of the applicant's books, which were alleged to contain obscene images, did not amount to deprivation since the seizure was temporary and

---

[263]The right to property under ECHR, A guide to the implementation of the right to property, Human rights hand book no 10

[264] CASE OF PAPAMICHALOPOULOS AND OTHERS v. GREECE (ARTICLE 50, Application no. 14556/89)

[265] CASE OF HANDYSIDE v. THE UNITED KINGDOM, (Application no. 5493/72)

was within the powers of the state under A1P1. The difference with CPO housing estate demolition affected parties and the facts or ruling in this case is that expropriation of estate regeneration homes is usually permanent as opposed to mere control. Therefore, this provision would not adversely affect any potential applicants faced with estate regeneration under CPOs. The overarching point here is that although there could be legitimate justifications for interference in an owner's property rights, under A1P1, depriving someone of their property can only be justified in exceptional circumstances as evident in *Lithgow et al,*[266]*where* deprivation of property was held to have happened under a CPO process. A similar ruling was held in *Sporrong and Lonnroth*, where the 'expropriation of building permits and building restrictions enforcement for specific durations was held to be interference in the applicants' enjoyment of their land amounting to deprivation of property.[267] These rulings affirm the protection under A1P1, for estate regeneration affected parties who are deprived of their property due to CPOs by local authorities.

However, it is important to emphasise that any potential applicants would need to prove that this was in fact deprivation not mere restrictions,[268] temporary deprivation or interference in the use or enjoyment of the property. Deprivation could be further proven where there is a partial loss of a significant or substantial part of a landowner's right, which amounts to deprivation without full expropriation. The rulings in *Sporrong and Lithgow* above appear to confirm the protection under ECHR the rights of those affected by CPOs where deprivation or even partial deprivation is found to have occurred by the court. CPO affected estate regeneration residents experience significant restrictions caused by CPOs, such as exposure to construction hazards like noise, fumes, vibration or contaminants or the restriction to sell to the open market as a willing buyer.[269]Residents could argue that this amounts to deprivation or partial deprivation under A1P1.

Deprivation could also be potentially established where there are two competing owners who already have rights in the property as opposed to the familiar practice of the acquiring authority taking over the property. This is illustrated in the case of *James v UK,*[270] where the court found that individuals with leases under the

---

[266] Lithgow v United Kingdom, Merits, App no 9006/80, App no 9262/81, App no 9263/81, App no 9265/81, App no 9266/81, App no 9313/81, App no 9405/81, A/102, (1986) 8 EHRR 329, [1986] ECHR 8, IHRL 59 (ECHR 1986), 8th July 1986, European Court of Human Rights [ECHR]

[267] Sporrong and Lonnroth(1982)5 EHHR 35

[268] See Practical Law UK practice Note 8-385 5732

[269] Imrie, R., & Thomas, H. (1997). Law, Legal Struggles and Urban Regeneration: Rethinking the Relationships. *Urban Studies, 34*(9), 1401–1418. https://doi.org/10.1080/0042098975484

leasehold reform Act 1967, entitled to long leases, who could purchase freeholds of their leases, at a defined statutory price, deprived freeholders of their property, due to the inability to sell the property or set the sale price.[271]

Ironically such a principle laid down in *James v UK above,* could be utilised by CPO affected residents[272]to disentangle themselves from the acquiring authority, although the acquiring authority could still have significant statutory powers to initiate a CPO. The acquiring authority could do so by citing other grounds such as control, as highlighted in *Agosi V UK,*[273] where the main issue was seizure and forfeiture by customs of smuggled Kruegerrands and the court did not deem such an action by authorities to amount to deprivation.[274]

Therefore, CPO affected parties should be aware of claims of control as opposed to seizure by acquiring authorities. However, it is important to emphasise that although such a defence by the authorities could be entertained by the courts, there must be a clear need to balance community interests with the protection of the individual's right to peaceful enjoyment of his or her home, in order to justify controlling the use of property in the general interest. Otherwise, that would invite potential misuse of the significant latitude afforded to states under A1P1 as a defence against CPOs affected parties.[275] Therefore, a finding of deprivation under A1P1, is an important tool against authorities pursuing estate regeneration.

Proportionality

Another central tenet of A1P1 is the principle of proportionality, which emphasises a fair balance between the public interest and the property interests of the owners.[276] Simply put, if there is a valid legitimate and lawful interference then it has to be proportionate. However, such a need to demonstrate proportionality is arguably

---

[270] James V UK(1986) 8 EHRR 123

[271] See Practical Law UK practice Note 8-385 5732

[272] See Cressigham Gardens in Lambeth

[273] Agosi v UK(1987) 9 EHRR1

[274] Practical Law UK practice Note 8-385 5732

[275] See R Plant V LLBC(cite full)

[276] See James V UK App No 8793/79 (A/98) (Official Case No)

[1986] ECHR 2 (Neutral Citation) ; James and ors v United Kingdom, Decision on Merits, App no 8793/79, B/81, 11th May 1984, European Commission on Human Rights (historical) [ECHR]

undermined, in practice, by national authorities enjoying a wide margin of appreciation in determining the public or community interests within the law. [277]

There are several factors, which determine such a fair balance or proportionality. These include procedural safeguards of the owner's property rights, the nature of the penalty applied[278]the extent of interference, the duration or persistence of interference,[279] the actual fault of the owner with its consequential significance and the irrationality or arbitrary nature of the statute.[280]

However, even if a threshold that satisfies proportionality is met by those affected, the need for proportionality in control cases is not a basis for compensation but simply indicates a need for a fair balance to be found.[281] Nevertheless, such interference may only be justified legally, if it's consistent with the public interest.[282]

As already mentioned, while the need to demonstrate the proportionality of the authorities' actions is a key protection measure for CPO affected residents, wider latitudes provided to the states arguably weaken those protections. Under A1P1 states are allowed a margin of appreciation in implementation of decisions associated with legitimate objectives of public interest [283]through proportionate measures designed to achieve greater social justice. While that appears to be a noble objective, in principle, such wide latitude leaves room for authorities to justify actions that are disproportionate to the affected residents whose homes are expropriated via schemes[284] like the wide scale demolition of homes with little[285] or no visible public interest.[286]

---

[277] Practical Law UK practice Note 8-835 57

[278] International Transport Roth v HS(2002) EWCA Civ 158

[279] Sporrong and Lonnroth

[280] R(Kensall) v SOS for Environment(2003) Admin 2003

[281] See Practical Law UK practice Note 8-385 5732

[282] In Tesco Stores Ltd v SOS

[283] James v UK above

[284] The Costs of Estate Regeneration: A Report by Architects for Social Housing, 7 SEPTEMBER 2018

[285] Knock it Down or Do it Up? The challenge of estate regeneration February 2015

[286] David Dewar, The implications of the SoS's rejection of an estate regeneration on grounds of social housing loss https://www.planningresource.co.uk, regeneration-grounds-social-housing-loss ,January 2019

The wider powers afforded to the states under the margin of appreciation, are made even more difficult to challenge by potential applicants due to the inherent institutional impediments faced by any potential applicants. Simply explained, in order for affected parties to challenge the proportionality of actions that amount to interference of property rights, such actions should be foreseeable[287] and authorities need to be accessible and provide clear simple comprehensible communication of reasons for their actions. In the absence of such communication, accessibility and foreseeability, by an authority, it would be extremely cumbersome, almost an obstruction on part of the authority, for estate regeneration CPO affected parties to timely, fairly and justly secure their property and associated rights.

However, in practice, authorities delay, obfuscate, deduct and withhold information[288] from potential applicants which clearly disadvantages estate regeneration affected residents, as mentioned above in various reports and discussed in more detail under ART 6. For instance, campaigners like those on Westbury estate in Lambeth[289] among others cited in reports above, refer to the woeful inadequacy of social rent homes and the ubiquitous use of s106[290] between public authorities like Lambeth et al, as evidence of a potential manipulation of the margin of appreciation left to states under A1P1. This illustrates the almost vacuous nature of the protection under A1P1 when authorities appear to manipulate the margin of appreciation to suit their interests. The case of *Tesco Stores Ltd v SOS*[291] *for Environment and Transport,* concretises the public interest argument as well as the margin of appreciation highlighted above. In this case, Sullivan J emphasised the need for a *'fair balance to be struck between the public interest such as redevelopment and the individual's right to a peaceful and quiet enjoyment of his possessions. Adding that such interference ought to be proportionate and necessary to meet the 'compelling case in the public interest' reflecting the necessary element of that balance'.*[292] The difficulty lies in determining what the clear public interest is and where the limits of its

---

[287] Hentrich V France(1994 18 EHRR 440 (1994)ECHR 29 Lithgow,

[288] LAMBETH COUNCIL REFUSE TO ANSWER FOI QUESTIONS MADE BY NEWS FROM CRYSTAL PALACE, https://newsfromcrystalpalace.wordpress.com/2018/11/26/lambeth-council-refuse-to-answer-foi-questions-made-by-news-from-crystal-palace

[289] https://en-gb.facebook.com/Save-Westbury-Estate-SW8-486344558188042/

[290] S106 and public interest requirements are discussed in detail under the chapter of the CPO process.

[291] J.P.L 2010,3 298-309

[292] Also see R (Clays Lane Housing cooperative ltd v Housing corp(2005),R (Pascoe v SOS(2007), R (Hall) v First SOS(2008) J.P.L 63 at 15

application end, especially in relation to taking or demolishing one's home with the spiral effect that follow as highlighted in numerous reports above.

The above comments by Sullivan J appear consistent with another observation made by the court in Chesterfield properties v Secretary of State, [293]that 'only another interest, a public interest, of greater force may override it'. In that CPO inspector's report,[294]objectors argued that as the Leaseholders' Article 1 and 8 rights have been breached, it is incumbent upon the Acquiring Authority to justify that breach in terms of proportionality. The objectors referred to, the case of R (Clays Lane) v Housing Corporation, where, Maurice Kay J stated that 'the appropriate test of proportionality requires a balancing exercise' between 'a decision which is justified on the basis of a compelling case in the public interest as being reasonably necessary' may not be 'obligatorily the least intrusive of Convention rights.' Adding that some leaseholders no longer have mortgages and many are no longer in employment, as a consequence of the CPO they will be separated from their family and friends and they will be unable to afford to return to the estate'.

During the stated CPO examination process the inspector agreed that, 'Paragraph 12 of the Guidance states that an acquiring authority should be sure that the purposes for which the compulsory purchase order is made justify interfering with the human rights of those with an interest in the land affected. They would need to invest considerable personal resources in addition to any compensation they would receive for their properties; the CPO would not only deprive them of their dwelling but also their financial security. If they chose not to pursue this option, they would inevitably need to leave the area and this would have implications for their family life, including the lives of that dependant on the…. together with the failure of the scheme to fully achieve the social, economic and environmental well-being. The interference with human rights would not be proportionate having regard to the level. The public benefits that the scheme would bring… a compelling case in the public interest has not been proved'.

These observations were reiterated in the Aylesbury estate case in Southwark, stated in the chapters above, where the inspector and subsequently the secretary of state found that the CPO backed estate regeneration was inconsistent with the

[293] Chesterfield Properties Plc v Secretary Of State For Environment & Ors [1997] EWHC Admin 709 (24th July, 1997), *http://www.bailii.org/ew/cases/EWHC/Admin/1997/709.html*
Cite as: 76 P & CR 117, (1997) 76 P & CR 117, [1997] EWHC Admin 709

[294] *CPO Report NPCU/CPO/A5840/74092 ,www.planningportal.gov.uk/planning inspectorate Page 73*

human rights of residents. Although it appears that the parties have since reached some sort of accommodation. The cases and comments above by both courts and the inspectors emphasise human rights as a fundamental consideration for CPO schemes not simply a peripheral matter.

How that is implemented on the ground to minimise or eliminate such human rights breaches appears to be almost impossible task. Therefore a finding of a breach A1P1 does not in effect protect applicants from dispossession. An approach that combines direct negotiations, political actions such as lobbying, and campaigns in parallel with any legal action appears to be more practically fruitful as opposed to relying on the protections of A1P1.

Justification

Despite the court rulings above, authorities could still potentially assert justification as a defence for the interference or deprivation of property rights. In other words, even if there was interference or a taking, the authorities could argue that they were within the law or legitimately justified to take the action they took.

Tax enforcement is one such route where that justification this could be applicable. As reiterated, a state has a right to enforce laws deemed necessary to control the use of property in accordance with the general interest to secure payment of taxes, penalties or lawful regulations, as long as the power is exercised rationally and proportionately, such as in the regulation of a sex shop.[295]

Nevertheless, despite such justification, the court could still find a breach where that justification is considered disproportionate or where there is a discretionary, unfair procedure creating an excessive burden born by the applicant and can further intervene in the absence of a reasonable justification for interference with property rights. Such an example is in *the case of Davies* where the court held in the absence of fair compensation, there was a breach of the need to strike a fair balance between the public interest and the van owners confirming that therefore A1P1 had been engaged.[296] Which affirmed that natural or legal persons could only be deprived of property, such as contributory or non-contributory state benefits,[297] or other interests,[298]

---

[295] *Belfast CC v Miss Behavin' Ltd*,([2007] WLR 1420, [2007] 1 WLR 1420, [2007] 3 All ER 1007, [2007] UKHL 19, *http://www.bailii.org/uk/cases/UKHL/2007/19.html*

[296] R Mott v Environment Agency(2018) UKSC 10)

[297] Stec v UK (2005)41 EHRR SE18

subject to conditions provided by law and the general principles of international law. An affirmation that potential CPO effected estate regeneration residents could arguably rely on to enforce their legal rights. However, it is always important for CPO affected parties to bear in mind that it is possible to conclude that various actions fall under the margin of appreciation on part of the state, if there is a fair appeal system or if the interference is reasonable and proportionate as discussed above at length. It seems to be a high bar for often unrepresented, resource starved and distressed residents to overcome especially properly raised and if supported by evidence from the acquiring authorities.

Having explored in some detail the broader principles underpinning A1P1 namely, deprivation, legitimate expectation, proportionality, justification and the margin of appreciation, with relevant cases or examples, it is of paramount importance to discuss in detail some of the specific areas where estate demolition or confiscation supported by CPO processes, acutely affects those who occupy the homes or have interests in the properties. Such examples include issues like market rate, the right to buy, home environment/environment rehousing and compensation and the extent to which potential applicants under A1P1 both could pursue them de facto and de jure.

A1P1 fails to offer full protection and requires a margin of appreciation which arguably allows local authorities to effect property deprivations or interfere in peoples' enjoyment of their property. There is no clear limits of interpretations of the margin of appreciation and there is a concern that could be potentially used as a general defence by actions. Given the lack of resources and lack of parity between parties, those affected could simply give up an further challenges against the authorities because of the appearance of an arguably respectable explanation by the authorities without being fairly adjudicated in an impartial and fair tribunal process. The spiral effect of such an occurrence is that authorities get emboldened in pursuing CPOs in estate regeneration because there is no real meaningful challenges against them. Therefore, the margin of appreciation principle requires revisiting if not out right deletion from the A1P1 lest it becomes a default position even when its clear such a defence would not arise at all.

Chapter 8

---

298 Beyeler v Italy (2001) 33 EHRR 52

Other specific *notable CPO estate regeneration issues under A1P1*

It should not be a contention that protection against interference in a home environment is among the most important protections under A1P1.[299]As discussed at some length above, such interference has to be consistent with the added imposition of a positive obligation on the contracting states to ensure that such interference is proportional to the stated aim. The home environment protection under A1P1 could intersect with Art 8, which asserts protection against the violation of the respect for one's home.[300] Among other issues that require attention is environmental pollution, which could seriously interfere with one's private or family life and deprive personal enjoyment of amenities associated with one's home such as[301] the case of *Moreno v Spain*[302] where the court concluded that noise pollution violated articles 8 and 13 of ECHR. Such interference may affect a person's wellbeing and prevent them from enjoying their homes, family life and adversely affect their health. CPO affected residents[303] have complained of noise, pollution and toxic hazards associated with construction hazards.[304]The courts appear to disregard apparent mere concerns about protection of healthy environment[305]and consider serious detriments to the persons concerned. If there is a nexus to the cause of such a serious effect, a complaint may arise under Art 8 to determine[306] state actions and the failure to effect measures necessary to prevent harmful activity.[307]

Emphasis is placed on the need for a causal link to be established as opposed to prospective harm depending on the repetitive nature of the negative activity.[308]Furthermore, it's not the general deterioration of the environment", per se, but harmful

[299] Hatton and others V UK,

[300] https://echr.coe.int/Documents/Convention_ENG.pdf

[301] CASE OF MORENO GÓMEZ v. SPAIN, *Application no. 4143/02*

[302] CASE OF MORENO GÓMEZ v. SPAIN *(Application no. 4143/02)*

[303] https://www.theguardian.com/uk-news/2019/jul/07/court-challenge-homes-southall-london-gasworks-brownfield-development

[304] https://www.theguardian.com/environment/2019/may/04/brownfield-site-new-homes-building-wrecking-health-southall,

[305] *Kyrtatos v Greece*

[306] (*Hatton and Others v. the United Kingdom* [GC], § 96; *Moreno Gómez v. Spain*, § 53)

[307] https://www.theguardian.com/environment/2019/may/04/brownfield-site-new-homes-building-wrecking-health-southall,

[308] *Fadeyeva v. Russia*, § 69.

effects that would be disproportionate to the accepted standards consistent with living in modern metropolitan areas.[309] For many affected residents or parties, it would be an obvious aim for prevention to be effected before any harm or interference in the peaceful enjoyment for affected faced with CPOs parties although in practice this is not always the case.[310] In reaching its decision regarding a breach under Art 8, associated with pollution, the courts consider process and substance.[311] Paying due regard to any vague or overbroad interference without reasoned decisions, processes, any shortcomings in a state's obligation or whether the right balance has been struck between the resident and other interested or parties.[312] Such state measures need not include extensive reports but could include professional assessments to determine the harmful consequences of construction activities. However, a decision may be made in the absence of such information[313] if a fair balance between parties exists.

Additionally, a failure to rehouse residents during demolition, excavation, redevelopment, could violate Art 8,[314] because in effect that would tantamount to a failure to protect their health and wellbeing.[315] Such protective measures should include regulatory and administrative mechanisms. Paradoxically, the court confines itself to respect for a home hence the wisdom of such a decision needs to be closely examined.[316] This was discussed in more detail under Art 8 respect for a home above. Despite a lack of clear blanket provision protecting the environment, per se, under A1P1, courts could be creative in dealing with decisions that had the effect of remedying environmental detriments associated with a home or home environment.[317] Such as in a case where transparency was required when residents living at a dangerous site with sodium cyanide or in proximity to hazardous effects were not

---

[309] . (*Asselbourg and Others v. Luxembourg* (Dec.)).

(*Martínez Martínez and Pino Manzano v. Spain*, § 42) (*Hardy and Maile v. the United Kingdom*

[310] https://www.theguardian.com/environment/2019/may/04/brownfield-site-new-homes-building-wrecking-health-southall

[311] (*Hatton and Others v. the United Kingdom* [GC], § 99).

[312] *Moreno Gómez v. Spain*, § 55). (*Fadeyeva v. Russia*, § 93; *Hardy and Maile v. the United Kingdom*, § 218

[313] *Hatton and Others v. the United Kingdom* [GC], § 128)

[314] *Fadeyeva v. Russia*, § 133

[315] *Tătar v. Romania*, § 88).

[316] (*Hatton and Others v. the United Kingdom* [GC], §§ 100 and 122),

[317] *López Ostra v. Spain*, §§ 56-58, *Moreno Gómez v. Spain*, § 61. *Di Sarno and Others v. Italy*, § 112).in (*Giacomelli v. Italy*, § 83),

provided access to information or conclusions of the study to permit such a scheme.[318] Which was similarly reiterated, in the case of _Giacomelli v. Italy,_ the *'court found a violation in the absence of a prior environmental impact assessment and the failure to suspend the activities of a plant generating toxic emissions close to a residential area'.* Such a documented lack of transparency is consistent with the experiences of many residents living in CPO affected areas where there is a lack of independent impact environmental and equality impact assessments.[319]

A question arises whether authorities do not disclose such information because of the crucially potential benefit to affected residents because environmental impact damages may be linked to actual loss. A case in point, where such inference is raised, is where applicants, who lived near Heathrow,[320] were subjected to noise nuisance, which affected their property valuation, although it was concluded that there was no direct evidence to suggest that the value of the applicants' property was diminished or was unsalable.[321] The reasoning seems contradictory since such pollution could limit interest in the property and therefore drive down prices. Furthermore, apart from environmental pollution associated with construction hazards, bad housing conditions, disrepair or blight during CPOs related construction[322] may breach the quiet enjoyment and Art 8 in terms of respect for a home[323] which is intersectional with A1P1.

Although there are statutory obligations in the UK legal system to deal with such bad housing conditions, [324]there are doubts about local authorities' willingness to enforce their own statutory liability or potential culpability. Which therefore strengthens and necessitates the need for Art 8 intervention where there are unfit housing conditions but no adequate remedy.[325]

CPOs, right to buy and A1P1

[318] Hatton and Others v. the United Kingdom [GC] (§ 120),

[319] https://www.theguardian.com/environment/2019/may/04/brownfield-site-new-homes-building-wrecking-health-southall

[320] Hatton and Others v. the United Kingdom [GC] (§ 120),

[321] . However, a settlement was reached in one case in respect of Art 8, 13 and A1P1.

[322] Demolition or refurbishment of social housing?, https://www.ucl.ac.uk/engineering-exchange/research-projects, 2018

[323]https://www.echr.coe.int/Documents/Guide_Art_8_ENG.pdf

[324] Housing/repairs-in-rented-housing/disrepair-what-are-your-options-if-you-are-a-social-housing-tenant/disrepair-what-are-the-landlord-s-responsibilities, /https://www.citizensadvice.org.uk/

[325] HA1985 s604,

Another key area that needs consideration is the impact of CPOs on what is known as the right to buy for secure tenants and the protections under A1P1. The relevant context in this case is where estate regeneration can be argued to effectively interfere with the right to buy of the secure residents. Not the overall discussion of the advantages or disadvantages of the right to buy per se.

The case of R Plant v LLBC[326] highlights this issue, which affects secure tenants faced with a CPO and interference in their right to buy under A1P1. In this particular case, a central issue was whether A1P1 was engaged and breached by the council's decision to demolish the estate using CPOs. The claimant among other issues appears to have alleged breach of A1P1 due to interference with S118 of HA 1985, right to buy and S84 (1) rights, which prevent the court from issuing a possession order on such a property except on legal grounds in schedule 2 of the Act and other provisional requirements.[327] The court held that A1P1 was not applicable to the council's cabinet decision, concluding that, *'A1P1 was not engaged and was indistinguishable from other authorities.[328]* Noting that 'if *engaged, it need only be considered in relation to the statutory right to buy when the authority commences County Court proceedings to obtain an order for possession of a particular home'.*

Notably, the court appeared to base its decision to the fact that the claimant had not already exercised his right to buy. However, it appears that the existence of that option and its removal clearly appeared to interfere in the claimant's property rights, hence engaging A1P1.

Nevertheless, it appears the court indirectly appeared to acknowledge that A1P1 was engaged but not breached, at least up to the point when steps would be taken to revoke it or a determination made as to whether it was breached. Stating that, *'If, contrary to the clear view I have reached, I had concluded that A1P1 was engaged in LLBC's decision, reached on 21 March 2016....the issue of whether it was breached would have been a matter for the Court to determine.'[329] This* Invites the question as to when the right time or forum would be for the claimant to enforce his rights under A1P1 if not at that specific court and that specific time. Moreover, If not why not?

---

[326] *R Plant v LLBC, [2016] EWHC 3324 (Admin)*

[327] *R Plant v LLB [2016] EWHC 3324 (Admin)*

[328] *Kay v Lambeth LBC [2005] QB 352 and Austin v Southwark LBC [2010] HLR 1'.*

[329] Citing *Belfast City Council v Miss Behavin' Ltd [2007] 1 WLR 1420 at paragraphs 13 to 15)'.*

However, questions remain after this ruling and it is not clear that those questions were adequately addressed by the court. Moreover, the unfortunate refusal to appeal closed down testing the *decision related to secure tenancy, CPOs and A1P1.*

However, a significant positive takeaway for CPO affected residents, especially with the right to buy, the court appears to have acknowledged their rights if they chose to move away. They would be secure tenants being provided with new secure tenancies if they decide to move elsewhere but not if they wish to be rehoused in a new home on their current location. In which case they would only be granted an assured tenancy.

Market Rate, CPOs and A1P1

Another extremely important issue for consideration by CPO affected estate regeneration residents that could be in violation of A1P1 is the inherent default prevention of applicants from selling their properties at market value. Such interference via CPOs therefore appears disproportionate since compensation should be reasonably related to the wider market value of the locality, taking into account the totality of the full circumstances associated with displacement and removal from a home or a locality. Furthermore, it would appear, A1P1 does not guarantee a right to full compensation in every situation since a margin of appreciation is allowed to the nation state in this respect.[330]

However, it must be emphasised that the issue, here is beyond market value per se. Market rate, in this context is disputed and is described as 'a euphemism for imposing compensation' on an unwilling seller.[331]Where owners are compelled to sell to a specific party, at a specific time, at a price largely determined by the same interested party usually the acquiring local authority also the arbiter of the planning decisions which appears to be a prima facie manifest conflict of interest.[332]

---

[330] See Lithgow and Practical Law UK Practice Note 8-385 5732

[331] Guy Roots et al, 2nd edition

[332]Neil Gray Libby Porter, By Any Means Necessary: Urban Regeneration and the "State of Exception" in Glasgow's Commonwealth Games 2014

The no scheme principle[333] and the equivalence principle[334] often cited in the government guidance regarding CPO compensation[335] appear woefully unrealistic since CPO affected areas face blight, crime, antisocial behaviour and disrepair which affect the market price.[336] Furthermore, those affected cannot simply move or sell to the open market due to the costs involved or the inability to sell in case of leaseholders. The compensation awarded does not often meet the prices or housing costs in the private sector within the locality. Not to mention the resulting severe emotional distress that affects the wellbeing, health, and avoidable psychological insecurity.

Additionally, residents largely buy or rent properties without any forthcoming knowledge of a CPO. In the case of Local authorities, leases can be for 125 years while life tenure with succession rights is routine for many local authority secure tenancies. Residents envisaged this as a safety net both as a home and for leaseholders as a potential long-term capital investment, which is crucial for social mobility.

Therefore, the reference to the so-called market price or apparent resemblance to market price does not reflect the necessary just, fair and equitable compensation for residents' families or other affected parties. There is a recognisable strong argument that compensation per se should be beyond statutory requirements and a central measure in assessing or the proportionate nature of the burden put on any CPO affected party.[337]

Chapter 9

Compensation and A1P1

---

[333] David Elvin, QC, the no scheme principle under s6a of LCA 1961, https://www.landmarkchambers.co.uk/wp-content/uploads/2018/08/CPO-Presentation-Seminar-25-Sept-2017-DEQC.pdf

[334] http://www.legislation.gov.uk/ukpga/Eliz2/9-10/33/section/5

[335] https://assets.publishing.service.gov.uk/government/uploads/system/uploads/attachment_data/file/817392/CPO_guidance_-_with_2019_update.pdf

[336] Loretta Lees, Mara Ferreri, Resisting gentrification on its final frontiers: Learning from the Heygate Estate in London (1974–2013),Cities, Volume 57,2016,Pages 14-24, https://doi.org/10.1016/j.cities.2015.12.005.(http://www.sciencedirect.com

[337] Deborah Rook, Property and Human Rights, 2001

As indicated above, compensation no doubt remains a contentious issue in CPO related matters and is set by statute as highlighted by the DCLG guidance.[338]The guidance cited above refers to market value plus home loss payments and disbursements,[339] apparently disregarding the value of the scheme on the value of the land in question. Instead, compensation assumes a willing seller without compulsion. This is via monetary payment at the open market value of the land, *'in so far as money can do it', to put one in the same position as land had not been taken from him…in so far as loss imposed on him in the public interest, but no greater'.*[340] However, this level of compensation does not cover the detrimental effects of being displaced from a settled community with the ensuing distress, fear and sense of powerlessness.[341] *Which would appear to resonate with A1P1 as reiterated In James v UK* and in *the former king of Greece et al v Greece*[342], where it was held that compensation that does not reasonably reflect the value of the property[343] could be deemed a disproportionate interference.[344]

A government review culminated into various law commission reports that were not implemented[345] leading to minimal changes.[346] DCLG guidance further explains this contentious and complex area'[347] stating that, *'compensation payable for the compulsory acquisition of an interest in land is based on the 'equivalence principle' (i.e. that the owner should be paid neither less nor more than their loss). The value*

---

[338]compulsory-purchase-process-and-the-crichel-down-rules-guidance

https://www.gov.uk/government/publications

[339]https://assets.publishing.service.gov.uk/government

[340] Lord justice Scott in Horn v Sunderland corporation

[341] Martine August, "It's all about power and you have none:" The marginalization of tenant resistance to mixed-income social housing redevelopment in Toronto, Canada,

Cities, Volume 57,2016, Pages 25-32, (http://www.sciencedirect.com

[342] Deborah Rook, Property Law and Human Rights, 2001

[343] Deborah Rook, Property Law and Human rights, 2001

[344] Holy Monasteries v Greece

[345] See urban renaissance report city university urban task force report, pg. 231,

[346] *Planning and Compulsory purchase Act 2004*

[347] DCLG guidance citing Part 1 Land compensation claims 1973

of land taken is the amount which it might be expected to realise if sold on the open market by a willing seller (Land Compensation Act 1961, section 5, rule 2), disregarding any effect on value of the scheme of the acquiring authority (known as the 'no scheme' principle); (see Land Compensation Act 1961, section 5, rule 5). Importantly, but unfortunate for those affected by CPOs, although it is implied under A1P1 that compensation will be paid,[348] the legitimate public interest may justify less than the financial equivalent to what the claimant lost based on the principle in *James*.[349] In addition, where rights to compensation are provided by statute, those provisions must be interpreted so as to be compatible with HRA 1998'.[350] Furthermore, A1P1 does not state how much compensation should be paid but states that *'the taking of property without any just compensation is justifiable only in exceptional circumstances'.* Compensation should be generous and proportionately beyond, market value or pecuniary loss given the spiral detriments including mental distress that befalls those affected by estate regeneration enforced by CPOs, as highlighted in the various reports above.

The compensation issue is best humorously articulated by John Pugh Smith,[351] who sums up the central concern for CPO affected landowners, as timely adequate compensation, *'especially for a welsh hill farmer'* as he put it.[352] This reference to the 'welsh farmer' could be arguably replicated to the majority of CPO affected parties or residents faced with the demolition of their homes under CPOs with the spiral affects which could be held as being in breach of A1P1. Therefore, it cannot be emphasised enough, the extent to which the expeditious nature and totality of compensation is central to the amicable resolutions of CPO related disputes or minimising the detrimental impact on residents. Acquiring authorities appear to seek to offer less compensation through a deliberately slow process, while livelihoods are on hold pending compensation.[353]

Rehousing

---

[348] Guy Roots et al, 2nd Edition

[349] James V UK, The Law of compulsory purchase, third edition, Guy Roots et al; *Thomas v Bridgend county council,*(2011), EWCA Civ 862, (2011) RVR 241

[350] Such as in *Thomas v Bridgend county council,*(2011), EWCA Civ 862, (2011) RVR 241, where the CA held that s19(3) of the Highway Act 1980, was incompatible with art 1 of the ECHR

[351] John Pugh –Smith, When is' enough ' legally enough, Encyclopaedia of Local government law bulletin,2015

[352] Saunders V Caerphilly CBC(2015)EWHC 1632 CH

[353] Alice Belotti, Estate regeneration and Community impact, LSE, 2016

S39 of the LCA 1973[354] sets out the grounds for rehousing which is summarised by the DCLG guidance[355]for many residents affected by estate regeneration enforced by CPOs, especially those with young children, finding secure and affordable accommodation is one of the most formidable barriers they face. Many are compelled either to live on potentially hazardous and dangerous protracted construction sites, such as asbestos contaminated land, move into temporary accommodation or move out of the locality entirely, which causes a series of detrimental impacts in all areas of their lives.[356]

The new properties tend to take many years[357]to build and are largely unaffordable. The new schemes such as shared ownerships, demote residents' property ownership interests, have stricter leases and diminish residents' equity, savings, home loss and disturbance. Residents who exercise any rights to stay as tenants are subjected to intrusive means testing or inquiries into unrelated areas of their lives despite the injustice of having one's home confiscated by the same acquiring authority.[358]

Additionally, the new housing may increase social divisions such as in a widely reported case, after estate demolition or regeneration, where children's playgrounds were segregated and there are familiar cases of 'poor doors'[359] depending on the housing tenure. Such division, it is strongly argued is incompatible with A1P1 in intersection with Art 14 of ECHR, which prohibits discrimination.[360] Primarily because

[354] http://www.legislation.gov.uk/ukpga/1973/26/contents

[355]https://assets.publishing.service.gov.uk/government/uploads/system/uploads/attachment_data/file/571453/booklet4.pdf

[356]PaulWatts,Its_not_for_us_Regeneration_the_2012_Olympics_and_the_gentrification_of_East_London_City_2013, http://www.academia.edu/6007431/;

Zoe Williams, the real cost of regeneration,http://www.execreview.com/2017/07/the-real-cost-of-regeneration/

[357] https://www.vice.com/en_uk/article/qkq4bx/every-flat-in-a-new-south-london-development-has-been-sold-to-foreign-investors

[358]PaulWatts,Its_not_for_us_Regeneration_the_2012_Olympics_and_the_gentrification_of_East_London_City_2013, http://www.academia.edu/6007431/;

Zoe Williams, the real cost of regenerationhttp://www.execreview.com

[359] https://www.newyorker.com/culture/cultural-comment/the-poor-door-and-the-glossy-reconfiguration-of-city-life

[360] /too-poor-to-play-children-in-social-housing-blocked-from-communal-playground

https://www.theguardian.com/cities/2019/mar/25

[361] Written by Jessica Perera, Institute of Race Relations, New IRR publication provides a fresh take on housing, policing and racism in London.

economic disadvantage tends to disproportionately affect women, racial minorities[361] and those with disabilities. All of which are protected characteristics under Art 14 of ECHR as well as EA2010 and HRA 98.

Therefore, taking into account of all the above issues, it is important that compensation should proportionately reflect the genuine or manifest public interest, [362] in individual circumstances and mirror the distinction between mere restrictions, which could amount to deprivation, and an actual taking of the physical property. Most CPO affected estate regeneration residents are affected by actual physical deprivation of property with associated emotional, social and financial detriments, both immediate and long-term. The statutory compensation does not appear to reflect the emotional or intangible but equally devastating detriments. Hence making the interference and deprivation acutely disproportionate and therefore in potential breach of A1P1 discussed in more detail above. Monetary compensation although helpful is not the panacea to displacement. It should be a package that includes mandatory adequate rehousing, take into account health implications, disruption to employment, education and support networks in balance with stated proven public interest for compulsory acquisition of one's home.

An issue that resonated with the US case of *Kelo,* [363]where the issue was a taking of a longstanding home by the local authorities. Justice Scalia noted that, 'yes you are paying for it, but you are giving the money to somebody, who does not want the money, who wants to live in the house that she's lived in her whole life. That counts for nothing? *'What this lady wants is not money. No amount of money is going to satisfy her. Living in this house her whole life. She does not want to move'.* That is the sense of deep injustice of the compulsory taking of homes, which are occupied especially in cases where residents have inculcated deep roots in the locality with a sense of cultural, economic and social attachments. That is not to minimise the more transient or temporary residents affected but there is no doubt that the impact is bound to be more damaging to those with entrenched roots in the community.

Chapter 10

[362] As stated in Trailer and Marina(leven) v Sec.of State 2004

[363] Kanner, Gideon. "Kelo v. New London: Bad Law, Bad Policy, and Bad Judgment." *The Urban Lawyer*, vol. 38, no. 2, 2006, pp. 201–235. *JSTOR*, www.jstor.org/stable/27895626.

Equal treatment under ART 14 and its convergence with A1P1

Equality[364] and fairness of treatment by those affected by CPOs, is critical to avoid breach of Art 14 in tandem with Art 8 and A1P1. Article 14 has no freestanding existence in absence of other rights. For Example in conjunction with Art 8, it was held that there was a breach of Art 14 where an 'occupant was prohibited from succeeding a tenancy after the death of his same-sex partner'.[365]

Therefore, CPO affected residents claiming art 14 protections could have to establish grounds for breach in other areas such as Art 8 or A1P1. The court appears to lay emphasis as to whether there are justiciable grounds within the scope of property rights. Such as in the case of *Marck v Belgium above,* where the court found in favour of a mother who alleged discrimination in relation to the freedom to dispose her property to so called illegitimate children although the court found no violation of A1P1 per se.

Similarly, in *Gaygusuz v Austria,* the court found a breach of Art 14 where there was a denial of assistance to an applicant who was not of Austrian Nationality.[366] Perhaps it could reflect the notably lower margin of appreciation in ART 14, which is very narrow, compared to A1P1. An applicant wishing to pursue a claim under ART 14 in relation to his or her property rights would have to prove elements of A1P1, such as possession but would not necessarily need to substantiate a violation of such rights to be able to make a claim of discrimination under Art 14. The applicant would be required to establish grounds under which his or rights under art 8 or A1P1 were breached and how such interference was different from other comparators in an unjustifiable manner.[367] Once the applicant establishes grounds for consideration of the claim under Art 14 and the associated Articles such as Art 8 or A1P1, the burden then falls on the state to justify the alleged discrimination in terms of its

---

[364] https://www.echr.coe.int/Documents/Convention_ENG.pdf

[365] (*Karner v. Austria*, §§ 41-43; *Kozak v. Poland*, § 99).

[366] The right to property, Human rights handbooks, No. 10

[367] Handbook No 10, property rights under ECHR

consistency with the law whether it is a legitimate aim and it is proportionate to that aim.

The interplay of art 14 and A1P1 also applies to Art 3[368] which is reiterated in the treaty of Rome as a free standing equal-treatment guarantee although the UK has not signed that treaty.

As far as Art 14 is specifically concerned, in terms of housing in general and estate demolition in particular, there are reports from bodies like the race audit and the Institute of race relations among others, [369]which cite disparity in housing and the disproportionate effects it has on racial minorities associated with estate regeneration.[370]

These have wider potentially intergenerational effects in terms of social mobility, access to opportunity and other social indicators where there are historical economic and social disadvantages among specific communities such as racial minorities, therefore national authorities have to pay close attention to the specific needs of minorities and those with protected characteristics which might require imposing certain conditions within certain limits.[371]

---

[368] Articles 2, 3 and 14, Equal access to justice in the case-law of the European Court of Human Rights on violence against women, https://www.echr.coe.int

[369] JESSICA PERERA,The London Clearances: Race, Housing and Policing, 2019

[370] https://www.ethnicity-facts-figures.service.gov.uk/

[371] (*Connors v. the United Kingdom*, § 84) Chapman v UK

United Kingdom [GC], § 96; *Yordanova and Others v. Bulgaria*, §§ 129-130 /(*Codona v. the United Kingdom*

[372] just-space-response-to-panel-note-7.3-20-may-2019.pdf, https://justspacelondon.files.wordpress.com/2019/04

[373]JESSICA PERERA, The London Clearances: Race, Housing and Policing, 2019

[374] CASE OF PINE VALLEY DEVELOPMENTS LTD AND OTHERS v. IRELAND, Application no. 12742/87

Specifically, in housing and estate regeneration, reports indicate that racial minorities[372] face a disproportionate detrimental impact.[373] This would appear to therefore be incompatible with the judgment In *Chapman,* for example, where the court affirmed that restricting the use of caravans, has an impact on the applicants' respect for their home. The applicant was notably from a racial minority group which is historically disadvantaged.

The ECHR has also held that there was discrimination and therefore a breach of Art 14 in the case of *Pine valley developments Ltd V Ireland*[374]*,* where the applicants complained of discrimination due to a refusal of planning permission in respect of the applicant in comparison to other landowners. A similar ruling found in favour of the applicant in respect of Art 14 and A1P1 in the case of *Chassgnou and others V France*[375], where it was held that legislation appeared to favour large landowners, who could use their land as they wished which put smaller farmers in a discriminatory position. A ruling that was consistent with the case *Larkos v Cyprus*[376] where *'the court held that offering differential protection to tenants against eviction – according to whether they are renting state-owned property or renting from private landlords, entailed a violation of Article 14 taken in conjunction with Article 8, due to the unjustifiable difference of treatment'.*

This would be consistent with the residents affected by CPOs who have cultural links or may be disadvantaged by being forced to areas whey they face racial discrimination.[377]In addition the ruling above is consistent with the need to treat residents fairly and equally, especially in relation to issues such as valuations of properties, rehousing and compensation, where racial minorities face a disproportionate detrimental impact on their lives. Emphasis appears to be put on a positive obligation for a member state to cultivate appropriate safeguards to the extent even a lack of legal capacity leading to dispossession without meaningful participation in the process or access to the final determination by the courts was held to be a violation of art 8, by the court having considered protection measures and their inadequacy in the national state law.[378]

---

[375] CASE OF CHASSAGNOU AND OTHERS v. FRANCE. Applications nos. 25088/94, 28331/95 and 28443/95)

[376] App no 29515/95 (Application No) ECHR 1999-I (Official Citation)

[377] (*Chapman v. the United Kingdom* [GC], § 73).

A principle that appears to have been emphasised by the UK Supreme Court,[379] where the court asserted that the EA2010 provided further protection to a group of people who fall under the protected characteristics category.[380] The implication here for CPO affected parties, especially resident occupiers, is that where there is evidence of discrimination without a legitimate and proportionate aim, there are grounds upon which Art 14 in conjunction with A1P1 or other articles like art 8 could be upheld in their favour. Thereby protecting their property rights and other associated rights.

As already discussed above, beyond ECHR and the HRA 1998, international conventions bar discrimination and other human rights abuses.

This is an extensive area that will be covered in a separate chapter under international law especially how estate regeneration enforced by CPOs is consistent with international human rights law in light of the recent criticisms of the UK by the United Nations[381] and other interventions by the UN rapporteurs[382] cited above. Therefore, the discussion of international law is in a brief context covering the universal declaration of human rights which has moral authority [383] with given legal effect under the international convention on civil and political rights.[384] Applicable to housing are articles 23, 22, 3, 14 and 26[385], inter alia, ratified by the UK in 1976.[386]It appears that clear protections against discrimination exert moral or political

---

[378] *Zehentner v. Austria*, §§ 63 and 65) / (*A.-M.V. v. Finland*, §§ 82-84 and 90).

[379] In Akerman –Livingston v Aster Communities Ltd(UKSC) 15,

[380]https://justspacelondon.files.wordpress.com/2019/04/just-space-response-to-panel-note-7.3-20-may-2019.pdf; https://www.london.gov.uk/nlp_ex_33_cover_report.pdf

[381] https://www.ohchr.org/EN/Issues/Poverty/Pages/SRExtremePovertyIndex.aspx

[382] https://www.ohchr.org/en/issues/housing/pages/housingindex.aspx

[383] http://www.un.org/en/universal-declaration-human-rights/

[384] https://www.ohchr.org/en/professionalinterest/pages/ccpr.aspx

[385] https://www.ohchr.org/en/professionalinterest/pages/ccpr.aspx

[386] our-human-rights-work/monitoring-and-promoting-un-treaties, https://www.equalityhumanrights.com/en/

diplomatic pressure on states and encouragement to implement adequate protections.[387]

It is however important to examine the provisions of art 10 1nd 11 that are relevant to the topic t hand namely estate regeneration enforced through CPOs.

Chapter 11

Art 10 and 11 of ECHR

Another aspect of ECHR that appears to be relevant to property rights and estate regeneration enforced by CPOs is the freedom of association and expression, which are covered, by Articles 10 and 11. Art 10 and 11 of ECHR are considered together here since the protections they provide are intrinsically linked.

Art 10[388] states that ...

1   *Everyone has the right to freedom of expression. This right shall include freedom to hold opinions and to receive and impart information and ideas without interference by public authority and regardless of frontiers. This Article shall not prevent States from requiring the licensing of broadcasting, television or cinema enterprises.*

2.   *The exercise of these freedoms, since it carries with it duties and responsibilities, may be subject to such formalities, conditions, restrictions or penalties as are prescribed by law and are necessary in a democratic society, in the interests of national security, territorial integrity or public safety, for the prevention of*

---

[387] (*Stenegry and Adam v. France* (Dec.)).

[388] https://www.echr.coe.int/Documents/Convention_ENG.pdf

66

disorder or crime, for the protection of health or morals, for the protection of the reputation or rights of others, for preventing the disclosure of information received in confidence, or for maintaining the authority and impartiality of the judiciary.

Chapter 12

Art 11 and property rights

Article 11 – states that:

1. 'Everyone has the right to freedom of peaceful assembly and to freedom of association with others, including the right to form and to join trade unions for the protection of his interests.

2. No restrictions shall be placed on the exercise of these rights other than such as are prescribed by law and are necessary in a democratic society in the interests of national security or public safety, for the prevention of disorder or crime, for the protection of health or morals or for the protection of the rights and freedoms of others. This Article shall not prevent the imposition of lawful restrictions on the exercise of these rights by members of the armed forces, of the police or of the administration of the State'[389].

ECHR rights of expression or association although protected may be restricted by state authorities with certain qualifications within the law such as in the interest maintaining order or public safety. Hence any limitations on these freedoms is placed on these rights in balance with public policy grounds.[390]Authorities must ensure that the property rights, which are the issues here, are infringed or interfered with without lawful justification such as in the case of CPOs under A1P1 or Art 8.

---

[389] https://www.echr.coe.int/Documents/Convention_ENG.pdf

[390] Observer and the Guardian v the United Kingdom (1991)

The case of *Handy side v UK*,[391] mentioned above highlights the relevant issues associated with property rights, which may be applicable to CPOs. In this case, the authorities seized books published by the applicant on grounds that they contained lewd content. It was held that since state authorities have a margin of appreciation under art 10, there was no breach of either Art 10 or A1P1. The implication here in relation to CPOs is that as long as states can justify and prove their activity within the margin of appreciation accorded to states based on the facts of the case, the court could potentially hold in the respective states favour.

However, in the later case of *Ozturk v Turkey*[392], the court found that the confiscation and destruction of the applicant's book was apparently related to his prior conviction by the authorities and was therefore in breach of art 10. In addition, the court further concluded that it was therefore not necessary to consider A1P1 in the circumstances.

This later case above highlights the fact that where there is an unjustifiable and permanent expropriation of property, or infringement of another associated rights such as art 10, the court could find a breach of ECHR. Therefore, residents or parties who are faced with having their [393]property rights being expunged as well as having other rights breached may have a potential route to challenge such alleged transgressions by the state authorities.

The wider relevance to CPO affected parties is that local authorities influence and diminish the affected communities' ability to meet, organise and express themselves during the process of consultation or the entire process of acquisition.[394]

---

[391] App No 5493/72 (Application No)

A/24 (Official Citation), [1976] ECHR 5 (Other Reference)

[392] *Ozturk v Turkey,* application no. 22479/93 ,*https://hudoc.echr.coe.int/eng"Ozturk v Turkey"],"documentcollectionid2":["GRAND Chamber*

[394] https://www.socialhousingsoundarchive.com/westbury-estate

This reportedly happens when traditionally elected bodies known as TRAs or leaseholders forums are disbanded, [395]undermined[396] or singled out for lack of funding among other practices.[397] Such as in Lambeth council where residents' elected groups have been suspended which limits effective, representative association without influence or manipulation by the authorities concerned.

TRAs tend to be more effective and organised in challenging Local Authority decisions but there are examples where such associations have been either suspended or marginalised,[398] residents' advocates complained of being singled out, targeted or victimised.[399] Such actions are bound to have a chilling effect on residents' ability to scrutinise or challenge the decisions, actions of such public bodies, [400]therefore jeopardising residents' ability to safeguard their human rights.[401]

In many reported areas, there is no evidence to justify curtailment of those rights in the context of CPOs[402] Another issue that requires consideration is Art 2. Although not an obvious issue under CPO estate regeneration Art 2 is arguably linked to the CPO estate regeneration activities that affect the health and wellbeing of residents[403] especially the vulnerable, elderly and children. In the chapters above, reference was made to various reports that document the social, economic and racial impact on the community and individuals. Such as reports from the Runnymede trust, [404]the

---

[395] https://lambethleaseholders.wordpress.com/

[396] https://newsfromcrystalpalace.wordpress.com/2017/11/08/housing-scandal-one-council-to-choose-who-represents-tenants-and-leaseholders-on-new-residents-assembly/

[397] Tenants and Residents Associations

[398]https://lambethleaseholders.wordpress.com

[399] leaseholders-chairman-quits-amid-council-bullying-claims-green-party-councilor-says-siege-mentality-exists-in-lambeth/://newsfromcrystalpalace.wordpress.com

[400] http://lambeth.network

[401] https://www.equalityhumanrights.com/en/human-rights-act/article-11-freedom-assembly-and-association

[402]what-are-human-rights/human-rights-act/article-11-right-protest, https://www.libertyhumanrights.org.uk/human-rights/

[403] https://newsfromcrystalpalace.wordpress.com/2019/06/10/council-has-refused-us-air-monitoring-systems-tenants-chief-tells-committee-his-wife-had-to-visit-a-and-e-three-times-with-lung-inflammation

[404] Faraha Elahi and Omar Khan Ethnic inequality, Capital for all, https://www.runnymedetrust.org

institute of race relations[405] among others. Those paragraphs simply explain how that is related to Art 2 of the ECHR as discussed below.

Chapter 13

Art 2

Article 2 of ECHR[406]of state that

"1. *Everyone's right to life shall be protected by law. No one shall be deprived of his life intentionally save in the execution of a sentence of a court following his conviction of a crime for which this penalty is provided by law.*

Art 2 protects life with defences specified in Art 2(2)[407]. It asserts that governments should protect citizens from the excess, failures or illegalities of industry, which among other detriments may harm the public.[408] As highlighted in Oneryildiz v Turkey, where violation of Art2 was found in respect of a lack of protection for citizens living near a garbage bin that led to an explosion, which caused loss of life.[409] Adding that Art 2 does not simply relate to use of force but in circumstances such as this, the authorities failed to do all they could were capable of doing to protect lives despite their knowledge of the danger to the victims. This is directly relevant to estate regeneration construction related activities where there is contamination and hazards elements, which authorities[410] are fully aware of but seem to be reluctant to take active measures to eliminate or minimise the risk to human health.[411].

---

[405] Jessica, Pereira, The London clearances, http://www.irr.org.uk

[406] https://www.echr.coe.int/Documents/Convention_ENG.pdf

[407] https://www.echr.coe.int/Documents/Convention_ENG.pdf

[408] Dimitri Xenos, Asserting the Right to life (Article 2, ECHR) in the Context of Industry 8 German L.J. 231 (2007)

[409] Oneryildiz v. Turkey, 2004-XII Eur. Ct. HR 79, First, Do No Harm: Human Rights and Efforts to Combat Climate Change 38 Ga. J. Int'l & Comp. L. 593 (2009-2010

Art 2 is therefore relevant due to the reported adverse impact on residents' well-being, health[412] and public safety during protracted large scale construction projects[413] associated with universally known potentially harmful effects such as vibration, fumes, noise, asbestos contamination,[414] that residents are subjected to for prolonged periods[415] which is clearly incompatible with Art2. However, enforcement remains a formidable impediment due to lack of resources and imbalance of power between affected residents and local authorities in concert with developers as observed by Anna Minton.[416]

Chapter 14

Art 3

As indicated under Art 2,[417] a similar observation arguably applies to CPO estate regeneration under Art 3, if there is evidence of an arguable link between aspects of inhuman or degrading treatment under art 3 and CPO estate regeneration activities.

---

[410] https://www.theguardian.com/environment/2019/may/04/brownfield-site-new-homes-building-wrecking-health-southall

[411] https://www.theguardian.com/environment/2019/may/04/brownfield-site-new-homes-building-wrecking-health-southall

[412] https://www.annaminton.com/groundcontrol

[413] https://www.theguardian.com/environment/2019/may/04/brownfield-site-new-homes-building-wrecking-health-southall

[414] John L Adgate, Sook Ja Cho, Bruce H Alexander, Gurmurthy Ramachandran, Katherine K Raleigh

Jean Johnson,, Rita B Messing, A L Williams, James Kelly & Gregory C Pratt

Modelling community asbestos exposure near a vermiculite processing facility: Impact of human activities on cumulative exposure, Journal Of Exposure Science And Environmental Epidemiology

2011/02/23

[415] Brownfield-site-new-homes-building-wrecking-health-southallhttps://www.theguardian.com/environment/2019/may/04

[416] Anna Minton, 'Scaring the living daylights out of people': The local lobby and the failure of democracy

1 Feb 2013

[417] Marcia Gibson, Hilary Thomson, Ade Kearns & Mark Petticrew (2011) Understanding the Psychosocial Impacts of Housing Type: Qualitative Evidence from a Housing and Regeneration Intervention, Housing Studies, 26:04, 555-573, DOI: 10.1080/02673037.2011.559724

Art 3 states that No one shall be subjected to torture or to inhuman or degrading treatment or punishment.

Art 3 prohibits torture as well as inhuman and degrading treatment. Treatment *can be considered inhuman when it causes physical or mental pain or degrading when it debases or humiliates a person beyond that is usual from punishment*[418]

In property or estate regeneration related cases,[419] if there is evidence of sustained actions that amount to inhuman and degrading treatment, associated with CPO activity,[420] like hazardous elements, it is arguable that those affected could bring action under these grounds. However, it appears that the bar in property related terms is too high for potential applicants to cross the admissibility threshold. For example, in *Predojevic and others v Solvenia,* the court found as inadmissible claims that deprivation of pension amounted to inhuman and degrading treatment.

In spite of a high bar or threshold to satisfy Art 3 requirements in association with property rights, its arguable, therefore that if there are clear or identifiable facts from which the court can infer inhuman or degrading treatment art 3 could be engaged. Such an example could be where construction hazards[421] like industrial dust, noise, lead, asbestos or other contaminants, which cause or are linked to illness or severe emotional distress.[422]Therefore, although it is likely that the rights under art 3 associated with CPOs and estate regeneration could require more hard evidence, it would appear that if there is a nexus between inhuman and degrading treatment, associated with estate regeneration, there could be circumstances where potential applicants can make an arguable case.

---

[418] https://www.libertyhumanrights.org.uk/human-rights/what-are-human-rights/human-rights-act/article-3-no-torture

[419] Wellbeing and Regeneration, reflection from Carpenter estate, Alexandre Apsan Frediani, Stephanie Butcher and Paul Watt

[420] Regeneration and Well-Being in East-London: Stories from Carpenters Estate

[421] https://www.theguardian.com/environment/2019/may/04/brownfield-site-new-homes-building-wrecking-health-southall

[422]https://www.theguardian.com/uk-news/2019/jul/07/court-challenge-homes-southall-london-gasworks-brownfield-development

Conclusion

The above observations are a starting point in terms of laying the foundation to examine the impact of housing estate regeneration or expropriation enforced through CPOs on residents, and its compatibility with human rights law. This would create a basis upon which a plausible determination of the effectiveness human rights law in challenging estate regeneration related human rights abuses could be made.

From the initial analysis so far, there appears to be emerging evidence or existing evidence of incompatibility with human rights law. However, further analysis is necessary to obtain a more rounded understanding of the issue and the mechanisms needed for residents to fight back and protect their human rights violated by those pursuing estate regeneration through the CPO process.

The upcoming editions will look into greater detail international law highlighting, the lived or documented experiences of specific communities as documented, and the different methods that residents have deployed so far in challenging estate regeneration, an assessment of the, the effectiveness of current remedies and then consider suggestions for reform. To ensure that, human rights law in this area has real teeth. Otherwise, if there is a perception that human rights law or indeed courts cannot protect residents against the interests of the powerful or some local authorities in concert with private entities, as mentioned above, then there is a real danger that faith in the legal or judicial system could further evaporate. Which will leave the decades of progress in human rights law and the protection it offers in real peril.

Bibliography

1. MHCLG: Guidance on compulsory purchase process and the Crichel down Rules for the disposal of surplus land acquired by, or under the threat of, compulsion,

https://www.gov.uk/government/publications/compulsory-purchase-process-and-the-crichel-down-rules-guidance.

2. The Implications of Kilo in Land Use Law, Symposium Articles: Keynote Address - Kelo, Lingle, and San Remo Hotel, Santa Clara Law Review, Vol. 46, Issue 4 (2006), pp. 787-810 Curtin, Daniel J. Jr

3. Globalization, Communities and Human Rights: Community-Based Property Rights and Prior Informed Consent,2006 Sutton Colloquium Article, Denver Journal of International Law and Policy, Vol. 35, Issue 3 & 4 (Summer-Fall 2007),pp. 413 428 https://heinonline.org/419

4. Human Rights and Property Rights [article] United States Law Review, Vol. 64, Issue 11 (November 1930), pp. 581-594 Blume, Fred H.

5. Equating Human Rights and Property Rights--The Need for Moral Judgement in an Economic Analysis of Law and Social Policy, Ohio State Law Journal, Vol. 47, Issue 1 (1986), pp. 163-200 Malloy, Robin Paul

6. Douglas Maxwell, Journal of planning & Environmental Law, Article 1 of the First protocol: A paper tiger in the face of compulsory purchase orders for private profit?

7. Towards a Compulsory Purchase Code: https://www.lawcom.gov.uk/project/towards-a-compulsory-purchase-code/

8. Compulsory acquisition of land: Developers, by PLC Property https://uk.practicallaw.thomsonreuters.com

9. Planning Act 2016: http://www.housing.org.uk/resource-library/browse/the-housing-and- planning-act-2016/

10. Kept in the Dark; https://www.transparency.org.uk

11. The Law of compulsory purchase, third edition, Guy Roots et al

12. Estate-regeneration-why-people-power-is-forcing-london-to-rethink-housing; developers-alarmed-at-khans-plans-to-give-estate-residents-power; https://www.architectsjournal.co.uk/news

13. Mayor-and-conservatives-dispute-latest-London-housing-stats; https://www.insidehousing.co.uk/news/news/ https://www.bbc.co.uk

14. Phil Hubbard, Loretta Lees. (2018) the right to community? *City* 22:1, pages 8-25.

15. https://www.transparency.org.uk/faulty-towers

16. https://architectsforsocialhousing.wordpress.com/2016/03/24/the-doomsday-book/).

17. Towards a paradigm of Southern urbanism Seth Schindler City Volume 21, 2017 - Issue 1Published online: 6 Mar 2017

18. Reconstructing Berlin: Materiality and meaning in the symbolic politics of urban space

19. Dominik Bartmanski et al.City Volume 22, 2018 - Issue 2 Published online: 17 Apr 2018

20. Editorial Editor-in-Chief's note: What/whose order is to be asserted in the city?

21. Bob Catterall City Volume 22, 2018 - Issue 2

22. Published online: 7 Jun 2018

23. The right to community?: Legal geographies of resistance on London's gentrification frontiers

24. Phil Hubbard et al. City Volume 22, 2018 - Issue 1 Published online: 15 Mar 2018 editorial

25. Editorial: The right to assert the order of things in the city Luke R. Barnesmoore City

26. Volume 22, 2018 - Issue 2 Published online: 7 Jun 2018

27. Stuart Hodkinson, Chris Essen, (2015) "Grounding accumulation by dispossession in everyday life: The unjust geographies of urban regeneration under the Private Finance Initiative", International Journal of Law in the Built Environment, Vol. 7 Issue: 1, pp.72-91, https://doi.org/10.1108/IJLBE-01-2014-0007

28. Towards a new perspective on the role of the city in social movements: Urban Policy after the 'Arab Spring' Raffael Beier City Volume 22, 2018 - Issue 2 Published online: 17 Apr 2018

29. Adonis, A., and B. Davies, eds. 2015. City Villages: More Homes, Better Communities. London: IPPR. https://www.ippr.org/publications/city-villages-more-homes-better-communities

30. The London Borough of Southwark (Aylesbury Estate Site 1B-1C) Compulsory Purchase Order 2014 ('the Order': http://35percent.org/img/Decision_Letter_Final.pdf

31. Prime minister pledges to transform sink estates: https://www.gov.uk/government/news/prime-minister-pledges-to-transform-sink-estates: 10 January 2016

32. 'Cameron time to demolish sink estates': https://www.bbc.co.uk/news/av/uk-politics-35275516/cameron-time-to-demolish-worst-sink-housing-estates, 10 January 2016

33. Compulsory purchase and Compensation: An Overview of the system in England and Wales, By Frances Plimmer.

34. Paul Watt & Anna Minton (2016) London's housing crisis and its activisms, City, 20:2, 204-221, https://doi.org/10.1080/13604813.2016.1151707

35. Participation in the right of access to adequate housing, 14 Tulsa J Comp. & Intl L 269 2006 -2007, Hein online

36. Republic of SA v Grootboom & others 2000(11) BCLR 1169

37. Evadne Grant, Enforcing Social and Economic Rights: The right to adequate housing in south Africa, 15 Afr, J, intl & Comp,L 1 (2007), Hein online

38. The requirements for a compelling case in the public interest to justify a CPO (High Court) by Practical Law Planning: In Horada v Secretary of State for Communities and Local Government [2015] EWHC 2512 (Admin), Volume: 25 issue: 1, page(s): 115-135

39. The privatization of council housing, Norman Ginsburg, Issue published: February 1, 2005 https://doi.org/10.1177%2F0261018305048970

40. Haringey Council votes to cancel development vehicle despite Lendlease warning 18 July 2018:https://www.insidehousing.co.uk/news/news/haringey-council-votes-to-cancel-development-vehicle-despite-lendlease-warning-57250:

41. Watt, P. 2015. "The IMD as a WMD in the Regeneration of London Council Estates: Tackling Spatial Inequalities and Producing Socio-spatial Injustice." Paper at Tackling Spatial Inequalities Conference, Sheffield, September 10

42. Paul Watt (2009) Housing Stock Transfers, Regeneration and State-Led Gentrification in London, Urban Policy and Research, 27:3, 229-242, https://doi.org/10.1080/08111140903154147

43. Pam Douglas & Joanne Parkes (2016) 'Regeneration' and 'consultation' at a Lambeth council estate, City, 20:2, 287-291, https://doi.org/10.1080/13604813.2016.1143683

44. Bracking V Secretary of state for works and pensions [2013] EWCA Civ 1345, [2014] Eq LR 60

45. Knock it down or Do it UP? The challenge of estate regeneration https://www.london.gov.uk/about-us/london-assembly/london-assembly-publications/knock-it-down-or-do-it

46. HPA 2016 and how it affects housing associations: http://www.lag.org.uk/magazine/2016/07/a-devastating-blow-to-social-housing-in-england.aspx

47. EA2010Equality Act 2010 (Specific Duties and Public Authorities) Regulations 2017. PSED: specific duties in England, Practical Law UK Practice Note

48. CPA 1965: Compulsory Purchase Act 1965.

49. CP (VD) A 1981: Compulsory Purchase (Vesting Declarations) Act 1981.

50. LCA 1961: Land Compensation Act 1961.

51. LCA 1973: Land Compensation Act 1973.

52. TCPA 1990: Town and Country Planning Act 1990

53. https://www.libertyhumanrights.org.uk/

54. https://www.equalityhumanrights.com/en/about-us

55. https://www.ohchr.org/en/professionalinterest/pages/ccpr.aspx

56. https://echr.coe.int/

57. British Institute of human rights www.Bihr.org.uk

58. Chartered Institute of Housing www. Cih.org

59. DCLG www.coommunites.gov.uk

60. Housing Law practitioners Association www. Hipa.org.uk

61. The Law Society www.lawsociety.org

62. https://savecressingham.wordpress.com/

63. http://www.insidehousing.co.uk/cressingham-gardens-regeneration-approved-in-high-court/7018185.article

64. http://35percent.org/2013-06-08-the-heygate-diaspora/

65. https://www.southwarknews.co.uk/news/council-given-permission-take-aylesbury-estate-cpo-case-high-court-disappointing-blow-campaigners/

66. http://www.shelter.org.uk

67. http://www.axethehousingact.org.uk/page/2/ on

68. Localism Act 2011, https://uk.practicallaw.thomsonreuters.com/1-504-2706

69. Housing and equality law, By Robert Brown, Arden Chambers

    a. https://uk.practicallaw.thomsonreuters.com/w-012-0034

70. https://www.ashurst.com/en/news-and-insights/legal-updates/compulsory-purchase-life-after-aylesbury/

71. https://www.birketts.co.uk/insights/legal-updates/compulsory-purchase-and-what-to-do-about-it

72. https://assets.publishing.service.gov.uk/government/uploads/system/uploads/attachment_data/file/551698/ECHR_Memorandum.pdf

73. https://www.burges-salmon.com/news-and-insight/legal-updates/alternative-development-proposals-how-do-they-affect-cpo-validity/

74. Housing and Regeneration Act 2008, Housing and Regeneration Act 2008

    a. http://www.opsi.gov.uk/acts/acts2008/ukpga_20080017_en_1

75. Donnelly, Jack. Universal human rights in theory and practice. Cornell University Press, 2013.

76. Human rights Act 1998: https://uk.practicallaw.thomsonreuters.com/0-506-9287

77. Lexis   Nexis:
    https://www.lexisnexis.com/uk/lexispsl/publiclaw/document/413481/5DF5-Dealing_with_a_human_rights_challengehttps://www.lexisnexis.com/uk/lexispsl/publicl

78. New law journal: https://www.newlawjournal.co.uk/

79. Practicallaw:https://uk.practicallaw.thomsonreuters.com/Browse/Home/Practice/PublicLaw

80. Hansard- https://hansard.parliament.uk/

81. https://www.leighday.co.uk/News/2015/November-2015/Cressingham-Gardens-tenant-wins-High-Court-legal

82. https://www.theguardian.com/commentisfree/2017/oct/25/labour-council-regeneration-housing-crisis-high-court-judge

83. The Secretary of states' ruling re: Town and Country Planning Act 1990 Section 226(1) (a), Acquisition of Land Act 1981 The London Borough of Southwark (Aylesbury Estate Site 1B-1C) Compulsory Purchase Order 2014 ('

84. https://hsfnotes.com/realestatedevelopment/2016/09/28/a-new-right-to-a-community-decision-by-the-secretary-of-state-not-to-confirm-the-cpo-for-aylesbury-estate/

85. Compulsory_purchase_process_and_the_Crichel_Down_Rules_-_guidance_updated_180228;https://assets.publishing.service.gov.uk/government/uploads/system/uploads/attachment_data/file/684529/

86. http://www.legislation.gov.uk/ukpga/2010/15/

87. https://www.burges-salmon.com/news-and-insight/legal-updates/the-neighbourhood-planning-act-2017/

88. https://www.legislation.gov.uk/ukpga/2010/15/section/149

89. https://assets.publishing.service.gov.uk/government/uploads/system/uploads/attachment_data/file/475271/cpo_guidance.pdf

90. Knock It Down Or Do It Up; https://www.london.gov.uk/sites/default/files/gla_migrate_files_destination/

91. London's Housing Crisis Worse for Ethnic Minorities 22 March 2016;;https://www.runnymedetrust.org/news/638/272

92. Dispossession the great social housing swindle: https://www.dispossessionfilm.com/

93. City Villages, More Homes, Better communities: https://www.ippr.org/files/publications/pdf/city-villages_Mar2015.pdf

94. Shelter. 2015. Homes for our Children. How much of the Housing Market is Affordable?,https://england.shelter.org.uk/Homes_for_our_Children.pdf

95. The-story-of-the-camberwell-submarine-4618, https://www.insidehousing.co.uk/insight/insight

96. Convention for the Protection of Individuals with regard to Automatic Processing of Personal Data Strasbourg, 28.I.1981 https://rm.coe.int/CoE

97. Legal Challenges to Implementing CPOs and Decisions under the Crichel down Rules by Tim Mould QC http://www.landmarkchambers.co.uk/userfiles/TM.pdf

98. The use of compulsory purchase powers for regeneration by Elvin QC, http://www.landmarkchambers.co.uk s. 149 of the Equality Act 2010

99. Land Compensation Claims: The Claimants Perspective by Simon Pickles Landmark Chambers http://www.landmarkchambers.co.uk/cases-compulsory_purchase_compensation.aspx

100. Compulsory purchase orders: stage 4, CPO compensation procedure: flowchart by Practical Law Planning, https://uk.practicallaw.thomsonreuters.com/2-629-7353

101. Twenty years later-Assessing the significance of the Human Rights Act 1998 to the residential possession proceedings, By Ian Loveland http://openaccess.city.ac.uk/17163/

102. Housing Act 1988 https://www.legislation.gov.uk/id/ukpga/1988/50

103. R on the application of Sainsbury's supermarket ltd) V Wolverhampton city Council (2010) UKSC

104. Waters v welsh development agency (2004)1WLR 1304

105. David Elvin QC paper, Use of compulsory purchase powers for regeneration, http://www.landmarkchambers.co.uk

106. Countryside Alliance v Attorney General [2007] UKHL 52

107. Article 1 of the first Protocol to the ECHR: protection of property, Practical Law UK Practice Note, https://uk.practicallaw.thomsonreuters.com/8-385-5732

108. Article 6 of the ECHR: right to a fair hearing Housing:

109. https://uk.practicallaw.thomsonreuters.com/2-385-8106

110. Part VII of the Housing Act 1996

111. Demolition or refurbishment of social housing? https://www.ucl.ac.uk/engineering-exchange/research-projects/2018/nov/demolition-or-refurbishment-social-housing

112. Stanton, J. (2014). The Big Society and Community Development: Neighbourhood Planning under the Localism Act. Environmental Law Review, 16(4), 262–276.

113. Murungaru v Home Secretary [2008] EWCA Civ 1015

114. Fazia Ali v The United Kingdom - 40378/10 Court (Fourth Section)) [2015] ECHR 924

115. Belfast City Council v Miss Behavin' Ltd [2007] UKHL 19

116. James V UK (A98 (1986 E.H.R.R 123 (ECHR)

117. Sporrong and Lönnroth [1982] 5 EHRR 35

118. Le Compte, Van Leuven and De Meyere v Belgium [1981] ECHR 3.

119.   Bryan v United Kingdom [1995] ECHR 50, (1996) 21 EHRR 342

120.   Begum v London Borough of Tower Hamlets [2003] UKHL 5

121.   Lithgow and others v UK [1986] 8 EHRR 329)

122.   Chapman v. the United Kingdom [GC], § 96;

123.   Yordanova and Others v. Bulgaria, §§ 129-130

124.   Zehentner v. Austria, §§ 63 and 65) / (A.-M.V. v. Finland, §§ 82-84 and 90).

125.   Qazi v Harrow LBC (2003 UKHL 43: (2004) 1 AC 983 (HL)

126.   Salvesen V Riddell(2013) UKSC 22: 2013 SC(U.K.S.C) 236(SC)

127.   López Ostra v. Spain, §§ 56-58,

128.   Moreno Gómez v. Spain, § 61.

129.   Di Sarno and Others v. Italy, § 112).

130.   Hatton and Others v. the United Kingdom [GC], § 96;

131.   Moreno Gómez v. Spain, § 53)

132.   Fadeyeva v. Russia, § 69.

133.   (Asselbourg and Others v. Luxembourg (dec.)).

134.   Martínez Martínez and Pino Manzano v. Spain,

135.   (Hardy and Maile v. the United Kingdom

136.   (Hatton and Others v. the United Kingdom [GC]

137.   https://www.facebook.com/Savewestburysw8-804075296314550/

138.   https://twitter.com/savewestburysw8

139.   WestburySW8 a diary of Housing Estate Expropriation and Displacement-A lived experience.